COMPUTERIZED ACCOUNTING WITH
QUICKBOOKS® 2019

Kathleen Villani, CPA
Queensborough Community College

James B. Rosa, CPA
Queensborough Community College

PARADIGM
EDUCATION SOLUTIONS

St. Paul

Vice President, Content and Digital Solutions: Christine Hurney
Director of Content Development, Computer Technology: Cheryl Drivdahl
Developmental Editor: Katie Werdick
Director of Production: Timothy W. Larson
Associate Production Editor/Project Manager: Melora Pappas
Senior Design and Production Artist: Julie Johnston
Copy Editor: Sweet Tea Editorial, LLC
Testers: Gary Chavez, Denise Seguin
Indexer: Terry Casey
Vice President, Director of Digital Products: Chuck Bratton
Digital Projects Manager: Tom Modl
Digital Solutions Manager: Gerry Yumul
Senior Director of Digital Products and Onboarding: Christopher Johnson
Supervisor of Digital Products and Onboarding: Ryan Isdahl
Vice President, Marketing: Lara Weber McLellan
Marketing and Communications Manager: Selena Hicks

Care has been taken to verify the accuracy of information presented in this book. However, the authors, editors, andpublisher cannot accept responsibility for web, email, newsgroup, or chat room subject matter or content, or forconsequences from the application of the information in this book, and make no warranty, expressed or implied, withrespect to its content.

Trademarks: Intuit and QuickBooks are trademarks and service marks of Intuit Inc., registered in the United States and other countries. Microsoft is a trademark or registered trademark of Microsoft Corporation in the United States and/or other countries. Some of the product names and company names included in this book have been used for identification purposes only and may be trademarks or registered trade names of their respective manufacturers and sellers. The authors, editors, and publisher disclaim any affiliation, association, or connection with, or sponsorship or endorsement by, such owners.

Paradigm Education Solutions is independent from Intuit and Microsoft Corporation and not affiliated with Intuit or Microsoft in any manner.

Cover Photo Credit: ©Tarchyshnik Andrei/Shutterstock.com

ISBN 978-0-76388-907-4 (print)
ISBN 978-0-76388-908-1 (digital)

© 2020 by Paradigm Publishing, LLC
875 Montreal Way
St. Paul, MN 55102
Email: CustomerService@ParadigmEducation.com
Website: ParadigmEducation.com

Printed in the United States of America

28 27 26 25 24 23 22 21 20 19   1 2 3 4 5 6 7 8 9 10

Brief Contents

Contents

Preface

Computerized Accounting with QuickBooks® 2019 teaches students how to use QuickBooks, a popular general ledger software package for small- and medium-sized businesses. With this program, businesses can maintain a general ledger; track vendor, customer, and inventory activities; process payroll for company employees; prepare bank reconciliations; track time for employees and jobs; and complete other key accounting procedures. In addition to learning how to use QuickBooks, students review the related accounting concepts as applied in the software.

QuickBooks® 2019 provides students with detailed instruction and extensive practice for learning how to use the software. To get the most out of this program, students should be familiar with basic accounting principles and practices. Students also should know how to use a personal computer and understand basic Windows terminology. Where knowledge of specific Windows procedures enhance the operation of QuickBooks, those procedures are explained. For effective use of this book, the chapter problems and case problems must be performed on a computer with QuickBooks 2019 software installed on it.

Course Objectives

A course that uses *QuickBooks® 2019* has two main objectives for students. The first objective is to know how to operate QuickBooks by entering common daily business transactions in the appropriate activity windows using sample company data. The second objective is to identify the behind-the-scenes accounting that QuickBooks is recording. This second objective is accomplished by reviewing the underlying accounting concepts through both narrative explanation and T-account illustrations. In the workplace, the better you understand the flow of the activity as it is recorded in the system, the more accurate and efficient you will be in operating the software.

After completing a course that uses *QuickBooks® 2019*, you should be able to do the following:

- Understand differences and similarities between a manual accounting system and QuickBooks
- Identify and execute the four levels of operation within QuickBooks: New Company Setup, Lists/Centers, Activities, and Reports
- Set up and maintain the Vendor, Customer, and Employee Centers and the Chart of Accounts, Items, and Payroll Item Lists
- Enter daily activities as appropriate in the Enter Bills, Pay Bills, Write Checks, Create Invoices, Receive Payments, Enter Sales Receipts, Make Deposits, Pay Sales Tax, Adjust Quantity/Value on Hand, Create Purchase Orders, Pay Employees, and Pay Liabilities windows

- Set up and customize a new company file using the Detailed Start and Express Start methods, with and without the QuickBooks Desktop Setup window
- Set up and process payroll
- Transfer funds between accounts, record and pay credit card charges, and prepare a bank reconciliation
- Record revenues and expenses by job, with and without the Time-Tracking feature
- View and print management reports, accounting reports, and financial statements
- Customize the desktop, Lists, Activities windows, and Reports

Instructional Design

QuickBooks® 2019 teaches you how to use the QuickBooks 2019 software by integrating the course content and a personal QuickBooks Accountant Desktop 2019 account.

QuickBooks® 2019 Course Content

QuickBooks® 2019 is organized to follow the four levels of operation in the QuickBooks 2019 software: New Company Setup, Lists/Centers, Activities, and Reports. As each level of operation is presented in the chapters, it is denoted with the appropriate margin icon shown at the left.

New Company Setup

Lists/Centers

Activities

Reports

You can learn the New Company Setup more effectively if you understand the basic operations of the QuickBooks software. Therefore, Chapters 1–5 present how to use QuickBooks following a normal business flow. After the basic software operations are mastered in Chapters 1–5, the New Company Setup level of operation is explained in Chapters 6 and 7. Chapters 8 and 9 discuss the setup and processing of payroll transactions. Throughout these chapters, you will view and print many management and accounting reports and financial statements. Upon successful completion of Chapters 1–9, you should have a thorough understanding of the four levels of operation in QuickBooks. Chapters 10–12 discuss banking, jobs accounting, time tracking, and customization features. The topics presented in each chapter build on the topics covered in previous chapters.

QuickBooks® Accountant Desktop 2019 Account

QuickBooks® 2019 comes with free, five-month access to QuickBooks Accountant Desktop 2019 sofware. The reports you create using the software are the best tools for measuring your comprehension and mastery of the procedures and concepts covered in this course. Building your own company file and completing the daily, monthly, and yearly accounting tasks will help ensure that you have experience completing essential accounting tasks using QuickBooks 2019.

Student Courseware

The following visual guide shows the rich features of *QuickBooks® 2019* that support mastery of skills and concepts.

Chapter Elements

Chapter openers present an overview of the skills you can learn by completing the chapter.

Objectives outline learning goals for the chapter.

Step-by-step procedures with screen captures guide you to the desired outcome for each accounting procedure. Screen captures illustrate what the screen should look like at key points.

Tables provide essential details about different links, buttons, and options in the various windows. Tables are also used to organize large amounts of data for entry in the software.

Hints in the margins provide alternative methods, reminders, and helpful tips for working in QuickBooks 2019.

Magenta text identifies material to type.

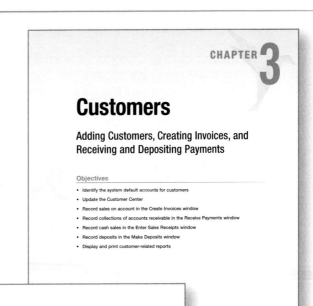

CHAPTER **3**

Customers

Adding Customers, Creating Invoices, and Receiving and Depositing Payments

Objectives

- Identify the system default accounts for customers
- Update the Customer Center
- Record sales on account in the Create Invoices window
- Record collections of accounts receivable in the Receive Payments window
- Record cash sales in the Enter Sales Receipts window
- Record deposits in the Make Deposits window
- Display and print customer-related reports

71

To view a specific customer file:
1. Move the mouse pointer to Alomar Company and double-click to open the file. If a window appears titled New Feature Add/Edit Multiple List Entries, insert a check mark in the box to the left of the *Do not display this message in the future* option and then click OK to close the window. The file opens in Edit Customer mode. See Figure 3–C.

FIGURE 3-C
Customer File—
Alomar Company
Selected

Table 3–2 describes the various parts of the customer's file.

TABLE 3–2
Customer File

Part	Description
Name page	Displays the customer's name, the customer's current balance, and three command buttons: OK, Cancel, and Help.
Address Info tab	Used to enter the customer's company name, billing and shipping address, contact person, telephone and mobile phone numbers, and email address. The Edit icon can be used to edit address information.
Payment Settings tab	Used to enter information such as the customer's account number, credit limit, payment terms, preferred delivery method, and credit card information.
Sales Tax Settings tab	Used to enter the customer's sales tax code and resale number.
Additional Info tab	Used to enter the customer type and to create customized fields.
Job Info tab	Used to enter information such as job status and start and end dates for a job for this customer.

2. Close the Edit Customer window.
3. Close the Customer Center.

CHAPTER 3 | Customers   **77**

Adding a Customer
Kristin Raina has just been hired by a new client, Maria Omari, to provide interior decorating services for Omari's new residence.

To add a new customer:
1. At the main menu bar, click Customers and then click *Customer Center*. The Customer Center opens, displaying a list of customers on the Customers & Jobs tab and information for the first customer on the list.
2. At the Customer Center window, click the New Customer & Job button and then select *New Customer*. The New Customer window appears. See Figure 3-D.

FIGURE 3-D
New Customer Window

HINT
To move from field to field, press the Tab key or Shift + Tab. In the *INVOICE/BILL TO* field, use the Down Arrow key to enter each line of the address.

3. Enter the following data on the Name page and Address Info tab. See Figure 3–E.

Name page	CUSTOMER NAME:	Omari, Maria
	OPENING BALANCE:	0 AS OF February 1, 2021
Address Info	FULL NAME:	
	First:	Maria
	Last:	Omari
	Main Phone:	612-555-9999
	Mobile:	612-555-9998
	Main Email:	MO@ppi-edu.net
	INVOICE/BILL TO:	210 NE Lowry Ave.
		Minneapolis, MN 54204

Accounting concepts accompany and summarize each transaction in the traditional debit and credit format illustrated with T-accounts.

Practice exercises provide an opportunity for you to repeat the preceding task or transaction without step-by-step guidance. Many practice exercises include a *QuickCheck* number, such as a report or a dollar amount.

QuickBooks level icons identify which level—New Company Setup, Activities, Lists/Centers, or Reports—is covered in each section of content.

Key terms and definitions in the margin provide quick reference for chapter vocabulary.

Chapter Review and Assessment Elements

The **procedure review** provides a summary of the QuickBooks steps discussed in the chapter.

Key concepts matching questions offer a quick assessment of comprehension.

Procedure check short- and long-answer questions encourage active and critical thinking.

Case problems help you master the topics of the chapter as you work with the company files for Lynn's Music Studio and Olivia's Web Solutions. Reports generated at the end of the case problems are the main assessment tools for each chapter.

SNAP for QuickBooks

SNAP

SNAP for QuickBooks is Paradigm's web-based training and assessment program and learning management system (LMS) for *QuickBooks® 2019*. SNAP for QuickBooks offers rich content, a sophisticated grade book, and robust scheduling and analytics tools. SNAP for QuickBooks courseware supports the *QuickBooks® 2019* content and provides access to the student courseware and Instructor eResources. The SNAP for QuickBooks resources are also available to export into any LMS that supports LTI tools.

Key features of SNAP for QuickBooks include chapter-based quizzes and exams with automatic scoring and gradebook entry; automatic feedback, scoring, and gradebook entry for case problem work; unique chapter-based video tutorials; and file management tools.

Online Quizzes and Exams

Chapter-based, multiple-choice quizzes and exams are preprogrammed in SNAP for QuickBooks with automatic feedback and gradebook entry. Instructors using other learning management systems will also have access to distance-learning cartridges to import chapter exams to their preferred LMS.

Automatic Feedback and Scoring Tool for Case Problem Reports

The end-of-chapter case problems in *QuickBooks® 2019* have been programmed for automatic feedback, scoring, and gradebook entry. At the end of each case problem, you can export your reports to Microsoft® Excel® and upload the Excel reports into SNAP for QuickBooks. SNAP for QuickBooks will instruct you to advance through the grading tool, as it compares your report against a model answer. SNAP for QuickBooks will then generate a score that is automatically added to the grade book and make your report available to the instructor.

Video Tutorials

Each chapter includes a video tutorial taught by Hector Garcia, CPA, that showcases the QuickBooks Accountant Desktop 2019 software interface and the procedures taught in the chapter. In addition to completing the procedures step-by-step, Hector demonstrates keyboard shortcuts and explains the functionality and capabilities of the software. Each tutorial is followed by a short, automatically graded quiz to assess comprehension.

File Management Tools

QuickBooks for SNAP allows you to upload homework assignments such as documents containing the short- and long-answer responses to the questions in each chapter's procedure check. The uploaded files are then available for your instructor to review and grade, if desired.

Instructor eResources

The Instructor eResources for *QuickBooks® 2019* are available through SNAP for QuickBooks.

- Planning resources, such as the "Course Planning" article and sample course syllabi
- Presentation resources, such as lecture notes
- Assessment resources, including model answers in PDF and QBW file format for chapter work and end-of-chapter activities, answer keys for evaluating student work, chapter-based exam banks in RTF file format for instructors who are not using SNAP, and the Comprehensive Problem solutions

About the Authors

Kathleen Villani is a professor of accounting and chairperson of the Business Department at Queensborough Community College of the City University of New York in Queens, New York. Kathleen received her bachelor's degree in accounting from Queens College of the City University of New York and her master's degree in business administration from Hofstra University. Since 1984, Kathleen has taught principles, intermediate, and cost accounting, along with accounting computer applications, microcomputer applications, and business organization and management. Kathleen has been included in *Who's Who Among America's Teachers* three times. She is a certified public accountant in the state of New York. Kathleen is a coauthor of *Computerized Accounting with QuickBooks® Pro 2000, 2003, 2005, 2007, 2008, 2009*, and *2010; Computerized Accounting with QuickBooks® 2011, 2012, 2013, 2014, 2015*, and *2018*; and *Computerized Accounting with QuickBooks® Online 2017* and *2018*—all published by Paradigm Education Solutions. Kathleen previously worked as an auditor for New York State and for Ernst and Young and was a financial controller of a health-care facility.

James B. Rosa is a professor of accounting at Queensborough Community College of the City University of New York in Queens, New York. Jim received his bachelor's degree in accounting from Queens College of the City University of New York and his master's degree in business administration from the Peter J. Tobin School of Business, St. John's University. Since 1987, Jim has taught principles and intermediate accounting, tax law, and accounting computer applications. Jim has been included in *Who's Who Among America's Teachers* three times. He is a certified public accountant in the state of New York. Jim is a coauthor of *Computerized Accounting with QuickBooks® Pro 2000, 2003, 2005, 2007, 2008, 2009*, and *2010; Computerized Accounting with QuickBooks® 2011, 2012, 2013, 2014, 2015*, and *2018*; and *Computerized Accounting with QuickBooks® Online 2017* and *2018*— all published by Paradigm Education Solutions.

Acknowledgments

The authors and editors are grateful to the accounting instructors who provided feedback on various aspects of this project, including the following:

Theodore Abah
Bamenda University of Science
    and Technology
Nkwen, Bamenda, Cameroon

Kevin Bauguess, MBA
International Career
    Development Center (ICDC)
Los Angeles, California

Anna Boulware, MBA, CMA
St. Charles Community College
St. Peters, Missouri

Colleen Ivancic, MS, CPA
Northwest College
Bridgeview, Illinois

Melody Hudson Kamerer
Butler County Community
    College
El Dorado, Butler Township,
    Pennsylvania

Glenn (Mel) McQueary II, CPA,
    CISA, CFE, CISM, CGMA
Houston Community College
Houston, Texas

Leah Moody
Cerritos College
Norwalk, California

Leslie Thompson, MS, CPA
Hutchinson Community College
Hutchinson, Kansas

We also thank Gary Chavez and Denise Seguin for testing activities and providing feedback on the content.

CHAPTER 1

QuickBooks 2019

Overview, Open a Company File, Create a Backup Copy, Restore a Backup Copy, and Change the Company Name

Objectives

- Describe the differences and similarities between manual and computerized accounting

- Identify the four levels of operation within QuickBooks

- Open QuickBooks

- Open a company file

- Make a backup copy of a company file

- Restore a backup copy of a company file

- Change the company name in a company file

accounting the process of recording, summarizing, and presenting the financial information of a company in the form of financial statements

Accounting for the financial activity of any company involves repetitive recording of day-to-day business activities. Recording common business activities such as paying bills, purchasing merchandise, selling merchandise, and processing payroll involves repeating the same steps again and again. Many of these activities can occur several times in the course of one day, requiring much repetitive recording.

When mainframe computers were introduced, certain processes such as payroll became simple to perform. Companies were created to process payrolls for local businesses using mainframe computers. Eventually, mainframe computers were used to process other accounting activities, such as maintaining the general ledger and journals. As personal computers became more common, computerized accounting software enabled routine business activities—including paying bills, buying and selling merchandise, and paying employees—to be processed without the need for a mainframe computer.

financial statements summaries of the financial information of a company, the most common of which are the income statement and the balance sheet

With a computerized accounting software package, as business activities are recorded, all necessary reports—from the journals to the general ledger to the payroll reports and the financial statements—are instantly prepared. This makes them available on a more timely basis. Also, if an error is noticed, it can be easily corrected and a revised report immediately printed.

Originally, only people trained in accounting commonly used accounting software. As more people began to use personal computers, business owners and non-accountants started to record business activities on their own using accounting software.

QuickBooks® 2019 is an example of an accounting software package used to record all types of business and accounting activities and prepare a variety of reports, including financial statements. However, unlike many accounting software products, it is designed with the non-accountant in mind. Many of the data entry windows are described in everyday, non-accounting terms. Behind the scenes, QuickBooks uses traditional accounting procedures to record, summarize, and report financial information. Therefore, a basic understanding of accounting terms and procedures allows you to operate the software more efficiently. Throughout the text, to clarify the accounting principles behind the QuickBooks features, accounting terms are defined in the margins, and accounting concepts are presented after each QuickBooks activity.

transaction a monetary business event or activity

general journal the document in which transactions are initially recorded chronologically; at the end of the month, transactions in the general journal are posted (rewritten) to the general ledger

general ledger the document in which transactions are summarized by account

Accounting with QuickBooks versus Manual and Other Computerized Accounting Systems

In accounting, every transaction that involves money must be recorded. In a manual accounting system, all transactions are recorded chronologically in a general journal. At the end of the month, these transactions are posted (rewritten) in a book called the *general ledger*. The general ledger summarizes the information by descriptive names, called *accounts*. Examples of accounts are Cash, Accounts Receivable, and Inventory (assets); Accounts Payable and Notes Payable (liabilities); Capital and Drawings, and Stock and Retained Earnings (equity); Fees Earned and Sales (revenue); and Rent, Insurance, Salaries, and Depreciation (expenses). After routine transactions and any necessary adjustments are recorded in the journal and posted to the general ledger, a **trial balance** is prepared to confirm that the general ledger is in balance, and then the financial statements are prepared.

To facilitate the recording of so many transactions in a manual accounting system, several journals are used. Similar transactions are recorded in each journal. Typically, a purchases journal is used to record purchases of merchandise on account; a sales journal is used to record sales of merchandise on account; a cash receipts journal is used to record collections of sales on account, cash sales, and any other cash receipt activity; and a cash payments journal is used to record payment of purchases on account, cash purchases, and any other cash payment activity. These journals are often referred to as **special journals**. Any transaction that is not appropriately recorded in a special journal is recorded in the general journal. Month-end adjusting journal entries and fiscal year-end closing entries are recorded in the general journal.

Many computerized accounting software packages follow the procedures used in a manual accounting system. Transactions are recorded in special journals and the general journal as appropriate, and transactions from the journals are then posted to the general ledger. Users of other accounting software packages need to analyze the transaction, determine the correct journal in which to record the transaction, enter the data, view the journal entry for correctness, and then post the journal entry to the general ledger.

QuickBooks, on the other hand, is designed for the non-accountant as well as the accountant. QuickBooks does not do its recording in special journals; instead, it identifies transactions by business function: vendors, customers, employees, and banking. The language used in recording transactions is common business language: enter bills, pay bills, create invoices, receive payments, and so on. The user enters the transaction based on the nature of the activity, and then, behind the scenes, the software updates the appropriate accounting reports—the journal, general ledger, and trial balance—and financial statements, based on the activity entered into the system.

Four Levels of Operation

Although much of the accounting is conducted behind the scenes in Quick-Books, an understanding of the accounting concepts used by the software will help you determine how to record financial information correctly. The operations conducted by QuickBooks can be classified into four levels: New Company Setup, Lists/Centers, Activities, and Reports. See Figure 1–A.

FIGURE 1–A
Four Levels of Operation in QuickBooks

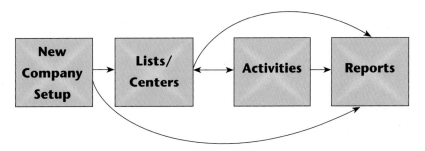

New Company Setup → Lists/Centers ↔ Activities → Reports

New Company Setup

The first level of operation is creating and setting up a new company file with the background information for the new company. This involves recording the company name, address, identification numbers, fiscal periods, type of business, accounts, and balances.

The second level of operation is recording background information in Lists and Centers. These Lists and Centers include Chart of Accounts, Item, Fixed Asset Item, Price Level, Billing Rate Level, Sales Tax Code, Payroll Item, Customer, Vendor, Employee, and so on. Information is initially recorded in Lists and Centers as part of New Company Setup, but it can be revised by adding, deleting, or editing information.

The Lists/Centers in QuickBooks function similarly to a database. Certain information is stored in these Lists/Centers, and as business activities involving any item in the Lists/Centers are processed, the information can simply be recalled and plugged into the windows rather than requiring you to retype the data.

In QuickBooks 2019, the difference between Lists and Centers lies in how the List information is accessed. For the Customer, Vendor, and Employee Lists, the information is accessed through their respective Centers. For the Chart of Accounts, Item, Fixed Asset Item, Price Level, Billing Rate Level, Sales Tax Code, and Payroll Item Lists, the Lists are accessed by clicking Lists on the main menu bar.

The third level of operation is recording daily business activities in QuickBooks. This is where most of the routine accounting work is processed. Activities are identified using common language such as enter bills, write checks, create invoices, and receive payments. In addition, the information in Lists/Centers is frequently used to eliminate repetitive entering of data while recording daily activities.

At certain times, it is necessary to display and print a variety of reports and financial statements based on information entered into QuickBooks. The fourth level of operation is using QuickBooks to display and print an assortment of Reports—for example, management reports related to each activity, such as vendor, customer, inventory, and payroll reports; accounting reports, such as the journal, general ledger, and trial balance; and financial statements, including the income statement and balance sheet.

Information that appears on the Reports is gathered during other operations within QuickBooks. As data is entered in the New Company Setup, Lists/Centers, and Activities levels of operation, the information is simultaneously recorded in the Reports level. QuickBooks provides for simple as well as more elaborate reporting. All the Reports can be customized according to the user's needs.

Installing the Student Trial Edition of QuickBooks 2019

HINT

If you purchased only digital access to this textbook, you will receive your license and product numbers in a separate email.

Enclosed with this book is a QuickBooks 2019 Software card that provides access to the Student Trial Edition of QuickBooks 2019. This is a complete version of the software that will be used to learn computerized accounting as presented in this text. The Student Trial Edition of QuickBooks allows you to use the software for five months.

Included on this QuickBooks 2019 Software card are a license number and a product number. You will download the Student Trial Edition of QuickBooks 2019 via the internet. During the process, you will be required to enter the license number and product number. After you do so, store the card in a safe place.

HINT

The installation process takes a while to complete.

HINT

Step 4 may vary depending on the internet browser you use.

To install the Student Trial Edition of QuickBooks 2019 on your computer:

1. Open the QuickBooks 2019 Software card packaged with this textbook. Note the license and product numbers. Do not discard the QuickBooks 2019 Software card; you will use the numbers on the card in Step 8 below.

Note: Replacement cards are available for purchase from Paradigm Education Solutions at CustomerService@ParadigmEducation.com or 800-535-6865.

2. Open an internet browser, type https://QB19.ParadigmEducation.com/QuickBooksDownloadPage into the address bar, and then press the Enter key or the Go arrow. If an Intuit - Great to see you message appears, click No Thanks. You are moved to the Intuit QuickBooks Download & Updates window.

3. In the QuickBooks Desktop Accountant 2019 section, click the Download button.

4. At the *Do you want to run or save Setup_QuickBooksPremier2019 .exe from http-download.intuit.com?* message, click Run.

5. At the User Account Control message, click Yes. The Intuit Download Manager window appears. It will take a while for the files to download.

6. When the download is complete, confirm that the Intuit Download Manager window has closed. Close the Intuit QuickBooks Support browser window.

7. Confirm that the QuickBooks Financial Software 2019 - InstallShield Wizard window is displayed on the screen. Follow the instructions on the screen.

8. When prompted, enter the license number and product number. These numbers are on the QuickBooks 2019 Software card.

9. After entering these numbers, continue to follow the instructions on the screen to complete the installation. At the last window—Congratulations!—click Open QuickBooks, if you can, and then move to Step 11.

   You may be able to only click the Close button because you need to restart your computer. If so, click Close and restart your computer.

10. If you restarted your computer, then locate the app QuickBooks Premier - Accountant Edition 2019 in your Start menu, tiles, or list of applications, and click to open QuickBooks, or double-click the QuickBooks icon on your desktop.

11. If you receive a message that states how QuickBooks uses your internet connection, click OK. If the QuickBooks Desktop Setup window appears, close the window.

12. If you are prompted to register QuickBooks, do this immediately.

Note: If you do not register the Student Trial Edition of QuickBooks within 30 days, you will no longer be able to use the software.

13. Close QuickBooks. If the Exiting QuickBooks message appears, click Yes.
14. Store the QuickBooks 2019 Software card in a safe place.

Installing the Company Files Needed for This Text

QuickBooks must be installed on your computer for you to use this book. In addition, you will need to download the company files that accompany this textbook. You will use the company files to learn the topics presented in each chapter and to complete the two case problems at the end of each chapter. There are company files for all chapters except Chapters 6 and 7, where you will learn to create a new company file.

By default, QuickBooks stores company files in the following path:

C:\Users\Public\Public Documents\Intuit\QuickBooks\Company Files.

HINT

You are not required to use this path. You can download the company files to a folder of your choice on your hard drive or network.

You do not need to use this path. The textbook assumes that you will store company files in the subfolder Company Files. However, your instructor can also install the company files in some other directory on your hard drive or on a network.

To download the company files, click the link in your SNAP course if you are a SNAP user, or use the link in your student ebook. After downloading the company files, you should save the files on your network or hard drive. Refer to your instructor for information on extracting company files from a zipped folder.

Opening QuickBooks

HINT

There are many ways to open QuickBooks. You can use the tiles or icons as illustrated in Figure 1–B, or you can use the Start menu and then choose the QuickBooks Premier - Accountant Edition 2019 program.

FIGURE 1–B

Sample Start
Screen Tile

To open QuickBooks:

1. In Windows 10, click the Start button and then click the QuickBooks Premier - Accountant Edition 2019 tile, or click the Start button, scroll through the list of applications, click the drop-down arrow next to QuickBooks, and then click QuickBooks Premier - Accountant Edition 2019. See Figure 1–B.

QuickBooks Premier - Accountant Edition 2019 tile shown on the Windows 10 start screen

In Windows 8, on the Start screen, click the QuickBooks Premier - Accountant Edition 2019 tile, or on the Desktop screen, click the QuickBooks Premier - Accountant Edition 2019 icon.

In Windows 7, click the QuickBooks Premier - Accountant Edition 2019 icon.

2. If you receive a message that states how QuickBooks uses your internet connection, click OK. If the QuickBooks Setup window appears, close the window.

QuickBooks opens and the QuickBooks main window appears. In addition, the No Company Open window appears. See Figure 1–C.

Note: If a company file was previously used on this computer, the company file may automatically be opened. In this case, click File and then click Close Company. If the QuickBooks Desktop Login window appears, click Cancel. You should see a window like the one shown in Figure 1–C.

In the No Company Open window, the first time QuickBooks is opened, no company files are listed. Thereafter, company files previously opened are listed; you can use this window to select a company name and then click the Open button. If companies are listed, notice under the box listing the company files that the location path is indicated. This path will be useful later as you begin to open several different company files. You also have three additional choices: Create a new company, Open or restore an existing company, and Open a sample file.

FIGURE 1–C

QuickBooks Main Window—No Company Open Window

title bar

main menu bar

QuickBooks main window

In Chapters 1–5 and 8–12, you will open an existing company file from those provided in the *Student Resources* that you have installed on the hard drive of your computer. In Chapters 6 and 7, you will learn how to create a new company file.

Using Drop-Down Menus and Dialog Boxes

Whether or not a company file is open, notice the QuickBooks main window shown in Figure 1–C. Along the top is the QuickBooks title bar, which includes a company name when a company file is open. Below the title bar is the main menu bar, which includes the menu choices of File, Edit, View, Lists, Favorites, Accountant, Company, Customers, Vendors, Employees, Banking, Reports, Window, and Help. When no company is open, only the menus File and Help are active and can be chosen. You can choose a menu by clicking the menu name or by pressing the Alt key and the underlined letter from the menu name on the keyboard. Whenever you choose a menu, a drop-down menu appears that lists additional choices or commands. Choices on the menus vary depending on the data entered into the company file and depending on which of the open windows is active.

At the main menu bar, click File. The File drop-down menu appears, displaying commands or choices. See Figure 1–D.

FIGURE 1–D

File Menu in QuickBooks

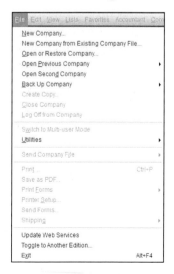

When you choose a command followed by an ellipsis (…), a window called a *dialog box* appears. Additional information must be entered in the dialog box for the command to be processed. Included in dialog boxes are command buttons (such as Open, Cancel, and Help). The active command button may be a different color, such as blue, or have a slightly darker line around it. You can activate a command button by clicking it. If the button is active, you can also activate the command by pressing the Enter key.

When you choose a command followed by an arrow (▸) from the File drop-down menu, an additional drop-down menu called a *submenu* appears. Submenus list additional commands or choices.

Versions of QuickBooks

Intuit, the maker of QuickBooks, offers several versions of the Quick-Books software: Pro, Premier, and Enterprise Solutions. In addition, the QuickBooks Premier version is available in several editions: Accountant Edition, General Business Edition, Contractor Edition, and so on. The fundamentals of each version and edition of the QuickBooks software are the same. QuickBooks Pro is the basic version of the software with Premier and Enterprise Solutions offering additional features. Usually, small business owners will use QuickBooks Pro. Larger businesses, businesses that have large inventories, and specific industries may use the QuickBooks Enterprise Solutions or QuickBooks Premier versions of the software. The QuickBooks Premier Accountant Edition is often used by accountants who have clients that use various versions or editions of QuickBooks. The QuickBooks Premier Accountant Edition software allows accountants to toggle (switch) to different versions and editions of QuickBooks to view their clients' accounting records using their clients' version or edition of QuickBooks.

QuickBooks also offers an online version of the software for a monthly fee. There are four versions available: QuickBooks Online Self-Employed, QuickBooks Online Simple Start, QuickBooks Online Essentials, and QuickBooks Online Plus. Although the functionality of the online version is similar to the traditional QuickBooks, the graphic interface of the menus, data entry windows, and reports differs significantly.

This book was written using the QuickBooks Premier Accountant Edition, which is the version provided with this textbook. When schools purchase the Education packs of the software to install in computer laboratories, Intuit provides the schools with the QuickBooks Premier Accountant Edition version of the software.

To toggle to other versions or editions of QuickBooks in the QuickBooks Premier Accountant Edition:
1. At the main menu bar, click File.
2. On the File menu, click *Toggle to Another Edition*. The Select Quick-Books Desktop Industry-Specific Edition dialog box appears. See Figure 1–E.

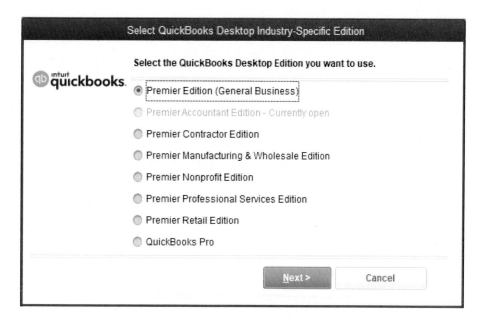

3. In the Select QuickBooks Desktop Industry-Specific Edition dialog box, click the desired version or edition of QuickBooks.

4. Click Next. The next window confirms the version or edition of Quick-Books that you selected.

    If you click Toggle, QuickBooks Premier - Accountant Edition closes and then reopens in the version or edition of QuickBooks that you have selected. Since the text is prepared using QuickBooks Premier - Accountant Edition, do not change to another version of the software.

5. Click Cancel.

There are several ways to determine which version or edition of Quick-Books you are using. The QuickBooks version or edition is listed in the title bar. In Figure 1–C on page 7, note that the title bar displays Quick-Books Accountant Desktop 2019. If you toggle to a different edition of QuickBooks, the title bar changes to reflect which version or edition you are using.

You can also determine the version or edition that is currently open in the Select QuickBooks Desktop Industry-Specific Edition dialog box. See Figure 1–E, which notes that the Premier Accountant Edition is currently open.

The Help menu also displays the version or edition of QuickBooks you are using.

To determine the version or edition of QuickBooks using the Help menu:

1. At the main menu bar, click Help.

2. At the drop-down menu, notice the last command.

    The last command on the drop-down Help menu displays the version or edition of QuickBooks that is open.

3. Click Help to remove the Help drop-down menu.

Opening a Company File

The sample company that came with this textbook, Kristin Raina Interior Designs, is used to illustrate the topics in each chapter.

HINT

To *select* is to highlight something by clicking it once. To *choose* is to activate a command, sometimes with one click and sometimes by double-clicking.

To open the CH1 Kristin Raina Interior Designs company file:

1. With QuickBooks open, at the No Company Open window, click the Open or restore an existing company button, or at the main menu bar, click File and then click *Open or Restore Company*. The Open or Restore Company window appears.

2. At the Open or Restore Company window, select *Open a company file*. See Figure 1–F.

FIGURE 1–F
Open or Restore Company Window—Open a Company File Selected

Open a company file

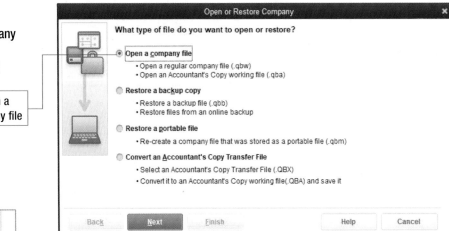

HINT

These are the company files downloaded from SNAP or your ebook. If you see a Download.zip folder or you do not see any company files, then you did not download or extract the company files. Refer to the instructions provided in SNAP or your ebook to download and extract the company files.

3. Click Next.

   The Open a Company dialog box appears. Most likely, the subfolder Company Files appears in the *Look in* text box. QuickBooks automatically assigns the extension .QBW to each company file.

4. In the Open a Company dialog box, in the *Look in* text box, choose the Company Files subfolder or the subfolder containing the company files.

5. Select the company file named **CH1 Kristin Raina Interior Designs.QBW**.

   When you select a company file name, the name also appears in the *File name* text box. See Figure 1–G.

FIGURE 1–G
Open a Company Dialog Box—CH1 Kristin Raina Interior Designs Company File Selected

HINT

Occasionally when opening a company file, you may receive a warning that QuickBooks encountered a problem. Click OK at the warning and then open the company file again.

6. Click Open.
7. At the QuickBooks Desktop Login window, in the *Password* text box, type Student1 and then click OK. Student1 is the password on all company files used in this textbook.

HINT

The password for all company files for this textbook is Student1. If you are prompted for the Security question, the Challenge Question is *First college room-mate's name*, and the Challenge Answer is *Friend*.

At various times when opening a company file or when operating QuickBooks, various pop-up messages will appear. In general, simply close the messages. On some occasions, you may be provided a choice not to show the message again. Also, in some situations, the QuickBooks default can be changed so the messages no longer appear. Throughout this book, suggestions are made to close the message, choose not to show the message again, or change the default.

For now, when opening a company file, if the Set Up an External Accountant User window appears, insert a check mark in the box to the left of *Don't show this again* and then click No to close the window. If the Accountant Center window appears, remove the check mark in the box to the left of *Show Accountant Center when opening a company file* and then click the X (close button) to close the window. If the Close Accountant Center window appears, click OK to close it. If the New Feature Tour window appears, click the X to close the window.

Once a company file is open, the QuickBooks main window changes. See Figure 1–H.

FIGURE 1–H
QuickBooks Main Window—Company File Open

title bar with company name

Left Icon bar

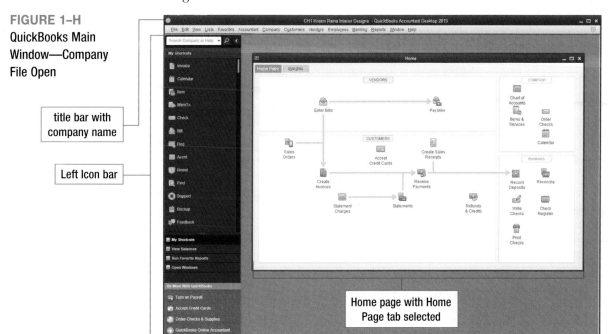

Home page with Home Page tab selected

The company name, CH1 Kristin Raina Interior Designs, is now displayed in the title bar. Along the left side of the window is the Left Icon bar. The remainder of the window displays the Home page. The Left Icon bar and the Home page can also be used to access information in QuickBooks as alternatives to using the main menu bar. In this text, only the main menu bar is used. If the WHAT'S NEW box appears on the edge of the Home page, click the X to close it. If the Help message appears, it will fade away in a few seconds.

In this textbook, the Left Icon bar and the Home page will be closed to allow more screen space for the windows.

HINT

Chapter 12 illustrates customizing and using the Home page and Icon bars.

HINT

In a computer laboratory, the Left Icon bar or Home page may not appear because another user has changed the default settings. To view the Left Icon bar, at the main menu bar, click View and then click *Left Icon Bar*. To view the Home page, at the main menu bar, click Company and then click *Home Page*.

To close the Left Icon bar:
1. At the main menu bar, click View.
2. At the View menu, click *Hide Icon Bar*.

To close the Home page:
1. Click the X on the Home page.

You can change the default if you do not want the Home page window to open each time QuickBooks is opened.

To change the default to close the Home page window:
1. At the main menu bar, click Edit.
2. At the Edit menu, click *Preferences.*
3. In the left panel, click the Desktop View icon.
4. Choose the My Preferences tab.
5. Remove the check mark to the left of *Show Home page when opening a company file.*
6. Click OK.

Multi-User and Single-User Mode

multi-user mode
a setting in QuickBooks that allows up to five users to access a company file at the same time, each on his or her own computer

single-user mode
a setting in QuickBooks that allows only one user on a single computer to access a company file at one time

HINT

See Appendix I for information about setting up multi-users in QuickBooks.

QuickBooks is designed so that several people can use one company file at the same time. Assume a business has three bookkeepers. When using QuickBooks, each bookkeeper can access the company records at the same time on his or her own computer. This is referred to as running the software in **multi-user mode**. Multi-user mode allows each bookkeeper to do his or her work individually, but at the same time, all the information entered individually updates the company file as a whole. QuickBooks Premier allows for up to five users at one time. When a QuickBooks company file is used only on a single computer, it is referred to as **single-user mode**.

In the computer laboratory, you will use QuickBooks in single-user mode. Each person is using the company file individually; your work is not and should not be connected to anyone else's work. When QuickBooks is in single-user mode, the menu choice in the File menu is *Switch to Multi-user Mode;* when in multi-user mode, the menu choice is *Switch to Single-user Mode.* Because you should work in single-user mode, the menu choice should be *Switch to Multi-user Mode.*

Backing Up a Company File

In business, it is advisable to make backup copies of records on a regular basis and store the backup copies in a safe place, separate from the business location. In the event of damage to a company's computers and/or files, the backup copies can be used to restore the lost or damaged data.

Why Backing Up a File Is Important

In this text, you will use the Back Up command for two purposes. First, Back Up will be used to make a copy of the original company file. As previously mentioned, company files are provided for the sample company Kristin Raina Interior Designs to illustrate topics in each chapter and for the two cases at the end of each chapter. To use the company files for practice, you will first open the company file and then make a copy of the company file using the Back Up command. The backup copy of the company file must then be restored for you to use it as a practice exercise. By making a backup copy of a company file and then restoring it, the original company file will then be preserved intact for others to use.

Second, as in business, you will use the Back Up command to make backup copies of your exercise company files on a removable storage device or a network directory. In the event your exercise company file is deleted from the hard drive that you are working on, you will have a backup copy. This copy will also be helpful in case you use a different computer each time in the computer laboratory.

Naming Backup Files

Two types of names are used in QuickBooks to identify a company file: the file name and the company name. When your backup copy is made and restored, it is recommended that you include your name or your initials as part of the company *file* name to distinguish your individual copy of the file from those of other students. In the restored copy (your exercise copy), the *company name* will also be changed to include your name or your initials to further identify the exercise copy of the company file as your copy.

In each chapter, the original company file name is preceded with the prefix CH1, CH2, and so on to represent the chapter number. The backup copies are assigned the prefixes EX1, EX2, and so on. EX stands for exercise.

QuickBooks automatically assigns the extension .QBB to a backup copy and condenses the file. Condensed backup copies cannot be used for work; they are strictly for use as stored copies.

Backup copies can be made to the Company Files subfolder, to a subfolder of your choice, or to a removable storage device. It is recommended that you create your own subfolder on the hard drive using File (or Windows) Explorer and that you use your subfolder to store your backup copy of the company file. The following instructions assume you have created your own subfolder.

To make a backup copy of the CH1 Kristin Raina Interior Designs company file:
1. At the main menu bar, click File and then click *Back Up Company.*
2. At the Back Up Company submenu, click *Create Local Backup.* The Create Backup window appears with the Do you want to save your backup copy online or locally? page displayed.
   At certain times in QuickBooks, the title in a window remains the same, but as you click the Next button, a series of pages within that window ask for or inform you of additional information.
3. At the Do you want to save your backup copy online or locally? page, confirm that *Local backup* is selected. See Figure 1–I.

FIGURE 1–I

Create Backup
Window—Do You Want to
Save Your Backup Copy
Online or Locally? Page

Options button

4. Click Next. The Backup Options window appears. See Figure 1–J.

FIGURE 1–J

Backup Options
Window

Add the date
and time option

Note: The first time you make a backup copy of a company file, the Backup Options window appears. For subsequent backup copies of the same file, this window will not appear; you will not need to do Steps 5–9 of this procedure.

5. At the Backup Options window, click the Browse button. The Browse for Folder window appears. See Figure 1–K.

FIGURE 1–K
Browse for Folder
Window

6. At the Browse for Folder window, choose your subfolder, a network directory designated by your instructor, or a removable storage device.
7. Click OK. You are returned to the Backup Options window, and the *Tell us where to save your backup copies (required)* field is completed.

    By default, the date and time are listed in the file name of the backup copy of a company file. When you make many backup copies of a company file, you will have several backup files, each with an individual date and time in the backup file name. You can remove this option by removing the check mark in the box to the left of *Add the date and time of the backup to the file name (recommended)*. See Figure 1–J. You then have only one backup copy of the file, which is replaced each time you update the backup copy. Additional settings can also be changed in this window.
8. Click OK.
9. At the QuickBooks message, click *Use this Location*. The Create Backup window—When do you want to save your backup copy? page appears. See Figure 1–L.

10. At the When do you want to save your backup copy? page, select *Save it now* and then click Next. The Save Backup Copy dialog box appears.

11. In the *Save in* field, choose your subfolder, a network directory designated by your instructor, or a removable storage device, if it is not correct.

12. In the *File name* text box, type EX1 *[Your Name]* Kristin Raina Interior Designs. See Figure 1–M.

13. Click Save.

If you use a file name that already exists, the message Confirm Save As appears and asks if you want to replace the existing file. If you want to replace or update the existing file, click Yes. If you do not want to replace the existing file, click No and then use a different file name in the Save Backup Copy dialog box.

If the QuickBooks message appears, click *Use this Location.*

14. At the QuickBooks Desktop Information message, click OK.

You have now made a backup copy of the company file, but the original file is still open. To work on the backup copy of the company file that you just created, you must restore the backup copy.

Restoring a Company File

You use the Restore command to open a backup copy of a company file. Recall that backup copies are automatically assigned the extension .QBB and that they are condensed copies of a company file. QuickBooks gives the restore copy a .QBW extension, which denotes the working copies of the company. If you are using removable storage devices to store your backup copies of company files, it is recommended that you use the hard drive for the exercises and use the removable storage devices only for backup. Using removable storage devices for the exercises may be slow, and all your work for one company file may not fit onto one removable storage device.

Restoring a backup file is a two-step process. In the first step, you determine which backup copy you wish to open (Open Backup Copy); in the second step, you indicate where you wish to restore the backup copy (Save Company File as). In business, the backup company file would be restored to the original company file name. In this book, however, the intent is to retain the original company file intact for others to use, so the backup company file will *not* be restored to the original company file name but rather to your exercise company file name.

To restore the backup copy of the company file:

1. At the main menu bar, click File and then click *Open or Restore Company.* The Open or Restore Company window—What type of file do you want to open or restore? page appears.

   This is the same window that appeared earlier in the chapter when you first opened the CH1 Kristin Raina Interior Designs company file, as seen in Figure 1–F on page 10. This window is now also used to restore a backup copy of a company file. Whenever you use this window, be clear about whether you are opening a company file or restoring a backup copy of a company file so you make the correct choice.

2. At the What type of file do you want to open or restore? page, select *Restore a backup copy.* See Figure 1–N.

FIGURE 1–N
Open or Restore Company Window—Restore a Backup Copy Selected

Restore a backup copy

3. Click Next. The Is the backup copy stored locally or online? page appears.
4. At the Is the backup copy stored locally or online? page, choose *Local backup* and then click Next. The Open Backup Copy dialog box appears.
5. In the *Look in* field, choose the location where you saved your backup copy.
6. Select the company file **EX1** *[Your Name]* **Kristin Raina Interior Designs (Backup).QBB**. See Figure 1–O.

FIGURE 1–O

Open Backup Copy
Dialog Box—EX1
[Your Name] Kristin
Raina Interior Designs
(Backup).QBB
Selected

Compare Figure 1–F on page 10 with Figure 1–N on page 17, and
compare Figure 1–G on page 10 with Figure 1–O above. When you
open a company file, at the Open or Restore Company window, you
choose the option *Open a company file*. See Figure 1–F. This window
is followed by the Open a Company dialog box. All the files in this
dialog box have the extension .QBW. See Figure 1–G.

Conversely, when you want to open a backup copy of a company
file, you must restore the file. At the Open or Restore Company
window, you choose the option *Restore a backup copy*. See Figure 1–N.
This window is followed by the Open Backup Copy dialog box. All the
files in this dialog box have the extension .QBB. See Figure 1–O.

You must use the Restore command to open a backup copy of a
file. If you do not see your backup copy file listed, you may be in the
wrong window or have the wrong file location. Go back to the Open
or Restore Company window, and be sure you selected the *Restore a
backup copy* option.

7. If the Open Backup Copy dialog box is correct, click Open. The
   Where do you want to restore the file? page appears.
8. At the Where do you want to restore the file? page, click Next. The
   Save Company File as dialog box appears.
9. In the *Save in* field, choose the subfolder where you will open and
   work on your copies of the company files.
10. In the *File name* text box, type EX1 *[Your Name]* Kristin Raina Inte-
    rior Designs. The prefix EX followed by the chapter number and
    your name or initials will be used for the restore copies as well as the
    backup copies. See Figure 1–P.

FIGURE 1–P
Save Company File as
Dialog Box

When a backup copy of a company file is restored, it becomes a working copy of the company file, and QuickBooks assigns it a .QBW extension.

11. If the information is correct, click Save.

If you use a file name that already exists, a Confirm Save As message appears to indicate that this company file exists and to ask if you want to replace it. If this is what you want to do, click Yes. You must type yes in the box in the Delete Entire File message and then click OK. If the name shown in the Confirm Save As message is not the correct file name, click No and then enter the correct file name in the Save Company File as dialog box.

12. At the QuickBooks Desktop Login window, in the *Password* text box, type Student1 and then click OK. If the Home page window appears, click the X to close it. If the Left Icon bar appears, click View at the main menu bar and then click *Hide Icon Bar* to remove it.

HINT

If you receive a QuickBooks Update Service message, click Install Later. See the following section on QuickBooks Updates for more information.

After your backup copy is successfully restored, your exercise copy of the company file appears in the QuickBooks window, but the title bar indicates the original company file name. Before you begin working, you should change the company name in the My Company window to match your exercise company file name. This further identifies this company file as your individual company file.

To change the company name:

1. At the main menu bar, click Company and then click *My Company.*
2. At the My Company window, click the Edit icon 🖉 in the upper middle part of the window. You are moved to the Company Information dialog box.
3. In the Company Information dialog box, in the *Company Name* text box, change the company name to EX1 *[Your Name]* Kristin Raina Interior Designs. See Figure 1–Q.

FIGURE 1–Q
Company Information
Dialog Box

4. If the information is correct, click OK.

You are returned to the My Company window with the company name updated. See Figure 1–R.

FIGURE 1–R
My Company Window—
Updated

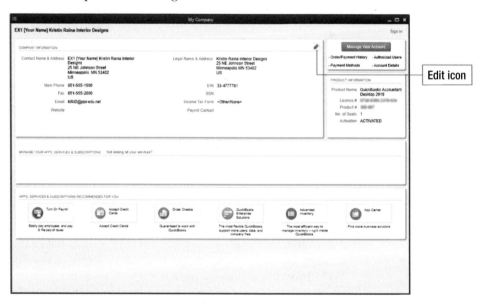

5. Close the My Company window.

HINT

The *file name* appears in the Open a Company, Backup, and Restore dialog boxes and File or Windows Explorer. The *company name* appears in the title bar of QuickBooks and the reports. It is recommended that you use the same name in both locations to more easily keep track of your files.

The company name is changed in the title bar. This company name now appears in the heading of the reports. The name in the title bar comes from the Company Information dialog box. The name of the company file in the Open a Company dialog box is based on the file name typed in the Backup and Restore dialog boxes. Be careful to type the same name in both places. Doing so will help you to more easily keep track of your files.

In business, backing up is used to maintain a copy of company financial records, and backup copies should be made on a regular basis. You would need to restore the backup copy only in the event your computer or files were damaged or you upgraded your computer system. An accountant may use backup and restore procedures when reviewing clients' accounting records.

Because you may work in a computer laboratory, where many students may work on the same company files, the backup and restore procedures are used to make your own personal copy of the company file so that you may practice the work in each chapter in your own file. You will also use the backup procedures to make a copy to your personal removable device in case your personal copy in a computer laboratory is deleted.

As you open company files and then do the backup and restore, you may become unsure as to which company file is open or in what location you are working. You can check the company file and the location path by viewing the Open Previous Company submenu.

To view which company file is open:
1. At the main menu bar, click File and then click *Open Previous Company*. The Open Previous Company submenu appears. The file listed at the top of the submenu list is the current file that is open. See Figure 1–S.

FIGURE 1–S
Open Previous Company Submenu

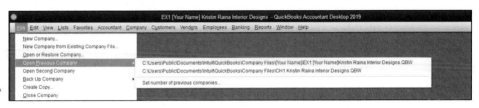

HINT

If you are unsure about the location of the company file in which you are working, click File and then click *Open Previous Company*. The file listed at the top of the submenu list is the current file that is open.

2. Click any open space on the computer screen to remove the File menu and Open Previous Company submenu.

QuickBooks Updates

QuickBooks occasionally provides product updates to the current version of software that you are using. Product updates, sometimes referred to as *maintenance releases* by QuickBooks, are delivered via the internet. Your computer can be set up so that the product updates are automatically downloaded (which is the default), or you can disable the automatic updates. If the updates are not automatic, when updates are available, a message should appear upon opening QuickBooks inquiring if you wish to update QuickBooks. You can also check for QuickBooks updates using the Help menu.

To update QuickBooks using the Help menu:
1. At the main menu bar, click Help.
2. At the drop-down menu, click *Update QuickBooks Desktop*. The Update QuickBooks Desktop window appears.
3. At the Update QuickBooks Desktop window, click the Update Now button on the Overview tab, or click the Update Now tab. See Figure 1–T.

FIGURE 1–T
Update QuickBooks
Desktop Window

4. On the Update Now tab, click the Get Updates button. If any updates are available, they will be downloaded. Follow the instructions to download the updates.
5. Close the Update QuickBooks Desktop window.

The product updates are noted by release numbers, such as R2 and R3. To determine the most recent update downloaded onto your computer, press the F2 function key on the keyboard or press Ctrl + 1, which displays the Product Information window. At the Product Information window, on the first line next to *Product*, the edition of QuickBooks is displayed along with the latest release number. See Figure 1–U.

FIGURE 1–U
Product Information
Window

product edition
and release
number

6. Close the Product Information window.

Exiting QuickBooks

Most work is automatically saved in QuickBooks when the correct command button is chosen. At the end of a session, it is recommended that you use the Back Up command to save your work onto a removable storage device or a network directory designated by your instructor. For the security of your work, you should also close your company file before exiting QuickBooks. However, it is not necessary to make a backup copy of the exercise file for this session.

At the end of each session, you should close the company file and then close QuickBooks.

To close the company file and exit QuickBooks:
1. At the main menu bar, click File and then click *Close Company*.
2. To exit QuickBooks, click the X on the QuickBooks title bar, or click File and then click *Exit*.

Chapter Review and Assessment

Procedure Review

To open a company file:
1. Open QuickBooks.
2. At the No Company Open window, click the Open or restore an existing company button, or at the main menu bar, click File and then click *Open or Restore Company.*
3. At the Open or Restore Company window, select *Open a company file* and then click Next.
4. In the Open a Company dialog box in the *Look in* text box, choose *Company Files* or the subfolder containing the company files for this course.
5. Select the company file **CH# Company Name.QBW.**
6. Click Open.
7. At the QuickBooks Desktop Login window, in the *Password* text box, type Student1 and then click OK.
8. If the New Feature Tour window appears, click the X (close button) to close the window. If the Help message appears, it will fade away in a few seconds. If the Set Up an External Accountant User window appears, insert a check mark in the box to the left of *Don't show this again* and then click No to close the window. If the Accountant Center window appears, remove the check mark in the box to the left of *Show Accountant Center when opening a company file* and then click the X to close the window. If the Home page window appears, click the X to close it. If the Left Icon bar appears, click View at the main menu bar and then click *Hide Icon Bar* to remove it.

To make a backup copy of a company file:
1. At the main menu bar, click File and then click *Back Up Company.*
2. At the Back Up Company submenu, click *Create Local Backup.*
3. At the Create Backup window–Do you want to save your backup copy online or locally? page, confirm that *Local backup* is selected and then click Next.

Note: The first time you make a backup copy of a company file, the Backup Options window appears. For subsequent backup copies of the same file, this window will not appear; you will not need to do Steps 4–7 of this procedure.

4. At the Backup Options window, click the Browse button.
5. At the Browse for Folder window, choose your subfolder, a network directory designated by your instructor, or a removable storage device and then click OK.
6. At the Backup Options window, if you do not want multiple backup copies of the company file, remove the check mark to the left of *Add the date and time of the backup to the file name* and then click OK.
7. At the QuickBooks message, click *Use this Location.*
8. At the Create Backup window–When do you want to save your backup copy? page, select *Save it now* and then click Next.
9. In the Save Backup Copy dialog box, in the *Save in* field, choose your subfolder, a network directory designated by your instructor, or a removable storage device if it is not correct.
10. In the *File name* text box, type EX# *[Your Name]* Company Name.

11. Click Save. If the QuickBooks message appears, click *Use this Location.*
12. At the QuickBooks Desktop Information message, click OK.

To restore the backup copy of the company file:
1. At the main menu bar, click File and then click *Open or Restore Company.*
2. At the Open or Restore Company window, at the What type of file do you want to open or restore? page, select *Restore a backup copy* and then click Next.
3. At the Is the backup copy stored locally or online? page, choose *Local backup* and then click Next.
4. In the Open Backup Copy dialog box, in the *Look in* field, choose the location where you saved your backup copy.
5. Select the company file **EX#** *[Your Name]* **Company Name.QBB**.
6. Click Open.
7. At the Where do you want to restore the file? page, click Next.
8. In the Save Company File as dialog box, in the *Save in* field, choose the subfolder in which you will open and work on your copies of the company files.
9. In the *File name* text box, type EX# *[Your Name]* Company Name.
10. Click Save.
11. At the QuickBooks Desktop Login window, in the *Password* text box, type Student1 and then click OK. If the Home page window appears, click the X to close it. If the Left Icon bar appears, click View at the main menu bar and then click *Hide Icon Bar* to remove it.

To change the company name:
1. At the main menu bar, click Company and then click *My Company.*
2. At the My Company window, click the Edit icon. You are moved to the Company Information dialog box.
3. In the Company Information dialog box, in the *Company Name* text box, type EX# *[Your Name]* Company Name.
4. Click OK. You are returned to the My Company window with the company name updated.
5. Close the My Company window. The company name is updated in the title bar of QuickBooks.

Key Concepts

Select the letter of the item that best matches each definition.

a. Company name
b. Ellipsis
c. Activities
d. QuickBooks
e. File name

f. Reports
g. New Company Setup
h. Main menu bar
i. Back Up Company
j. Lists/Centers

_____ 1. A software package used to record business and accounting activities, designed with the non-accountant in mind.
_____ 2. The level of operation that creates a new company file.
_____ 3. The level of operation that records background information.
_____ 4. The level of operation where most routine work is processed.

_____ 5. The level of operation where information can be displayed and printed.

_____ 6. Follows a command on a menu and means additional information must be entered in a second window called a *dialog box.*

_____ 7. The name that appears in the title bar of QuickBooks. The source is the My Company window.

_____ 8. The part of the QuickBooks window where the File, Edit, View, Lists, Favorites, Accountant, Company, Customers, Vendors, Employees, Banking, Reports, Window, and Help menus are displayed.

_____ 9. The name indicated in the Backup and Restore dialog boxes.

_____ 10. The command used to make a copy of the original company file.

Procedure Check

1. What is QuickBooks?
2. List the steps for opening a company file called Madeline's Shoe Club, which is stored in the Company Files subfolder on the hard drive.
3. Assume you are instructed to work on a company file named **CH1 Edward's Electronics**. List the steps to make a backup copy called **EX1 *[Your Name]* Edward's Electronics** and then restore the backup copy. Assume the company file is stored in the Company Files subfolder and backed up and restored in the *[Your Name]* subfolder. If you backed up the file to a removable storage device, how would the steps be different, and how would they be the same?
4. Assume you are working on a company file previously backed up and restored as **EX1 *[Your Name]* Travel Food Supplies** but are unable to finish the work today. When you return the next day to complete the work, explain how you would open the company file, assuming no additional backup copy was made.
5. Explain the difference between the file name and the company name.
6. Discuss the advantages of using a computerized accounting software package instead of using non-computerized accounting methods. Discuss the specific advantages of using QuickBooks.

Case Problems

Demonstrate your knowledge of the QuickBooks features discussed in this chapter by completing the following case problems.

Case Problem 1–1

On April 1, 2021, Lynn Garcia started her business, Lynn's Music Studio, as a music instructor.

1. Open the company file **CH1 Lynn's Music Studio.QBW**.
2. At the QuickBooks Desktop Login window, in the *Password* text box, type Student1 and then click OK.
3. Make a backup copy of the company file and name it **LMS1 *[Your Name]* Lynn's Music Studio**.

4. Restore the backup copy of the company file. In both the Open Backup Copy and Save Company File as dialog boxes, use the file name **LMS1** *[Your Name]* **Lynn's Music Studio** and enter Student1 as the password.
5. Change the company name to **LMS1** *[Your Name]* **Lynn's Music Studio**.
6. Close the company file.
7. Exit QuickBooks.

Case Problem 1–2

On June 1, 2021, Olivia Chen started her business, Olivia's Web Solutions, as an internet consultant and web page designer.

1. Open the company file **CH1 Olivia's Web Solutions.QBW**.
2. At the QuickBooks Desktop Login window, in the *Password* text box, type Student1 and then click OK.
3. Make a backup copy of the company file and name it **OWS1** *[Your Name]* **Olivia's Web Solutions**.
4. Restore the backup copy of the company file. In both the Open Backup Copy and Save Company File as dialog boxes, use the file name **OWS1** *[Your Name]* **Olivia's Web Solutions** and enter Student1 as the password.
5. Change the company name to **OWS1** *[Your Name]* **Olivia's Web Solutions**.
6. Close the company file.
7. Exit QuickBooks.

CHAPTER 2

Vendors

Adding Vendors and Creating and Paying Bills

Objectives

- Identify the system default accounts for vendors
- Update the Vendor Center
- Record purchases on account in the Enter Bills window
- Process credit memos in the Enter Bills window
- Record payments of accounts payable in the Pay Bills window
- Record cash purchases in the Write Checks window
- Display and print vendor-related reports

vendor someone from whom a company buys goods or services, either on account or for cash

QuickBooks allows you to track all vendor transactions. A **vendor** is someone from whom a company buys goods or services, either on account or for cash. You should establish a file for each vendor before entering transactions for that vendor. The collection of all vendor files comprises the vendor list, which is contained in the Vendor Center (Lists/Centers).

Once a vendor file is established, transactions (Activities) such as receiving a bill from a vendor, paying that bill, and paying for a cash purchase can be entered in the Enter Bills, Pay Bills, and Write Checks windows, respectively. As transactions are recorded in the activities windows, QuickBooks simultaneously updates the vendor's file in the Vendor Center, as well as any related reports (Reports), with information about the transaction for a particular vendor.

In this chapter, you will record and pay bills received by our sample company, Kristin Raina Interior Designs, for non-inventory purchases of goods and services, such as operating expenses and assets acquisitions. In addition, you will record cash purchases when bills have not been previously received or entered.

QuickBooks versus Manual Accounting: Vendor Transactions

purchases journal a journal used to record all purchases of goods on account; can be in a single-column or multi-column

In a manual accounting system, all purchases of goods on account are recorded in a multicolumn **purchases journal**. At the conclusion of the month, the totals are posted to the asset, expense, and liability (Accounts Payable) accounts affected by the transactions. As each purchase transaction is recorded, the appropriate vendor's account in the accounts payable subsidiary ledger is updated for the new liability on a daily basis. Payments for open accounts payable balances and payments for cash purchases of goods or services are recorded in a multicolumn **cash payments journal**.

cash payments journal a multicolumn journal used to record all cash payment activities, including payments of accounts payable

As in the purchases journal, monthly totals are posted to the general ledger accounts, while payment information is recorded daily in the vendor's subsidiary ledger record.

In QuickBooks, the Vendor Center serves as the accounts payable subsidiary ledger for the company. The Vendor Center contains a file for each company and individual from whom the company buys goods and services. Relevant information—such as name, address, contact person, and credit limit—should be entered at the time the vendor's file is created in the Vendor Center.

HINT

See Appendix B for a comparison of manual accounting versus QuickBooks.

When the company receives a bill for goods or services, you record the bill in the Enter Bills window. The Enter Bills window is equivalent to the multicolumn purchases journal. QuickBooks automatically updates the

Chart of Accounts List the list of accounts a company uses as it conducts its business

Chart of Accounts List and general ledger; at the same time, it updates the vendor's file in the Vendor Center for the new liability. When the bill is to be paid, you enter the transaction in the Pay Bills window. The Pay Bills window is equivalent to the part of the cash payments journal that records payments of open accounts payable. This transaction also updates the Chart of Accounts List and general ledger and at the same time updates the vendor's file in the Vendor Center for payment of the liability.

For a cash payment for a bill not previously entered, you use the Write Checks window. This is equivalent to the part of the cash payments journal that records payment for cash purchases of goods or services. Again, the Chart of Accounts List, the general ledger, and the vendor's file in the Vendor Center are updated simultaneously.

System Default Accounts

To process transactions expeditiously and organize data for reporting, Quick-Books establishes specific general ledger accounts as default accounts in each activity window. When you enter transactions, QuickBooks automatically increases or decreases certain account balances depending on the nature of the transaction. For example, when you enter a vendor invoice in the Enter Bills window, QuickBooks automatically increases (credits) the Accounts Payable account, because the Enter Bills window is used to record purchases on account. When you write a check in the Pay Bills window, QuickBooks automatically decreases (debits) the Accounts Payable account. Therefore, you do not have to enter the account numbers or names for these default accounts, because they have been pre-established by QuickBooks.

Throughout the text, the default accounts for each type of transaction, such as vendor, customer, inventory, and payroll, will be identified.

Chapter Problem

In this chapter, you will enter and track vendor transactions for Kristin Raina Interior Designs, a sole proprietorship that provides interior decorating and design services to both residential and commercial clients. The owner of the business, Kristin Raina, began operations on January 1, 2021 by investing $50,000 in the business. During January, Kristin Raina devoted most of her time to organizing the business, securing office space, and buying assets. Beginning February 1, 2021, she wishes to begin tracking vendor transactions. Information for several vendors has been entered in the Vendor Center. This information, along with February 1, 2021, beginning balances, is contained in the company file **CH2 Kristin Raina Interior Designs**.

To open the company file:
1. Open QuickBooks.
2. At the No Company Open window, click the Open or restore an existing company button, or click File and then click *Open or Restore Company*.
3. At the Open or Restore Company window, choose *Open a company file* and then click Next.
4. In the Open a Company dialog box, in the *Look in* field, choose the Company Files subfolder or the subfolder containing the company files.
5. Select the company file **CH2 Kristin Raina Interior Designs.QBW** and then click Open.
6. At the QuickBooks Desktop Login window, in the *Password* text box, type Student1 and then click OK.
7. Close all pop-up windows and messages.

> **HINT**
> Refer to Page 11 in Chapter 1 for steps to close all unnecessary windows and messages.

To make a backup copy of the company file:
1. At the main menu bar, click File and then click *Back Up Company*.
2. At the Back Up Company submenu, click *Create Local Backup*.
3. At the Create Backup window—Do you want to save your backup copy online or locally? page, confirm that *Local backup* is selected and then click Next.
4. At the Backup Options window, click the Browse button.
5. At the Browse for Folder window, choose your subfolder, a network directory designated by your instructor, or a removable storage device and then click OK.

> **HINT**
> The first time you make a backup copy of a company file, the Backup Options window appears. For subsequent backup copies of the same file, this window will not appear; you will not need to complete Steps 4–7 of this procedure.

HINT

QuickBooks automatical-
ly assigns the extension
.QBB to a backup copy.

6. At the Backup Options window, you can remove the check mark to the left of *Add the date and time of the backup to the file name* if you do not want multiple backup copies and then click OK.
7. At the QuickBooks message, click *Use this Location*.
8. At the Create Backup window—When do you want to save your backup copy? page, choose *Save it now* and then click Next.
9. In the Save Backup Copy dialog box, in the *Save in* field, choose your subfolder, a network directory designated by your instructor, or a removable storage device, if it is not correct.
10. In the *File name* text box, type EX2 *[Your Name]* Kristin Raina Interior Designs.
11. Click Save. If the QuickBooks message appears, click *Use this Location*.
12. At the QuickBooks Information message, click OK.

To restore the backup copy of the company file:
1. At the main menu bar, click File and then click *Open or Restore Company*.
2. At the Open or Restore Company window—What type of file do you want to open or restore? page, choose *Restore a backup copy* and then click Next.
3. At the Is the backup copy stored locally or online? page, choose *Local backup* and then click Next.
4. In the Open Backup Copy dialog box, in the *Look in* field, choose the location where you saved your backup copy.
5. Select the company file **EX2 *[Your Name]* Kristin Raina Interior Designs.QBB** and then click Open.
6. At the Where do you want to restore the file? page, click Next.
7. In the Save Company File as dialog box, in the *Save in* field, choose the subfolder in which you will open and work on your copies of the company file.
8. In the *File name* text box, type EX2 *[Your Name]* Kristin Raina Interior Designs and then click Save.
9. At the QuickBooks Desktop Login window, in the *Password* text box, type Student1 and then click OK
10. Close all pop-up windows and messages.

HINT

QuickBooks automatical-
ly assigns the extension
.QBW to a restored copy.

The backup copy has been restored, but the company name still reads CH2 Kristin Raina Interior Designs.

To change the company name:
1. At the main menu bar, click Company and then click *My Company*.
2. At the My Company window, click the Edit icon.
3. In the Company Information dialog box, change the company name to **EX2 *[Your Name]* Kristin Raina Interior Designs** and then click OK.
4. Close the My Company window.

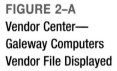 → **The Vendor Center**

The Vendor Center contains a file for each vendor with which the company does business. For example, the utility company that supplies electricity, the company that provides advertising, and the company from which equipment for the business is purchased are all vendors. The Vendor Center contains important information on each vendor, such as company name, address, contact person, type of vendor, terms, credit limit, tax identification number, and current balance owed. All the vendors with which the company does business should be included in the Vendor Center.

You should enter the information for each vendor in the Vendor Center before recording transactions. However, if you inadvertently omit a vendor, you can add that vendor during the Activities level of operation with minimal disruption.

You need to periodically revise the Vendor Center to add new vendors, delete vendors no longer used in the business, and make modifications as background information on vendors changes. Making these adjustments to the vendor files in the Vendor Center is referred to as *updating* the Vendor Center, and doing so is part of the second level of operation in QuickBooks.

Kristin Raina has entered information for existing and anticipated vendors in the Vendor Center of her company file.

To review the Vendor Center:

1. At the main menu bar, click Vendors and then click *Vendor Center*. If a window appears titled New Feature - Attach Documents to Quick-Books, click OK or the X to close the window. The Vendor Center appears with the vendor file for Galeway Computers displayed. See Figure 2–A.

FIGURE 2–A
Vendor Center—
Galeway Computers
Vendor File Displayed

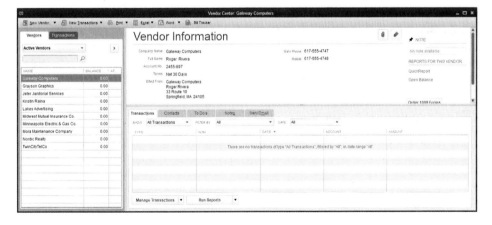

Table 2–1 describes the various parts of the Vendor Center.

TABLE 2–1
Vendor Center

Part	Description
Vendors tab	Lists all vendors with current balances owed. You can display all vendors, active vendors, or vendors with balances.
Transactions tab	Lists all transactions for a selected vendor. The Transactions tab in the Vendor Information section contains the same information.
New Vendor button	Used to add a new vendor or multiple vendors.
New Transactions button	Used to enter a bill or pay a bill.
Vendor Information section	Displays background and transaction information for the vendor selected on the Vendor tab.
Attach icon	Used to attach documents from your computer or scanner.
Edit icon	Used to edit background information for the vendor selected on the Vendors tab.
Reports for This Vendor section	Lists the reports available in the Vendor Center.
Contacts tab	Used to add a contact name for this vendor by clicking the Manage Contacts drop-down arrow and choosing *Add New*. You can designate the contact as primary, secondary, or additional.
To Do's tab	Used to view the To Do List for this vendor.
Notes tab	Used to include narrative information specific to a vendor.

In addition, after selecting a vendor, you can right-click the vendor name on the Vendors tab to display a shortcut menu to accomplish most vendor-related activities. See Figure 2–B.

FIGURE 2–B
Vendor Center Shortcut Menu

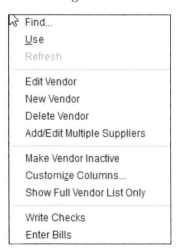

To view a specific vendor file:

1. Move the mouse pointer to *Jeter Janitorial Service* and then double-click to open the file. If a window appears titled New Feature Add/Edit Multiple List Entries, insert a check mark in the box to the left of the *Do not display this message in the future* option and then click OK to close the window. The file opens in Edit Vendor mode. See Figure 2–C.

FIGURE 2–C
Vendor File—Jeter
Janitorial Services

Table 2–2 describes the various parts of the vendor's file.

TABLE 2–2
Vendor File

Part	Description
Name page	Displays the vendor's name, the vendor's current balance, and three command buttons: OK, Cancel, and Help.
Address Info tab	Enter the vendor's company name, address, contact person, telephone and mobile numbers, and email address. The Edit icon can be used to edit address information.
Payment Settings tab	Enter information such as the vendor's account number, credit limit, payment terms, and name to be printed on checks.
Tax Settings tab	Enter the vendor's tax identification number and indicate if the vendor is to receive IRS Form 1099.
Account Settings tab	Identify up to three default general ledger posting accounts for each vendor. Once a vendor is selected in an activity window, the first account listed is identified as the general ledger posting account for that transaction. The use of this tab is optional.
Additional Info tab	Enter the vendor type and create customized fields.

2. Close the Edit Vendor window.
3. Close the Vendor Center.

Adding a Vendor

Kristin Raina has just hired a new accountant who will provide accounting services each month for the business. She wishes to add this vendor to the Vendor Center by creating a vendor file.

To add a new vendor:

1. At the main menu bar, click Vendors and then click *Vendor Center*. The Vendor Center opens with a list of vendors on the Vendor tab and information displayed for the first vendor on the list.
2. At the Vendor Center window, click the New Vendor button and select *New Vendor*. The New Vendor window appears. See Figure 2–D.

FIGURE 2–D
New Vendor Window

HINT

QuickBooks defaults to the current date. Be sure to change the date to match the problem. When entering a date, you can type the date instead of scrolling through the calendar.

HINT

Press the Tab key to move to the next field, or press Shift + Tab to move back a field. In the *BILLED FROM* field, at the end of each line in the address, use the Enter key or the Down Arrow key to move to the next line.

3. Enter the following data on the Name page and the Address Info tab. (The Edit button can be used to enter the address, but this is not necessary.)

Name page	*VENDOR NAME:*	*[Your Name]* Accounting Service
	OPENING BALANCE:	0 AS OF February 1, 2021
Address Info	*COMPANY NAME:*	*[Your Name]* Accounting Service
	FULL NAME:	
	First:	*[Your First Name]*
	Last:	*[Your Last Name]*
	Main Phone:	651-555-2222
	Mobile:	651-555-2223
	Main Email:	*[Your Initials]*@ppi-edu.net
	BILLED FROM:	One Main Plaza
		St. Paul, MN 53602

Your New Vendor window should look similar to Figure 2–E.

FIGURE 2–E
New Vendor Window—
Name Page and Address
Info Tab Completed

HINT

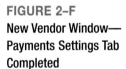

You can click the Edit
icon ✎ to access the
address information
window.

4. Click the Payment Settings tab and enter the following information.

Payment Settings	*ACCOUNT NO.:*	99-2021-XX
	PAYMENT TERMS:	Net 30 Days
	PRINT NAME ON CHECK AS:	*[Your Name]* Accounting Service

See Figure 2–F.

FIGURE 2–F
New Vendor Window—
Payments Settings Tab
Completed

5. Click the Account Settings tab and enter the following information.

Account Settings   Select account to pre-fill transactions:
6020 Accounting Expense

See Figure 2–G.

FIGURE 2–G
New Vendor Window—
Account Settings Tab
Completed

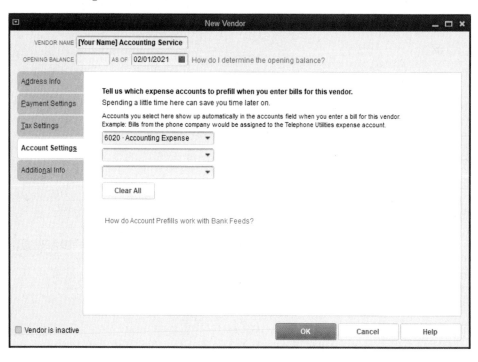

6. If the information is correct, click OK.
7. Close the Vendor Center.

Deleting a Vendor

Kristin Raina wishes to delete Lakes Advertising from the Vendor Center because the company has ceased to operate.

To delete a vendor:
1. At the main menu bar, click Vendors and then click *Vendor Center*.
2. At the Vendor Center window, select (highlight) *Lakes Advertising*, but do not open the file. See Figure 2–H.

FIGURE 2–H
Vendor Center—Lakes
Advertising Selected

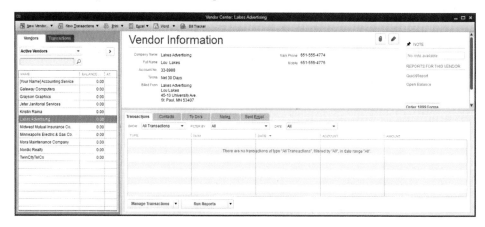

HINT
Remember, you must click OK to save the information. If you exit the window by clicking the X, the information will be lost.

3. At the main menu bar, click Edit and then click *Delete Vendor*.
4. At the Delete Vendor warning, click OK to delete the vendor file.
5. Close the Vendor Center.

QuickBooks cannot delete a vendor that has a balance or that has been part of a transaction for the fiscal period. If a vendor will no longer be used but there has been activity in the file for the period, you can insert a check mark in the *Vendor is inactive* box. The vendor's name is no longer displayed in the reports, but the vendor information is retained in Quick-Books and can be accessed as needed.

Editing a Vendor

HINT

An alternative method to access the Edit Vendor window is to select the vendor in the Vendor Center and then click the Edit icon.

Kristin Raina needs to edit the file for Minneapolis Electric & Gas Co. because the billing address has changed.

To edit a vendor file:
1. At the main menu bar, click Vendors and then click *Vendor Center*.
2. At the Vendor Center window, double-click *Minneapolis Electric & Gas Co.* The vendor file opens in Edit Vendor mode. See Figure 2–I.

FIGURE 2–I
Edit Vendor Window

3. Since this is an edit of an address, click the Edit icon [icon]. The Edit Address Information window appears. See Figure 2–J.

FIGURE 2–J
Edit Address Information
Window

4. At the *Address* field, delete the current street address; in its place, type 150 Douglas Ave. and then click OK. See Figure 2–K.

FIGURE 2–K
Edit Vendor Window—
Completed

5. If the information is correct, click OK.
6. Close the Vendor Center.

Practice Exercise 2–1

Add the following vendor:

Name page	*VENDOR NAME:*	Williams Office Supply Company
	OPENING BALANCE:	0 AS OF February 1, 2021
Address Info	*COMPANY NAME:*	Williams Office Supply Company
	FULL NAME:	
	First:	Bernard
	Last:	Williams
	Main Phone:	612-555-2240
	Mobile:	612-555-2241
	Main Email:	Wilsup@ppi-edu.net
	BILLED FROM:	15 Grand Ave. S.
		Minneapolis, MN 55404
Payment Settings	*ACCOUNT NO.:*	55-8988
	PAYMENT TERMS:	Net 30 Days
	PRINT NAME ON CHECK AS:	Williams Office Supply Company

Delete the following vendor:
  Mora Maintenance Company

Edit the following vendor:
  New phone/mobile for Grayson Graphics:

Main Phone:	612-555-0002
Mobile:	612-555-0003

QuickCheck: The updated Vendor Center appears in Figure 2–L.

FIGURE 2–L Updated Vendor Center

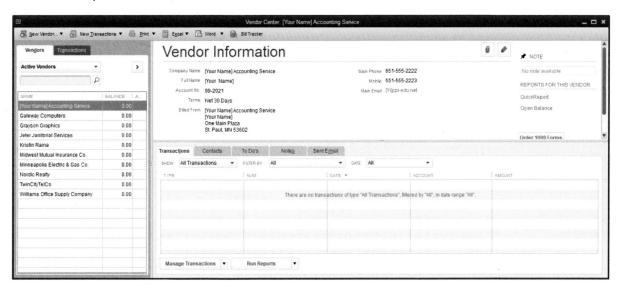

The Enter Bills Window

purchase on account
when a company
receives a bill for goods
or services from a vendor
but plans to pay it at a
later date

In QuickBooks, the Enter Bills window is used to record a **purchase on account**. This window allows you to identify the vendor sending the bill, the invoice date, due date, terms of payment, and nature of purchase (expense, asset, or item). QuickBooks uses the default Accounts Payable account from the Chart of Accounts to post all open bill liabilities. Certain recurring bills can be set up to be recorded automatically as they become due. In addition, you can use this window to record credit memos.

QuickBooks records a transaction that is a purchase on account as follows:

	Asset/Expense/Drawings	XXX		
	Accounts Payable			XXX

At the same time, QuickBooks updates the vendor's file in the Vendor Center to reflect the new liability.

Recall from Chapter 1 that the third level of operation in QuickBooks is Activities. In this case, the Activity is the recording of purchases on account in the Enter Bills window. Accounts Payable is the default general ledger posting account. All transactions entered in this window will result in a credit to the Accounts Payable account. The *ACCOUNT* field in this window is used to indicate the asset, expense, or drawings account to be debited.

The Enter Bills window appears in Figure 2–M.

FIGURE 2–M
Enter Bills Window—Expenses Tab

The Enter Bills window has two tabs: Main and Reports. The Main tab allows you to select a vendor from the Vendor Center, enter a bill reference number, indicate whether it is a bill or credit, and indicate the expense or item purchased. On the Main tab, there are two subtabs: Expenses and Items. The Expenses tab should be the active tab.

The Reports tab allows you to access various transactions reports. Most icons and data fields are self-explanatory, but take special note of the parts of the Main tab described in Table 2–3.

TABLE 2–3

Enter Bills Window, Main Tab

Part	Description
Find button, Previous/ Next arrows	Used to move from the current transaction to the previous or next transaction. The current transaction is saved before moving to the previous or next window. Also used to find previously recorded bills by vendor, date range, reference number, or amount.
New button	Used to open a blank transactions window and save a current transaction.
Delete button	Used to delete or void a transaction.
Clear Splits button	Used to erase entries on the Expenses and Items tabs.
Recalculate button	Used to add up multiple entries on the Expenses and Items tabs to fill the *AMOUNT DUE* field.
Pay Bill button	Used to open the Pay Bills window.
Bill Received check box	Indicates that the bill has been received for this expense or item. If unchecked, the expense or item was received, but the bill will follow at a later date.
Expenses/Items tabs	For non-item purchases, such as expenses and non-inventory assets, click the Expenses tab. For the purchase of an item, such as inventory, click the Items tab. The Items tab is covered in Chapter 5.
Save & Close button	Used to save (post) the transaction and close the window.
Save & New button	Used to save (post) the transaction and clear the window for a new transaction.
Clear button	Used to clear the entire screen if errors are made.
Vendor Name/ Transaction tabs	Displays a summary of information about the vendor, recent transactions, and notes. Click the > arrow to hide the information, and click the < arrow to display it.
Edit icon	Allows you to edit vendor information while remaining in the Enter Bills window. The icon appears when a vendor is selected.
SUMMARY section	Lists the phone number, email address, and open balance for the selected vendor.
RECENT TRANSACTIONS section	Displays recent transactions for the selected vendor. Also allows you to access a Quick Report for this vendor.
NOTES section	Clicking the Edit icon allows you to post notes concerning the selected vendor.

Entering a Bill

On February 2, 2021, Kristin Raina received a bill for utilities services from Minneapolis Electric & Gas Co. in the amount of $350, Ref. No. 125-55. The bill is due March 4, 2021, terms **Net 30 Days.**

Net 30 Days full payment of an invoice requested within 30 days of the invoice date

To enter a bill:

1. At the main menu bar, click Vendors and then click *Enter Bills.*
2. Click the *Bill* option and the *Bill Received* check box, if necessary.
3. At the *VENDOR* field, click the down arrow to display the VENDOR drop-down list and then click *Minneapolis Electric & Gas Co.*
4. At the *DATE* field, choose *02/02/2021.* (Click the Calendar icon, click through the months to find February 2021, and then click *2.*)
5. At the *REF. NO.* field, type 125-55.
6. At the *AMOUNT DUE* field, type 350.
7. At the *BILL DUE* field, choose *03/04/2021.*
8. At the *TERMS* field, click *Net 30 Days*, if necessary.
9. Click the Expenses tab, if necessary, and then in the *ACCOUNT* field, click the first line to display the drop-down list arrow. At the account drop-down list, click *6500 Utilities Expense.* See Figure 2–N.

FIGURE 2–N

Enter Bills Window Completed

HINT

Click the > arrow on the vendor Name/ Transaction tabs to hide the tabs. Click the < arrow to display the tabs.

10. If the information is correct, click the Save & Close button.

Recall that the Save & Close button saves the information and closes the window. Clicking the Next arrow saves the information and then clears the fields for the next transaction. Clicking the Previous arrow displays the window for the previous transaction. Since this is the first transaction, the Previous arrow cannot yet be used.

For a purchase of an expense on account, the general ledger posting is as follows:				In addition, the vendor file (subledger) for Minneapolis Electric & Gas Co. reflects the new liability:	
6500 Utilities Exp		2010 Accts Payable		Minn Electric & Gas	
Dr	Cr	Dr	Cr	Dr	Cr
350			350		350

Updating the Vendor Center While in an Activities Window

On February 2, 2021, Kristin Raina received a bill for prepaid advertising services from Cuza and Carl Associates in the amount of $600, Invoice No. X-145. The bill is due March 4, 2021, terms Net 30 Days. Cuza and Carl Associates is a new vendor.

To update the Vendor Center from the Enter Bills window:
1. At the main menu bar, click Vendors and then click *Enter Bills*.
2. At the VENDOR drop-down list, click *< Add New >*. The New Vendor window appears. This is the same window that appears after choosing the New Vendor button in the Vendor Center window.
3. Enter the following information for the new vendor.

Name page	*VENDOR NAME:*	Cuza and Carl Associates
	OPENING BALANCE:	0 AS OF February 2, 2021
Address Info	*COMPANY NAME:*	Cuza and Carl Associates
	FULL NAME:	
	First Name:	Carrie
	Last Name:	Cuza
	Main Phone:	651-555-8855
	Mobile:	651-555-8856
	Main Email:	CC@ppi-edu.net
	BILLED FROM:	23 W. University Ave. St. Paul, MN 53603
Payment Settings	*ACCOUNT NO.:*	KR569
	TERMS:	Net 30 Days
	PRINT NAME ON CHECK AS:	Cuza and Carl Associates

HINT
You can display transactions previously entered by clicking the Previous arrow ◄ above the Find button; any errors can then be corrected. Clicking the Next arrow ► returns you to the current transaction or brings you to a clear window.

4. Click OK to save the information and then exit the New Vendor window. The new vendor is now listed in the *VENDOR* field.
5. Complete the remaining fields of the Enter Bills window.
6. On the Expenses tab, click the account *1410 Prepaid Advertising* and key 600 in the *AMOUNT* field, if necessary.

   You use the Expenses tab to indicate which account should be debited. The account can be an asset, expense, or drawings account. Remember when using this window that by default, Accounts Payable is the account credited. See Figure 2–O.

FIGURE 2–O
Enter Bills Window—
Completed

7. If the information is correct, click the Save & New button.

Correcting Errors

There are several ways to correct an error in a recorded transaction. One way is to open the window that contains the transaction and use the Previous arrow ⬅ above the Find button to view it. You can then make the necessary correction and save the transaction by choosing the Save button at the top of the window. As an alternative to correcting an error in a transaction, you can delete the transaction by clicking the Delete button (in this example) or by selecting Edit at the main menu bar, clicking *Delete Bill*, and reentering the transaction correctly.

Assume that on February 2, 2021, Kristin Raina inadvertently records a Prepaid Advertising amount for $300, realizes the correct amount is $600, and further realizes the invoice had already been recorded. The bill is from Cuza and Carl Associates, Invoice No. X-145, due March 4, 2021, terms Net 30 Days.

To record an erroneous transaction, make corrections, and delete the transaction:
1. At the main menu bar, click Vendors and then click *Enter Bills* if the Enter Bills window is not already open.
2. At the VENDOR drop-down list, click *Cuza and Carl Associates*.
3. Enter information at the *DATE, REF. NO., BILL DUE, TERMS,* and *ACCOUNT* fields.
4. At the *AMOUNT DUE* field, type 300.
5. Click the Save & New button.
6. You will receive a warning that the Reference No. has already been used. This means that you are incorrectly recording an invoice for the second time. For now, ignore the warning and click Keep Number. The transaction is recorded.
7. Click the Previous arrow ⬅.
   Upon reviewing the transaction, you realize the correct amount should have been $600.

8. At the *AMOUNT DUE* field, change the amount to 600. The *AMOUNT* field, on the Expenses tab, will automatically update. Click the Save & New button.

9. A message appears that says *You have changed the transaction. Do you want to record your changes?* Click Yes.

    If a window appears that asks *Want to reclassify several transactions at once?*, click OK to close the window. The corrected transaction is then saved with the new amount. But you now realize that this transaction is a duplicate transaction, and you wish to delete the transaction completely.

10. Click the Previous arrow to view the transaction.

11. Click the X on the Delete button.

12. You will receive another warning message that asks *Are you sure you want to delete this transaction?* Click OK. The duplicate transaction is deleted.

Practice Exercise 2–2

Record the following transactions in the Enter Bills window:

Feb. 3	Received bill from Nordic Realty for February rent, Invoice No. F-21, $800. Due date February 13, 2021 (charge to Rent Expense Account No. 6400).
Feb. 6	Received bill from Williams Office Supply Company for purchase of office supplies, Invoice No. K-222, $475. Due date March 8, 2021 (charge to Office Supplies Account No. 1305).
Feb. 9	Received bill from Midwest Mutual Insurance Co. for one-year insurance policy, Invoice No. 01-21, $2,400. Due date March 11, 2021 (charge to Prepaid Insurance Account No. 1420).
Feb. 13	Received bill from Galeway Computers for new computer, Invoice No. 556588, $3,600. Due date March 15, 2021 (charge to Computers, Cost Account No. 1825).
Feb. 23	Received bill from *[Your Name]* Accounting Service for accounting service, Invoice No. Feb21, $300. Due date March 25, 2021. (Note that Account 6020—Accounting Expense automatically filled the general ledger posting account line on the Expenses tab because the Account Settings tab was completed for this vendor.)

Processing a Credit Memo

credit memo
a reduction of Accounts Payable as a result of a return or an allowance by a vendor

QuickBooks allows you to process a **credit memo** from a vendor using the Enter Bills window. The resulting credit reduces the balance owed to that vendor.

On February 24, 2021, Kristin Raina returned $75 of damaged office supplies to Williams Office Supply Company for credit, using credit memo CM-245.

To record a vendor credit:

1. At the main menu bar, click Vendors and then click *Enter Bills* if the Enter Bills window is not already open.
2. At the VENDOR drop-down list, click *Williams Office Supply Company*. Note on the Vendor tab the open balance and the bill for the purchase of supplies dated 02/06/21.
3. Click the *Credit* option. When this option is chosen, the default entry is a debit to Accounts Payable.
4. Enter the appropriate information at the *DATE, REF. NO.*, and *CREDIT AMOUNT* fields.
5. At the *MEMO* field, type Return damaged office supplies.
6. On the Expenses tab, in the *ACCOUNT* field, click *1305 Office Supplies*. See Figure 2–P. Click the Save & Close button.

FIGURE 2–P
Credit Memo—
Completed

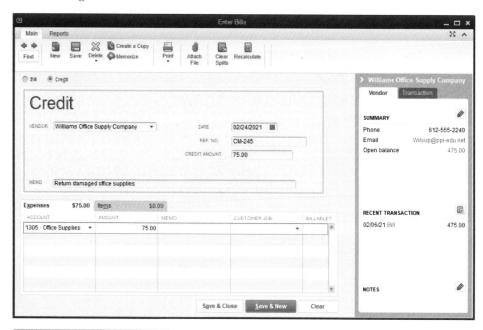

ACCOUNTING CONCEPT

For a return of office supplies for credit, the general ledger posting is as follows:

2010 Accts Payable		1305 Office Supplies	
Dr	Cr	Dr	Cr
75			75

In addition, the vendor file for Williams Office Supply Company reflects the reduced liability amount:

Williams Office Supply Co.		
Dr		Cr
CM 75	Bill	475
	Bal	400

The Pay Bills Window

In QuickBooks, the Pay Bills window is used to record a **payment on account**. These are the bills previously recorded in the Enter Bills window. This window displays all open bills as of a selected date. Bills can be paid in full, or a partial payment can be made. Payment can be in the form of check, credit card, or online payment. In addition, several bills can be paid at one time.

The Pay Bills window is designed only for payments of existing bills. The default accounts are Accounts Payable and Cash. The transaction is recorded as follows:

		Accounts Payable	XXX	
		Cash		XXX

At the same time, the vendor's file in the Vendor Center is updated to reflect the payment. The QuickBooks Pay Bills window appears in Figure 2–Q.

FIGURE 2–Q Pay Bills Window

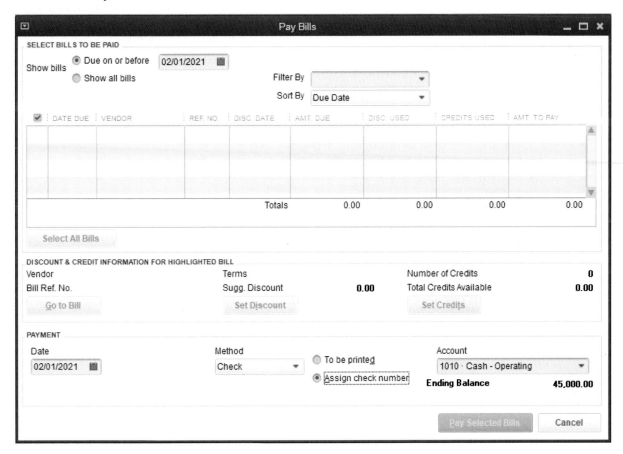

This window allows you to select a bill or bills to be paid, pay all or part of each bill, and designate checks to be printed by the computer. Table 2–4 describes the various parts of the Pay Bills window.

TABLE 2-4
Pay Bills Window

Part	Description
Show bills section	Allows you to display all bills or bills due by a certain date.
Filter By field	Allows you to display bills for all vendors or a selected vendor from the drop-down list.
Sort By field	Allows you to list bills by due date, discount date, vendor, or amount due.
Go to Bill button	Allows you to view the selected bill in the Enter Bills window.
Set Discount/Set Credits buttons	Used to activate any discount or credit for a bill selected for payment.
PAYMENT Date field	Indicates the date of payment that will appear on the payment check and on all reports.
PAYMENT Account field	Lists accounts from which this payment can be made.
Show bills section	Allows you to display all bills or bills due by a certain date.
Filter By field	Allows you to display bills for all vendors or a selected vendor from the drop-down list.

If you make an error in this window and have clicked the Pay Selected Bills button, you cannot correct the error in this window. However, you can correct the error in the Write Checks window, as will be explained later.

Activities identified as purchases on account were recorded in the Enter Bills window. Subsequently, activities identified as payment of the outstanding accounts payable (previously recorded in the Enter Bills window) are then recorded in the Pay Bills window. Accounts Payable and Cash are the default general ledger posting accounts. All transactions entered in this window result in a debit to the Accounts Payable account and a credit to the Cash account.

Paying a Bill in Full

On February 10, 2021, Kristin Raina wishes to pay Nordic Realty Corp. for the rent bill received on February 3, 2021 (Check No. 1). Do not print the check.

To pay a bill:
1. At the main menu bar, click Vendors and then click *Pay Bills.*
2. In the Show bills section, click *Show all bills.*
3. At the *Filter By* field, choose *Nordic Realty.*
4. At the *PAYMENT Date* field, choose *02/10/2021.*
5. At the *PAYMENT Method* field, choose *Check* and then *Assign check number.*
6. Confirm that the *PAYMENT Account* field reads *1010 Cash - Operating.*
7. Choose the bill from *Nordic Realty* by inserting a check mark in the box (❑) to the left of *Nordic Realty.* See Figure 2–R.

FIGURE 2–R
Pay Bills Window—
Vendor Bill Selected

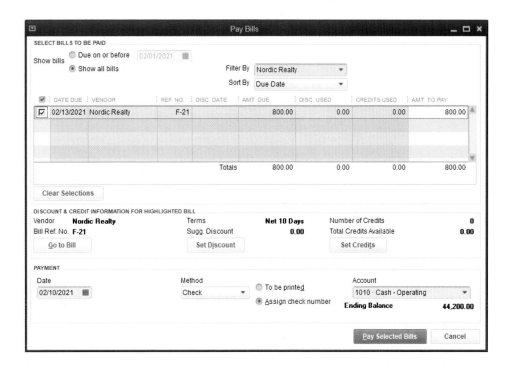

8. Click the Pay Selected Bills button. The Assign Check Numbers window appears.
9. Click the *Let me assign the check numbers below* option.
10. In the *CHECK* field, type 1. See Figure 2–S.

FIGURE 2–S
Assign Check Numbers
Window

11. Click OK.
12. The Payment Summary window appears. See Figure 2–T.

HINT

If the information is incorrect, it cannot be corrected here. It can be corrected later in the Write Checks window.

FIGURE 2–T
Payment Summary
Window

13. Click the Done button.

ACCOUNTING CONCEPT

For a payment of an existing Accounts Payable, the general ledger posting is as follows:					In addition, the vendor file (sub-ledger) for Nordic Realty Corp. reflects the payment:	
2010 Accts Payable		**1010 Cash - Operating**			**Nordic Realty Corp.**	
Dr	Cr	Dr	Cr		Dr	Cr
800			800		Pay 800	800 Bill
						0

Even though a check is not printed, for accounts payable and general ledger purposes, the bill is now considered paid. The vendor balance owed has been reduced along with the cash balance. Each time you click Pay Selected Bills in this window, the Assign Check Numbers window appears. After assigning the first check number, you can either use the foregoing procedure and indicate a check number, or you can click the *Let QuickBooks assign check numbers* option. Subsequent check numbers will then be assigned in sequence. You will not see a check number in this window, but you will see the check numbers for these transactions in the Write Checks window and reports.

Making a Partial Payment of a Bill

QuickBooks allows a partial payment to be made toward an outstanding bill. On February 23, 2021, Kristin Raina wishes to make a partial payment of $200 toward the Cuza and Carl Associates outstanding bill of $600 (Check No. 2).

To make a partial payment:
1. At the main menu bar, click Vendors and then click *Pay Bills.*
2. In the Show bills section, click *Show all bills* to display all the bills.
3. At the *Filter By* field, choose *Cuza and Carl Associates.*
4. At the *PAYMENT Date* field, set the payment date for *02/23/2021.*

5. At the *PAYMENT Method* field, choose *Check*, if necessary; the *Assign check no.* option should be selected. Accept *1010 Cash - Operating* in the *PAYMENT Account* field.

6. In the *AMT. TO PAY* field, on the line for the Cuza and Carl Associates bill, type 200.

When you move to another field, the bill is automatically checked off for payment. See Figure 2–U.

FIGURE 2–U
Pay Bills Window—
Partial Payment

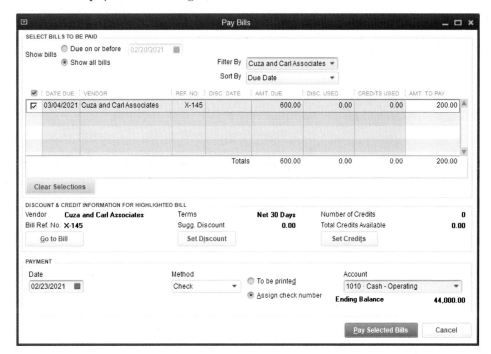

7. Click the Pay Selected Bills button.
8. At the Assign Check Numbers window, click the *Let QuickBooks assign check numbers* option.
9. Click OK.
10. At the Payment Summary window, notice the check number is 2.
11. Click Done.

Practice Exercise 2–3

HINT

Use the Scroll Down arrow if you do not see the invoice in the Pay Bills window.

Record the following transactions at the Pay Bills window:

Feb. 27	Paid *[Your Name]* Accounting Service bill in full (Check No. 3).
Feb. 27	Made a partial payment of $1,000 toward Galeway Computers bill of $3,600 (Check No. 4).

The Write Checks Window

In QuickBooks, the Write Checks window is used to record a **cash purchase** that has not been previously entered into the system. The Write Checks window is useful for companies that usually pay on account but occasionally receive bills and remit payments immediately and for companies that do not purchase goods or services on account and therefore do not need to track vendor data. Accounts Payable is not used, which allows for a cash purchase to be recorded in one step. The data fields in this window are similar to those in the Enter Bills window: payee (vendor name), date, expense, asset, and item purchased.

The Write Checks window is used for all cash purchases, whether the payment is by check, PayPal, electronic transfer, or debit card. The default account is Cash. The transaction is recorded as follows:

	Asset/Expense/Drawing	XXX	
	Cash		XXX

A transaction entered in this window is not tracked through the *Accounts Payable* or *Vendor* reports.

Activities identified as cash purchases are recorded in the Write Checks window. In this window, the Cash account is the default credit posting account because all transactions result in a cash payment. The account field in this window is used to indicate the asset, expense, or drawings account to be debited.

On February 28, 2021, Kristin Raina receives a bill for $125 for monthly janitorial services from Jeter Janitorial Services. She pays it with Check No. 5.

To write a check:

1. At the main menu bar, click Banking and then click *Write Checks.*
2. At the *BANK ACCOUNT* field, confirm that *1010 Cash - Operating* displays. Click to remove the check mark in the *Print Later* box, and in the check number field, type 5, if necessary.
3. At the *DATE* field, choose *02/28/2021.*
4. At the PAY TO THE ORDER OF drop-down list, click *Jeter Janitorial Services.*
5. At the *$* field, type 125.
6. On the Expenses tab, in the *ACCOUNT* field, click *6300 Janitorial Expenses* at the drop-down list. See Figure 2–V.

FIGURE 2-V

Write Checks Window—
Completed

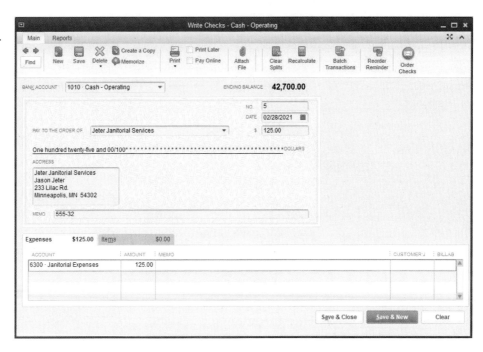

7. If the information is correct, click the Save & New button. Even though a check is not printed, the bill is now considered paid.

ACCOUNTING CONCEPT

For a cash payment of an expense, the general ledger posting is as follows:

6300 Janitorial Expenses		1010 Cash - Operating	
Dr	Cr	Dr	Cr
125			125

The vendor file is unaffected because payment was made immediately.

If you click the Previous arrow at this time, you will see the payments recorded in this window as well as the payments recorded in the Pay Bills window. Activities recorded in the Pay Bills window are actually checks written that subsequently appear in the Write Checks window, in addition to the checks written in the Write Checks window. The payments are recorded in check number sequence. Since checks are not being printed, the program automatically assigns the next check number. Any errors recorded in the Pay Bills window cannot be corrected in the Pay Bills window, but they can be corrected in the Write Checks window.

To see an example of this, click the Previous arrow several times. Each time, notice that the payments include those entered in both the Write Checks and Pay Bills windows. As you scroll through the windows, notice the window is different for payments made in the Write Checks and Pay Bills windows. Notice also that the check numbers are in sequence.

HINT

Make sure the *Print Later* box is not checked.

Record the following transactions in the Write Checks window:

Feb. 28	Received bill from Grayson Graphics for design supplies, $200. Pay immediately with Check No. 6 (charge to Design Supplies Account No. 1300).
Feb. 28	Received bill from TwinCityTelCo for telephone service for February, $275. Pay immediately with Check No. 7 (charge to Telephone Expense Account No. 6450).
Feb. 28	The owner, Kristin Raina, withdrew $400 for personal use. Pay immediately with Check No. 8 (charge to Kristin Raina, Drawings Account No. 3020).

As previously mentioned, the Write Checks window is used for all cash payments, including those made with a debit card. The steps to enter a purchase by debit card or online payment are the same as the steps for payment by check, except instead of entering a check number in the *NO.* field, another identifier (such as DC-1 or DC-2) is used. All other steps are the same.

Reports

Vendor Reports and Accounting Reports

Reports, the fourth level of operation in QuickBooks, reflect the information and activities recorded in the various Lists/Centers and Activities windows. QuickBooks can display and print a variety of internal management reports as well as typical accounting and financial reports, many of which should be printed monthly.

Viewing and Printing Vendor Reports

The Accounts Payable and vendor-related reports help a company manage its liability payments, ensure timely and correct remittances, control cash flow, and retain an accurate record of all vendor-related transactions. Among these reports are the *Unpaid Bills Detail* report, the *Vendor Balance Detail* report, and the *Vendor Contact List* report.

Unpaid Bills Detail Report

The *Unpaid Bills Detail* report lists all unpaid bills for each vendor at a specific date. The report lists each open bill (with date and invoice number) for a vendor, along with any credit memos applied. The report may be customized to show all vendors or only those with outstanding bills.

To view and print the *Unpaid Bills Detail* report:
1. At the main menu bar, click Reports and then click *Vendors & Payables.*
2. At the Vendors & Payables submenu, click *Unpaid Bills Detail.*
3. At the *Date* calendar, choose *02/28/2021.* The *Unpaid Bills Detail* report appears. See Figure 2–W.

FIGURE 2–W
Unpaid Bills Detail Report

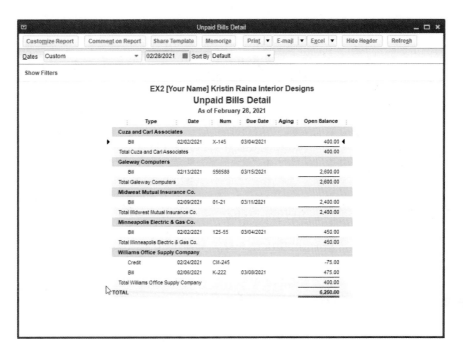

Along the top of the *Unpaid Bills Detail* report window are several buttons (e.g., Customize Report, Comment on Report, Share Template, Memorize, Print). Notice the vertical dotted bar before each column heading in the report text. If you wish to change the width of a column, you can click and drag the crossed arrows that appear in either direction.

4. To print the report, click the Print button at the top of the report and then click *Report*.

   If you receive a message about Printing Features, insert a check mark in the box to the left of the *Do not display this message in the future* option and then click OK. The Print Reports dialog box appears. See Figure 2–X.

FIGURE 2–X
Print Reports Dialog Box

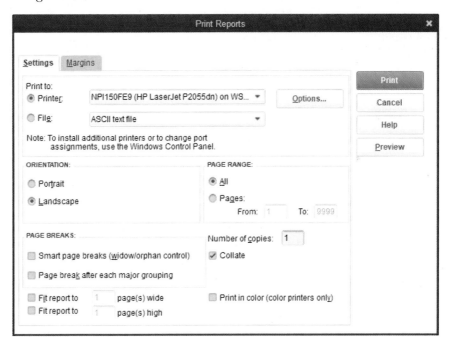

In the Print Reports dialog box, the settings and margins can be changed based on your printer. The orientation of the report can also be changed. There is a Preview button if you wish to preview the report before printing. At this time, do not change any settings other than the orientation. For most reports, the portrait orientation is fine, but for some wider reports, the landscape orientation may be more useful.

5. In the Print Reports dialog box, choose *Portrait* in the Orientation section and then click Print.
6. Close the report.

If you receive a Memorize Report message, insert a check mark in the box to the left of the *Do not display this message in the future* option and then click No.

Vendor Balance Detail Report

The *Vendor Balance Detail* report displays all transactions for each vendor and shows the remaining balance owed. This report is similar to an accounts payable subsidiary ledger in a manual system. The report shows all vendor-related transactions—that is, all bills, payments, and credit memos for each vendor—in chronological order.

To view and print the *Vendor Balance Detail* report:

1. At the main menu bar, click Reports and then click *Vendors & Payables.*
2. At the Vendors & Payables submenu, click *Vendor Balance Detail.*
3. Click the Print button at the top of the report and then click *Report.*
4. In the Print Reports dialog box, choose *Portrait* orientation and then click Print. Your printout should look like Figure 2–Y.

FIGURE 2–Y
Vendor Balance Detail Report

HINT

The columns in this figure have been widened to better display the data.

EX2 [Your Name] Kristin Raina Interior Designs
Vendor Balance Detail
All Transactions

Type	Date	Num	Account	Amount	Balance
[Your Name] Accounting Service					
Bill	02/23/2021	Feb21	2010 · Accounts Payable	300.00	300.00
Bill Pmt -Check	02/27/2021	3	2010 · Accounts Payable	-300.00	0.00
Total [Your Name] Accounting Service				0.00	0.00
Cuza and Carl Associates					
Bill	02/02/2021	X-145	2010 · Accounts Payable	600.00	600.00
Bill Pmt -Check	02/23/2021	2	2010 · Accounts Payable	-200.00	400.00
Total Cuza and Carl Associates				400.00	400.00
Galeway Computers					
Bill	02/13/2021	556588	2010 · Accounts Payable	3,600.00	3,600.00
Bill Pmt -Check	02/27/2021	4	2010 · Accounts Payable	-1,000.00	2,600.00
Total Galeway Computers				2,600.00	2,600.00
Midwest Mutual Insurance Co.					
Bill	02/09/2021	01-21	2010 · Accounts Payable	2,400.00	2,400.00
Total Midwest Mutual Insurance Co.				2,400.00	2,400.00
Minneapolis Electric & Gas Co.					
Bill	02/02/2021	125-55	2010 · Accounts Payable	350.00	350.00
Total Minneapolis Electric & Gas Co.				350.00	350.00
Nordic Realty					
Bill	02/03/2021	F-21	2010 · Accounts Payable	800.00	800.00
Bill Pmt -Check	02/10/2021	1	2010 · Accounts Payable	-800.00	0.00
Total Nordic Realty				0.00	0.00
Williams Office Supply Company					
Bill	02/06/2021	K-222	2010 · Accounts Payable	475.00	475.00
Credit	02/24/2021	CM-245	2010 · Accounts Payable	-75.00	400.00
Total Williams Office Supply Company				400.00	400.00
TOTAL				**6,150.00**	**6,150.00**

5. Close the report.

Vendor Contact List **Report**

HINT

The *Vendor Contact List* report may also be accessed from the Vendors & Payables submenu.

The *Vendor Contact List* report displays information for all vendors that has been entered in each vendor's file. This report displays the name of each vendor, along with the vendor's account number, address, contact person, and telephone and mobile numbers. It also shows the present balance owed.

To view the *Vendor Contact List* report:

1. At the main menu bar, click Reports and then click *List*.
2. At the List submenu, click *Vendor Contact List*. The *Vendor Contact List* report appears. See Figure 2–Z.

FIGURE 2–Z
Vendor Contact List

HINT

The format of your reports may vary slightly from the figures in the textbook. The reports in the figures are customized to display certain information. Chapter 12 will discuss customizing reports.

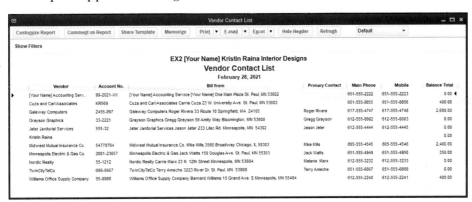

3. Close the report.

Drilling Down to a Transaction Window

HINT

You can view a vendor file by choosing the vendor name from the *Vendor Contact List* or by "drilling down" to the vendor file from within a vendor report.

While viewing reports, it is frequently helpful to see the originating transaction or document that gave rise to the report figures. Most of the reports provide a drill-down feature. When reviewing a report, Quick-Books, like many computerized accounting programs, allows you to "drill down" from a report to the original window where data has been entered. If the transaction is incorrect, you can edit or remove the transaction at that time. Any changes to the transactions are automatically reflected in subsequent reports.

When Kristin Raina reviewed the *Unpaid Bills Detail* report, she discovered that the bill from Minneapolis Electric & Gas Co. was entered incorrectly as $350, while the correct amount was $450.

To drill down from a report and correct an error:

1. At the main menu bar, click Reports and then click *Vendors & Payables*.
2. At the Vendors & Payables submenu, click *Unpaid Bills Detail*.
3. Set the date for *02/28/2021*.
4. Place the mouse pointer over the Minneapolis Electric & Gas Co. bill. Notice that the pointer turns into a magnifying glass with a Z in the center. This is called the *zoom glass*.

5. With the zoom glass positioned over the Minneapolis Electric & Gas Co. bill, double-click the bill. The original bill entry appears. See Figure 2–AA.

6. At the *AMOUNT DUE* field, change the amount to 450.
7. After completing the change, click the Save & Close button.
8. At the Recording Transaction window, click Yes.
9. If the Report needs to be refreshed window appears, click Yes. You will be returned to the report with the corrected figure in place. See Figure 2–BB.

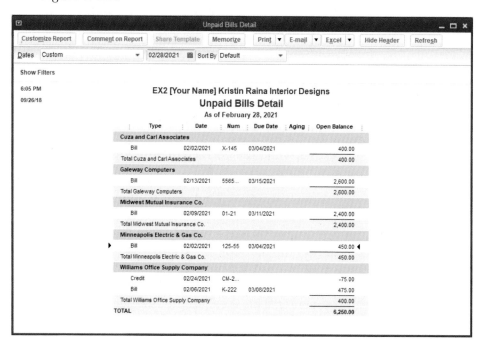

10. To print the corrected report, click the Print button at the top of the report.

11. In the Print Reports dialog box, choose *Landscape* orientation and then click Print.
12. Close the report.

Viewing and Printing Accounting Reports

As activities are entered in the windows, behind-the-scenes accounting activity is recorded in general journal format and posted to the general ledger, and then it flows into the financial statements. QuickBooks can display and print these standard accounting reports, such as the *Journal* report. The *Journal* report displays, in general journal format, all transactions recorded during a specified period of time.

To view and print the *Journal* report:
1. At the Reports menu, click *Accountant & Taxes*.
2. At the Accountant & Taxes submenu, click *Journal*.
3. At the *From* and *To* fields, choose *02/01/2021* and *02/28/2021*. The *Journal* report is displayed.
4. To print the report, click the Print button at the top of the report and then click *Report*.
5. In the Print Reports dialog box, choose *Landscape* orientation and then click Print. See Figure 2–CC.

FIGURE 2–CC
Journal Report

EX2 [Your Name] Kristin Raina Interior Designs
Journal
February 2021

Trans #	Type	Date	Num	Name	Memo	Account	Debit	Credit
3	Bill	02/02/2021	125-55	Minneapolis Electric & Ga...		2010 · Accounts Payable		450.00
				Minneapolis Electric & Ga...		6500 · Utilities Expense	450.00	
							450.00	450.00
4	Bill	02/02/2021	X-145	Cuza and Carl Associates		2010 · Accounts Payable		600.00
				Cuza and Carl Associates		1410 · Prepaid Advertising	600.00	
							600.00	600.00
6	Bill	02/03/2021	F-21	Nordic Realty		2010 · Accounts Payable		800.00
				Nordic Realty		6400 · Rent Expense	800.00	
							800.00	800.00
7	Bill	02/06/2021	K-222	Williams Office Supply Co...		2010 · Accounts Payable		475.00
				Williams Office Supply Co...		1305 · Office Supplies	475.00	
							475.00	475.00
8	Bill	02/09/2021	01-21	Midwest Mutual Insurance ...		2010 · Accounts Payable		2,400.00
				Midwest Mutual Insurance ...		1420 · Prepaid Insurance	2,400.00	
							2,400.00	2,400.00
9	Bill	02/13/2021	556588	Galeway Computers		2010 · Accounts Payable		3,600.00
				Galeway Computers		1825 · Computers, Cost	3,600.00	
							3,600.00	3,600.00
10	Bill	02/23/2021	Feb21	[Your Name] Accounting S...		2010 · Accounts Payable		300.00
				[Your Name] Accounting S...		6020 · Accounting Expense	300.00	
							300.00	300.00
11	Credit	02/24/2021	CM-245	Williams Office Supply Co...	Return damaged off...	2010 · Accounts Payable	75.00	
				Williams Office Supply Co...	Return damaged off...	1305 · Office Supplies		75.00
							75.00	75.00
12	Bill Pmt -Check	02/10/2021	1	Nordic Realty	55-1212	1010 · Cash - Operating		800.00
				Nordic Realty	55-1212	2010 · Accounts Payable	800.00	
							800.00	800.00
13	Bill Pmt -Check	02/23/2021	2	Cuza and Carl Associates	KR569	1010 · Cash - Operating		200.00
				Cuza and Carl Associates	KR569	2010 · Accounts Payable	200.00	
							200.00	200.00
14	Bill Pmt -Check	02/27/2021	3	[Your Name] Accounting S...	99-2021	1010 · Cash - Operating		300.00
				[Your Name] Accounting S...	99-2021	2010 · Accounts Payable	300.00	
							300.00	300.00
15	Bill Pmt -Check	02/27/2021	4	Galeway Computers	2455-897	1010 · Cash - Operating		1,000.00
				Galeway Computers	2455-897	2010 · Accounts Payable	1,000.00	
							1,000.00	1,000.00
16	Check	02/28/2021	5	Jeter Janitorial Services	555-32	1010 · Cash - Operating		125.00
				Jeter Janitorial Services	555-32	6300 · Janitorial Expenses	125.00	
							125.00	125.00
17	Check	02/28/2021	6	Grayson Graphics	33-2221	1010 · Cash - Operating		200.00
				Grayson Graphics	33-2221	1300 · Design Supplies	200.00	
							200.00	200.00
18	Check	02/28/2021	7	TwinCityTelCo	666-6667	1010 · Cash - Operating		275.00
				TwinCityTelCo	666-6667	6450 · Telephone Expense	275.00	
							275.00	275.00
19	Check	02/28/2021	8	Kristin Raina		1010 · Cash - Operating		400.00
				Kristin Raina		3020 · Kristin Raina, Drawi...	400.00	
							400.00	400.00
TOTAL							12,000.00	12,000.00

6. Close the report.

QuickBooks automatically assigns transaction numbers (Trans #). You cannot change them. Notice in Figure 2–CC that there is no transaction number 5 because this transaction was deleted earlier in the chapter. The software deletes the transaction but moves to the next transaction number for the next transaction. When comparing your work to the solutions, do not be concerned if you have different transaction numbers as long as you have the correct journal entries.

HINT

See Appendix C for a summary of journal report types.

The *Type* column in Figure 2–CC indicates the window where the activity was recorded. In this column, the *Bill* entries represent transactions entered in the Enter Bills window. Notice that each *Bill* transaction has a credit to Accounts Payable because this is the default for that account. The *Credit* entry represents the credit memo entered in the Enter Bills window. Recall that when the credit memo option is chosen, the default account becomes a debit to Accounts Payable. The *Bill Pmt–Check* entries represent transactions entered in the Pay Bills window. Each of these transactions is a debit to Accounts Payable and a credit to Cash; these two accounts are the defaults for this window. The *Check* entries are from the Write Checks window. Each has a credit to Cash because that is the default account for this window.

Exiting QuickBooks

After completing this session, you should make a backup copy of your exercise company file on a removable storage device or network directory using the backup procedures explained in Chapter 1. When you back up to a removable storage device, be sure to change the *Save in* field to the location where you keep your backup files and then carefully type in the correct file name.

Close the company file and then exit QuickBooks.

Chapter Review and Assessment

Procedure Review

To add a vendor:
1. At the main menu bar, click Vendors and then click *Vendor Center.*
2. At the Vendor Center window, click the New Vendor button and then select *New Vendor.*
3. Enter the background data for the vendor.
4. Click OK.
5. Close the Vendor Center window.

To delete a vendor:
1. At the main menu bar, click Vendors and then click *Vendor Center.*
2. At the Vendor Center window, select the vendor you wish to delete.
3. At the main menu bar, click Edit and then click *Delete Vendor.*
4. Click OK at the warning.
5. Close the Vendor Center window.
    You cannot delete a vendor that has a balance or that was used in a transaction during the period.

To edit a vendor:
1. At the main menu bar, click Vendors and then click *Vendor Center.*
2. At the Vendor Center window, select the vendor you wish to edit and then double-click the vendor name.
3. Change the appropriate information.
4. Click OK.
5. Close the Vendor Center window.

To enter a bill:
1. At the main menu bar, click Vendors and then click *Enter Bills.*
2. Click the *Bill* option.
3. At the VENDOR drop-down list, click the vendor name.
4. Enter the bill date in the *DATE* field.
5. Enter the invoice number in the *REF. NO.* field.
6. Enter the amount in the *AMOUNT DUE* field.
7. Enter the due date in the *BILL DUE* field.
8. Select the terms in the *TERMS* field.
9. Select the account to be debited on the Expenses tab.
10. Click Save & Close.

To update the Vendor Center while in an Activity window:
1. At the main menu bar, click Vendors and then click *Enter Bills.*
2. At the VENDOR drop-down list, click *< Add New >.*
3. Follow the procedures to add a vendor.
4. Click OK.

To correct an error in an Activity window:
1. Open the Activity window containing the error.
2. Use the Previous arrow to locate the transaction.
3. Make the necessary corrections.
4. Click the Save & Close button.

To process a credit memo:
1. At the main menu bar, click Vendors and then click *Enter Bills*.
2. Click the *Credit* option.
3. Follow the procedures for entering a bill.

To pay a bill:
1. At the main menu bar, click Vendors and then click *Pay Bills*.
2. Click *Show all bills*.
3. At the *Filter By* field, choose the appropriate vendor whose bill you wish to pay.
4. Enter the payment date in the *PAYMENT Date* field.
5. At the *PAYMENT Method* field, choose *Check* and the *Assign check no.* option.
6. At the *PAYMENT Account* field, choose the appropriate cash account.
7. Choose the bill to be paid by inserting a check mark in the box (❑) to the left of the bill. Accept the full amount or enter a partial amount.
8. Click the Pay Selected Bills button. The Assign Check Numbers dialog box appears.
9. Click the *Let me assign the check numbers below* option.
10. Enter the check number.
11. Click OK.
12. At the Payment Summary window, click Done.

To record a cash purchase:
1. At the main menu bar, click Banking and then click *Write Checks*.
2. At the *BANK ACCOUNT* field, choose the appropriate account.
3. Enter the payment date in the *DATE* field. Enter the check or identifying number in the *NO.* field.
4. Choose the payee from the PAY TO THE ORDER OF drop-down list.
5. At the *$* field, enter the amount of the payment.
6. On the Expenses tab, choose the account to be debited.
7. Click Save & Close.

To view and print vendor reports from the Reports menu:
1. At the main menu bar, click Reports and then click *Vendors & Payables*.
2. At the Vendors & Payables or List submenu, choose a report.
3. Indicate the appropriate dates for the report and then click the Refresh button at the top of the report.
4. Click the Print button at the top of the report and then click *Reports*.
5. In the Print Reports dialog box, review the settings and then click Print.
6. Close the report.

Key Concepts

Select the letter of the item that best matches each definition.

a. *Journal* report
b. Write Checks window
c. System default account
d. Vendor Center
e. *Unpaid Bills* report

f. Credit memo
g. Pay Bills window
h. Vendor
i. Enter Bills window
j. *Vendor Contact List* report

_____ 1. Someone from whom the business buys goods or services.
_____ 2. Contains a file for all vendors with whom the company does business.
_____ 3. A report that lists all unpaid vendor bills at a specific date.
_____ 4. Processed through the Enter Bills window to reflect a reduction of the vendor's liability due to a credit for return or allowance.
_____ 5. Activity window used to record vendor bills to be paid at a later date.
_____ 6. Activities displayed in general journal format for a specified period of time.
_____ 7. Report that lists all vendors from which the company buys goods and services.
_____ 8. A pre-identified general ledger account that increases or decreases automatically, depending on the type of transaction entered.
_____ 9. Activity window used to record a cash purchase of goods or services from a vendor.
_____ 10. Activity window used to pay bills previously entered in the Enter Bills window.

Procedure Check

1. Your company has changed its telephone carrier. Describe the steps to add the new vendor to the system.
2. Upper management requests a list of all businesses from which the company buys goods or services. How would you use QuickBooks to quickly produce this information?
3. You receive a batch of bills that must be paid immediately. You do not need to maintain an Accounts Payable record of these payments. How would you use QuickBooks to expeditiously enter these payments into the system and write the appropriate payment checks?
4. A vendor calls your company to complain that a bill sent 45 days ago remains unpaid. How would you use QuickBooks to verify this complaint?
5. You wish to view all the bills received from a vendor and all payments made to that vendor. How would you use QuickBooks to obtain the required information?
6. Compare and contrast a manual accounting system with a computerized accounting system for processing vendor transactions. How does the accounts payable subsidiary ledger compare with the Vendor Center?

Case Problems

Demonstrate your knowledge of the QuickBooks features discussed in this chapter by completing the following case problems.

Case Problem 2–1

On April 1, 2021, Lynn Garcia started her business, Lynn's Music Studio, as a music instructor. She began by depositing $10,000 cash in a bank account in the business name. She also contributed a piano and some guitars. The musical instruments have an outstanding note balance of $2,000, which will now be assumed by the business. The cash, musical instruments, note payable, and capital have all been recorded in the opening balances of the books. Lynn anticipates setting up her studio in the beginning of the month and expects to provide piano and guitar lessons later in the month. Record the transactions listed below for the month of April.

1. Open the company file **CH2 Lynn's Music Studio.QBW**.
2. At the QuickBooks Desktop Login window, in the *Password* text box, type Student1 and then click OK.
3. Make a backup copy of the company file and name it **LMS2** *[Your Name]* **Lynn's Music Studio** and enter the password.
4. Restore the backup copy of the company file. In both the Open Backup Copy and Save Company File as dialog boxes, use the file name **LMS2** *[Your Name]* **Lynn's Music Studio** and enter the password.
5. Change the company name to **LMS2** *[Your Name]* **Lynn's Music Studio**.
6. Add the following vendors to the Vendor Center:

VENDOR NAME:	Pioneer Phone
OPENING BALANCE:	0 AS OF April 1, 2021
COMPANY NAME:	Pioneer Phone
First Name:	Customer
Last Name:	Service
Main Phone:	570-555-6000
Mobile:	570-555-6500
Main Email:	pioph@ppi-edu.net
BILLED FROM:	1000 Route 6
	Carbondale, PA 18407
PAYMENT TERMS:	Net 15 Days

VENDOR NAME:	Steamtown Electric
OPENING BALANCE:	0 AS OF April 1, 2021
COMPANY NAME:	Steamtown Electric
First Name:	Customer
Last Name:	Service
Main Phone:	570-555-2500
Mobile:	570-555-3000
Main Email:	steam@ppi-edu.net
BILLED FROM:	150 Vine Lane
	Scranton, PA 18501
PAYMENT TERMS:	Net 15 Days

Delete the following vendor:
   Universal Electric

Edit the following vendor:
   Mutual Insurance Company main telephone number: 570-555-5600

7. Using the appropriate window, record the following transactions for April 2021:

Apr. 2   Received bill for rent for the month of April from Viewhill Realty, $600, paid immediately, Check No. 1. Do not print check.

Apr. 2   Received a bill for a one-year insurance policy on account from Mutual Insurance Company, Invoice No. 4010102, $1,200, Net 30 Days.

Apr. 5   Purchased furniture on account from Mills Family Furniture, Invoice No. 1257, $2,500, Net 30 Days.

Apr. 6   Purchased a computer system on account from Computer Town, Invoice No. X234, $3,000, Net 30 Days.

Apr. 9   Purchased music supplies on account from Strings, Sheets, & Such, Invoice No. 1290, $500, Net 15 Days.

Apr. 9   Received bill for tuning of piano and guitars from Tune Tones, $100, paid immediately, Check No. 2. Tune Tones is a new vendor:

VENDOR NAME:	Tune Tones
OPENING BALANCE:	0 AS OF April 1, 2021
COMPANY NAME:	Tune Tones
First Name:	Tony
Last Name:	Tune
Main Phone:	570-555-1111
Mobile:	570-555-2222
Main Email:	TUNE@ppi-edu.net
BILLED FROM:	500 Monroe Ave. Dunmare, PA 18512
PAYMENT TERMS:	Net 30 Days

Apr. 9   Purchased office supplies on account from Paper, Clips, and More, Invoice No. 01-1599, $400, Net 30 Days.

Apr. 12   Received the telephone bill from Pioneer Phone, Invoice No. pp401, $50, Net 15 Days.

Apr. 13   Received utilities bill from Steamtown Electric, Invoice No. SE401, $70, Net 15 Days.

Apr. 20   Paid in full Strings, Sheets, & Such, Invoice No. 1290 (Check No. 3). Do not print check.

Apr. 23   Received a credit memo from Paper, Clips, and More, Invoice No. CM250, $50, for office supplies returned. Apr. 26   Paid in full Pioneer Phone, Invoice No. pp401 (Check No. 4).

Apr. 27   Paid in full Steamtown Electric, Invoice No. SE401 (Check No. 5).

Apr. 30   Made a partial payment of $1,000 to Mills Family Furniture (Check No. 6).

Apr. 30   Made a partial payment of $1,000 to Computer Town (Check No. 7).

Apr. 30   The owner, Lynn Garcia, withdrew $1,000 for personal use (Check No. 8).

8. Display and print the following reports for April 1, 2021, to April 30, 2021.
   a. *Unpaid Bills Detail*
   b. *Vendor Balance Detail*
   c. *Vendor Contact List*
   d. *Journal*

Case Problem 2–2

On June 1, 2021, Olivia Chen started her business, Olivia's Web Solutions, as an internet consultant and web page designer. She began by depositing $25,000 cash in a bank account in the business name. She also contributed a computer system. The computer has an outstanding note balance of $2,500 that will be assumed by the business. The cash, computer, note payable, and capital have all been recorded in the opening balances of the books. Olivia anticipates setting up her office in the beginning of the month and expects to provide web design and internet consulting services later in the month. You will record the transactions listed below for the month of June.

1. Open the company file **CH2 Olivia's Web Solutions.QBW**.
2. At the QuickBooks Desktop Login window, in the *Password* text box, type Student1 and then click OK.
3. Make a backup copy of the company file and name it **OWS2 *[Your Name]* Olivia's Web Solutions**.
4. Restore the backup copy of the company file. In both the Open Backup Copy and Save Company File as dialog boxes, use the file name **OWS2 *[Your Name]* Olivia's Web Solutions** and enter the password.
5. Change the company name to **OWS2 *[Your Name]* Olivia's Web Solutions**.
6. Add the following vendors to the Vendor Center:

VENDOR NAME:	Comet Computer Supplies
OPENING BALANCE:	0 AS OF June 1, 2021
COMPANY NAME:	Comet Computer Supplies
First Name:	Customer
Last Name:	Service
Main Phone:	631-555-4444
Mobile:	631-555-4455
Main Email:	CometCs@ppi-edu.net
BILLED FROM:	657 Motor Parkway
	Center Island, NY 11488
PAYMENT TERMS:	Net 15 Days
VENDOR NAME:	Chrbet Advertising
OPENING BALANCE:	0 AS OF June 1, 2021
COMPANY NAME:	Chrbet Advertising
First Name:	Chris
Last Name:	Chrbet
Main Phone:	212-555-8777
Mobile:	212-555-8778
Main Email:	Cadv@ppi-edu.net

BILLED FROM:	201 East 10th Street
	New York, NY 10012
PAYMENT TERMS:	Net 30 Days

Delete the following vendor:
   Johnson Ad Agency

Edit the address for Martin Computer Repairs:
   366 North Franklin Street
   Garden City, NY 11568

7. Using the appropriate window, record the following transactions for June 2021:

Jun. 1	Received bill for rent for the month of June from ARC Management, $800, paid immediately. Check No. 1. Do not print check.
Jun. 4	Received a one-year insurance policy on account from Eastern Mutual Insurance, Invoice No. 87775, $1,800, Net 30 Days.
Jun. 4	Purchased software on account from Netsoft Development Co., Invoice No. 38745, $3,600, Net 30 Days.
Jun. 7	Purchased office furniture on account from Lewis Furniture Co., Invoice No. O9887, $3,200, Net 30 Days.
Jun. 8	Purchased six months of advertising services on account from Chrbet Advertising, Invoice No. O-989, $1,200, Net 30 Days.
Jun. 11	Purchased computer supplies on account from Comet Computer Supplies, Invoice No. 56355, $600, Net 15 Days.
Jun. 14	Received bill for online internet services from Systems Service, $150, paid immediately (Check No. 2). Systems Service is a new vendor:

VENDOR NAME:	Systems Service
OPENING BALANCE:	0 AS OF June 1, 2021
COMPANY NAME:	Systems Service
First Name:	Jeremy
Last Name:	Jones
Main Phone:	516-555-2525
Mobile:	516-555-2526
Main Email:	Sysser@ppi-edu.net
BILLED FROM:	36 Sunrise Lane
	Hempstead, NY 11004
PAYMENT TERMS:	Net 30 Days

Jun. 15	Purchased office supplies on account from Office Plus, Invoice No. 3665, $450, Net 30 Days.
Jun. 18	Received telephone bill from Eastel, Invoice No. 6-2568, $350, Net 30 Days.
Jun. 21	Received utilities bill from LI Power Company, Invoice No. OWS-23556, $125, Net 15 Days.

Jun. 21	Returned office supplies to Office Plus for $75 credit, CM789.
Jun. 21	Paid in full Eastern Mutual Insurance, Invoice No. 87775 (Check No. 3). Do not print check.
Jun. 25	Paid in full Comet Computer Supplies, Invoice No. 56355 (Check No. 4).
Jun. 28	Paid in full LI Power Company, Invoice No. OWS-23556 (Check No. 5).
Jun. 30	Made a partial payment of $2,000 to Netsoft Development Co. (Check No. 6).
Jun. 30	Made partial payment of $1,500 to Lewis Furniture Co. (Check No. 7).
Jun. 30	The owner, Olivia Chen, withdrew $500 for personal use (Check No. 8).

8. Display and print the following reports for June 1, 2021, to June 30, 2021:
   a. *Unpaid Bills Detail*
   b. *Vendor Balance Detail*
   c. *Vendor Contact List*
   d. *Journal*

To change the company name:
1. At the main menu bar, click Company and then click *My Company.*
2. At the My Company window, click the Edit icon.
3. In the Company Information dialog box, change the company name to **EX3** *[Your Name]* **Kristin Raina Interior Designs** and then click OK.
4. Close the My Company window.

The Customer Center

The Customer Center contains a file for each customer to whom the company sells goods or services. Each file contains important information, such as company name, address, contact person, type of customer, terms, credit limit, preferred payment method, and current balance owed. You should include all customers with which the company does business in the Customer Center.

Recall from Chapter 1 that the second level of operation in QuickBooks is recording background information in Lists/Centers. The Customer Center is revised periodically when new customers are added, customers not used in the business are deleted, and modifications are made to customer information. Making these adjustments to the customer files is referred to as *updating* the Customer Center.

As previously stated, the Customer Center contains a file for each customer with whom the company does business. You should try to enter the information for each customer in the Customer Center before recording transactions. However, if you inadvertently omit a customer, you can add that customer during the Activities level of operation with minimal disruption.

Kristin Raina has entered information for existing and anticipated customers in the Customer Center.

To view the Customer Center:
1. At the main menu bar, click Customers and then click *Customer Center.* If a window appears titled New Feature - Attach Documents to Quick-Books, click OK or click the X to close it.

    The Customer Center appears with the customer file for Alomar Company displayed. See Figure 3–A.

FIGURE 3–A
Customer Center—
Alomar Company File
Displayed

Table 3–1 describes the various parts of the Customer Center.

TABLE 3–1
Customer Center

Part	Description
Customers & Jobs tab	Lists all customers and jobs with current balances due. You can display all customers, active customers, or only customers with balances.
Transactions tab	Lists all transactions for a selected customer. The Transactions tab in the Customer Information section contains the same information.
New Customer & Job button	Used to add a new customer or job.
New Transactions button	Used to create invoices and to enter sales receipts, payments, and credit memos.
Customer Information section	Displays background and transaction information for the customer selected on the Customers & Jobs tab.
Attach icon	Used to attach documents via the QuickBooks Document Management feature.
Contacts tab	Used to add a contact name for this customer by clicking the Manage Contacts drop-down arrow and choosing *Add New*. You can designate the contact as primary, secondary, or additional.
Edit icon	Used to edit background information for the customer selected on the Customers & Jobs tab.
To Do's tab	Used to view the To Do List for this customer.
Notes tab	Used to include narrative information specific to a customer.
Reports for This Customer section	Lists the reports available in the Customer Center.

In addition to the foregoing, once a customer is selected, you can right-click the customer name on the Customers & Jobs tab to display a shortcut menu, as shown in Figure 3–B. Use this menu to perform most customer-related activities.

FIGURE 3–B
Customer Center
Shortcut Menu

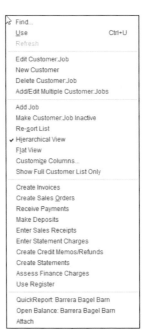

To view a specific customer file:

1. Move the mouse pointer to Alomar Company and double-click to open the file. If a window appears titled New Feature Add/Edit Multiple List Entries, insert a check mark in the box to the left of the *Do not display this message in the future* option and then click OK to close the window. The file opens in Edit Customer mode. See Figure 3–C.

FIGURE 3–C
Customer File—
Alomar Company
Selected

Name page

tabs

Table 3–2 describes the various parts of the customer's file.

TABLE 3–2
Customer File

Part	Description
Name page	Displays the customer's name, the customer's current balance, and three command buttons: OK, Cancel, and Help.
Address Info tab	Used to enter the customer's company name, billing and shipping address, contact person, telephone and mobile phone numbers, and email address. The Edit icon can be used to edit address information.
Payment Settings tab	Used to enter information such as the customer's account number, credit limit, payment terms, preferred delivery method, and credit card information.
Sales Tax Settings tab	Used to enter the customer's sales tax code and resale number.
Additional Info tab	Used to enter the customer type and to create customized fields.
Job Info tab	Used to enter information such as job status and start and end dates for a job for this customer.

2. Close the Edit Customer window.
3. Close the Customer Center.

Add the following customer:

Name page	*CUSTOMER NAME:*	Berger Bakery Company
	OPENING BALANCE:	0 AS OF February 1, 2021
Address Info	*COMPANY NAME:*	Berger Bakery Company
	First Name:	Barry
	Last Name:	Berger
	Main Phone:	612-555-2240
	Mobile:	612-555-2241
	Main Email:	BBC@ppi-edu.net
	INVOICE/BILL TO:	18 N Grand Ave.
		Minneapolis, MN 55403
Payment Settings	*ACCOUNT NO:*	R1825
	CREDIT LIMIT:	10,000
	PAYMENT TERMS:	Net 30 Days
	PREFERRED DELIVERY METHOD:	None
	PREFERRED PAYMENT METHOD:	Check
Additional Info	*CUSTOMER TYPE:*	Commercial

Delete the following customer:
    Lever Land Company

Edit the following customer:
    New phone/mobile for Barrera Bagel Barn:

Main Phone:	612-555-1233
Mobile:	612-555-1234

QuickCheck: The updated Customer Center appears in Figure 3–J.

FIGURE 3–J Updated Customer Center

The Create Invoices Window

Recall from Chapter 1 that the third level of operation in QuickBooks is Activities. In QuickBooks, Activities identified as **sales on account** are recorded in the Create Invoices window. Accounts Receivable is the default general ledger posting account. All transactions entered in this window result in a debit to the Accounts Receivable account. The account to be credited, usually a revenue account, is determined based on the item chosen.

sale on account
occurs when a company sells goods or services to a customer but does not receive payment until a future date

QuickBooks records a sales-on-account transaction as follows:

| | | Accounts Receivable | | XXX | | | |
| | | Revenue | | | | XXX | |

At the same time, QuickBooks updates the customer's file in the Customer Center to reflect the new receivable. The QuickBooks Create Invoices window appears in Figure 3–K.

FIGURE 3–K
Create Invoices Window

The Create Invoices window has four tabs: Main, Formatting, Send/Ship, and Reports. The Main tab allows you to select a customer from the Customer Center, enter an invoice number and terms of payment, and identify items sold or services provided. The Formatting tab allows you to customize the design and presentation of invoices. Customizing invoices will be covered in Chapter 12. The Send/Ship tab allows you to select a carrier for a shipment. The Reports tab accesses various transaction reports. Most icons and data fields are self-explanatory, but take special note of the various parts on the Main tab, as described in Table 3–3.

The Find button; Previous and Next arrows; and New, Save, Delete, Save & Close, Save & New, and Clear buttons all have the same functions in this window as in the Enter Bills window.

TABLE 3–3
Create Invoices
Window, Main Tab

Part	Description
TEMPLATE field	QuickBooks allows for eight types of invoice formats. Choose the one that best describes the items sold. For this chapter, the Intuit Service Invoice will be used. In addition, you can customize and download additional formats.
ITEM field	When you click in the *ITEM* field, a drop-down arrow appears, which allows you to access the Item List. Choose the item of service or inventory sold from the drop-down list. Once an item is selected, the description and rate are filled in automatically based on data entered in the Item List window.
Print button	Used to print this invoice immediately rather than using the Print Forms submenu of the File menu.
Customer Name/ Transaction tabs	Displays a summary of information about the customer, recent transactions, and notes. Click the > arrow to hide this information; click the < arrow to display it.
Edit icon	Used to edit customer information while remaining in the Create Invoices window.
SUMMARY section	Lists phone number, email address, credit limit, and open balance for the selected customer.
CUSTOMER PAYMENT section	Used to edit customer payment preferences.
RECENT TRANSACTIONS section	Displays recent transactions for the selected customer.
NOTES section	Used to post notes concerning the selected customer.

Items

Kristin Raina Interior Designs has established two service revenue items in the Item List: Decorating Services and Design Services. Decorating Services represent interior decorating consulting and are billed at a rate of $50 per hour. Design Services represent interior design work on specific projects and are billed at a rate of $60 per hour.

To view items:

1. At the main menu bar, click Lists and then click *Item List.* The Item List window appears. See Figure 3–L.

FIGURE 3–L
Item List Window

NAME	DESCRIPTION	TYPE	ACCOUNT	ON	PRICE	ATTACH
◆ Decorating Services	Decorating Services	Service	4020 · Decorating Services		50.00	
◆ Design Services	Design Services	Service	4010 · Design Services		60.00	

2. To view the data for the Decorating Services item, double-click the item. The Edit Item window appears. See Figure 3–M.

FIGURE 3–M
Edit Item Window—
Decorating Services

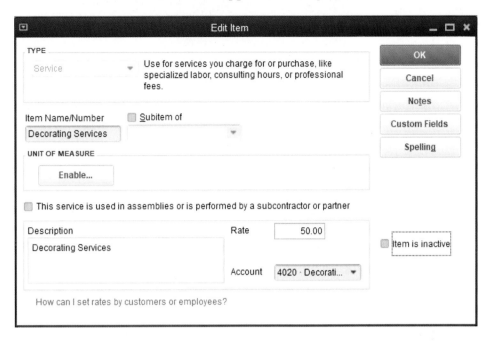

Decorating Services is indicated as a service item (rather than inventory or payroll). The window also contains a description, rate per unit (hour), and default general ledger posting account. QuickBooks uses this data when you create an invoice for a customer for this service.

3. Close the Edit Item and Item List windows.

Creating an Invoice

On February 1, 2021, Kristin Raina provided 12 hours of decorating services on account to Beverly Jones.

HINT

In the event a new customer needs to be added while you are in the Create Invoices window, click < *Add New* > from the CUSTOMER:JOB drop-down list.

To create an invoice:

1. At the main menu bar, click Customers and then click *Create Invoices*.
2. At the CUSTOMER:JOB drop-down list, click *Jones, Beverly*.
3. At the TEMPLATE drop-down list, accept the default choice, *Intuit Service Invoice*.
4. At the *DATE* field, choose *02/01/2021*.
5. At the *INVOICE #* field, type 1001.
6. At the TERMS drop-down list, accept the default choice, *Net 30 Days*.
7. At the *ITEM* field, click the first line to display the drop-down Item List and then click *Decorating Services*. The data from the Decorating Services file in the Item List complete the *DESCRIPTION* and *RATE* fields. See Figure 3–N.

FIGURE 3–N
Create Invoices
Window—Partially
Completed

8. At the *QUANTITY* field, type 12.

   When you move to the next field, the *AMOUNT* box is completed based on the hourly rate times the hours invoiced.

9. At the top of the window, confirm that the *Print Later* and *Email Later* boxes do not contain check marks. In the lower left part of the window, the *Your customer can't pay this invoice online* command should remain off. See Figure 3–O.

FIGURE 3–O
Create Invoices
Window—Completed

HINT

You can display transactions previously entered by clicking the Previous arrow. You can correct errors in a transaction, or you can remove a transaction by clicking the Delete button and then either deleting or voiding the invoice.

As stated earlier, the default account to debit in the Create Invoices window is Accounts Receivable. An account to be credited is not indicated in this window. The item for Decorating Services in the Item List indicated the revenue account that should be credited when entering this item in an activity window. Once you choose the Decorating Services item in the Create Invoices window, QuickBooks knows from the Item List to credit the revenue account Decorating Services for this transaction.

10. If the information is correct, click the Save & Close button.

For a sale of decorating services on account, the general ledger posting is as follows:

1200 Accts Rec			4020 Decor Serv	
Dr	Cr		Dr	Cr
600				600

In addition, the customer file (subledger) for Beverly Jones reflects the new receivable:

Jones, Beverly	
Dr	Cr
600	

Practice Exercise 3-2

Record the following transactions at the Create Invoices window:

Feb. 6	Provided 16 hours of design services to Jennie Guthrie on account. Invoice No. 1002. *QuickCheck:* $960
Feb. 13	Provided 8 hours of decorating services and 16 hours of design services to Cook Caterers. Invoice No. 1003. *QuickCheck:* $1,360
Feb. 17	Provided 24 hours of design services to Franco Films Co. Invoice No. 1004. *QuickCheck:* $1,440
Feb. 23	Provided 24 hours of decorating services to Berger Bakery Company. Invoice No. 1005. *QuickCheck:* $1,200
Feb. 27	Provided 6 hours of decorating services and 15 hours of design services to Cook Caterers. Invoice No. 1006. *QuickCheck:* $1,200

The Receive Payments Window

In QuickBooks, the Receive Payments window is used to record the **collection of accounts receivable** from customers previously invoiced in the Create Invoices window. This window displays all open invoices for a specific customer. Payment can be in the form of cash, check, credit/debit card, or e-check. In addition, customer credit memos can be recorded.

The Receive Payments window is designed only for the collection of existing invoices. The default accounts are Accounts Receivable and Cash or Undeposited Funds (discussed later in this chapter). The transaction is recorded as follows:

collection of accounts receivable
occurs when a customer pays part or all of the outstanding balance due the company; sometimes referred to as *payment of accounts receivable*

			Cash (or Undeposited Funds)		XXX			
			Accounts Receivable				XXX	

At the same time, the customer's file in the Customer Center is updated to reflect the payment. The QuickBooks Receive Payments window appears in Figure 3–P.

FIGURE 3–P
Receive Payments Window

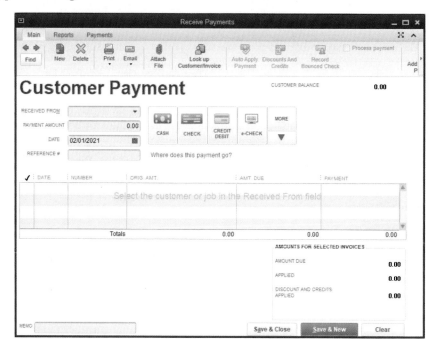

Once a customer is identified, a list of open invoices is displayed. Table 3–4 describes the various parts of the Receive Payments window.

TABLE 3–4
Receive Payments Window, Main Tab

Part	Description
CUSTOMER BALANCE field	Indicates the balance owed by the selected customer for all open invoices.
PAYMENT AMOUNT field	Used to enter the current payment. When an amount is entered, it is applied to the oldest invoice, and a check mark appears to the left of the invoice line. If you wish to have the payment applied to an alternate invoice, you need to select that invoice by inserting a check mark to the left of it.
CASH, CHECK, CREDIT/DEBIT, e-CHECK, MORE buttons	Used to indicate the customer's method of payment.
Look up Customer/ Invoice button	Used to search for all open invoices. The search can be by invoice number, customer name, amount, date, and so on.
Auto Apply/Un-Apply Payment button	Auto Apply Payment is the default button. If no invoice has been selected, Auto Apply automatically applies a payment to the oldest invoice. When a payment is applied, the button switches to Un-Apply Payment, which allows you to select the invoice to be paid.
Discounts and Credits button	Used to apply discounts for early payments and unused credits.

Activities identified as sales on account were recorded in the Create Invoices window. Subsequently, Activities identified as collection of an outstanding account receivable (previously recorded in the Create Invoices window) are now recorded in the Receive Payments window. Cash or Undeposited Funds and Accounts Receivable are the default general ledger posting accounts. All transactions entered in this window result in a debit to the Cash or Undeposited Funds account and a credit to the Accounts Receivable account.

Receiving a Payment in Full

On February 13, 2021, Kristin Raina receives a $600 payment from Beverly Jones for Invoice No. 1001, her Check No. 6544.

To record a receipt of payment:
1. At the main menu bar, click Customers and then click *Receive Payments.*
2. At the RECEIVED FROM drop-down list, click *Jones, Beverly.* All the open invoices for Beverly Jones are displayed. See Figure 3–Q.

FIGURE 3–Q
Receive Payments
Window—Beverly Jones

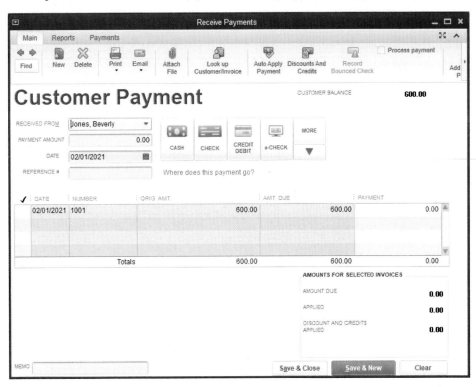

3. At the *PAYMENT AMOUNT* field, type 600.
   Once the amount is entered and you move to the next field, a check mark appears next to open Invoice No. 1001, indicating the $600 payment will be applied to that invoice automatically (since this is the only open invoice).
4. At the *DATE* field, choose *02/13/2021.*
5. Click the CHECK button.
6. At the *CHECK* # field, type 6544. See Figure 3–R.

FIGURE 3–R
Receive Payments
Window—Completed

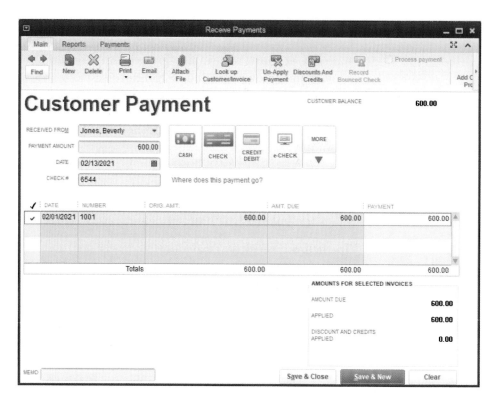

7. Click the Save & Close button.

Save & Close returns you to the main window. If you wish to remain in the Receive Payments window after posting, click the Save & New button or the Next arrow. This posts the transaction and clears the window for the next entry.

ACCOUNTING CONCEPT

For a payment of an existing account receivable, the general ledger posting is as follows:

In addition, the customer file (subledger) for Beverly Jones reflects the payment:

Beverly Jones	
Dr	Cr
Inv 600	Pay 600
0	

Entering a Partial Payment of an Invoice

The Receive Payments window allows you to record partial payments of open invoices. On February 20, 2021, Franco Films remits $500 toward its open Invoice No. 1004 in the amount of $1,440, its Check No. 1255. No discount is allowed.

To record a partial payment of an invoice:

1. At the main menu bar, click Customers and then click *Receive Payments.*
2. At the RECEIVED FROM drop-down list, click *Franco Films Co.* The open invoice is displayed along with the unpaid amount of $1,440 in the *CUSTOMER BALANCE* field.
3. At the *PAYMENT AMOUNT* field, type 500.

   When you move to the next field, the amount appears in the *PAY-MENT* field. The *UNDERPAYMENT* box appears, indicating that $940 remains underpaid and asking if you want to leave it as an underpayment or write off the balance. Choose the *LEAVE THIS AS AN UNDERPAYMENT* option.
4. At the *DATE* field, choose *02/20/2021.*
5. Click the CHECK button.
6. At the *CHECK # field,* type 1255. See Figure 3–S.

FIGURE 3–S
Receive Payments Window—Partial Payment

7. Click the Save & Close button.

Receiving Payment for More Than One Invoice

QuickBooks allows you to record the payment of several invoices at the same time. On February 27, 2021, Cook Caterers remits $2,560 in full payment of Invoice Nos. 1003 and 1006, its Check No. 655.

To record payment of more than one invoice:

1. At the main menu bar, click Customers and then click *Receive Payments.*
2. At the RECEIVED FROM drop-down list, click *Cook Caterers.* All the open invoices are displayed. See Figure 3–T.

FIGURE 3–T
Receive Payments
Window—Invoices
Displayed

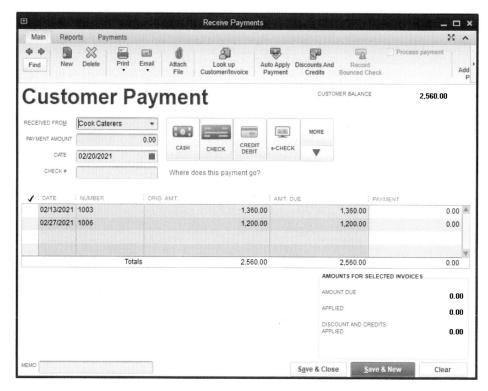

3. At the *PAYMENT AMOUNT* field, type 2560. When you move to the next field, the amount is applied to the two invoices.
4. At the *DATE* field, choose *02/27/2021*. See Figure 3–U.

FIGURE 3–U
Receive Payments
Window—Payment
Applied

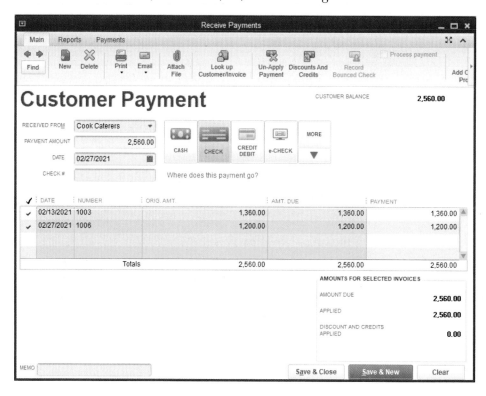

5. Click the payment method button and complete the *CHECK* # field. See Figure 3–V.

FIGURE 3–V
Receive Payments
Window—Completed

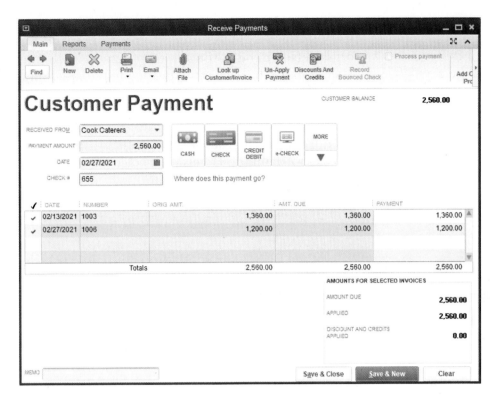

6. If the information is correct, click the Save & New button.

Practice Exercise   3–3

Record the following transactions at the Receive Payments window:

Feb. 28	Received $960 from Jennie Guthrie in full payment of Invoice No. 1002, her Check No. 674.
Feb. 28	Received $600 from Berger Bakery Company in partial payment of Invoice No. 1005. Leave as underpayment, its Check No. 12458.

Activities

The Enter Sales Receipts Window

In QuickBooks, you use the Enter Sales Receipts window to record sales for which the payments are received immediately. Since you do not use Accounts Receivable, this window allows you to record a **cash sale** in one step. The data fields in this window are similar to those in the Create Invoices window: customer, date, item sold, service provided, and so on.

cash sale a sale for which payment is received immediately

The Enter Sales Receipts window is used for all cash sales of goods and services. As with the Receive Payments window, the default account is Cash or Undeposited Funds. The transaction is recorded as follows:

	Cash (or Undeposited Funds)	XXX	
	Revenue		XXX

A transaction entered in this window is not tracked through the *Accounts Receivable* or *Customer* reports.

Activities identified as cash sales are recorded in the Enter Sales Receipts window. In this window, the Cash or Undeposited Funds account is the default debit posting account because each transaction results in a cash receipt. The account to be credited is based on the item selected. As in the Create Invoices window, when an item is selected, QuickBooks uses the information from the Item List window to determine which account should be credited.

On February 24, 2021, Kristin Raina provided eight hours of design services to Hamilton Hotels on Invoice No. 1007. Hamilton Hotels issued Check No. 25546 in full payment.

To record a cash sale:

1. At the main menu bar, click Customers and then click *Enter Sales Receipts.*
2. At the CUSTOMER:JOB drop-down list, click *Hamilton Hotels.*
3. In the *DATE* field, enter the appropriate date and then in the *SALE NO.* field, type 1007.
4. Click the CHECK button.
5. At the *CHECK NO.* field, type 25546 and then confirm that the *Print Later* and *Email Later* boxes do not contain check marks.
6. Complete the remainder of the window in the same manner as you would complete an invoice. See Figure 3–W.

HINT

After entering the quantity, you must move to another field for the amount to be computed.

FIGURE 3–W
Enter Sales Receipts Window—Completed

7. If the information is correct, click the Save & Close button.

The customer file is unaffected because the payment was received at the point of sale.

ACCOUNTING CONCEPT

For a cash sale, the general ledger posting is as follows:

1250 Undeposited Funds		4010 Design Serv	
Dr	Cr	Dr	Cr
480			480

The Make Deposits Window

Most accounting textbooks assume that when cash is received, it is immediately posted to the Cash account. However, many businesses post to the Cash account only when funds are actually deposited in the checking account. This may occur several days after the funds are received. For these businesses, the receipt of funds is posted to a current asset account, titled Undeposited Funds, until a deposit is made. At that point, a second transaction is recorded to show the undeposited funds transferred to the Cash - Operating account. Debits to the Cash - Operating account should coincide with deposits recorded on the bank statement. This allows the company to more easily track deposits during the month-end bank reconciliation process.

When the Undeposited Funds account is used, cash receipts are recorded as follows:

		Undeposited Funds		XXX		
		Accounts Receivable/Revenue				XXX

This entry results from activities entered in the Receive Payments and Enter Sales Receipts windows.

When funds previously received and recorded in the Receive Payments or Sales Receipts windows are subsequently deposited in the bank, the Make Deposits window is used. The default accounts are Cash and Undeposited Funds. The transaction is recorded as follows:

		Cash		XXX		
		Undeposited Funds				XXX

Activities identified as deposits of funds are recorded in the Make Deposits window. In this window, Cash and Undeposited Funds are the default general ledger posting accounts. Each transaction entered in this window results in a debit to the Cash account and a credit to the Undeposited Funds account.

In the Receive Payments and Enter Sales Receipts windows, the default posting account for the receipt of cash is the Undeposited Funds account, rather than the Cash - Operating account. If you wish to allow for alternate debit posting accounts, you can change this default in the Payments Preferences of the Edit menu.

In this chapter, Kristin Raina will deposit all the receipts at one time at month-end. In a real-world setting, deposits are made more frequently depending on collection volume. Using this window allows you either to deposit each receipt individually or deposit several receipts or to deposit all the receipts at one time. On February 28, 2021, Kristin Raina deposits all the collections for the month.

To deposit all receipts collected and previously recorded as Undeposited Funds:

1. At the main menu bar, click Banking and then click *Make Deposits*. The Payments to Deposit window is displayed, showing all undeposited receipts.
2. At the Sort payments by drop-down list, click *Date*. See Figure 3–X.

> **HINT**
>
> In this text, the Undeposited Funds account will remain the default debit posting account.

FIGURE 3–X

Payments to Deposit
Window

3. Because all the receipts will be deposited, click the Select All button. All the receipts are checked for deposit. See Figure 3–Y.

FIGURE 3–Y

Payments to Deposit
Window—All Receipts
Selected

4. If the information is correct, click OK. You are forwarded to the Make Deposits window.
5. At the Deposit To drop-down list, click *1010 Cash - Operating*.
6. At the *Date* field, choose *02/28/2021*. See Figure 3–Z.

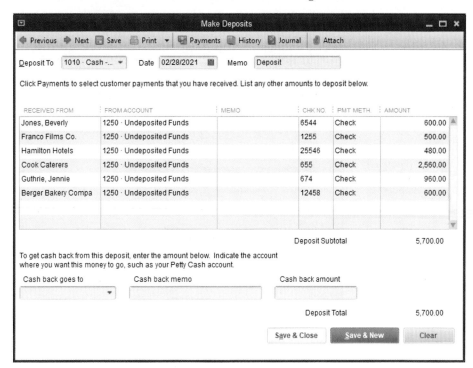

7. If the information is correct, click the Save & Close button.

The deposit of receipts as a separate transaction is recorded as follows:

1010 Cash - Operating		1250 Undeposited Funds	
Dr	Cr	Dr	Cr
5,700		5,700	5,700
			0

Customer Reports and Accounting Reports

Recall from Chapter 1 that Reports, the fourth level of operation, display the information and activities recorded in the various Lists/Centers and Activities windows. QuickBooks can display and print a variety of internal management reports as well as typical accounting and financial reports, many of which should be printed monthly.

Viewing and Printing Customer Reports

The Accounts Receivable and customer-related reports help the company to manage its collections, control cash flow, and retain an accurate record of all customer-related transactions. Among these reports are the *Open Invoices* report, the *Customer Balance Detail* report, and the *Customer Contact List* report.

Open Invoices Report

The *Open Invoices* report lists all unpaid invoices for each customer at a specific date. The report lists each open invoice, with the date and invoice number, for a customer; it also lists the terms and due date. The report may be customized to show all customers or only those with outstanding bills.

To view and print the *Open Invoices* report:
1. At the main menu bar, click Reports and then click *Customers & Receivables.*
2. At the Customers & Receivables submenu, click *Open Invoices.*
3. At the *Date* field, choose *02/28/2021.*
4. At the top of the report, click the Refresh button. The report is displayed. See Figure 3–AA.

FIGURE 3–AA

Open Invoices Report

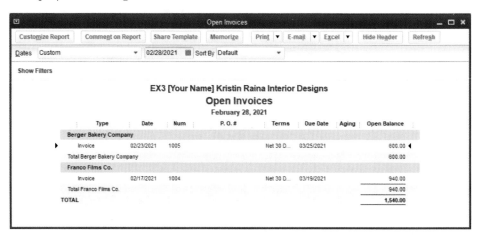

5. To print the report, click the Print button at the top of the report.
6. In the Print Reports dialog box, choose *Landscape* orientation and then click Print.
7. Close the report.

Customer Balance Detail Report

The *Customer Balance Detail* report displays all transactions for each customer with the remaining balance owed. This report is similar to an accounts receivable subsidiary ledger in a manual accounting system.

To view and print the *Customer Balance Detail* report:
1. At the main menu bar, click Reports and then click *Customers & Receivables.*
2. At the Customers & Receivables submenu, click *Customer Balance Detail.* The report shows all invoices, payments, and credit memos for each customer in chronological order.
3. To print the report, click the Print button at the top of the report and then click *Report.*
4. In the Print Reports dialog box, choose *Landscape* orientation and then click Print. Your printout should look like Figure 3–BB.

HINT

To change the width of a column, click and drag the vertical dotted bars between the column headings.

HINT

The format of your reports may vary slightly from the figures in the textbook. The reports in the figures are customized to display specific information. Chapter 12 will discuss customizing reports.

FIGURE 3-BB Customer Balance Detail Report

EX3 [Your Name] Kristin Raina Interior Designs
Customer Balance Detail
All Transactions

Type	Date	Num	Account	Amount	Balance
Berger Bakery Company					
Invoice	02/23/2021	1005	1200 · Accounts Receivable	1,200.00	1,200.00
Payment	02/28/2021	12458	1200 · Accounts Receivable	-600.00	600.00
Total Berger Bakery Company				600.00	600.00
Cook Caterers					
Invoice	02/13/2021	1003	1200 · Accounts Receivable	1,360.00	1,360.00
Invoice	02/27/2021	1006	1200 · Accounts Receivable	1,200.00	2,560.00
Payment	02/27/2021	655	1200 · Accounts Receivable	-2,560.00	0.00
Total Cook Caterers				0.00	0.00
Franco Films Co.					
Invoice	02/17/2021	1004	1200 · Accounts Receivable	1,440.00	1,440.00
Payment	02/20/2021	1255	1200 · Accounts Receivable	-500.00	940.00
Total Franco Films Co.				940.00	940.00
Guthrie, Jennie					
Invoice	02/06/2021	1002	1200 · Accounts Receivable	960.00	960.00
Payment	02/28/2021	674	1200 · Accounts Receivable	-960.00	0.00
Total Guthrie, Jennie				0.00	0.00
Jones, Beverly					
Invoice	02/01/2021	1001	1200 · Accounts Receivable	600.00	600.00
Payment	02/13/2021	6544	1200 · Accounts Receivable	-600.00	0.00
Total Jones, Beverly				0.00	0.00
TOTAL				**1,540.00**	**1,540.00**

5. Close the report.

Customer Contact List Report

The *Customer Contact List* report displays the information that has been entered in each customer's file in the Customer Center. This report displays the customer name, billing address, contact person, main phone and fax numbers, and present balance due.

HINT

The *Customer Contact List* report may also be accessed from the Customers & Receivables submenu.

To view the *Customer Contact List* report:
1. At the main menu bar, click Reports and then click *List.*
2. At the List submenu, click *Customer Contact List.* The Customer Contact List appears. See Figure 3–CC.

FIGURE 3-CC Customer Contact List Report

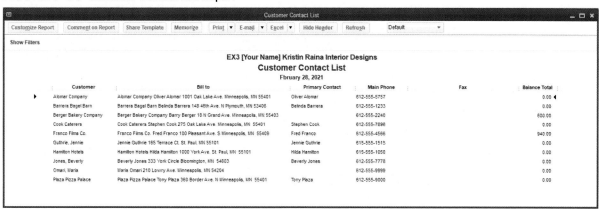

3. Close the report.

Viewing and Printing Accounting Reports

HINT

You can "drill down" from the reports to the activity window if you need to make any corrections.

As activities are entered in the windows, behind-the-scenes accounting activity is recorded in general journal format, posted to the general ledger, and flowed into the financial statements. You can display and print standard accounting reports showing these activities, such as the *Journal* report. The *Journal* report displays, in general journal format, all transactions recorded during a specified period of time.

To view and print the *Journal* report:

HINT

QuickBooks assigns transaction numbers that cannot be changed. Do not be surprised if your transaction numbers differ from those shown in the textbook, because you deleted transactions. The important thing is to make sure that the journal entries are correct.

1. At the main menu bar, click Reports and then click *Accountant & Taxes*.
2. At the Accountant & Taxes submenu, click *Journal*.
3. At the *From* and *To* fields, choose *02/01/2021* to *02/28/2021*.
4. At the top of the report, click the Refresh button. The *Journal* report is displayed.
5. To print the report, click the Print button at the top of the report and then click *Report*.
6. In the Print Reports dialog box, choose *Landscape* orientation and then click Print. The last part of your printout should look like Figure 3–DD.
7. Close the report.

HINT

If the name field displays *Multiple*, you can click the Expand button at the top of the report to display more detail.

Notice on your printout that all the activity for February is displayed in the order that it was entered. The earlier transactions are the vendor activities recorded in Chapter 2. The later transactions are the customer activities recorded in this chapter. Scroll down to the transactions for this chapter, and look in the *Type* column. This indicates the window where the activity was recorded. The *Invoice* type is from the Create Invoices window. Each of these transactions has a debit to Accounts Receivable, because this is the default for that window. The *Payment* type is from the Receive Payments window. Each of these transactions is a debit to Undeposited Funds and a credit to Accounts Receivable, which are the default accounts for this window. The *Sales Receipt* type is from the Enter Sales Receipts window. Each of these transactions has a debit to Undeposited Funds, because that is the default account for this window. The *Deposit* type is from the Make Deposits window. Each of these transactions by default is a debit to Cash and a credit to Undeposited Funds.

Exiting QuickBooks

Upon completing this session, make a backup copy of your practice exercise company file to a removable storage device using the Back Up command. Be sure to change the *Save in* field to the removable storage device and then carefully type the correct file name. Close the company file and then exit QuickBooks.

FIGURE 3–DD Journal Report—Partial

EX3 [Your Name] Kristin Raina Interior Designs
Journal
February 2021

Trans #	Type	Date	Num	Adj	Name	Memo	Account	Debit	Credit
25	Invoice	02/27/2021	1006		Cook Caterers		1200 · Accounts Receivable	1,200.00	
					Cook Caterers	Decorating Services	4020 · Decorating Services		300.00
					Cook Caterers	Design Services	4010 · Design Services		900.00
								1,200.00	1,200.00
26	Payment	02/13/2021	6544		Jones, Beverly		1250 · Undeposited Funds	600.00	
					Jones, Beverly		1200 · Accounts Receivable		600.00
								600.00	600.00
27	Payment	02/20/2021	1255		Franco Films Co.		1250 · Undeposited Funds	500.00	
					Franco Films Co.		1200 · Accounts Receivable		500.00
								500.00	500.00
28	Payment	02/27/2021	655		Cook Caterers		1250 · Undeposited Funds	2,560.00	
					Cook Caterers		1200 · Accounts Receivable		2,560.00
								2,560.00	2,560.00
29	Payment	02/28/2021	674		Guthrie, Jennie		1250 · Undeposited Funds	960.00	
					Guthrie, Jennie		1200 · Accounts Receivable		960.00
								960.00	960.00
30	Payment	02/28/2021	12458		Berger Bakery Company		1250 · Undeposited Funds	600.00	
					Berger Bakery Company		1200 · Accounts Receivable		600.00
								600.00	600.00
31	Sales Receipt	02/24/2021	1007		Hamilton Hotels		1250 · Undeposited Funds	480.00	
					Hamilton Hotels	Design Services	4010 · Design Services		480.00
								480.00	480.00
32	Deposit	02/28/2021				Deposit	1010 · Cash - Operating	5,700.00	
					-MULTIPLE-	Deposit	1250 · Undeposited Funds		5,700.00
								5,700.00	5,700.00
TOTAL								**30,160.00**	**30,160.00**

Chapter Review and Assessment

Procedure Review

To add a customer:
1. At the main menu bar, click Customers and then click *Customer Center.*
2. At the Customer Center window, click the New Customer & Job button and then select *New Customer.*
3. Enter the background data for the customer.
4. Click OK.
5. Close the Customer Center window.

To delete a customer:
1. At the main menu bar, click Customers and then click *Customer Center.*
2. At the Customer Center window, select the customer you wish to delete.
3. At the main menu bar, click Edit and then click *Delete Customer:Job.*
4. Click OK at the warning.
5. Close the Customer Center window.
    You cannot delete a customer who has a balance or who was used in a transaction during the current accounting period.

To edit a customer:
1. At the main menu bar, click Customers and then click *Customer Center.*
2. At the Customer Center window, double-click to select the customer you wish to edit.
3. Change the appropriate information.
4. Click OK.
5. Close the Customer Center window.

To create an invoice:
1. At the main menu bar, click Customers and then click *Create Invoices.*
2. At the CUSTOMER:JOB drop-down list, click the customer name.
3. At the TEMPLATE drop-down list, accept *Intuit Service Invoice.*
4. At the *DATE* field, enter the invoice date.
5. At the *INVOICE* # field, enter the invoice number.
6. At the TERMS drop-down list, select the terms.
7. At the *ITEM* field, click the first line to display the drop-down Item List and then click the appropriate item(s).
8. At the *QUANTITY* field, enter the quantity.
9. At the top of the window, confirm that the *Print Later* and *Email Later* boxes do not contain check marks. In the lower left part of the window, the *Your customer can't pay this invoice online* command should remain off.
10. Click the Save & Close button.

To receive a payment:
1. At the main menu bar, click Customers and then click *Receive Payments.*
2. At the RECEIVED FROM drop-down list, click the customer name.
3. At the *PAYMENT AMOUNT* field, enter the amount.
4. At the *DATE* field, enter the payment date.

5. Click the CHECK button.
6. At the *CHECK #* field, enter the check number.
7. Click the Save & Close button.

To enter a cash sale:
1. At the main menu bar, click Customers and then click *Enter Sales Receipts.*
2. At the CUSTOMER:JOB drop-down list, click the customer name.
3. Click the CHECK button and then enter the check number.
4. Complete the remainder of the window in the same manner as an invoice.
5. Click the Save & Close button.

To make a deposit:
1. At the main menu bar, click Banking and then click *Make Deposits.*
2. At the Payments to Deposit window, click Select All to deposit all the receipts.
3. Click OK.
4. At the Make Deposits window, at the Deposit To drop-down list, accept or choose the *1010 Cash - Operating* account.
5. Enter the deposit date in the *Date* field.
6. Click the Save & Close button.

To view and print customer reports from the Reports menu:
1. At the main menu bar, click Reports and then click *Customers & Receivables.*
2. At the Customers & Receivables submenu, choose a report.
3. Choose the appropriate dates for the report and then click the Refresh button at the top of the report.
4. Click the Print button at the top of the report and then click *Report.*
5. In the Print Reports dialog box, review the settings and then click Print.
6. Close the report.

Key Concepts

Select the letter of the item that best matches each definition.

a. Customer Center
b. Receive Payments window
c. Cash sales
d. Create Invoices window
e. *Open Invoices* report

f. Customer
g. Undeposited Funds
h. Enter Sales Receipts window
i. Deposit Funds window
j. *Customer Balance Detail* report

_____ 1. Contains a file for each customer with whom the company does business.
_____ 2. A report that displays all the transactions for a customer.
_____ 3. Window used to deposit funds collected.
_____ 4. A person or business to which the company provides services or sells a product.
_____ 5. Window used to record the payment of invoices.

_____ 6. Sales for which payment is received immediately.
_____ 7. Window used to record sales on account.
_____ 8. Collections not yet deposited in the bank.
_____ 9. A report that lists all the unpaid invoices for each customer.
_____ 10. Window used to record sales for cash.

Procedure Check

1. Your company has obtained a new major client. Describe the steps to add the new client to the system.
2. Your company has the type of business that makes cash sales to many customers and rarely tracks accounts receivable. How would you use QuickBooks to record your sales?
3. Your business wishes to track all the deposits made to the bank to facilitate the month-end bank reconciliation process. How would you record the collection of funds to accomplish this?
4. You wish to determine the oldest unpaid invoices. How would you use QuickBooks to obtain that information?
5. You wish to view all the invoices and collection activity for a customer. How would you use QuickBooks to obtain the required information?
6. Compare and contrast a manual accounting system with a computer-ized accounting system for processing customer transactions. Include an explanation of how the accounts receivable subsidiary ledger com-pares with the Customer Center.

Case Problems

Demonstrate your knowledge of the QuickBooks features discussed in this chapter by completing the following case problems.

Case Problem 3–1

On April 1, 2021, Lynn Garcia started her business, Lynn's Music Studio. Lynn began by depositing $10,000 cash in a bank account in the business name. She also contributed a piano and some guitars. The musical instru-ments have an outstanding note balance of $2,000 that has been assumed by the business. The cash, musical instruments, note payable, and capital have all been recorded in the opening balances of the books. During the first part of the month, Lynn set up her studio. She has now begun provid-ing piano and guitar lessons. Piano lessons are billed at $35 per hour, and guitar lessons are billed at $30 per hour. You will record the transactions listed below for the month of April. The company file for this chapter includes the beginning information for Lynn's Music Studio along with the transaction balances from Chapter 2.

1. Open the company file **CH3 Lynn's Music Studio.QBW**.
2. At the QuickBooks Desktop Login window, in the *Password* text box, type Student1 and then click OK.
3. Make a backup copy of the company file and name it **LMS3 *[Your Name]* Lynn's Music Studio**.

4. Restore the backup copy of the company file. In both the Open Backup Copy and Save Company File as dialog boxes, use the file name **LMS3** *[Your Name]* **Lynn's Music Studio** and enter the password.

5. Change the company name to **LMS3** *[Your Name]* **Lynn's Music Studio**.

6. Add the following customer to the Customer Center:

CUSTOMER NAME:	Musical Youth Group
OPENING BALANCE:	0 AS OF April 1, 2021
COMPANY NAME:	Musical Youth Group
First Name:	Dana
Last Name:	Thompson
Main Phone:	570-555-6642
Mobile:	570-555-6700
Main Email:	myg@ppi-edu.net
INVOICE/BILL TO:	550 Marion Lane
	Scranton, PA 18504
CREDIT LIMIT:	20,000
PAYMENT TERMS:	Net 30 Days
TYPE:	Group

Delete the following customer:
   Rivera Family

7. Using the appropriate window, record the following transactions for April 2021:

Apr. 9	Provided 15 hours guitar lessons and 10 hours piano lessons on account to Jefferson High School, Invoice No. 2001, Net 10 Days. Be sure the Intuit Service Invoice is the active template.
Apr. 12	Provided 3 hours piano lessons to the Schroeder Family, Invoice No. 2002. Received payment immediately, Check No. 478.
Apr. 13	Provided 12 hours piano lessons to Highland School, Invoice No. 2003, Net 30 Days.
Apr. 16	Provided 8 hours guitar lessons and 5 hours piano lessons to Twin Lakes Elementary School, Invoice No. 2004, Net 30 Days.
Apr. 16	Provided 6 hours guitar lessons to the Patterson Family, Invoice No. 2005. Received payment immediately, Check No. 208.
Apr. 20	Provided 5 hours guitar lessons and 7 hours piano lessons to Mulligan Residence, Invoice No. 2006, Net 30 Days.
Apr. 20	Received payment in full from Jefferson High School for Invoice No. 2001, Check No. 28759.

Apr. 23   Provided 5 hours piano lessons to Douglaston Senior
            Center, Invoice No. 2007, Net 30 Days. Douglaston
            Senior Center is a new client:

CUSTOMER NAME:	Douglaston Senior Center
OPENING BALANCE:	0 AS OF April 1, 2021
COMPANY NAME:	Douglaston Senior Center
First Name:	Herbie
Last Name:	Richardson
Main Phone:	570-555-7748
Mobile:	570-555-8800
Main Email:	DSC@ppi-edu.net
INVOICE/BILL TO:	574 S Beech Street
	Scranton, PA 18506
CREDIT LIMIT:	25,000
PAYMENT TERMS:	Net 30 Days
TYPE:	Group

Apr. 23   Provided 10 hours guitar lessons and 10 hours piano
            lessons to the Musical Youth Group, Invoice No. 2008.
            Received payment immediately, Check No. 578.

Apr. 26   Provided 15 hours guitar lessons and 10 hours piano
            lessons on account to Jefferson High School, Invoice
            No. 2009, Net 10 Days.

Apr. 26   Received payment in full from Highland School for
            Invoice No. 2003, Check No. 75281.

Apr. 27   Provided 2 hours guitar lessons for the Patel Family,
            Invoice No. 2010. Received payment immediately,
            Check No. 629.

Apr. 30   Provided 8 hours guitar lessons and 5 hours piano les-
            sons to Twin Lakes Elementary School, Invoice No.
            2011, Net 30 Days.

Apr. 30   Received partial payment of $145 from Mulligan Resi-
            dence for Invoice No. 2006, Check No. 715.

Apr. 30   Deposited all receipts for the month.

8. Display and print the following reports for April 1, 2021, to April 30, 2021:
   a. *Open Invoices*
   b. *Customer Balance Detail*
   c. *Customer Contact List*
   d. *Journal*

Case Problem 3–2

On June 1, 2021, Olivia Chen began her business, Olivia's Web Solutions. Olivia began by depositing $25,000 cash in a bank account in the business name. She also contributed a computer. The computer has an outstanding note balance of $2,500 that has been assumed by the business. The cash, computer, note payable, and capital have all been recorded in the opening balances of the books. During the first part of the month, Olivia set up her office. She has now begun providing web design and internet consulting services to individuals and small businesses. The Web Page Design Services are billed at $125 per hour, and the Internet Consulting Services are billed at $100 per hour. You will record the transactions listed below for the month of June. The company file includes the beginning information for Olivia's Web Solutions along with the transaction balances from Chapter 2.

1. Open the company file **CH3 Olivia's Web Solutions.QBW**.
2. At the QuickBooks Desktop Login window, in the *Password* text box, type Student1 and then click OK.
3. Make a backup copy of the company file and name it **OWS3 *[Your Name]* Olivia's Web Solutions**.
4. Restore the backup copy of the company file. In both the Open Backup Copy and Save Company File as dialog boxes, use the file name **OWS3 *[Your Name]* Olivia's Web Solutions** and enter the password.
5. Change the company name to **OWS3 *[Your Name]* Olivia's Web Solutions**.
6. Add the following customer to the Customer Center:

CUSTOMER NAME:	Thrifty Stores
OPENING BALANCE:	0 AS OF June 1, 2021
COMPANY NAME:	Thrifty Stores
First Name:	William
Last Name:	Way
Main Phone:	718-555-2445
Mobile:	718-555-2446
Main Email:	Thrifty@ppi-edu.net
INVOICE/BILL TO:	23 Boston Ave.
	Bronx, NY 11693
CREDIT LIMIT:	25,000
PAYMENT TERMS:	Net 30 Days
TYPE:	Commercial

Delete the following customer:
   Printers Group

7. Using the appropriate window, record the following transactions for June 2021:

Jun. 11	Provided 8 hours Internet Consulting Services and 10 hours Web Page Design Services on account to Long Island Water Works, Invoice No. 1001, Net 30 Days. Be sure the Intuit Service Invoice is the active template.
Jun. 14	Provided 8 hours Web Page Design Services on account to Sehorn & Smith, Invoice No. 1002, Net 30 Days.
Jun. 15	Provided 8 hours Web Page Design Services on account to the Schneider Family, Invoice No. 1003, Net 15 Days.
Jun. 17	Provided 4 hours Internet Consulting Services and 8 hours Web Page Design Services on account to Miguel's Restaurant, Invoice No. 1004, Net 30 Days.

Jun. 18	Provided 4 hours Internet Consulting Services to the Singh Family, Invoice No. 1005. Received payment immediately, Check No. 687.
Jun. 21	Provided 8 hours Web Page Design Services on account to Breathe Easy, Invoice No. 1006, Net 30 Days.
Jun. 25	Received payment in full from Long Island Water Works for Invoice No. 1001, Check No. 124554.
Jun. 25	Provided 12 hours Web Page Design Services on account to Thrifty Stores, Invoice No. 1007, Net 30 Days.
Jun. 28	Provided 8 hours Internet Consulting Services on account to Artie's Auto Repair, Invoice 1008, Net 30 Days. Artie's Auto Repair is a new client:

CUSTOMER NAME:	Artie's Auto Repair
OPENING BALANCE:	0 AS OF June 1, 2021
COMPANY NAME:	Artie's Auto Repair
First Name:	Leon
Last Name:	Artie
Main Phone:	516-555-1221
Mobile:	516-555-1231
Main Email:	ArtieAuto@ppi-edu.net
INVOICE/BILL TO:	32 West 11th Street
	New Hyde Park, NY 11523
CREDIT LIMIT:	25,000
PAYMENT TERMS:	Net 30 Days
TYPE:	Commercial

Jun. 28	Received payment in full from Sehorn & Smith for Invoice No. 1002, Check No. 3656.
Jun. 29	Provided 12 hours of Internet Consulting Services on account to South Shore School District, Invoice No. 1009, Net 30 Days.
Jun. 29	Received payment in full from Miguel's Restaurant for Invoice No. 1004, Check No. 3269.
Jun. 30	Provided 8 hours of Internet Consulting Services on account to Sehorn & Smith, Invoice No. 1010, Net 30 Days.
Jun. 30	Received partial payment of $250 from Breathe Easy for Invoice No. 1006, Check No. 1455.
Jun. 30	Deposited all receipts for the month.

8. Display and print the following reports for June 1, 2021, to June 30, 2021:
   a. *Open Invoices*
   b. *Customer Balance Detail*
   c. *Customer Contact List*
   d. *Journal*

CHAPTER 4

Period-End Procedures

Making General Journal Entries

Objectives

- Update the Chart of Accounts List
- Record adjustments in the Make General Journal Entries window
- View the effect of period-end adjustments on the trial balance
- Display and print period-end accounting reports
- Change the reports display using the Customize Report button
- Display and print accounting reports and financial statements

QuickBooks allows you to record journal entries in general journal format. As shown in Chapters 2 and 3, QuickBooks records daily activities in windows such as Enter Bills, Pay Bills, Write Checks, Create Invoices, Receive Payments, and so on. However, behind the scenes, QuickBooks also records the activities in general journal format using debits and credits. The accounts used to record the activities come from the Chart of Accounts (Lists/Centers).

At times, some account balances (Activities) will need to be adjusted based on information that does not appear in the daily activities so that the financial statements can be properly prepared in accordance with **generally accepted accounting principles (GAAP)**. These adjustments to the accounts are **adjusting journal entries**, and they are recorded in the Make General Journal Entries window. As you record the daily activities and adjusting journal entries, QuickBooks simultaneously updates the accounting records and financial statements (Reports).

In this chapter, our sample company, Kristin Raina Interior Designs, will make the necessary adjusting journal entries for February—the end of the first month of operations.

QuickBooks versus Manual Accounting: General Journal Entries

In a manual accounting system, the general journal is the document in which transactions are initially recorded chronologically. For each transaction, the dollar value of at least one account must be recorded as a **debit** amount, and the dollar value of at least one account must be recorded as a **credit** amount. The total dollar value of debits must equal the total dollar value of credits. A company has the option of recording all transactions exclusively in the general journal or, alternatively, for frequent similar transactions, in special journals. In either case, at month-end, the transactions from all journals are posted to the general ledger.

Periodically, certain adjustments that are not daily business activities must be made to the accounts to update the balances. These adjustments, called *adjusting journal entries*, are always recorded in the general journal. They are then posted to the general ledger to update the balances in the accounts. The adjusted balances are used to prepare the financial statements. These adjusting journal entries must always be made on the date the financial statements are prepared, but they can be recorded more often. Most large companies typically prepare the adjusting journal entries monthly.

QuickBooks does not follow the format of the special journals for daily transactions. Instead, each activity is recorded in a different window depending on the nature of the activity. Behind the scenes, QuickBooks records the activity in general journal format, as seen in the *Journal* report. However, for adjusting journal entries, QuickBooks uses the Make General Journal Entries window in a manner similar to that of a manual accounting system. As you save the information entered in each window, including the Make General Journal Entries window, the general ledger balances, the Chart of Accounts List balances, the trial balance, and the financial statements are updated simultaneously. Because balances are easily updated in a computerized accounting system, even small companies can record adjusting journal entries monthly.

---

generally accepted accounting principles (GAAP) principles used to prepare a company's financial statements, which consist of both formal accounting regulations and procedures mandated by regulatory agencies and traditionally used accounting procedures

adjusting journal entries adjustments made to accounts at certain periods, such as the end of the month or the end of the fiscal year, to bring the balances up to date

debit a dollar amount recorded in the *left* column of an account, which, depending on the account, either increases or decreases the balance in the account

credit a dollar amount recorded in the *right* column of an account, which, depending on the account, either increases or decreases the balance in the account

Chapter Problem

In this chapter, you will record the adjusting journal entries for the end of the first month of business, February 28, 2021, for Kristin Raina Interior Designs. The February 1, 2021, beginning balances, along with all the vendor and customer activities for the month of February, as illustrated in Chapters 2 and 3, are contained in the company file **CH4 Kristin Raina Interior Designs**.

Before you begin, open the company file **CH4 Kristin Raina Interior Designs.QBW**. Enter the password, *Student1*. Make a backup copy of the file, name it **EX4 *[Your Name]* Kristin Raina Interior Designs**, and then restore the file. Enter the password, *Student1*. Finally, change the company name in the file to **EX4 *[Your Name]* Kristin Raina Interior Designs**.

Lists/Centers

The Chart of Accounts List

Recall from Chapter 1 that the second level of operation in QuickBooks is recording background information in Lists/Centers. Lists and Centers need to be revised periodically when new accounts need to be added, accounts not used in the business need to be deleted, or modifications need to be made to an account. When you make these revisions to the accounts, you are updating the Chart of Accounts List.

Chart of Accounts List the list of accounts a company uses as it conducts its business

general ledger the document in which transactions are summarized by account

The Chart of Accounts List is the list of accounts a company uses as it conducts its business. In a manual accounting system, all the individual accounts are placed together in a book called the general ledger. Each account in the general ledger shows all the increases and decreases in the account, reflected as debits and credits, and the balance in each account. In computerized accounting systems, a general ledger is also maintained showing the increases and decreases in each account, reflected as debits and credits, and the balance for each account. In addition, the Chart of Accounts List displays the balance next to each account name. Because of this, the Chart of Accounts List has become synonymous with the general ledger in computerized systems, although it indicates the balances for only the assets, liabilities, and equity accounts and does not display all the detail activities.

In QuickBooks, the Chart of Accounts List consists of the account numbers, names, types, and balances. The account numbers are optional but are used in this text. The name you assign an account is the name that appears in the windows and reports. The balance is determined by the original amount entered (if any) when the account is first created and then subsequently updated by Activities entered in the windows.

The software uses account types to determine where to place each account name and balance on the financial statements and to establish the system default accounts. The account types consist of:

Assets:
- Bank
- Accounts Receivable
- Other Current Asset
- Fixed Asset
- Other Asset

Liabilities:
- Accounts Payable
- Credit Card
- Other Current Liability
- Long-Term Liability

Equity:
- Equity

Income and Expenses:
- Income
- Cost of Goods Sold
- Expense
- Other Income
- Other Expense

As shown in Chapters 2 and 3, QuickBooks identifies certain accounts as system default accounts and uses them to identify the transactions recorded in the windows. For example, the Accounts Payable account type is used to identify the Accounts Payable liability account when transactions are recorded in the Enter Bills window. The Accounts Receivable account type is used to identify the Accounts Receivable asset account when transactions are recorded in the Create Invoices window. When QuickBooks looks for an account, it looks for the account type, not the account name.

Kristin Raina previously entered information to establish the Chart of Accounts List, which was then used for the February activities recorded in Chapters 2 and 3.

To review the Chart of Accounts List:
1. At the main menu bar, click Reports and then click *List*.
2. At the List submenu, click *Account Listing*. The *Account Listing* report is displayed. See Figure 4–A.

FIGURE 4–A Account Listing Report

Account	Type	Balance Total	Description	Accnt. #	Tax Line
1010 · Cash - Operating	Bank	47,400.00		1010	<Unassigned>
1200 · Accounts Receivable	Accounts Receivable	1,540.00		1200	<Unassigned>
1250 · Undeposited Funds	Other Current Asset	0.00		1250	<Unassigned>
1300 · Design Supplies	Other Current Asset	200.00		1300	<Unassigned>
1305 · Office Supplies	Other Current Asset	400.00		1305	<Unassigned>
1410 · Prepaid Advertising	Other Current Asset	600.00		1410	<Unassigned>
1420 · Prepaid Insurance	Other Current Asset	2,400.00		1420	<Unassigned>
1700 · Furniture and Fixtures	Fixed Asset	12,000.00		1700	<Unassigned>
1700 · Furniture and Fixtures:1725 · Furniture, Cost	Fixed Asset	12,000.00		1725	<Unassigned>
1700 · Furniture and Fixtures:1750 · Accum. Dep., Furniture and Fix	Fixed Asset	0.00		1750	<Unassigned>
1800 · Computers	Fixed Asset	3,600.00		1800	<Unassigned>
1800 · Computers:1825 · Computers, Cost	Fixed Asset	3,600.00		1825	<Unassigned>
1800 · Computers:1850 · Accum. Dep., Computers	Fixed Asset	0.00		1850	<Unassigned>
2010 · Accounts Payable	Accounts Payable	6,250.00		2010	<Unassigned>
2020 · Notes Payable	Other Current Liability	7,000.00		2020	<Unassigned>
2030 · Interest Payable	Other Current Liability	0.00		2030	<Unassigned>
3010 · Kristin Raina, Capital	Equity	50,000.00		3010	<Unassigned>
3020 · Kristin Raina, Drawings	Equity	-400.00		3020	<Unassigned>
3030 · Accumulated Earnings	Equity			3030	<Unassigned>
4010 · Design Services	Income			4010	<Unassigned>
4020 · Decorating Services	Income			4020	<Unassigned>
6020 · Accounting Expense	Expense			6020	<Unassigned>
6030 · Administrative Expense	Expense			6030	<Unassigned>
6175 · Deprec. Exp., Furniture	Expense			6175	<Unassigned>
6200 · Insurance Expense	Expense			6200	<Unassigned>
6300 · Janitorial Expenses	Expense			6300	<Unassigned>
6350 · Promotion Expense	Expense			6350	<Unassigned>
6400 · Rent Expense	Expense			6400	<Unassigned>
6450 · Telephone Expense	Expense			6450	<Unassigned>
6500 · Utilities Expense	Expense			6500	<Unassigned>

HINT

Recall that in a report, you can click and drag the vertical dotted bar before the column heading to change the width of the column.

In QuickBooks, the account balances that flow into the financial statements are based on the account types. If you want to subtotal two or more accounts on the financial statements, you can identify an account as a subaccount. A subaccount shows a subtotal amount on the financial statements in addition to the regular account balances. A parent account is an account that has a subaccount.

In Kristin Raina's Chart of Accounts List, the asset cost and accumulated depreciation accounts were marked as subaccounts of the related asset account. This was done to see the accumulated depreciation account as a deduction from the cost of an asset on the financial statements and to display the net amount.

At the *Account Listing* report, when parent and subaccounts are used, subaccount names by default display the parent account name left-aligned and the subaccount name to the right of the parent account name all on one line. Review the *Account Listing* report in Figure 4–A on page 112. Look at the 1700 Furniture and Fixtures account. The accounts below it are 1700 Furniture and Fixtures: 1725 - Furniture, Cost and 1700 Furniture and Fixtures: 1750 - Accum. Dep., Furniture and Fix. This means accounts 1725 and 1750 are subaccounts of 1700. Account 1700 is a parent account because it has subaccounts. Notice the same setup with accounts 1800, 1825, and 1850 in the *Account Listing* report.

To view a specific account:

1. With the *Account Listing* report open, place the zoom glass over the Cash - Operating account.
2. Choose *Cash - Operating* by double-clicking it. The Edit Account window for Cash - Operating is displayed. See Figure 4–B.

FIGURE 4–B
Edit Account Window

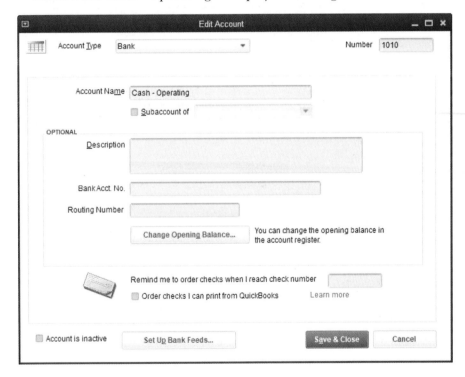

Table 4–1 describes the account information contained in the Edit Account window.

TABLE 4–1
Edit Account Window

Field	Description
Account Type	Use the drop-down list to display and choose the account type. QuickBooks uses the account type for system default accounts in windows and for placement on financial statements.
Number	An account number is optional. Account numbers will be used in this text and have been established in the company files.
Account Name	Enter an account name of your choice. The software uses the account type, not the account name, for necessary identification (default accounts and placement on financial statements). The name typed in this field appears in the windows and on reports.
Subaccount of	An account can be identified as a subaccount of another account. To activate this field, click to insert a check mark in the box. Once this box is activated, use the drop-down list to determine in which account this will become a subaccount.
Description	This field is optional. A description entered here appears on certain reports.
Bank Acct. No. and Routing Number	These fields are optional. They are listed as references for the user.

3. Close the Edit Account window.
4. At the *Account Listing* report, double-click *1800 Computers: 1850 - Accum. Dep., Computers.* At the Edit Account window, notice how this account is marked as a subaccount of 1800 - Computers. See Figure 4–C.

FIGURE 4–C
Edit Account Window—
Subaccount Checked

Subaccount of check box

5. Close the Edit Account window.
6. Close the *Account Listing* report.

Adding an Account

In preparation for recording month-end adjusting journal entries, Kristin Raina has determined that she needs to add an Advertising Expense account to the Chart of Accounts List.

To add a new account:

1. At the main menu bar, click Lists and then click *Chart of Accounts*. The Chart of Accounts List window appears. See Figure 4–D.

FIGURE 4–D
Chart of Accounts List Window

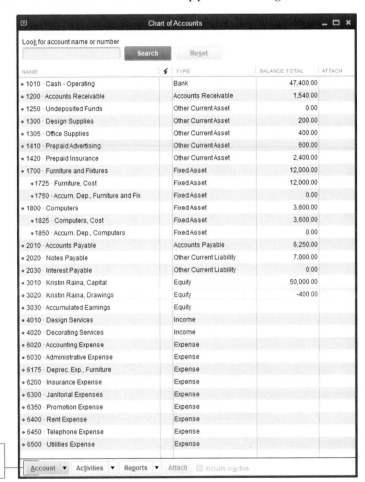

List window drop-down menu buttons

Notice that most of the account names are left-aligned. In the Chart of Accounts List window, when parent and subaccounts are used, by default the parent account name is left-aligned, and the subaccount names are indented under the parent account name. For example, account 1700 is the parent account, and subaccounts 1725 and 1750 are indented under account 1700.

The presentation of parent accounts and subaccounts in the Chart of Accounts List window is different from the presentation of parent and subaccounts on the *Account Listing* report. Recall that in the *Account Listing* report in Figure 4–A on page 112, for each subaccount listed, both the parent account and subaccount are listed on one line, with the parent account name left-aligned and the subaccount name listed to the right of the parent account name.

The Chart of Accounts List is displayed in a List window. Each List window has drop-down menu buttons at the bottom of the window.

The first menu button in all List windows represents the name of the list—in this case, Account. In almost all List windows, there is also a Reports button. The remaining buttons vary according to the List window displayed. In the Chart of Accounts List window, the first menu button is Account, the second menu button is Activities, the third menu button is Reports, and the fourth menu button is Attach. The Activities and Reports buttons are shortcuts you can use instead of using the main menu bar drop-down menus to access commands. The Attach button can be used to attach documents using the Quick-Books Doc Center feature. The Attach button may or may not be an active button.

2. At the Chart of Accounts List window, click the Account menu button. A drop-down menu appears. See Figure 4–E.

FIGURE 4–E
Account Drop-Down
Menu

3. At the Account button drop-down menu, click *New*. The Add New Account: Choose Account Type window appears. You can click the drop-down arrow at the *Other Account Types* field to display additional account types. See Figure 4–F.

FIGURE 4–F
Add New Account:
Choose Account Type
Window

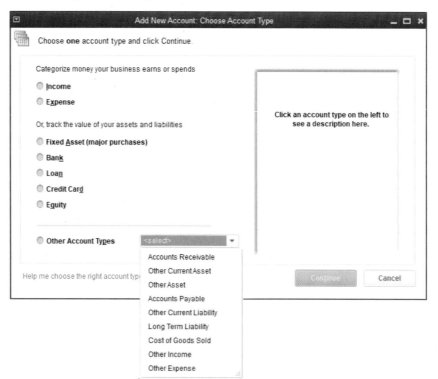

4. Click *Expense* and then click Continue. The Add New Account window appears with the Account Type drop-down list completed with *Expense.* See Figure 4–G.

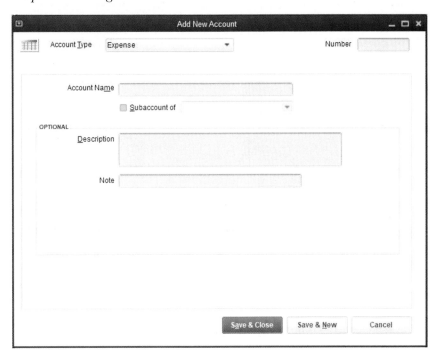

If you chose an incorrect account type, you can simply change it here. Click the Account Type arrow and a drop-down list displays all the account types. See Figure 4–H.

FIGURE 4–H
Account Type
Drop-Down List

5. Enter the following data as the account number and name.

Number: 6050
Account Name: Advertising Expense

See Figure 4–I.

FIGURE 4–I
Add New Account
Window—Completed

6. If the information is correct, click the Save & Close button. Notice the account was added to the Chart of Accounts List.
7. Close the Chart of Accounts List window.

Deleting an Account

Kristin Raina has decided the Promotion Expense account is not necessary and should be deleted.

To delete an account:

1. At the main menu bar, click Lists and then click *Chart of Accounts.*
2. At the Chart of Accounts List window, select (highlight) *6350 Promotion Expense.* See Figure 4–J.

FIGURE 4–J
Chart of Accounts List
Window—Promotion
Expense Selected

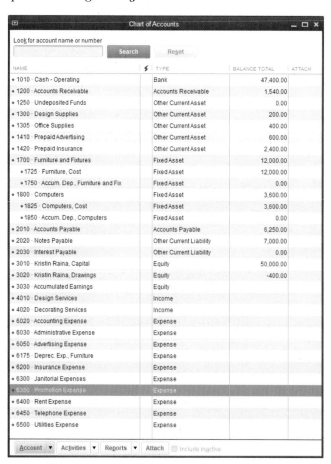

3. Click the Account menu button.
4. At the Account button drop-down menu, click *Delete Account*.
5. When the Delete Account warning appears, click OK. The account is deleted.
6. Close the Chart of Accounts List window.

HINT

If you delete the wrong account, immediately click Edit on the main menu bar and then click *Undo Delete Account*; if you do not do this immediately, you will not be able to undo the deletion.

An account with a balance or an account that has been used in a transaction cannot be deleted. It can instead be marked inactive and will no longer appear in reports.

Editing an Account

Kristin Raina has decided to change the account name Furniture and Fixtures to simply Furniture.

HINT

To edit an account, you must click the Account menu button and then click *Edit Account*. Do *not* double-click the account name in the Chart of Accounts List window.

To edit an account:
1. Open the Chart of Accounts List and select the *1700 Furniture and Fixtures* account.
2. At the Chart of Accounts List window, click the Account menu button.
3. At the Account button drop-down menu, click *Edit Account*. The Edit Account window appears.
4. At the *Account Name* field, delete the text *and Fixtures*. See Figure 4–K.

FIGURE 4–K
Edit Account Window—Completed

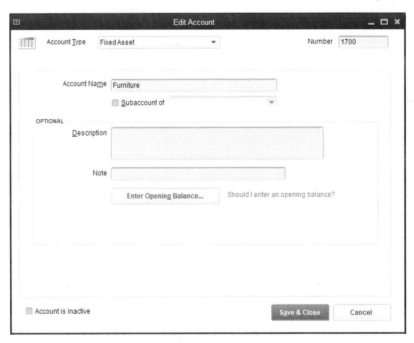

5. If the information is correct, click the Save & Close button.
6. Close the Chart of Accounts List window.

Add the following accounts:

Type: Expense
Number: 6325
Name: Office Supplies Expense

Type: Other Expense
Number: 7000
Name: Interest Expense

Delete the following account:
    6030 Administrative Expense

Edit the following account:
    Change the name of account 1750 to *Accum. Dep., Furniture.*

QuickCheck: The updated Chart of Accounts List window appears in Figure 4–L.

FIGURE 4–L
Updated Chart of
Accounts List Window

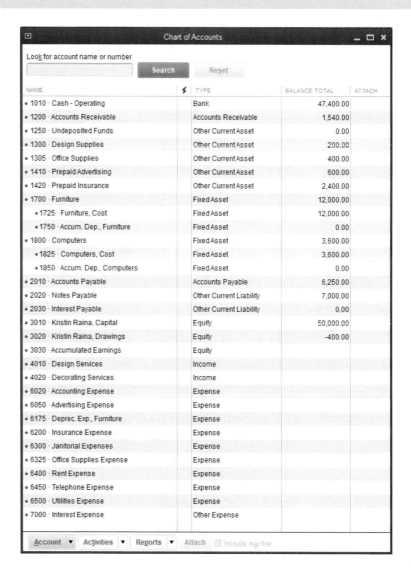

The Trial Balance

In a manual accounting system, errors can occur when journal entries are recorded and posted to the general ledger or when doing arithmetic computations. The **trial balance** is used to verify that the total debits equal the total credits, which means the general ledger is in balance. In a computerized system, on the other hand, there is less chance of the accounts being out of balance because the postings to the general ledger and arithmetic computations occur automatically.

But a trial balance is still useful. It allows you to view the accounts and their debit or credit balances without having to look at all the details in the general ledger. It is often useful to review the trial balance before recording the adjusting journal entries.

trial balance a report containing all the general ledger account names, their debit or credit balances, and the total debits and credits

To view and print the trial balance:

1. At the main menu bar, click Reports and then click *Accountant & Taxes*.
2. At the Accountant & Taxes submenu, click *Trial Balance*.
3. At the *From* and *To* fields, choose *01/01/2021* and *02/28/2021* and then click the Refresh button at the top of the report. The trial balance is displayed. See Figure 4–M.

FIGURE 4–M
Trial Balance Report

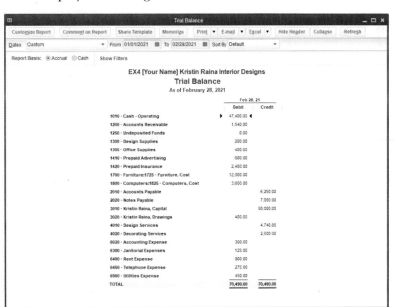

HINT

Print the trial balance at this time. Once you record adjusting journal entries, you will no longer be able to view and print a preadjusted trial balance.

4. Print the report.
5. Close the report.

The Make General Journal Entries Window

To adjust account balances based on accounting rules, you usually need to enter adjusting journal entries before preparing financial statements. In QuickBooks, adjusting journal entries are recorded in the Make General Journal Entries window. This window is set up similarly to that for a manual accounting system. It lists the account and amount of the debit entry, the account and amount of the credit entry, and an explanation.

The QuickBooks Make General Journal Entries window is shown in Figure 4–N.

FIGURE 4–N
Make General Journal
Entries Window

Table 4–2 describes the various parts of the Make General Journal Entries window.

TABLE 4–2
Make General Journal
Entries Window

Part	Description
ADJUSTING ENTRY	Identifies the journal entry as an adjusting journal entry when checked. Adjusting journal entries appear on the *Adjusted Trial Balance* (worksheet) report and the *Adjusting Journal Entries* report. In the *Journal* report, any adjusting entry will be noted with a check mark.
ACCOUNT	Indicates the general ledger account to be adjusted.
DEBIT	Indicates the amount to debit to the account.
CREDIT	Indicates the amount to credit to the account.
MEMO	This field is optional. Any memo entry recorded here will appear in reports.
List of Selected General Journal Entries	Displays a list of journal entries recorded in the Make General Journal Entries window. If the journal entry was checked off as an adjusting entry, it will have a check mark in this list.
Hide List button	Click this button to hide the List of Selected General Journal Entries. When you hide the List of Selected General Journal Entries, the button changes to Show List.

As you recall from Chapter 1, the third level of operation in QuickBooks is Activities. Activities identified as adjustments to account balances are entered in the Make General Journal Entries window. There are no default accounts in this window because each adjusting journal entry is different. The account to debit and the account to credit must be indicated. Adjusting journal entries are usually dated the last day of the month.

The first adjusting journal entry Kristin Raina makes on February 28, 2021, is to record (debit) Advertising Expense and reduce (credit) the Prepaid Advertising account for one month of service. The prepaid advertising was originally purchased on February 1 for $600 and represents a six-month prepayment. One month of Advertising Expense is $100 ($600/6 months).

HINT

Look at the Trial Balance in Figure 4–M on page 121. Notice the Prepaid Advertising account with a balance of $600.

To record an adjusting journal entry:

HINT

In QuickBooks Premier Accountant Edition, the *Make General Journal Entries* choice is also available on the Accountant menu.

1. At the main menu bar, click Company and then click *Make General Journal Entries.*

   The Assigning Numbers to Journal Entries message may appear. As you know, QuickBooks automatically assigns a transaction number (Trans #) to each transaction recorded in each window. You cannot change the transaction number. If a transaction is deleted, that transaction number is also deleted; the next transaction is assigned the next transaction number in sequence. QuickBooks allows the user to assign a journal entry number to each transaction. In this book, journal entry numbers are used for the adjusting journal entries. Once you start a sequence of numbers in the Make General Journal Entries window, QuickBooks automatically assigns the next adjusting journal entry number in sequence; however, you can edit or delete the automatically assigned journal entry number. If you receive the message box, insert a check mark in the box to the left of *Do not display this message in the future* and then click OK.

   The Make General Journal Entries window appears.

2. At the *DATE* field, choose *02/28/2021.*
3. At the *ENTRY NO.* field, type AJE1.
4. Insert a check mark in the box to the left of *ADJUSTING ENTRY,* if necessary.

HINT

Use the scroll arrow in the drop-down list to find the account.

5. In the first line of the *ACCOUNT* field, click the drop-down arrow, scroll down, and then click *6050 Advertising Expense.*
6. At the *DEBIT* field, type 100.
7. Move to the second line in the *ACCOUNT* field, click the drop-down arrow, and then click *1410 Prepaid Advertising.*
8. At the *CREDIT* field, type 100, if necessary.
9. At the *MEMO* field, type To record one month of advertising expense. The *MEMO* field is optional; you do not have to enter an explanation. See Figure 4–O.

FIGURE 4–O

Make General Journal Entries Window— Completed

As in the other windows, the Find button and Previous and Next arrows can be used to view previous and subsequent journal entries. Choosing one of the arrows saves the entry. The Save & New button can be used when entering more than one journal entry.

For this adjusting journal entry, the general ledger posting is as follows:

6050 Advertising Exp		1410 Prepaid Advertising	
Dr	Cr	Dr	Cr
100		Bill 600	100 Adj
		Bal 500	

10. If the entry is correct, click the Save & Close button.

In each journal entry, the total dollar value of debits must equal the total dollar value of credits. At the Make General Journal Entries window, if you attempt to save an entry that is not in balance, a warning window appears that gives you the opportunity to correct the journal entry. If the journal entry is not corrected, you will not be able to save it.

Practice Exercise 4–2

HINT

If the Tracking Fixed Assets on Journal Entries message appears, insert a check mark in the box to the left of *Do not display this message in the future* and then click OK.

Record the following adjusting journal entries in the Make General Journal Entries window. Record each adjusting journal entry separately, and continue with the *ENTRY NO.* sequence of AJE2, AJE3, and so on:

Feb. 28	Record one month of insurance expense. The insurance was purchased for $2,400 in February and recorded as Prepaid Insurance. It is a one-year policy effective February 1. *QuickCheck:* $200
Feb. 28	Record the depreciation expense on the Furniture of $100 per month.
Feb. 28	Record the depreciation expense on the Computer of $60 per month. Add the new account 6185 Deprec. Exp., Computers while in the Make General Journal Entries window.
Feb. 28	Record one month of interest expense on the note payable of $50. (Credit Interest Payable.)
Feb. 28	The office supplies on hand totaled $225. Refer to the Office Supplies account on the Trial Balance to determine the amount of the adjustment. *QuickCheck:* $175

HINT

In the event a new account needs to be added while in the Make General Journal Entries window, click < *Add New* > from the *ACCOUNT* drop-down list. This opens the Add New Account: Choose Account Type window and allows you to add the new account to the list without exiting the Make General Journal Entries window.

After all the adjusting journal entries are recorded, if the *List of Selected General Journal Entries* field is displayed, the journal entries identified as adjusting entries are noted with check marks. You may need to change the range of the List to *All.* See Figure 4–P.

Period-End Accounting Reports and Financial Statements

Reports, the fourth level of operation in QuickBooks, reflect the activities and adjustments recorded in the windows as well as the information compiled in the Lists/Centers. When you complete the adjusting journal entries, you should display and print the period-end accounting reports and financial statements.

Viewing and Printing Accounting Reports

The period-end accounting reports consist of the *Journal*, the *General Ledger*, and the *Adjusted Trial Balance* reports. These reports should be printed at the end of each month.

Journal Report

In the previous chapters, the *Journal* report was printed for the entire month. However, it is not necessary to reprint all the journal entries when you wish to view only the adjusting journal entries. All reports can be customized to modify the appearance of the report or the fields of information to be displayed. In this case, we will customize the report using the Filter feature, which displays only the adjusting journal entries in the *Journal* report.

To view and print only the adjusting journal entries in the *Journal* report:
1. At the main menu bar, click Reports and then click *Accountant & Taxes*.
2. At the Accountant & Taxes submenu, click *Journal*.

Note: Do not choose the Adjusting Journal Entries *report at this time.*

3. At the *From* and *To* fields, choose *02/01/2021* and *02/28/2021* and then click the Refresh button at the top of the report. The *Journal* report is displayed.

   All transactions for February, from all windows, are displayed. Scroll to the bottom of the entries. Notice the account type General Journal on the last six journal entries. These are the adjusting journal entries entered in the Make General Journal Entries window.

4. Click the Customize Report button at the top of the report. The Modify Report: Journal dialog box appears.
5. Click the Filters tab.
6. At the *FILTER* field, scroll down and click *Transaction Type*. The box to the right of the *FILTER* field changes to *Transaction Type*.
7. At the Transaction Type drop-down list, click *Journal*. See Figure 4–Q.

FIGURE 4–Q
Modify Report: Journal—
Filters Tab—Completed

8. Click OK. Only the journal entries recorded in the Make General Journal Entries window are displayed.
9. Above the heading of the report, click Show Filters. The Filters bar indicates that in this report, a *Custom* date is used and only *Journal* transaction type entries are displayed. See Figure 4–R.

FIGURE 4–R
Journal Report—
Adjusting Journal Entries

Show Filters/
Hide Filters

10. To remove the Filters bar, click Hide Filters.
11. Print the report.
12. Close the report.

Because it is usually the accountant who views the adjusting journal entries, instead of displaying the *Journal* report and filtering the adjusting journal entries, QuickBooks Premier Accountant Edition provides an *Adjusting Journal Entries* report.

To view and print the *Adjusting Journal Entries* report in QuickBooks Premier Accountant Edition:

1. At the main menu bar, click Reports and then click *Accountant & Taxes*.
2. At the Accountant & Taxes submenu, click *Adjusting Journal Entries*.
3. At the *From* and *To* fields, choose *02/01/2021* and *02/28/2021* and then click the Refresh button at the top of the report. The *Adjusting Journal Entries* report is displayed.

   This report displays the adjusting journal entries recorded in the Make General Journal Entries window that were checked off as an Adjusting Entry. The adjusting journal entries are the same entries displayed in the *Journal* report in Figure 4–R on page 126. Notice, however, that in this report, the title of the report is *Adjusting Journal Entries*, and the columns labeled *Trans #*, *Type*, and *Adj* are not displayed.
4. Print the report.
5. Close the report.

General Ledger Report

All transactions recorded in any of the windows are posted to the general ledger. The *General Ledger* report displays all the activity in each account as a debit or a credit and then lists the balance after each activity.

To view and print the *General Ledger* report:

1. At the main menu bar, click Reports and then click *Accountant & Taxes*.
2. At the Accountant & Taxes submenu, click *General Ledger*.
3. At the *From* and *To* fields, choose *01/01/2021* and *02/28/2021* and then click the Refresh button at the top of the report. The general ledger is displayed. See Figure 4–S.

FIGURE 4–S
General Ledger Report—
Partial

4. Print the report.
5. Close the report.

Adjusted Trial Balance Report

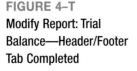

HINT

Once you record the adjusting journal entries, you can no longer create a pre-adjusted trial balance.

The trial balance of February 28, 2021 (Figure 4–M, page 121), was reviewed before the adjusting journal entries were prepared. Typically, the trial balance is printed again after the adjusting journal entries have been recorded. The second trial balance is referred to as the *Adjusted Trial Balance* report. To distinguish between the two printed trial balances, you will modify the report by changing the name in the heading of the second trial balance to *Adjusted Trial Balance*.

To view and print the *Adjusted Trial Balance* report:
1. At the main menu bar, click Reports and then click *Accountant & Taxes.*
2. At the Accountant & Taxes submenu, click *Trial Balance.*

Note: Do not choose the Adjusted Trial Balance *report at this time.*

3. At the *From* and *To* fields, choose *01/01/2021* and *02/28/2021* and then click the Refresh button at the top of the report. The trial balance is displayed. Notice that the heading includes the default heading *Trial Balance.* You will use the Customize Report button to change the heading to *Adjusted Trial Balance.*
4. At the top of the report, click the Customize Report button. The Modify Report: Trial Balance dialog box appears.
5. Click the Header/Footer tab.
6. At the *Report Title* field, type the word Adjusted before the text *Trial Balance.* See Figure 4–T.

FIGURE 4–T

Modify Report: Trial Balance—Header/Footer Tab Completed

7. If the information is correct, click OK. The *Trial Balance* heading is now displayed as *Adjusted Trial Balance*. See Figure 4–U.

FIGURE 4–U

Trial Balance Report—
Renamed Adjusted
Trial Balance

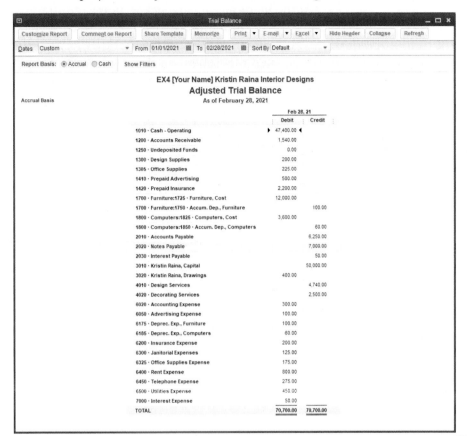

8. Print the report.
9. Close the report.

Compare the effect of the adjusting journal entries on the account balances by comparing the trial balance (Figure 4–M, page 121) to the adjusted trial balance (Figure 4–U).

Note: The trial balance showed $70,490, while the adjusted trial balance now shows $70,700.

Once again, the text is using the Accountant edition of the QuickBooks software. So instead of displaying the *Trial Balance* report and modifying the report to display the name *Adjusted Trial Balance*, QuickBooks Premier Accountant Edition provides an *Adjusted Trial Balance* (worksheet) report. Not only does this report have the name *Adjusted Trial Balance*, but it also displays the original trial balance, the adjusting journal entries, and the adjusted trial balance. It is similar to a worksheet an accountant might prepare.

To view, make a correction, and print the *Adjusted Trial Balance* (worksheet) report in QuickBooks Premier Accountant Edition:

1. At the main menu bar, click Reports and then click *Accountant & Taxes.*
2. At the Accountant & Taxes submenu, click *Adjusted Trial Balance.*
3. At the *From* and *To* fields, choose *01/01/2021* and *02/28/2021* and then click the Refresh button at the top of the report. The *Adjusted Trial Balance* report is displayed. See Figure 4–V.

FIGURE 4–V
Adjusted Trial Balance (Worksheet) Report

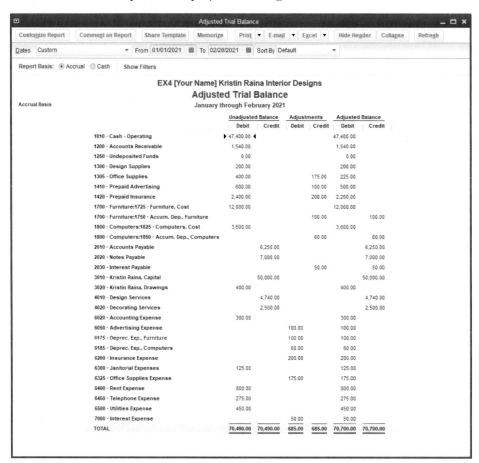

Look at the first two columns labeled *Unadjusted Balance.* This is the original trial balance of February 28, 2021. Compare this balance to the one in Figure 4–M on page 121. Next, look at the third and fourth columns, which are labeled *Adjustments.* These are the adjusting journal entries displayed in the *Journal* report in Figure 4–R on page 126. Finally, look at the fifth and sixth columns of this report. This is the adjusted trial balance that was displayed in Figure 4–U on page 129.

Recall that in most reports in QuickBooks, you can "drill down" to the original window where an activity was recorded and make any necessary changes. This can also be done in this report. Assume that you realize the Office Supplies on hand is $250, not $225 as noted in the practice exercise on page 124. The last adjusting journal entry originally recorded as $175 needs to be changed to $150 ($400 Office Supplies – $250 supplies on hand = $150 Supplies Expense).

4. In the *Adjustments - Debit* column, on the line that displays *6325 Office Supplies Expense*, double-click *175.00*. This drills down to the *Transactions by Account* report.
5. In the *Transactions by Account* report, on the line that displays *AJE6*, double-click *175.00*. This drills down to the Make General Journal Entries window, where the adjusting journal entry for Supplies Expense was originally recorded.
6. Change the amount to *150.00* in both the *DEBIT* column and the *CREDIT* column. See Figure 4–W.

FIGURE 4–W
Make General Journal
Entries Window—
Correction Completed

The List of Selected General Journal Entries still displays *175* for *AJE6*. This list will be updated after the change to the adjusting journal entry is saved.

7. If the information is correct, click the Save & Close button. At the Recording Transaction message, click Yes.
8. You are returned to the *Transactions by Account* report with the adjusting journal entry updated for the correction. Close the *Transactions by Account* report.

9. You are returned to the *Adjusted Trial Balance* (worksheet) report. Click the Refresh button. The report is updated. See Figure 4–X.

FIGURE 4–X
Adjusted Trial Balance
(Worksheet) Report—
Correction Completed

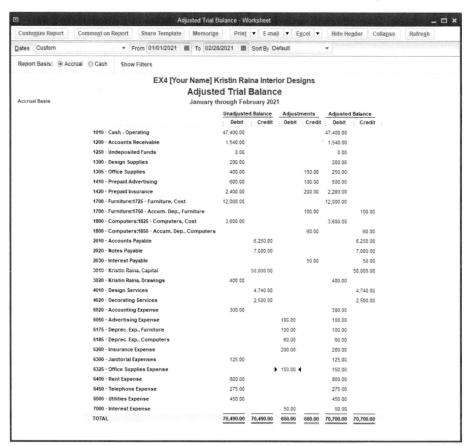

HINT

Compare the *Adjusted Trial Balance* (work-sheet) report to Figure 4–R on page 126, Figure 4–U on page 129, and Figure 4–V on page 130. Notice the TOTALs in the *Adjustments* columns have changed due to the change in AJE6. Notice the TOTALs in the *Adjusted Balance* columns are the same, but the balances in the Office Supplies account and the Office Supplies Expense account have changed.

10. Print the report.
11. Close the report.

Viewing and Printing Financial Statements

The financial statements include the income statement and the balance sheet. A company must prepare financial statements at least once a year, but they can be prepared more frequently, such as quarterly or even monthly.

Profit & Loss Standard Report (Income Statement)

The income statement is known as the *Profit & Loss* report in QuickBooks. The *Profit & Loss* report displays revenue and expenses for a specified period of time. The *Profit & Loss* report can be displayed in a standard or comparative format. In addition, a detailed *Profit & Loss* report can be produced that lists all the transactions affecting a particular item on the report.

To view and print a year-to-date *Profit & Loss Standard* report:
1. At the main menu bar, click Reports and then click *Company & Financial.*
2. At the Company & Financial submenu, click *Profit & Loss Standard.*
3. At the *From* and *To* fields, choose *01/01/2021* and *02/28/2021* and then click the Refresh button at the top of the report. The report for the period is displayed. See Figure 4–Y.

FIGURE 4–Y

Profit & Loss Standard Report

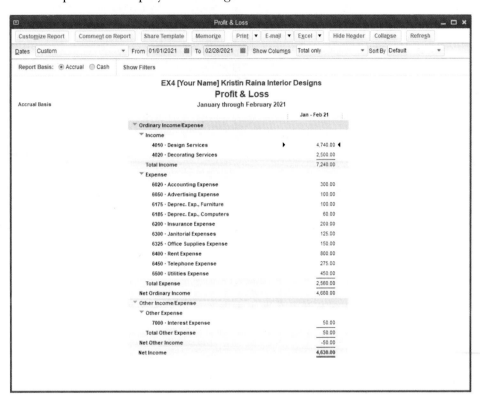

4. Print the report.
5. Close the report.

Balance Sheet Standard Report

In QuickBooks, the *Balance Sheet* report, which shows the assets, liabilities, and equity balances as of a certain date, may be displayed in a standard, summary, or comparative format. In addition, a detailed report, showing all the transactions affecting balance sheet accounts, can be produced.

To display and print a *Balance Sheet Standard* report:
1. At the main menu bar, click Reports and then click *Company & Financial.*
2. At the Company & Financial submenu, click *Balance Sheet Standard.*
3. At the *As of* field, choose *02/28/2021* and then click the Refresh button at the top of the report. The balance sheet in standard format is displayed.

4. Print the report. See Figure 4–Z.

FIGURE 4–Z

Balance Sheet Standard Report

EX4 [Your Name] Kristin Raina Interior Designs
Balance Sheet

Accrual Basis   As of February 28, 2021

	Feb 28, 21
ASSETS	
Current Assets	
Checking/Savings	
1010 · Cash - Operating	47,400.00
Total Checking/Savings	47,400.00
Accounts Receivable	
1200 · Accounts Receivable	1,540.00
Total Accounts Receivable	1,540.00
Other Current Assets	
1300 · Design Supplies	200.00
1305 · Office Supplies	250.00
1410 · Prepaid Advertising	500.00
1420 · Prepaid Insurance	2,200.00
Total Other Current Assets	3,150.00
Total Current Assets	52,090.00
Fixed Assets	
1700 · Furniture	
1725 · Furniture, Cost	12,000.00
1750 · Accum. Dep., Furniture	-100.00
Total 1700 · Furniture	11,900.00
1800 · Computers	
1825 · Computers, Cost	3,600.00
1850 · Accum. Dep., Computers	-60.00
Total 1800 · Computers	3,540.00
Total Fixed Assets	15,440.00
TOTAL ASSETS	**67,530.00**
LIABILITIES & EQUITY	
Liabilities	
Current Liabilities	
Accounts Payable	
2010 · Accounts Payable	6,250.00
Total Accounts Payable	6,250.00
Other Current Liabilities	
2020 · Notes Payable	7,000.00
2030 · Interest Payable	50.00
Total Other Current Liabilities	7,050.00
Total Current Liabilities	13,300.00
Total Liabilities	13,300.00
Equity	
3010 · Kristin Raina, Capital	50,000.00
3020 · Kristin Raina, Drawings	-400.00
Net Income	4,630.00
Total Equity	54,230.00
TOTAL LIABILITIES & EQUITY	**67,530.00**

HINT

This is a printout of the *Balance Sheet Standard* report. The Fixed Assets section of the *Balance Sheet Standard* report on the computer screen lists the balances of all Fixed Assets—parent and subaccounts—in a single column.

Look at the Fixed Assets section on the printout of the *Balance Sheet Standard* report. Recall that in the Chart of Accounts List, parent and subaccounts were used for the fixed assets. When parent and subaccounts flow into the financial statements, the parent account name becomes a heading and a total for the related subaccounts. Under the parent account name heading, the subaccount names are indented on the financial statements. The account balances for the subaccounts are displayed and subtotaled and then shown as the total for the parent account. For example, the parent account 1700 Furniture is a heading; the subaccounts 1725 Furniture, Cost and 1750 Accum. Dep., Furniture are indented and displayed under the parent account; and then the parent account 1700 Furniture is again displayed, this time as the total for the subaccounts. On the printout of the report, the balances of the subaccounts (12,000 and –100) are displayed to the left of the dollar-value column, and the subtotal of these subaccounts (11,900) is displayed in the dollar-value column and labeled as the total for the parent account.

5. Close the report.

Registers

Because QuickBooks is designed for the non-accountant, it includes an alternative method for reviewing daily activity by using registers. Registers are available for any balance sheet account—that is, any asset, liability, or equity account. Registers are not available for income and expense accounts.

The register format is similar to that of a personal checkbook, but the information displayed in a register is similar to the information displayed in the general ledger.

To view a register:
1. At the main menu bar, click Lists and then click *Chart of Accounts.*
2. At the Chart of Accounts List window, double-click the *1010 Cash - Operating* account. The 1010 Cash - Operating register appears. See Figure 4–AA.

FIGURE 4–AA
1010 Cash - Operating Register

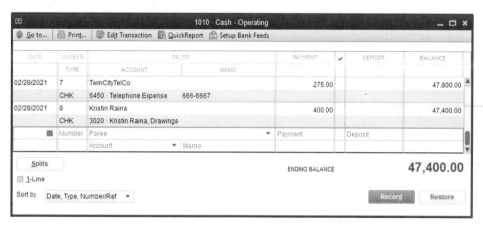

HINT
An alternative method of displaying the register is to select *1010 Cash - Operating* in the Chart of Accounts List window, click the Activities menu button, and then click *Use Register.*

Transactions that were entered in any of the other windows that affected the 1010 Cash - Operating account are also displayed in the register. Scroll through the transactions and compare them with those in the 1010 Cash - Operating account in the general ledger (see Figure 4–S on page 127). You can use the register to correct any activity already recorded by "drilling down" to the source of the activity.

To "drill down" using the register:

1. At the 1010 Cash - Operating register, double-click the *February 23, Cuza and Carl Associates* transaction. The Bill Payments(Check) window appears. See Figure 4–BB.

FIGURE 4–BB
Bill Payments(Check) Window

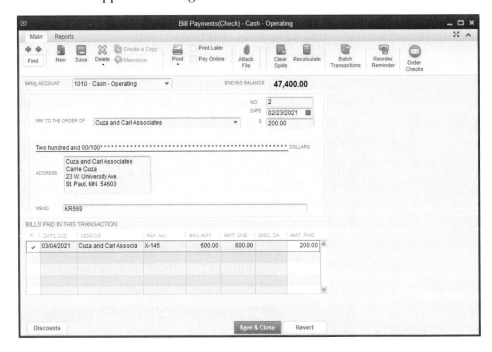

HINT

An alternative method of "drilling down" from the register to the activity window is to select the transaction in the register and then click Edit Transaction in the register.

This transaction was originally recorded in the Pay Bills window. Recall that after a transaction is saved in the Pay Bills window, it cannot subsequently be edited in that window. However, the Write Checks window shows all payments, both those entered through the Pay Bills window and those entered in the Write Checks window. So even though this transaction was initially recorded in the Pay Bills window, you can "drill down" to the Bill Payments(Check) - Cash - Operating window and correct any errors, if necessary.

2. Close all the windows.

Registers are available only for balance sheet accounts. For income statement accounts—that is, income and expenses—registers are not available, but an *Account QuickReport* is available that displays all the activity to the account—again, similar to the general ledger information.

To view an income *Account QuickReport*:
1. At the main menu bar, click Lists and then click *Chart of Accounts*.
2. At the Chart of Accounts window, double-click *4020 Decorating Services*.
3. At the *From* and *To* fields, choose *02/01/2021* and *02/28/2021* and then click the Refresh button at the top of the report. The *Account QuickReport* is displayed, listing all the activity to this account during the time period chosen. See Figure 4–CC.

FIGURE 4–CC Account QuickReport

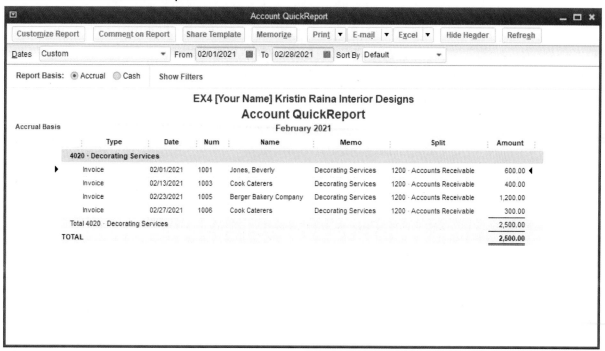

From this report, as with others, you can "drill down" to the window where the original activity was recorded.
4. Close the report.
5. Close the Chart of Accounts List window.

Exiting QuickBooks

Upon completing this session, make a backup copy of your practice exercise company file to a removable storage device using the Back Up command. Be sure to change the *Save in* field to the removable storage device and then carefully type the correct file name. Close the company file and then exit QuickBooks.

Chapter Review and Assessment

Procedure Review

To add a new account:
1. At the main menu bar, click Lists and then click *Chart of Accounts*.
2. At the Chart of Accounts List window, click the Account menu button.
3. At the Account button drop-down menu, click *New*.
4. At the Add New Account: Choose Account Type window, choose the account type and then click Continue.
5. At the Add New Account window, enter the data for the account.
6. Click the Save & Close button.
7. Close the Chart of Accounts List window.

To delete an account:
1. At the main menu bar, click Lists and then click *Chart of Accounts*.
2. At the Chart of Accounts List window, select the account you wish to delete.
3. Click the Account menu button.
4. At the Account button drop-down menu, click *Delete Account*. Note that you cannot delete an account that has a balance or has been used in a transaction.
5. Click OK at the Delete Account warning.
6. Close the Chart of Accounts List window.

To edit an account:
1. At the main menu bar, click Lists and then click *Chart of Accounts*.
2. At the Chart of Accounts List window, select the account you wish to edit.
3. Click the Account menu button.
4. At the Account button drop-down menu, click *Edit Account*.
5. Change the appropriate information.
6. Click the Save & Close button.
7. Close the Chart of Accounts List window.

To record an adjusting journal entry:
1. At the main menu bar, click Company and then click *Make General Journal Entries*.
2. At the *DATE* field, enter the date.
3. At the *ENTRY NO.* field, type in the original journal entry number, if necessary; thereafter, QuickBooks assigns the entry numbers in sequence.
4. Insert a check mark in the box to the left of *ADJUSTING ENTRY*.
5. In the first line of the *ACCOUNT* field, click once to access the drop-down list of accounts and then choose the account to debit.
6. Enter the amount to debit at the *DEBIT* field.
7. On the second line in the *ACCOUNT* field, from the drop-down list of accounts, choose the account to credit.
8. At the *CREDIT* field, enter the amount to credit.
9. At the *MEMO* field, type in a brief explanation (optional).
10. Click the Save & Close button.

To view and print accounting reports from the Reports menu:

1. At the main menu bar, click Reports and then click *Accountant & Taxes.*
2. At the Accountant & Taxes submenu, choose a report.
3. Choose the appropriate dates for the report and then click the Refresh button at the top of the report.
4. Print the report.
5. Close the report.

To view and print financial statements from the Reports menu:

1. At the main menu bar, click Reports and then click *Company & Financial.*
2. At the Company & Financial submenu, choose a financial statement.
3. Choose the appropriate dates for the statement and then click the Refresh button at the top of the report.
4. Print the report.
5. Close the report.

To filter the information displayed in a report or financial statement:

1. Open a report or financial statement, enter the correct dates, and then click the Refresh button.
2. At the top of the report, click the Customize Report button.
3. In the Modify Report dialog box, click the Filters tab.
4. At the *FILTER* field, select the category of information you wish to filter—for example, transaction type. The field to the right changes to the filter chosen.
5. Choose the specific information you wish to filter; for example, in transaction type, you might choose *Journal.*
6. Click OK. The report now displays the information chosen on the Filters tab.
7. Above the heading of the report, click *Show Filters.* The filters selected for this report are displayed.
8. To remove the Filters bar, click *Hide Filters.*
9. Close the report.

To change the heading in a report or financial statement:

1. Open a report or financial statement, enter the correct dates, and then click the Refresh button.
2. At the top of the report, click the Customize Report button.
3. In the Modify Report dialog box, click the Header/Footer tab.
4. At the *Report Title* field, change the name of the report to the desired title.
5. Click OK. The report now displays the new title of the report.
6. Close the report.

To view and print a register or *Account QuickReport* from the Lists menu:

1. At the main menu bar, click Lists and then click *Chart of Accounts.*
2. Double-click the account for which you want the register or *Account QuickReport.* (Registers are used for assets, liabilities, and equity accounts; *Account QuickReports* are used for revenues and expenses accounts.)

    c. *Trial Balance:* Change name in header of the report to *Adjusted Trial Balance* (June 1, 2021–June 30, 2021)

    d. *Profit & Loss Standard* (June 1, 2021–June 30, 2021)

    e. *Balance Sheet Standard* (June 30, 2021)

CHAPTER 5

Inventory

Receiving and Selling Items, Processing Sales Discounts, Adjusting Quantity/Value on Hand, and Paying Sales Tax

Objectives

- Identify the two inventory systems
- Update the Item List
- Record purchases of inventory items in the Enter Bills and Write Checks windows
- Identify transactions requiring sales tax
- Process sales discounts
- Record adjustments to inventory items in the Adjust Quantity/Value on Hand window
- Record payment of sales tax in the Pay Sales Tax window
- Display and print inventory-related reports
- Display and print accounting reports and financial statements

QuickBooks allows you to track inventory transactions. **Inventory** is ready-made merchandise that is sold to customers for a profit. Before you can enter inventory transactions, you must establish a file for each inventory item. Inventory item files are included in the Item List (Lists/Centers).

Once you establish an inventory item file, transactions for the item (Activities) can be entered in the Enter Bills, Write Checks, Create Invoices, Enter Sales Receipts, and Adjust Quantity/Value on Hand activity windows in much the same manner as was done in prior chapters. Every time the company receives merchandise for resale, sells merchandise, or adjusts the inventory because of loss or damage, QuickBooks records that information in the Item List. This allows you to accurately determine inventory quantity, value, and profit on sales. In addition, QuickBooks automatically changes balance sheet and income statement accounts based on the inventory information in the Item List (Reports).

In this chapter, our sample company, Kristin Raina Interior Designs, begins purchasing and selling decorative accessories to clients in addition to providing design and decorating services. This means that Kristin Raina must now be concerned with keeping an inventory.

QuickBooks versus Manual Accounting: Inventory Transactions

As discussed in previous chapters, in a manual accounting system, purchases on account are recorded in a purchases journal while sales on account are recorded in a sales journal. This is true whether the purchase or sale is for services or for merchandise. Cash transactions are recorded in the cash receipts or cash payments journals, again for both inventory and non-inventory items.

In QuickBooks, the Item List serves as an inventory subsidiary ledger for the company. The list includes all the items the company sells, both inventory and service items. Relevant information for each inventory item, such as name/number, type, description, cost, sales price, and related general ledger accounts, is entered at the time the item file is created and is updated as necessary.

When the company purchases an inventory item from a vendor on account, the transaction is recorded in the Enter Bills activity window in much the same manner as non-inventory purchases have been recorded. When the inventory items are sold on account, the invoice is recorded in the Create Invoices activity window in a manner similar to that for other revenues. When you enter these transactions, QuickBooks updates the Chart of Accounts List (general ledger) and at the same time updates each vendor and customer file. In addition, it updates the Item List to reflect the purchase and sale of the inventory items. Cash purchases of inventory items are recorded in the Write Checks activity window, while cash sales of inventory are recorded in the Enter Sales Receipts activity window. Changes in inventory that are not the result of a sale or purchase are recorded in the Adjust Quantity/Value on Hand window. In each instance when inventory items are purchased, sold, or adjusted, the Item List is updated to reflect the new inventory quantity and value.

Accounting for Inventory Transactions

periodic inventory system values the inventory periodically based on a physical count of the merchandise; usually done once a year

There are two types of inventory systems: periodic and perpetual. Under the **periodic inventory system**, separate records are *not* maintained for inventory items, and no attempts are made to adjust the inventory account for purchases and sales. Instead, inventory is counted periodically to determine inventory quantity, value, cost of goods sold, and gross profit. In the past, the periodic system was often used by businesses that sold high-volume, low-cost goods, for which keeping individual inventory records was not practical.

perpetual inventory system values the inventory after every purchase and sale of inventory items

Under the **perpetual inventory system**, accounting records are maintained that continuously show the current inventory quantity and value. When inventory is purchased, the inventory (asset) account is increased. When inventory is sold, the inventory account is reduced. In addition, the cost of goods sold is simultaneously computed to arrive at gross profit. Before the availability of low-cost computer hardware and software, only businesses with low-volume, high-cost goods used the perpetual system. Now, with computers pervasive in business, most companies are able to use a perpetual inventory system.

QuickBooks, like almost all general ledger accounting software programs, uses the perpetual system for two reasons. It not only allows the user to know the current inventory quantity and value at any given moment, but it also calculates the cost of goods sold and gross profit after each sale without the need for a periodic physical inventory count.

Chapter Problem

In this chapter, you will track inventory transactions for Kristin Raina Interior Designs, which will begin selling decorative inventory items in addition to providing decorating and design services. Information for inventory items has been entered in the Item List. This information, along with the March 1, 2021, beginning balances, is contained in the company file **CH5 Kristin Raina Interior Designs**.

Before you begin, open the company file **CH5 Kristin Raina Interior Designs.QBW**. Enter the password, *Student1*. Make a backup copy of the file, name it **EX5 *[Your Name]* Kristin Raina Interior Designs**, and then restore the file. Enter the password, *Student1*. Finally, change the company name in the file to **EX5 *[Your Name]* Kristin Raina Interior Designs**.

Lists/Centers

The Item List

Recall from Chapter 1 that the second level of operation in QuickBooks is to record background information in Lists/Centers. The Item List contains a file for each type of service or inventory item sold by the company. If the item sold is an inventory product, QuickBooks calls this an *inventory part* as opposed to a *service item.* You should enter the information for each inventory item in the Item List before recording transactions. This will make the Activities function run more smoothly. However, if you inadvertently omit an item, you can add that item during the Activities level of operation with minimal disruption.

The Item List contains important information on each product, such as type of item; number; descriptions; cost; general ledger posting accounts for inventory asset, cost of goods sold, and sales; preferred vendor; and sales tax status. All products or services sold by the company should be included in the Item List. Periodically, these files need to be updated as products are added or discontinued or as background information changes.

Kristin Raina has entered information for various inventory items in the Item List.

To review the Item List:
1. At the main menu bar, click Lists and then click *Item List.* The Item List appears. See Figure 5–A.

FIGURE 5–A Item List

To view a specific inventory item file:
1. Double-click the *Carpets* item name. The inventory item file opens in Edit Item mode. See Figure 5–B.

FIGURE 5–B
Edit Item Window

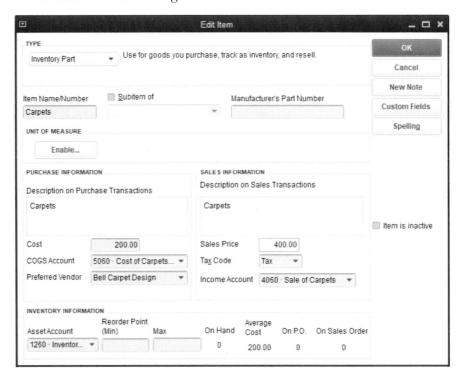

Table 5–1 describes the various fields of the Edit Item window.

TABLE 5–1
Edit Item Window

Field	Description
TYPE	If this is an inventory item, select *Inventory Part*. Other selections include *Service* for service revenue items, *Non-inventory Part* for products sold that are not maintained in inventory, *Inventory Assembly, Other Charge*, and so on.
Item Name/Number	Used to assign an identifying name or number to each item.
Subitem of	Used if an item is a component of another item, such as in a construction or manufacturing company.
Description on Purchase Transactions/Description on Sales Transactions	Used to enter a description of the item for the purchase or sales activity windows.
Cost	Used to enter the typical unit cost for the item. This amount will appear in the purchase activity windows (Enter Bills and Write Checks) as the default cost amount. Can override this entry as needed.
COGS Account	Lists the default general ledger posting account for cost of goods sold when the item is sold. Can override this account as needed.
Sales Price	This is the default unit-selling price that appears in the sales activity windows (Create Invoices and Enter Sales Receipts). Can override this entry as needed.
Tax Code	Used to indicate if the item is taxable or nontaxable for sales tax purposes.
Income Account	This is the default general ledger posting account for revenue when the item is sold. Can override this account as needed.
Asset Account	This is the default general ledger posting account for the inventory balance sheet account when an item is purchased. Can override this entry as needed.

2. Close the Edit Item window.
3. Close the Item List window.

The Item List is revised periodically when new inventory items are added, unused items are deleted, or modifications are made to inventory items. Making these adjustments to the inventory item files is referred to as *updating the Item List*.

Adding an Item

The company has decided to sell a line of modern lamps to its clients and needs to add this inventory item to the Item List.

To add an item:

1. At the main menu bar, click Lists and then click *Item List*.
2. At the Item List window, click the Item menu button. The Item drop-down menu appears. See Figure 5–C.

FIGURE 5–C
Item Drop-Down Menu

3. At the Item button drop-down menu, click *New*. The New Item window appears. See Figure 5–D.

FIGURE 5–D
New Item Window

4. At the TYPE drop-down list, click *Inventory Part*.
5. Complete the remainder of the window with the following information:

Item Name/Number:	Lamps
Description on	
Purchase/Sales Transactions:	Lamps
Cost:	100
COGS Account:	5070 Cost of Lamps Sold
Preferred Vendor:	Lumiare Lighting Company
Sales Price:	200
Tax Code:	Tax – Taxable Sales
Income Account:	4070 Sale of Lamps
Asset Account:	1270 Inventory of Lamps
Date:	March 1, 2021

Your screen should look like Figure 5–E.

FIGURE 5–E
New Item Window—
Completed

6. If the information is correct, click OK.
7. Close the Item List window.

Deleting an Item

Kristin Raina wishes to delete Tapestries from the Item List because the company has decided not to sell this product.

To delete an item:
1. At the main menu bar, click Lists and then click *Item List.*
2. At the Item List window, select *Tapestries* but do not open the file. See Figure 5–F.

FIGURE 5–F
Item List—Tapestries
Selected

3. Click the Item menu button. At the Item button drop-down menu, click *Delete Item.*
4. A warning screen appears. Click OK. The item file is deleted.
5. Close the Item List window.

You cannot delete an item with a balance or an item that has been part of a transaction for the period.

Editing an Item

Kristin Raina needs to edit the file for Draperies because the unit cost has increased to $125 and the sales price to $250.

To edit an item file:
1. At the main menu bar, click Lists and then click *Item List.*
2. Double-click the *Draperies* item file. The file opens in Edit Item mode. See Figure 5–G.

FIGURE 5–G
Edit Item Window—
Draperies

3. At the *Cost* and *Sales Price* fields, delete the current information and then enter the new amounts shown in Figure 5–H.

FIGURE 5–H
Edit Item Window—
Draperies—Updated

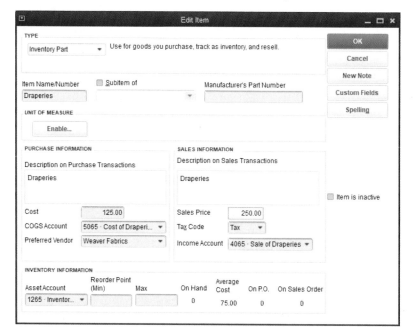

4. If the information is correct, click OK.
5. Close the Item List window.

Practice Exercise   5–1

Add the following item:

Type:	Inventory Part
Item Name/Number:	Mirrors
Description on Purchase/Sales Transactions:	Decorative Mirrors
Cost:	150
COGS Account:	5075 Cost of Mirrors Sold
Preferred Vendor:	Ace Glass Works
Sales Price:	300
Tax Code:	Tax – Taxable Sales
Income Account:	4075 Sale of Mirrors
Asset Account:	1275 Inventory of Mirrors
Date:	March 1, 2021

Delete the following item:

    Wall Units

QuickCheck: The updated Item List appears in Figure 5–I.

FIGURE 5–I Updated Item List

Inventory Center

Many of the procedures reviewed in this chapter, such as adding and editing an inventory item and recording a sale of inventory, can be accomplished through the Inventory Center. The Inventory Center can be found by clicking the Vendors menu, clicking *Inventory Activities,* and then clicking *Inventory Center.* See Figure 5–J.

The Inventory Center window is similar to the Vendor Center and Customer Center windows. The Inventory Center window contains a file for each inventory item. Each file contains important information, such as inventory item name, description, cost, sales price, and quantity on hand. The Inventory Center duplicates the information contained in the Item List. However, the Inventory Center maintains only files for Inventory Part items as seen on the Item List. The Inventory Center does not display non-inventory part items from the Item List.

FIGURE 5-J Inventory Center

Purchasing Inventory

Recall from Chapter 1 that the third level of operation in QuickBooks is Activities, in which you record the daily business activities. Activities identified as purchases of inventory items on account are recorded in the Enter Bills window. Activities identified as purchases of inventory items for cash are recorded in the Write Checks window.

Recording Inventory Purchases Using the Enter Bills Window

In Chapter 2, you used the Enter Bills activity window when goods and services were purchased on account from a vendor. There are two subtabs on the Main tab of the Enter Bills window: Expenses and Items. When you chose *Enter Bills* from the Vendors drop-down menu, you used the Expenses tab to record your non-inventory purchases. When a company wishes to use the inventory feature, the Vendors drop-down menu offers an additional choice of *Receive Items and Enter Bill.* When you click *Receive Items and Enter Bill,* the Enter Bills window opens, but you use the Items tab to record an inventory purchase. In the Enter Bills window, the Items tab is similar to the Expenses tab but provides for additional fields that relate to inventory. In addition, you will find buttons that can be used when purchase orders are used in the purchase of inventory.

In some instances, items are received before the vendor forwards a bill. If this occurs, a different procedure is employed to record the transactions. However, for this chapter, it is assumed that a bill from the vendor accompanies the receipt of the inventory item and that you will record the transaction in the Enter Bills window—Items tab by clicking Vendors on the main menu bar and then *Receive Items and Enter Bill.* See Figure 5–K.

FIGURE 5–K
Enter Bills Window—
Items Tab

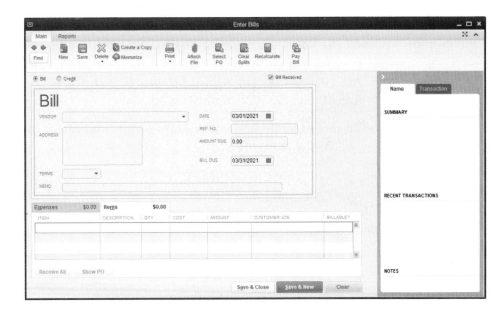

Table 5–2 describes the various fields on the Items tab in the Enter Bills window.

TABLE 5–2
Enter Bills Window—
Items Tab

Field	Description
ITEM	Click the inventory item purchased from the drop-down list. Once an item is chosen, the *DESCRIPTION* and *COST* fields are automatically filled based on information in the item file.
QTY	Enter the quantity purchased. QuickBooks multiplies the quantity purchased by the unit cost to arrive at the *AMOUNT* and *AMOUNT DUE* figures. In the *QTY* field, an icon appears. Clicking the icon allows you to view the current availability information for this item, such as quantity available and quantity on purchase order. You can enter the quantity amount in the field while this icon is displayed. This icon appears any time an inventory part item is selected.

Notice that a field for the general ledger accounts is not displayed. Recall that when you entered items in the Item List, the general ledger accounts for the purchase (inventory asset account) and sale (income account and COGS account) of inventory items were indicated. QuickBooks uses the information in the Item List and the information entered in the Enter Bills window to adjust the correct accounts automatically.

The Enter Bills window—Items tab is designed for purchases of inventory items on account. The default accounts are the Inventory asset account and the Accounts Payable account. QuickBooks uses the information on the Item List to correctly record the amount and account for the inventory asset. The transaction is recorded as follows:

	Inventory		XXX		
		Accounts Payable			XXX

Recording a Purchase and Receipt of an Inventory Item on Account

On March 1, 2021, Kristin Raina purchases and receives 10 mirrors from Ace Glass Works at a cost of $150 each, its Invoice No. K-588. The bill is due March 31, 2021, terms Net 30 Days.

To record a purchase and receipt of inventory items on account:

1. At the main menu bar, click Vendors and then click *Receive Items and Enter Bill.*
2. At the VENDOR drop-down list, click *Ace Glass Works.*
3. Complete the *DATE, REF. NO., BILL DUE,* and *TERMS* fields in the same way you would for a non-inventory purchase. Make sure the Items tab is the active tab. See Figure 5–L.

FIGURE 5–L
Enter Bills Window—
Partially Completed

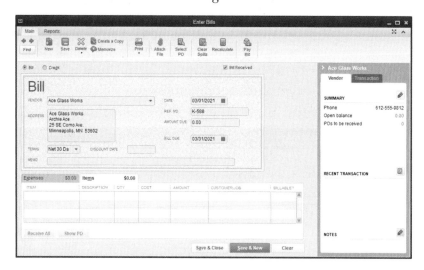

4. At the ITEM drop-down list, click *Mirrors.* The *DESCRIPTION* and *COST* fields fill automatically.
5. At the *QTY* field, type 10 and then move to the next field. The *AMOUNT* and *AMOUNT DUE* fields are completed automatically. See Figure 5–M.

FIGURE 5–M
Enter Bills Window—
Completed

HINT

Remember: You can enter the quantity while the inventory icon is displayed.

For a purchase of inventory on account, the general ledger posting is as follows:

1275 Mirrors Inventory		2010 Accts Payable	
Dr	Cr	Dr	Cr
1,500			1,500

In addition, the vendor file (subledger) for Ace Glass Works reflects the new liability.

Ace Glass Works	
Dr	Cr
	1,500

6. If all the data is correct, click the Save & Close button.

In addition to the general ledger and vendor file changes, this transaction updates the item file for Mirrors to reflect a quantity of 10 on hand with an inventory value of $1,500.

Recording Inventory Purchases Using the Write Checks Window

Like the Enter Bills window, the Write Checks window has an Expenses tab and an Items tab. For the purchase of inventory items for cash, you switch to the Items tab after opening the Write Checks window. The fields in which to enter information for inventory items in the Write Checks window—Items tab are similar to those in the Enter Bills window—Items tab.

The Write Checks window—Items tab is designed for purchases of inventory items for cash. The default accounts are the Inventory asset account and the Cash account. QuickBooks uses the information on the Item List to correctly record the amount and account for the inventory asset. The transaction is recorded as follows:

		Inventory		XXX		
		Cash			XXX	

Recording a Purchase and Receipt of an Inventory Item for Cash

On March 2, 2021, Kristin Raina purchases and receives 16 lamps from Lumiare Lighting Company at a cost of $100 each, its Invoice No. 6844, paid with Check No. 9.

To record a purchase and receipt of inventory items for cash:
1. At the main menu bar, click Banking and then click *Write Checks*.
2. At the Write Checks window, confirm that the *Print Later* and *Pay Online* boxes are not checked; at the *BANK ACCOUNT* field, confirm that *1010 Cash - Operating* is displayed; and at the *NO.* field, confirm that *9* is displayed.
3. At the *DATE* field, choose *03/02/2021*.
4. At the PAY TO THE ORDER OF drop-down list, click *Lumiare Lighting Company*.

5. Click the Items tab.
6. At the ITEM drop-down list, click *Lamps*.
7. At the *QTY* field, type 16 and then move to the next field. Quick-Books completes the *AMOUNT* field. See Figure 5–N.

FIGURE 5–N
Write Checks Window—Completed

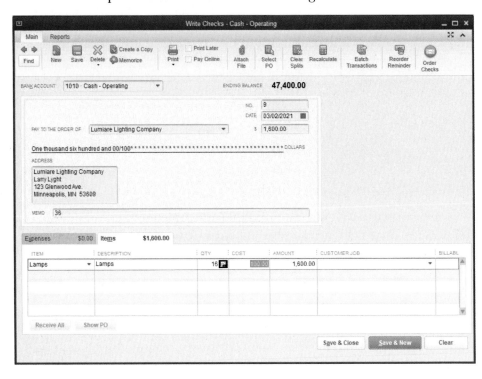

8. Click the Save & Close button.

ACCOUNTING CONCEPT

For a cash payment for the purchase of inventory, the general ledger posting is as follows:

1270 Lamps Inventory		1010 Cash - Operating	
Dr	Cr	Dr	Cr
1,600			1,600

In addition, the item file for Lamps is updated to reflect the new purchase.

Practice Exercise   **5–2**

Record the following transactions at the Enter Bills or Write Checks window:

Mar. 6	Purchased and received 10 carpets from Bell Carpet Design at a cost of $200 each, its Invoice No. 12-5585. The bill is due April 5, 2021. *QuickCheck:* $2,000
Mar. 13	Purchased and received 12 sets of draperies from Weaver Fabrics at a cost of $125 each. Pay immediately with Check No. 10. *QuickCheck:* $1,500

HINT

Many companies use purchase order forms to order inventory items from their suppliers. After completing Chapter 5, refer to Appendix D to see how QuickBooks uses purchase orders as part of the inventory purchase cycle.

Sales Tax

sales tax an amount charged on the sale of merchandise (usually a percentage of the sales price) that the company collects as part of the sale and later remits to the appropriate government agency

When a company sells a product to a customer, it is usually required to collect **sales tax** on the sale. The sales tax amount charged is added to the invoice price of the product. For example, a customer purchases an item with a retail price of $1,000, and the applicable sales tax rate is 6%. The retailer adds $60 to the invoice and collects $1,060 from the customer. At a later date, the retailer remits the tax collected from this and other customers to the appropriate state sales tax collection agency. Rules for applying and collecting sales tax are complex and beyond the scope of this text. For examples and cases in this text, assume every customer pays sales tax. QuickBooks, like most general ledger software programs, is equipped to track sales-taxable transactions and to facilitate the collection and payment of taxes due.

In this chapter, Kristin Raina Interior Designs will sell decorative accessories to its customers. All sales of these products are subject to a sales tax charge of 7%, which is added to the invoice total. The tax will be payable to the Minnesota Department of Revenue at the end of each month. Sales tax will not be collected on services (decorating and design) in this text, because services generally are not subject to sales tax. Note, however, that in some localities, services also are subject to sales tax.

As you know from Chapter 3, a sale on account is recorded in the Create Invoices window, and a sale for cash is recorded in the Enter Sales Receipts window. The default account in the Create Invoices window is a debit to Accounts Receivable, and the default account in the Enter Sales Receipts window is a debit to Cash or Undeposited Funds. When sales tax is charged on the sale of an item, a default Sales Tax Payable account is credited in both the Create Invoices and Enter Sales Receipts windows. The sale of taxable products either for cash or on account results in the following general ledger posting:

Accounts Receivable/Cash (or Undeposited Funds)	XXX				
Sales			XXX		
Sales Tax Payable			XXX		

Sale of Inventory

Activities

Activities identified as sales of inventory items on account are recorded in the Create Invoices window. Activities identified as sales of inventory items for cash are recorded in the Enter Sales Receipts window. Activities recorded in these windows are similar to those in Chapter 3, but additional fields in the window are used that relate to inventory.

Inventory Sales on Account in the Create Invoices Window

When you record the sale of inventory items in the Create Invoices window, you use a template to access the additional fields needed for inventory items. In Chapter 3, for the sale of services, you used the Intuit Service Invoice Template. For the sale of inventory items on account, you will use the Intuit Product Invoice Template.

The Create Invoices window—Intuit Product Invoice is designed for the sale of inventory items on account. The default accounts are Accounts Receivable, Cost of Goods Sold, Inventory, Sales Tax Payable, and Sales.

QuickBooks uses the inventory Item List to determine the correct amount and account for the Cost of Goods Sold, Inventory, and Sales accounts. If an item is marked as taxable, QuickBooks uses the Item List to determine the correct amount of sales tax to be recorded in the Sales Tax Payable account. The transaction is recorded as follows:

Accounts Receivable	XXX			
Cost of Goods Sold	XXX			
Inventory			XXX	
Sales Tax Payable			XXX	
Sales			XXX	

Recording a Sale of an Inventory Item on Account

On March 15, 2021, Kristin Raina sells the following items to Jennie Guthrie on account, Invoice No. 1008, Terms 2/10, Net 30 Days:

2 lamps	$ 400.00
3 carpets	1,200.00
1 mirror	300.00
Total sale of merchandise	$ 1,900.00
sales tax (0.07 × $1,900)	133.00
decorating services (8 hours)	400.00
Total sale on account	$ 2,433.00

To record a sale of inventory on account:

1. At the main menu bar, click Customers and then click *Create Invoices*.
2. At the CUSTOMER:JOB drop-down list, click *Guthrie, Jennie*.
3. At the TEMPLATE drop-down list, click *Intuit Product Invoice*. Additional fields for inventory item information appear.
4. Enter the information listed above for the *DATE* and *INVOICE* # fields.
5. At the TERMS drop-down list, click *2/10, Net 30 Days*, if necessary.
6. At the *QUANTITY* field, type 2.
7. Click the *ITEM CODE* field. At the ITEM CODE drop-down list, click *Lamps*. QuickBooks automatically fills the *DESCRIPTION, PRICE EACH, AMOUNT*, and *TAX* fields. See Figure 5–O.

FIGURE 5–O

Create Invoices Window—Partially Completed

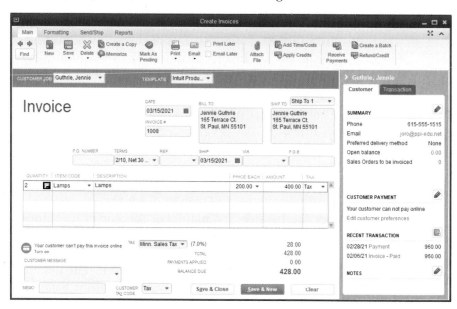

Note that the word *Tax* should appear in the *TAX* field for the taxable items, and *Non* should appear for the nontaxable service item. If the correct coding for the tax does not appear, use the drop-down list in the field to indicate the correct tax code.

8. Move to the second line of the *QUANTITY* field and type 3.
9. At the ITEM CODE drop-down list, click *Carpets*. QuickBooks fills the *DESCRIPTION, PRICE EACH, AMOUNT,* and *TAX* fields.
10. Move to the third line of the *QUANTITY* field and type 1.
11. At the ITEM CODE drop-down list, click *Mirrors*. QuickBooks fills the remaining fields.
12. Move to the fourth line of the *QUANTITY* field and type 8.
13. At the ITEM CODE drop-down list, click *Decorating Services*. QuickBooks fills the remaining fields. Note that the *TAX* field indicates *Non* because Decorating Services are not subject to sales tax.
14. Click the arrow at the TAX drop-down list and then click *Minn. Sales Tax*, if necessary. Confirm that the *Print Later* and *Email Later* boxes do not contain check marks. The *Your customer can't pay this invoice online* command should remain off. At the CUSTOMER TAX CODE drop-down list, confirm that *Tax* is selected. See Figure 5–P.

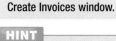

You may need to press the Tab key to move to additional lines in the Create Invoices window, or you can enlarge the Create Invoices window.

HINT

If you miss an item, click *Insert Line* from the Edit menu; if you wish to erase a line, click *Delete Line* from the Edit menu.

FIGURE 5–P
Create Invoices
Window—Completed

15. If the information is correct, click the Save & Close button.

For a sale of inventory products on account, the general ledger posting is as follows:

1200 Accts Receivable			4060-4075 Sale of Inventory			
Dr	Cr		Dr	Cr	2 lamps @ 200 =	400
2,433				1,900	3 carpets @ 400 =	1,200
					1 mirror @ 300 =	300
						1,900

2200 Sales Tax Payable			4010-4020 Service Revenue	
Dr	Cr		Dr	Cr
	133			400

The cost of the inventory sold and resulting decline in the inventory is recorded as follows:

5060-5075 Cost of Goods Sold			1260-1275 Inventory			
Dr	Cr		Dr	Cr	2 lamps @ 100 =	200
950				950	3 carpets @ 200 =	600
					1 mirror @ 150 =	150
						950

Inventory Sales for Cash in the Enter Sales Receipts Window

The Enter Sales Receipts window is designed for cash received for both the sale of services and the sale of inventory items for cash. Once an inventory item is chosen, QuickBooks uses the information from the Item List to correctly record the Cost of Goods Sold, Inventory, and Sales accounts. If an item is marked as taxable, QuickBooks uses the Item List to determine the correct amount of sales tax to be recorded in the Sales Tax Payable account. The transaction is recorded as follows:

Cash (or Undeposited Funds)	XXX		
Cost of Goods Sold	XXX		
Inventory			XXX
Sales Tax Payable			XXX
Sales			XXX

Recording a Sale of an Inventory Item for Cash

On March 22, 2021, Kristin Raina sells the following items to Beverly Jones, Invoice No. 1009, receiving payment immediately, her Check No. 5477.

1 carpet	$ 400.00
2 draperies	500.00
Total sale of merchandise	$ 900.00
sales tax $(0.07 \times \$900)$	63.00
decorating services (4 hrs)	200.00
Total sale for cash	$ 1,163.00

To record a sale of inventory for cash:

1. At the main menu bar, click Customers and then click *Enter Sales Receipts.*
2. At the CUSTOMER:JOB drop-down list, click *Jones, Beverly.*
3. Choose the appropriate date and then type 1009 in the *SALE NO.* field.
4. Click the CHECK button and then type 5477 in the *CHECK NO.* field. Confirm that the *Print Later* and *Email Later* boxes do not contain check marks and that *Tax* is selected in the CUSTOMER TAX CODE drop-down list.
5. Complete the remainder of the Enter Sales Receipts window for each item in the same manner as you would in the Create Invoices window. See Figure 5–Q.

FIGURE 5–Q Enter Sales Receipts Window—Completed

6. If all the information is correct, click the Save & Close button.

Companies that have cash sales of numerous low-cost items use the Sales Receipts window to enter these sales in batches on a periodic basis, such as weekly or semimonthly.

For a sale of inventory products for cash, the general ledger posting is as follows:

1250 Undeposited Funds		
Dr	Cr	
1,163		

4060-4075 Sale of Inventory	
Dr	Cr
	900

(1 carpet @ 400 = 400
2 draperies @ 250 = 500
900)

2200 Sales Tax Payable	
Dr	Cr
	63

4010-4020 Service Revenue	
Dr	Cr
	200

The cost of the inventory sold and resulting decline in the inventory is recorded as follows:

5060-5075 Cost of Goods Sold	
Dr	Cr
450	

1260-1275 Inventory	
Dr	Cr
	450

(1 carpet @ 200 = 200
2 draperies @ 125 = 250
450)

Practice Exercise 5–3

Record the following transactions at the Create Invoices or Enter Sales Receipts window:

Mar. 27	Sold the following on account to Hamilton Hotels, Invoice No. 1010, Terms 2/10, Net 30 Days:
	2 mirrors $ 600.00
	2 carpets 800.00
	Total sale of merchandise $ 1,400.00
	sales tax (0.07 × $1,400) 98.00
	decorating services (6 hrs) 300.00
	Total sale on account $ 1,798.00
Mar. 29	Sold the following for cash to Franco Films Co., Invoice No. 1011, its Check No. 1361:
	4 lamps $ 800.00
	2 draperies 500.00
	Total sale of merchandise $ 1,300.00
	sales tax (0.07 × $1,300) 91.00
	design services (4 hrs) 240.00
	Total sale for cash $ 1,631.00

Sales Discounts

sales discount
a reduction in the selling price that is offered if the invoice payment is made shortly after the invoice date

Sales discounts are offered to customers to encourage early payment of outstanding invoices. Generally, companies provide for a 1% or 2% reduction of the invoice amount if the payment is made within 10 days of the invoice date. The terms, written as *2/10, Net 30*, would indicate a 2% discount within 10 days with the entire amount due in 30 days.

On March 23, 2021, Kristin Raina receives full payment from Jennie Guthrie for Invoice No. 1008, her Check No. 2453, less the appropriate discount.

To record a receipt of payment within the discount period:
1. At the main menu bar, click Customers and then click *Receive Payments.*
2. At the RECEIVED FROM drop-down list, click *Guthrie, Jennie.* The open invoice in the full amount for Jennie Guthrie appears.
3. At the *DATE* field, choose *03/23/2021.* Select the payment method and then enter the check number. See Figure 5–R.

FIGURE 5–R

Receive Payments Window—Jennie Guthrie—Partially Completed

4. Select the invoice by clicking in the ✓ field next to the open invoice. The Automatically Calculate Payments window warning appears, inquiring if the *Automatically calculate payments* option should be selected in the Company Preferences for Payments. Insert a check mark in the box to the left of *Do not display this message in the future* and then click Yes. If you choose No in error, go to Edit, click *Preferences*, and then choose Payments. On the Company Preferences tab, insert a check mark next to the *Automatically calculate payments* option.

5. Click the Discounts and Credits button. The Discount and Credits window appears.

   This window displays information concerning the selected invoice, including the date the discount is available. The window computes the default discount amount based on information contained in the customer file.
6. At the Discount Account drop-down list, click *4100 Sales Discounts.* See Figure 5–S.

FIGURE 5–S
Discount and Credits
Window

7. Click Done to accept the discount calculation. You are returned to the Receive Payments window with the amount due recalculated based on the discount and the net due placed in the *PAYMENT AMOUNT* and *PAYMENT* fields.
8. At the ✓ field, insert a check mark next to the selected invoice again, if necessary. See Figure 5–T.

FIGURE 5–T
Receive Payments
Window—Completed

HINT

See Appendix E for the steps to record a customer credit for returned inventory and to write off uncollectable receivables.

9. If the information is correct, click the Save & Close button.

HINT

If you make an error on the payment, you can correct changes and resave, or you can click Edit and then *Delete Payment* and start over.

ACCOUNTING CONCEPT

For a collection of an accounts receivable with a sales discount, the general ledger posting is as follows:

1010 Cash - Operating		1200 Accts Receivable		4100 Sales Discounts	
Dr	Cr	Dr	Cr	Dr	Cr
2,384.34		Bill 2,433	Coll 2,433	48.66	
		Bal 0			

In addition, the customer file (subledger) for Jennie Guthrie reflects the new collection.

Practice Exercise   5–4

Record the following transaction at the Receive Payments window:

Mar. 30	Received full payment from Hamilton Hotels for Invoice No. 1010, its Check No. 6555, less applicable discount. *QuickCheck:* $1,762.04

Activities

The Adjust Quantity/Value on Hand Window

In QuickBooks, you use the Adjust Quantity/Value on Hand activity window to record changes in the inventory from events other than purchases or sales. If inventory items are lost, stolen, damaged, or spoiled, the resulting change in the inventory quantity and/or value is recorded in this window as an **inventory adjustment**. The reduction is considered a loss or expense with a corresponding reduction in the inventory asset account. The account used to record the reduction to inventory is the Inventory Adjustment account. This is a cost of goods sold account, and it will be included in the cost of goods sold section of the income statement.

Activities identified as adjustments to inventory are recorded in the Adjust Quantity/Value on Hand window. Each transaction entered in this window results in a debit to the Inventory Adjustment account and a credit to the appropriate inventory asset account. QuickBooks records the transaction as follows:

			Inventory Adjustment (Loss/Expense)		XXX			
			Inventory (Asset)				XXX	

On March 31, 2021, Kristin Raina discovers that a mirror is damaged and cannot be returned to the manufacturer.

To record an inventory adjustment:

1. At the main menu bar, click Vendors and then click *Inventory Activities.*
2. At the Inventory Activities submenu, click *Adjust Quantity/Value on Hand.*
3. At the Adjustment Type drop-down list, choose *Quantity and Total Value.*
4. At the *Adjustment Date* field, choose *03/31/2021.*
5. At the *Reference No.* field, type Inv. Adj. 1.
6. At the Adjustment Account drop-down list, click *5900 Inventory Adjustment.* If the Income or Expense expected window appears, insert a check mark next to *Do not display this message in the future* and then click OK.
7. At the ITEM drop-down list, click *Mirrors.* The description and current quantity are displayed. See Figure 5–U.

FIGURE 5–U
Adjust Quantity/Value on Hand Window

8. At the *NEW QUANTITY* field, type 6. When you move to the next field, QuickBooks fills the *QTY DIFFERENCE* and *NEW VALUE* fields and enters the Total Value of Adjustment amount. See Figure 5–V.

FIGURE 5–V
Adjust Quantity/Value on Hand Window—Completed for Quantity

9. If the information is correct, click the Save & Close button.

HINT

If you make an error in this window, click Edit and then *Delete Inventory Adjustment* and redo the transaction.

If the inventory adjustment was a result of a change in value only, without a change in quantity, you would choose *Total Values* at the Adjustment Type drop-down list. This allows you to adjust the value without changing the quantity.

ACCOUNTING CONCEPT

For an adjustment to inventory, the general ledger posting is as follows:

5900 Invent Adj		1275 Inv of Mirrors	
Dr	Cr	Dr	Cr
150		Prev Bal 1,050	Adj 150
		Bal 900	

In addition, the item file (subledger) for Mirrors reflects the new balance.

The Pay Sales Tax Window

In QuickBooks, the Pay Sales Tax window is used to record the remittance of sales tax charged to customers to the proper tax agency. QuickBooks uses the default accounts Sales Tax Payable and Cash.

The Pay Sales Tax window is designed for Activities identified as payment of sales tax charged to customers. The default accounts are Sales Tax Payable and Cash. QuickBooks records the transaction as follows:

	Sales Tax Payable	XXX		
	Cash			XXX

At the conclusion of each month, Kristin Raina remits the sales tax collected from customers to the appropriate state agency.

To pay the sales tax collected:
1. At the main menu bar, click Vendors and then click *Sales Tax.*
2. At the Sales Tax submenu, click *Pay Sales Tax.* The Pay Sales Tax window appears. See Figure 5–W.

FIGURE 5–W

Pay Sales Tax Window

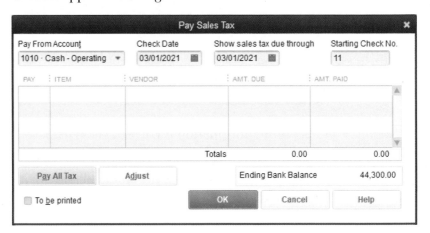

3. At the *Check Date* field, choose *03/31/2021.* In the *Pay From Account* field, confirm that the *1010 Cash - Operating* account is selected. Confirm that the *To be printed* box does not contain a check mark.
4. Confirm that the *Starting Check No.* is *11.*
5. At the *Show sales tax due through* field, choose *03/31/2021.*
6. Click the Pay All Tax button to select the liability. The sales tax liabilities to date is displayed.
7. At the *PAY* field, insert a check mark, if necessary. See Figure 5–X.

FIGURE 5–X
Pay Sales Tax Window—
Liabilities Displayed

8. If the information is correct, click OK. The liability is now paid.

ACCOUNTING CONCEPT

For a payment of sales tax, the general ledger posting is as follows:

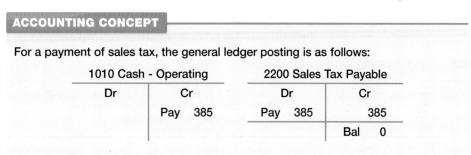

Make Deposits

Recall from Chapter 3 that Kristin Raina Interior Designs deposits all funds collected from customers at the end of the month. Before the reports for the month are reviewed, the deposits should be recorded.

Practice Exercise 5–5

Record the following transaction at the Make Deposits window:

Mar. 31	Deposit all undeposited funds to the Cash - Operating account. *QuickCheck:* $6,940.38

Inventory Reports, Accounting Reports, and Financial Statements

Recall from Chapter 1 that Reports, the fourth level of operation, reflect the activities recorded in the various Lists/Centers and Activities windows. Inventory activities entered in the various windows flow into the reports, many of which should be displayed and printed at the end of the month.

Viewing and Printing Inventory Reports from the Reports Menu

Inventory reports, such as the *Inventory Valuation Detail* report, *Inventory Stock Status by Item* report, and *Purchases by Item Detail* report, help the company track and manage its inventory.

Inventory Valuation Detail Report

The *Inventory Valuation Detail* report displays the transactions affecting each inventory item along with the quantity and value on hand for each.

To view and print the *Inventory Valuation Detail* report:
1. At the main menu bar, click Reports and then click *Inventory*.
2. At the Inventory submenu, click *Inventory Valuation Detail*.
3. At the *From* and *To* fields, choose *03/01/2021* and *03/31/2021* and then click the Refresh button at the top of the report. The report for the period is displayed.
4. Print the report. Your printout should look like Figure 5–Y.

FIGURE 5–Y Inventory Valuation Detail Report

EX5 [Your Name] Kristin Raina Interior Designs
Inventory Valuation Detail
March 2021

Type	Date	Name	Num	Qty	Cost	On Hand	Avg Cost	Asset Value
Inventory								
Carpets (Carpets)								
Bill	03/06/2021	Bell Carpet ...	12-5585	10	2,000.00	10	200.00	2,000.00
Invoice	03/15/2021	Guthrie, Je...	1008	-3		7	200.00	1,400.00
Sales Receipt	03/22/2021	Jones, Bev...	1009	-1		6	200.00	1,200.00
Invoice	03/27/2021	Hamilton H...	1010	-2		4	200.00	800.00
Total Carpets (Carpets)						4.00		800.00
Draperies (Draperies)								
Check	03/13/2021	Weaver Fa...	10	12	1,500.00	12	125.00	1,500.00
Sales Receipt	03/22/2021	Jones, Bev...	1009	-2		10	125.00	1,250.00
Sales Receipt	03/29/2021	Franco Film...	1011	-2		8	125.00	1,000.00
Total Draperies (Draperies)						8.00		1,000.00
Lamps (Lamps)								
Check	03/02/2021	Lumiare Lig...	9	16	1,600.00	16	100.00	1,600.00
Invoice	03/15/2021	Guthrie, Je...	1008	-2		14	100.00	1,400.00
Sales Receipt	03/29/2021	Franco Film...	1011	-4		10	100.00	1,000.00
Total Lamps (Lamps)						10.00		1,000.00
Mirrors (Decorative Mirrors)								
Bill	03/01/2021	Ace Glass ...	K-588	10	1,500.00	10	150.00	1,500.00
Invoice	03/15/2021	Guthrie, Je...	1008	-1		9	150.00	1,350.00
Invoice	03/27/2021	Hamilton H...	1010	-2		7	150.00	1,050.00
Inventory Adjust	03/31/2021		1	-1		6	150.00	900.00
Total Mirrors (Decorative Mirrors)						6.00		900.00
Total Inventory						28.00		3,700.00
TOTAL						**28.00**		**3,700.00**

5. Close the report.

Inventory Stock Status by Item Report

The *Inventory Stock Status by Item* report displays the on-hand status of each inventory item. The report indicates whether an item should be ordered based upon on-hand quantity and the reorder amount.

To view and print the *Inventory Stock Status by Item* report:
1. At the main menu bar, click Reports and then click *Inventory*.
2. At the Inventory submenu, click *Inventory Stock Status by Item*.
3. At the *From* and *To* fields, choose *03/01/2021* and *03/31/2021* and then click the Refresh button at the top of the report. The report for the period is displayed. See Figure 5–Z.

FIGURE 5–Z
Inventory Stock Status
by Item Report

4. Print the report.
5. Close the report.

Purchases by Item Detail Report

The *Purchases by Item Detail* report displays all purchase information for each inventory item. The report shows the vendor name, cost per unit, quantity purchased, and total cost.

To view and print the *Purchases by Item Detail* report:
1. At the main menu bar, click Reports and then click *Purchases*.
2. At the Purchases submenu, click *Purchases by Item Detail*.
3. At the *From* and *To* fields, choose *03/01/2021* and *03/31/2021* and then click the Refresh button at the top of the report. The report for the period is displayed.
4. Print the report. Your printout should look like Figure 5–AA.

FIGURE 5–AA Purchases by Item Detail Report

EX5 [Your Name] Kristin Raina Interior Designs
Purchases by Item Detail
March 2021

Accrual Basis

Type	Date	Num	Memo	Source Name	Qty	Cost Price	Amount	Balance
Inventory								
Carpets (Carpets)								
Bill	03/06/2021	12-5585	Carpets	Bell Carpet Design	10	200.00	2,000.00	2,000.00
Total Carpets (Carpets)					10		2,000.00	2,000.00
Draperies (Draperies)								
Check	03/13/2021	10	Draperies	Weaver Fabrics	12	125.00	1,500.00	1,500.00
Total Draperies (Draperies)					12		1,500.00	1,500.00
Lamps (Lamps)								
Check	03/02/2021	9	Lamps	Lumiare Lighting Co...	16	100.00	1,600.00	1,600.00
Total Lamps (Lamps)					16		1,600.00	1,600.00
Mirrors (Decorative Mirrors)								
Bill	03/01/2021	K-588	Decorative Mirrors	Ace Glass Works	10	150.00	1,500.00	1,500.00
Total Mirrors (Decorative Mirrors)					10		1,500.00	1,500.00
Total Inventory					48		6,600.00	6,600.00
TOTAL					**48**		**6,600.00**	**6,600.00**

This report, like several of those reviewed in prior chapters, allows you to "drill down" to view the source transaction. Kristin Raina wishes to see the detail of the purchase of carpets on March 6, 2021.

To "drill down" to the purchase transaction of carpets:
1. Hover the mouse pointer over the carpet purchase transaction until the zoom glass appears.
2. Double-click the transaction. The Enter Bills window for this transaction is displayed.
3. Close the Enter Bills window and the report.

Viewing and Printing Inventory Reports from the Lists Menu

QuickBooks allows you to view and print several inventory reports from the Lists windows. Once a list is accessed, a report list is available that is accessed by clicking the Reports menu button in the List window.

The *Sales by Item Detail* report shows sales of all inventory items both on account and for cash.

To view and print an Item List report such as *Sales by Item Detail*:

1. At the main menu bar, click Lists and then click *Item List*.
2. At the Item List window, click the Reports menu button.
3. At the Reports menu, click *Reports on All Items*.
4. At the Reports on all Items submenu, click *Sales Reports*.
5. At the Sales Reports submenu, click *By Item Detail*.
6. At the *From* and *To* fields, choose *03/01/2021* and *03/31/2021* and then click the Refresh button at the top of the report. The report for the period is displayed.
7. Print the report. Your printout should look like Figure 5–BB.

FIGURE 5–BB Sales by Item Detail Report

EX5 [Your Name] Kristin Raina Interior Designs
Sales by Item Detail
March 2021

Accrual Basis

Type	Date	Num	Memo	Name	Qty	Sales Price	Amount	Balance
Inventory								
Carpets (Carpets)								
Invoice	03/15/2021	1008	Carpets	Guthrie, Jennie	3	400.00	1,200.00	1,200.00
Sales Receipt	03/22/2021	1009	Carpets	Jones, Beverly	1	400.00	400.00	1,600.00
Invoice	03/27/2021	1010	Carpets	Hamilton Hotels	2	400.00	800.00	2,400.00
Total Carpets (Carpets)					6		2,400.00	2,400.00
Draperies (Draperies)								
Sales Receipt	03/22/2021	1009	Draperies	Jones, Beverly	2	250.00	500.00	500.00
Sales Receipt	03/29/2021	1011	Draperies	Franco Films Co.	2	250.00	500.00	1,000.00
Total Draperies (Draperies)					4		1,000.00	1,000.00
Lamps (Lamps)								
Invoice	03/15/2021	1008	Lamps	Guthrie, Jennie	2	200.00	400.00	400.00
Sales Receipt	03/29/2021	1011	Lamps	Franco Films Co.	4	200.00	800.00	1,200.00
Total Lamps (Lamps)					6		1,200.00	1,200.00
Mirrors (Decorative Mirrors)								
Invoice	03/15/2021	1008	Decorative Mirrors	Guthrie, Jennie	1	300.00	300.00	300.00
Invoice	03/27/2021	1010	Decorative Mirrors	Hamilton Hotels	2	300.00	600.00	900.00
Total Mirrors (Decorative Mirrors)					3		900.00	900.00
Total Inventory					19		5,500.00	5,500.00
Service								
Decorating Services (Decorating Services)								
Invoice	03/15/2021	1008	Decorating Services	Guthrie, Jennie	8	50.00	400.00	400.00
Sales Receipt	03/22/2021	1009	Decorating Services	Jones, Beverly	4	50.00	200.00	600.00
Invoice	03/27/2021	1010	Decorating Services	Hamilton Hotels	6	50.00	300.00	900.00
Total Decorating Services (Decorating Services)					18		900.00	900.00
Design Services (Design Services)								
Sales Receipt	03/29/2021	1011	Design Services	Franco Films Co.	4	60.00	240.00	240.00
Total Design Services (Design Services)					4		240.00	240.00
Total Service					22		1,140.00	1,140.00
TOTAL					**41**		**6,640.00**	**6,640.00**

8. Close the report and the Item List.

In addition to the *Sales* reports, *Purchase, Inventory, Item,* and *Price* reports can be viewed from the Reports menu of the Item List.

Viewing and Printing Accounting Reports and Financial Statements

At the end of each month, the *Journal, Profit & Loss Standard* (or *Income Statement*), and *Balance Sheet Standard* reports should be viewed and printed. Your printouts should look like Figures 5–CC, 5–DD, and 5–EE, respectively.

FIGURE 5–CC Journal Report—Partial March 1, 2021–March 31, 2021

EX5 [Your Name] Kristin Raina Interior Designs
Journal
March 2021

Trans #	Type	Date	Num	Name	Memo	Account	Debit	Credit
39	Bill	03/01/2021	K-588	Ace Glass Works		2010 · Accounts Payable		1,500.00
				Ace Glass Works	Decorative Mirrors	1275 · Inventory of Mirrors	1,500.00	
							1,500.00	1,500.00
40	Check	03/02/2021	9	Lumiare Lighting Company	36	1010 · Cash - Operating		1,600.00
				Lumiare Lighting Company	Lamps	1270 · Inventory of Lamps	1,600.00	
							1,600.00	1,600.00
41	Bill	03/06/2021	12-5585	Bell Carpet Design		2010 · Accounts Payable		2,000.00
				Bell Carpet Design	Carpets	1260 · Inventory of Carpets	2,000.00	
							2,000.00	2,000.00
42	Check	03/13/2021	10	Weaver Fabrics	9878	1010 · Cash - Operating		1,500.00
				Weaver Fabrics	Draperies	1265 · Inventory of Draperies	1,500.00	
							1,500.00	1,500.00
43	Invoice	03/15/2021	1008	Guthrie, Jennie		1200 · Accounts Receivable	2,433.00	
				Guthrie, Jennie	Lamps	4070 · Sale of Lamps		400.00
				Guthrie, Jennie	Lamps	1270 · Inventory of Lamps		200.00
				Guthrie, Jennie	Lamps	5070 · Cost of Lamps Sold	200.00	
				Guthrie, Jennie	Carpets	4060 · Sale of Carpets		1,200.00
				Guthrie, Jennie	Carpets	1260 · Inventory of Carpets		600.00
				Guthrie, Jennie	Carpets	5060 · Cost of Carpets Sold	600.00	
				Guthrie, Jennie	Decorative Mirrors	4075 · Sale of Mirrors		300.00
				Guthrie, Jennie	Decorative Mirrors	1275 · Inventory of Mirrors		150.00
				Guthrie, Jennie	Decorative Mirrors	5075 · Cost of Mirrors Sold	150.00	
				Guthrie, Jennie	Decorating Services	4020 · Decorating Services		400.00
				Minn. Dept. of Revenue	Sales Tax	2200 · Sales Tax Payable		133.00
							3,383.00	3,383.00
44	Sales Receipt	03/22/2021	1009	Jones, Beverly		1250 · Undeposited Funds	1,163.00	
				Jones, Beverly	Carpets	4060 · Sale of Carpets		400.00
				Jones, Beverly	Carpets	1260 · Inventory of Carpets		200.00
				Jones, Beverly	Carpets	5060 · Cost of Carpets Sold	200.00	
				Jones, Beverly	Draperies	4065 · Sale of Draperies		500.00
				Jones, Beverly	Draperies	1265 · Inventory of Draperies		250.00
				Jones, Beverly	Draperies	5065 · Cost of Draperies Sold	250.00	
				Jones, Beverly	Decorating Services	4020 · Decorating Services		200.00
				Minn. Dept. of Revenue	Sales Tax	2200 · Sales Tax Payable		63.00
							1,613.00	1,613.00
45	Invoice	03/27/2021	1010	Hamilton Hotels		1200 · Accounts Receivable	1,798.00	
				Hamilton Hotels	Decorative Mirrors	4075 · Sale of Mirrors		600.00
				Hamilton Hotels	Decorative Mirrors	1275 · Inventory of Mirrors		300.00
				Hamilton Hotels	Decorative Mirrors	5075 · Cost of Mirrors Sold	300.00	

...continues

FIGURE 5–CC Journal Report...*continued*

EX5 [Your Name] Kristin Raina Interior Designs
Journal
March 2021

Trans #	Type	Date	Num	Name	Memo	Account	Debit	Credit
				Hamilton Hotels	Carpets	4060 · Sale of Carpets		800.00
				Hamilton Hotels	Carpets	1260 · Inventory of Carpets		400.00
				Hamilton Hotels	Carpets	5060 · Cost of Carpets Sold	400.00	
				Hamilton Hotels	Decorating Services	4020 · Decorating Services		300.00
				Minn. Dept. of Revenue	Sales Tax	2200 · Sales Tax Payable		98.00
							2,498.00	2,498.00
46	Sales Receipt	03/29/2021	1011	Franco Films Co.		1250 · Undeposited Funds	1,631.00	
				Franco Films Co.	Lamps	4070 · Sale of Lamps		800.00
				Franco Films Co.	Lamps	1270 · Inventory of Lamps		400.00
				Franco Films Co.	Lamps	5070 · Cost of Lamps Sold	400.00	
				Franco Films Co.	Draperies	4065 · Sale of Draperies		500.00
				Franco Films Co.	Draperies	1265 · Inventory of Draperies		250.00
				Franco Films Co.	Draperies	5065 · Cost of Draperies Sold	250.00	
				Franco Films Co.	Design Services	4010 · Design Services		240.00
				Minn. Dept. of Revenue	Sales Tax	2200 · Sales Tax Payable		91.00
							2,281.00	2,281.00
47	Payment	03/23/2021	2453	Guthrie, Jennie		1250 · Undeposited Funds	2,384.34	
				Guthrie, Jennie		1200 · Accounts Receivable		2,433.00
				Guthrie, Jennie		4100 · Sales Discounts	48.66	
							2,433.00	2,433.00
48	Payment	03/30/2021	6555	Hamilton Hotels		1250 · Undeposited Funds	1,762.04	
				Hamilton Hotels		1200 · Accounts Receivable		1,798.00
				Hamilton Hotels		4100 · Sales Discounts	35.96	
							1,798.00	1,798.00
49	Inventory Adjust	03/31/2021	1			5900 · Inventory Adjustment	150.00	
					Mirrors Inventory Adju...	1275 · Inventory of Mirrors		150.00
							150.00	150.00
50	Sales Tax Pay...	03/31/2021	11	Minn. Dept. of Revenue		1010 · Cash - Operating		385.00
				Minn. Dept. of Revenue		2200 · Sales Tax Payable	385.00	
							385.00	385.00
51	Deposit	03/31/2021			Deposit	1010 · Cash - Operating	6,940.38	
				-MULTIPLE-	Deposit	1250 · Undeposited Funds		6,940.38
							6,940.38	6,940.38
TOTAL							**28,081.38**	**28,081.38**

EX5 [Your Name] Kristin Raina Interior Designs
Profit & Loss
January through March 2021

Accrual Basis

	Jan - Mar 21
Ordinary Income/Expense	
Income	
4010 · Design Services	4,980.00
4020 · Decorating Services	3,400.00
4060 · Sale of Carpets	2,400.00
4065 · Sale of Draperies	1,000.00
4070 · Sale of Lamps	1,200.00
4075 · Sale of Mirrors	900.00
4100 · Sales Discounts	-84.62
Total Income	13,795.38
Cost of Goods Sold	
5060 · Cost of Carpets Sold	1,200.00
5065 · Cost of Draperies Sold	500.00
5070 · Cost of Lamps Sold	600.00
5075 · Cost of Mirrors Sold	450.00
5900 · Inventory Adjustment	150.00
Total COGS	2,900.00
Gross Profit	10,895.38
Expense	
6020 · Accounting Expense	300.00
6050 · Advertising Expense	100.00
6175 · Deprec. Exp., Furniture	100.00
6185 · Deprec. Exp., Computers	60.00
6200 · Insurance Expense	200.00
6300 · Janitorial Expenses	125.00
6325 · Office Supplies Expense	150.00
6400 · Rent Expense	800.00
6450 · Telephone Expense	275.00
6500 · Utilities Expense	450.00
Total Expense	2,560.00
Net Ordinary Income	8,335.38
Other Income/Expense	
Other Expense	
7000 · Interest Expense	50.00
Total Other Expense	50.00
Net Other Income	-50.00
Net Income	8,285.38

FIGURE 5–EE Balance Sheet Standard Report March 31, 2021

EX5 [Your Name] Kristin Raina Interior Designs
Balance Sheet
As of March 31, 2021

Accrual Basis

	Mar 31, 21
ASSETS	
Current Assets	
Checking/Savings	
1010 · Cash - Operating	50,855.38
Total Checking/Savings	50,855.38
Accounts Receivable	
1200 · Accounts Receivable	1,540.00
Total Accounts Receivable	1,540.00
Other Current Assets	
1260 · Inventory of Carpets	800.00
1265 · Inventory of Draperies	1,000.00
1270 · Inventory of Lamps	1,000.00
1275 · Inventory of Mirrors	900.00
1300 · Design Supplies	200.00
1305 · Office Supplies	250.00
1410 · Prepaid Advertising	500.00
1420 · Prepaid Insurance	2,200.00
Total Other Current Assets	6,850.00
Total Current Assets	59,245.38
Fixed Assets	
1700 · Furniture	
1725 · Furniture, Cost	12,000.00
1750 · Accum. Dep., Furniture	-100.00
Total 1700 · Furniture	11,900.00
1800 · Computers	
1825 · Computers, Cost	3,600.00
1850 · Accum. Dep., Computers	-60.00
Total 1800 · Computers	3,540.00
Total Fixed Assets	15,440.00
TOTAL ASSETS	**74,685.38**
LIABILITIES & EQUITY	
Liabilities	
Current Liabilities	
Accounts Payable	
2010 · Accounts Payable	9,750.00
Total Accounts Payable	9,750.00
Other Current Liabilities	
2020 · Notes Payable	7,000.00
2030 · Interest Payable	50.00
Total Other Current Liabilities	7,050.00
Total Current Liabilities	16,800.00
Total Liabilities	16,800.00
Equity	
3010 · Kristin Raina, Capital	50,000.00
3020 · Kristin Raina, Drawings	-400.00
Net Income	8,285.38
Total Equity	57,885.38
TOTAL LIABILITIES & EQUITY	**74,685.38**

Exiting QuickBooks

Upon completing this session, make a backup copy of your practice exercise company file to a removable storage device using the Back Up command. Be sure to change the *Save in* field to the removable storage device and then carefully type the correct file name. Close the company file and then exit QuickBooks.

Chapter Review and Assessment

Procedure Review

To add an item:
1. At the main menu bar, click Lists and then click *Item List*.
2. At the Item List window, click the Item menu button.
3. At the Item button drop-down menu, click *New*.
4. Enter the background data for the item.
5. Click OK.
6. Close the Item List window.

To delete an item:
1. At the main menu bar, click Lists and then click *Item List*.
2. At the Item List window, select the item you wish to delete.
3. Click the Item menu button.
4. At the Item button drop-down menu, click *Delete Item*.
5. Click OK at the warning.
6. Close the Item List window.
     You cannot delete an item that has a balance or is used in a transaction.

To edit an item:
1. At the main menu bar, click Lists and then click *Item List*.
2. At the Item List window, select the item you wish to edit.
3. Click the Item menu button.
4. At the Item button drop-down menu, click *Edit Item*.
5. Change the appropriate information.
6. Click OK.
7. Close the Item List window.

To record a purchase and receipt of an inventory item on account:
1. At the main menu bar, click Vendors and then click *Receive Items and Enter Bill*.
2. At the VENDOR drop-down list, click the vendor name.
3. Enter data into the *DATE, REF. NO., BILL DUE,* and *TERMS* fields in the usual manner.
4. Click the item from the ITEM drop-down list.
5. Enter the quantity; the *AMOUNT* and *AMOUNT DUE* fields fill automatically.
6. Click the Save & Close button.

To record a purchase and receipt of an inventory item for cash:
1. At the main menu bar, click Banking and then click *Write Checks*.
2. At the Write Checks window, click the appropriate bank account.
3. Enter the check date in the *DATE* field.
4. Click the vendor from the PAY TO THE ORDER OF drop-down list.
5. Click the Items tab.
6. Click the item from the ITEM drop-down list.
7. Enter the quantity. The *AMOUNT* field fills automatically.
8. Click the Save & Close button.

To record a sale of inventory on account:
1. At the main menu bar, click Customers and then click *Create Invoices.*
2. At the CUSTOMER:JOB drop-down list, click the customer name.
3. At the TEMPLATE drop-down list, click *Intuit Product Invoice.*
4. Enter data into the *DATE, INVOICE #,* and *TERMS* fields in the usual manner.
5. Enter the quantity.
6. Click the item from the ITEM drop-down list; the *DESCRIPTION, PRICE EACH,* and *AMOUNT* fields fill automatically.
7. At the TAX drop-down list, click the applicable sales tax. Make sure that *Tax* from the CUSTOMER TAX CODE drop-down list is selected.
8. Click the Save & Close button.

To enter a cash sale of inventory:
1. At the main menu bar, click Customers and then click *Enter Sales Receipt.*
2. At the CUSTOMER:JOB drop-down list, click the customer name.
3. Enter the date, invoice number, payment method, and check number.
4. Complete the remainder of the window in the same manner as a sale on account.
5. Click the Save & Close button.

To record a receipt of payment within the discount period:
1. At the main menu bar, click Customers and then click *Receive Payments.*
2. At the RECEIVED FROM drop-down list, click the customer name.
3. Enter the payment date in the *DATE* field. Enter the payment method and check number.
4. Select the invoice by clicking in the ✓ field next to the open invoice.
5. Click Yes at the warning and then click the Discounts and Credits button.
6. At the Discount Account drop-down list, click the *Sales Discounts* account.
7. Click Done to accept the discount calculation.
8. At the ✓ field, insert a check mark next to the selected invoice again, if necessary.
9. Click the Save & Close button.

To record an inventory adjustment:
1. At the main menu bar, click Vendors and then click *Inventory Activities.*
2. At the Inventory Activities menu, click *Adjust Quantity/Value on Hand.*
3. At the Adjustment Type drop-down list, choose *Quantity and Total Value.*
4. Enter data into the *DATE* and *REFERENCE NO.* fields.
5. At the Adjustment Account drop-down list, click *Inventory Adjustment.*
6. Select the item from the drop-down list.
7. Enter the new quantity in the *NEW QUANTITY* field.
8. Click the Save & Close button.

To pay sales tax:
1. At the main menu bar, click Vendors and then click *Sales Tax.*
2. At the Sales Tax submenu, click *Pay Sales Tax.*
3. Enter the payment date.
4. Click the *Cash* account.
5. Enter the correct date in the *Show sales tax due through* field.
6. Click the Pay All Tax button.
7. Insert a check mark in the *PAY* field.
8. Click OK.

To view and print inventory reports from the Reports menu:
1. At the main menu bar, click Reports and then click *Inventory.*
2. At the Inventory submenu, choose a report.
3. Indicate the appropriate dates for the report.
4. Click the Print button at the top of the report and then click *Report.*
5. Print the report.
6. Close the report.

To view and print inventory reports from the Lists menu:
1. At the main menu bar, click Lists and then click *Item List.*
2. Click the Reports menu button.
3. Click *Reports on All Items.*
4. From the submenu, click a category.
5. From the second submenu, click a report.
6. Indicate the appropriate dates for the report.
7. Click the Print button at the top of the report.
8. Print the report.
9. Close the report.

Key Concepts

Select the letter of the item that best matches each definition.

a. Enter Bills window—Items tab
b. Adjust Quantity/Value on Hand activity window
c. Item List
d. Sales discounts
e. *Purchases by Item Detail* report
f. Sales tax
g. Pay Sales Tax window
h. *Inventory Valuation Detail* report
i. *Sales by Item Detail* report
j. *Inventory Stock Status by Item* report

_____ 1. Report that displays all transactions affecting each inventory item.
_____ 2. Reduction of the invoice amount due when the customer pays by a specific date.
_____ 3. Window used to record purchases and receipt of inventory items.
_____ 4. Window used to adjust the quantity or value of inventory as a result of damage or loss.
_____ 5. Contains a file of all inventory items.
_____ 6. Window used to remit sales tax collected from customers to the appropriate state tax agency.

_____ 7. Report that displays each purchase transaction for inventory items.
_____ 8. Report that displays the on-hand status of each inventory item.
_____ 9. Report from the Item List that shows sales information for each inventory item.
_____ 10. Tax collected by a retailer from a customer on the sales of goods.

Procedure Check

1. Your company will be selling a new product. Describe the steps that must be taken to add the new item to the system.
2. Explain the difference between using *Enter Bills* or *Receive Items and Enter Bills* from the Vendors drop-down menu.
3. Your company wishes to determine which inventory items generate the most revenue. How could you use QuickBooks to develop this information?
4. At year-end, you wish to confirm the quantity on hand for each inventory item. How would you use QuickBooks reports to determine the quantity and value of the ending inventory?
5. Your company wishes to view the profitability of each inventory item. How could you use QuickBooks to develop this information?
6. Discuss the advantages of using a computerized accounting system to maintain a perpetual inventory system.

Case Problems

Demonstrate your knowledge of the QuickBooks features discussed in this chapter by completing the following case problems.

Case Problem 5–1

On April 1, 2021, Lynn Garcia began her business, Lynn's Music Studio. In the first month of business, Lynn set up the music studio, provided guitar and piano lessons, and recorded month-end activity. In May, the second month of business, Lynn will purchase and sell inventory items of guitars, keyboards, music stands, and sheet music. For customers that purchase merchandise inventory, the terms of payment are 2/10, Net 30 Days. For illustration purposes, assume a 7% sales tax is charged on the sales of all inventory items. The company file includes the information for Lynn's Music Studio as of May 1, 2021.

1. Open the company file **CH5 Lynn's Music Studio.QBW**.
2. At the QuickBooks Desktop Login window, in the *Password* text box, type Student1 and then click OK.
3. Make a backup copy of the company file and name it **LMS5 [*Your Name]* Lynn's Music Studio** and enter the password.
4. Restore the backup copy of the company file. In both the Open Backup Copy and Save Company File as dialog boxes, use the file name **LMS5 [*Your Name]* Lynn's Music Studio**.
5. Change the company name to **LMS5 [*Your Name]* Lynn's Music Studio**.

6. Add the following inventory items to the Item List:

Type:	Inventory Part
Item Name/Number:	Keyboards
Description on	
Purchase/Sales Transactions:	Keyboards
Cost:	75
COGS Account:	5065 Cost of Keyboards Sold
Preferred Vendor:	Katie's Keyboards
Sales Price:	150
Tax Code:	Tax – Taxable Sales
Income Account:	4065 Sale of Keyboards
Asset Account:	1265 Inventory of Keyboards

Type:	Inventory Part
Item Name/Number:	Sheet Music
Description on	
Purchase/Sales Transactions:	Sheet Music
Cost:	3
COGS Account:	5075 Cost of Sheet Music Sold
Preferred Vendor:	Strings, Sheets & Such
Sales Price:	6
Tax Code:	Tax – Taxable Sales
Income Account:	4075 Sale of Sheet Music
Asset Account:	1275 Inventory of Sheet Music

Delete the following inventory item:
    Harmonicas

7. Using the appropriate window, record each of the following transactions for May:

May 3	Purchased 30 guitars on account from Music Instruments, Inc., at $50 each, its Invoice No. GU75998.
May 3	Purchased 30 keyboards on account from Katie's Keyboards at $75 each, its Invoice No. 10089-30.
May 3	Purchased 30 music stands from Melody Music Equipment at $20 each, paid immediately, Check No. 9. Do not print check.
May 3	Purchased 300 sheets of music of various themes from Strings, Sheets & Such at $3 each, paid immediately, Check No. 10. Do not print check.
May 4	Sold 15 guitars for $100 each, 15 keyboards for $150 each, and 15 music stands for $40 each to Jefferson High School, Invoice No. 2012, terms 2/10, Net 30 Days. In addition, provided 15 hours of guitar lessons and 10 hours of piano lessons.
May 4	Sold 10 keyboards for $150 each to Highland School, Invoice No. 2013, terms 2/10, Net 30 Days. In addition, provided 12 hours of piano lessons.

May 7	Received full payment from Jefferson High School for Invoice 2009, Check No. 30531. (No discount.)
May 10	Record the weekly cash sales of sheet music, 75 sheets at $6 each, Sale No. 2014. Leave the *CUSTOMER:JOB* field blank.
May 11	Sold 3 guitars for $100 each, 3 keyboards for $150 each, and 3 music stands for $40 each to Mulligan Residence, Invoice No. 2015, terms 2/10, Net 30 Days. In addition, provided 5 hours of guitar lessons and 7 hours of piano lessons.
May 11	Received full payment net of discount from Jefferson High School for Invoice No. 2012, Check No. 30711.
May 14	Received full payment net of discount from Highland School, Check No. 76115.
May 17	Purchased 20 keyboards on account from Katie's Keyboard Company at $75 each, its Invoice No. 10758-20.
May 17	Purchased 10 music stands from Melody Music Equipment at $20 each, paid immediately, Check No. 11. Do not print check.
May 17	Record the weekly cash sales of sheet music, 100 sheets at $6 each, Sale No. 2016.
May 21	Sold 5 guitars for $100 each, 5 keyboards for $150 each, and 5 music stands for $40 each to Twin Lakes Elementary, Invoice No. 2017, terms 2/10, Net 30 Days. In addition, provided 8 hours of guitar lessons and 5 hours of piano lessons.
May 24	Received a payment of $830 from Twin Lakes Elementary for Invoice Nos. 2004 and 2011, Check No. 7266.
May 24	Record the weekly cash sales of sheet music, 115 sheets at $6 each, Sale No. 2018.
May 24	Purchased 300 sheets of music of various themes from Strings, Sheets, & Such at $3 each, paid immediately, Check No. 12. Do not print check.
May 25	Received full payment net of discount from Twin Lakes Elementary for Invoice No. 2017, Check No. 7384.
May 25	Paid in full Music Instruments, Inc. (Check No. 13). Do not print check.
May 25	Paid in full Katie's Keyboard Company, Invoice No. 10089-30 (Check No. 14). Do not print check.
May 31	Record the weekly cash sales of sheet music, 145 sheets at $6 each, Invoice No. 2019.
May 31	Upon reviewing the inventory, Lynn discovers that one guitar is damaged, through no fault of the manufacturer, and cannot be sold. Adjust the inventory on hand to remove the one guitar from the inventory. Inv. Adj. 1.
May 31	Remit all sales tax collected to the PA Dept. of Revenue, Check No. 15.
May 31	Deposit all undeposited funds to the Cash - Operating account.

8. Display and print the following reports for May 1, 2021, to May 31, 2021:
   a. *Inventory Valuation Detail*
   b. *Inventory Stock Status by Item*
   c. *Purchases by Item Detail*
   d. *Sales by Item Detail*
   e. *Journal*
   f. *Profit & Loss Standard* (April 1, 2021–May 31, 2021)
   g. *Balance Sheet Standard*

Case Problem 5–2

On June 1, 2021, Olivia Chen began her business, Olivia's Web Solutions. In the first month of business, Olivia set up the office, provided web page design and internet consulting services, and recorded month-end activity. In July, the second month of business, Olivia will purchase and sell inventory items of computer hardware and software. For customers that purchase merchandise inventory, the terms of payment are 2/10, Net 30 Days. For illustration purposes, assume an 8% sales tax is charged on the sales of all inventory items. The company file includes the information for Olivia's Web Solutions as of July 1, 2021.

1. Open the company file **CH5 Olivia's Web Solutions.QBW**.
2. At the QuickBooks Desktop Login window, in the *Password* text box, type Student1 and then click OK.
3. Make a backup copy of the company file and name it **OWS5 *[Your Name]* Olivia's Web Solutions**.
4. Restore the backup copy of the company file. In both the Open Backup Copy and Save Company File as dialog boxes, use the file name **OWS5 *[Your Name]* Olivia's Web Solutions** and enter the password.
5. Change the company name to **OWS5 *[Your Name]* Olivia's Web Solutions**.
6. Add the following inventory items to the Item List:

Type:	Inventory Part
Item Name/Number:	Scanners
Description on	
Purchase/Sales Transactions:	Scanners
Cost:	300
COGS Account:	5065 Cost of Scanners Sold
Preferred Vendor:	Scanntronix
Sales Price:	600
Tax Code:	Tax – Taxable Sales
Income Account:	4065 Sale of Scanners
Asset Account:	1265 Inventory of Scanners
Type:	Inventory Part
Item Name/Number:	Desktop Publishing Software
Description on	
Purchase/Sales Transactions:	Desktop Publishing Software
Cost:	100

COGS Account:	5075 Cost of Desktop Pub. Software
Preferred Vendor:	Textpro Software, Inc.
Sales Price:	200
Tax Code:	Tax – Taxable Sales
Income Account:	4075 Sale of Desktop Pub. Soft.
Asset Account:	1275 Inventory of Desktop Pub. Soft.

Delete the following inventory item:
  Printers

7. Using the appropriate window, record each of the following transactions for July:

Jul. 2	Purchased 10 computers on account from Computec Computers at $1,000 each, its Invoice No. 068788.
Jul. 2	Purchased 20 scanners on account from Scanntronix at $300 each, its Invoice No. 10089-30.
Jul. 2	Purchased 10 desktop publishing software packages from Textpro Software, Inc. at $100 each, paid immediately, Check No. 9. Do not print check.
Jul. 2	Purchased 20 HTML software packages from InterSoft Development Co. at $75 each, paid immediately, Check No. 10. Do not print check.
Jul. 5	Sold 3 computers for $2,000 each, 2 scanners for $600 each, and 1 desktop publishing software package for $200 on account to Long Island Water Works, Invoice No. 1011, terms 2/10, Net 30 Days. In addition, provided 10 hours of internet consulting services.
Jul. 6	Sold 2 computers on account to Miguel's Restaurant for $2,000 each, Invoice No. 1012, terms 2/10, Net 30 Days. In addition, provided 8 hours of web page design services.
Jul. 9	Sold 1 scanner for $600 and 1 desktop publishing software package for $200 to the Singh family, Invoice No. 1013. Received payment immediately, their Check No. 901.
Jul. 12	Sold 1 computer for $2,000, 2 scanners for $600 each, and 1 HTML software package for $150 on account to Breathe Easy, Invoice No. 1014, Net 30 Days. In addition, provided 12 hours of internet consulting services.
Jul. 13	Received full payment net of discount from Long Island Water Works for Invoice No. 1011, Check No. 125671.
Jul. 16	Purchased 5 computers on account from Computec Computers at $1,000 each, its Invoice No. 072445.
Jul. 16	Purchased 5 desktop publishing software packages from Textpro Software, Inc. at $100 each, paid immediately, Check No. 11. Do not print check.

Jul. 19	Sold 1 computer for $2,000 and 1 desktop publishing software package for $200 to the Schneider Family, Invoice No. 1015. Received payment immediately, their Check No. 899.
Jul. 20	Sold 3 computers for $2,000 each, 3 scanners for $600 each, and 2 desktop publishing software packages for $200 each to South Shore School District, Invoice No. 1016, terms 2/10, Net 30 Days. In addition, provided 16 hours of web page design services.
Jul. 26	Received full payment, no discount, from Miguel's Restaurant for Invoice No. 1012, Check No. 4110.
Jul. 27	Received full payment, no discount, from Breathe Easy for Invoice Nos. 1006 (remaining balance) and 1014, Check No. 1874.
Jul. 30	Purchased 5 computers on account from Computec Computers at $1,000 each, its Invoice No. 073111.
Jul. 30	Paid in full Computec Computers Invoice No. 068788 (Check No. 12). Do not print check.
Jul. 30	Paid in full Scanntronix, Invoice No. 10089-30 (Check No. 13). Do not print check.
Jul. 30	Upon reviewing the inventory, Olivia discovers one HTML software package was damaged, through no fault of the manufacturer, and cannot be sold. Adjust the inventory on hand to remove the one HTML software package from the inventory. Inv. Adj. 1.
Jul. 31	Remit all sales tax collected to New York State, Check No. 14.
Jul. 31	Deposit all undeposited funds to the Cash - Operating account.

8. Display and print the following reports for July 1, 2021, to July 31, 2021:
    a. *Inventory Valuation Detail*
    b. *Inventory Stock Status by Item*
    c. *Purchases by Item Detail*
    d. *Sales by Item Detail*
    e. *Journal*
    f. *Profit & Loss Standard* (June 1, 2021–July 31, 2021)
    g. *Balance Sheet Standard*

FIGURE 6–A

QuickBooks Desktop
Setup Window—Let's
Get Your Business Set
Up Quickly! Page

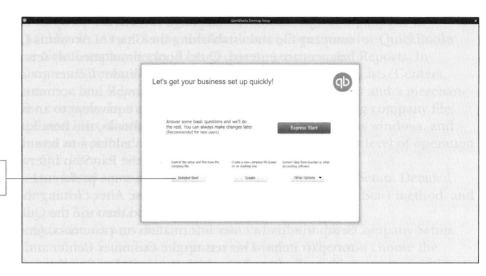

Detailed
Start button

Detailed Start and EasyStep Interview Window

In New Company Setup, the first level of operation in QuickBooks, you
will enter the information needed to create and set up a company file for
Kristin Raina Interior Designs using the Detailed Start method, which uses
the EasyStep Interview window.

The EasyStep Interview window is designed to guide you through the
steps needed to create and set up a new company file. (EasyStep Interview
is not the only way to create a company file in QuickBooks; an alternative
method is covered in Chapter 7.)

With EasyStep Interview, you proceed through a series of pages by clicking the Next button. On each page, you enter basic company information
and answer questions that QuickBooks uses to create the new company
file. As you answer the questions, QuickBooks establishes some preferences for your company. Company preferences enable or disable features
available in QuickBooks. When a feature is enabled, you will see that
choice listed on the drop-down menu and on the Home page. If a feature
is disabled, you will not see that choice on the drop-down menu or Home
page.

The company information can later be edited by clicking Company
and then *My Company*. The preferences can be edited by clicking Edit and
then *Preferences*.

At any time, you can click the Leave button to leave the EasyStep
Interview window. However, you are advised not to leave before saving the
company file. If you leave the window before saving the company file, all
the information will be lost.

If you leave the EasyStep Interview after saving the company file,
QuickBooks goes to the No Company Open window. The next time you
open the company file, you return to the EasyStep Interview window at the
same page you left.

To create a new company file using the Detailed Start method and the EasyStep Interview window:

1. At the QuickBooks Desktop Setup window, at the Let's get your business set up quickly! page, click the Detailed Start button. The EasyStep Interview window appears with the Enter your company information page displayed.

2. At the Enter your company information page, at the *Company name* field, type the company name CH6 *[Your Name]* Kristin Raina Interior Designs.

    When you tab to the *Legal name* field, the same name is automatically filled in. The legal name is the name that will be used on tax forms. If the company name and legal name are not the same, you can make any necessary changes. For our sample company, the company name and legal name are the same.

3. At the Enter your company information page, type the following information:

Tax ID:	33-4777781
Street address:	25 NE Johnson Street
City:	Minneapolis
State:	MN
Zip:	53402
Country:	U.S.
Phone:	651-555-1000
Fax:	651-555-2000
E-mail address:	KRID@ppi-edu.net

See Figure 6–B.

FIGURE 6–B

EasyStep Interview Window—Enter Your Company Information Page

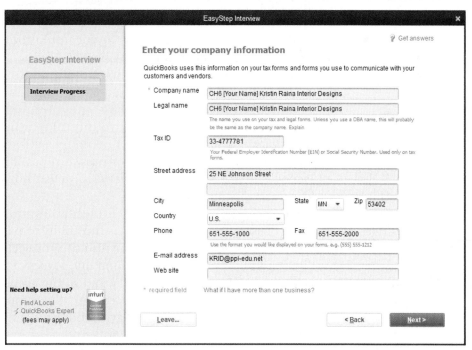

4. If the information is correct, click Next. You are moved to the Select your industry page.

5. At the Select your industry page, scroll down the INDUSTRY list and click *General Product-based Business.* See Figure 6–C.

FIGURE 6–C
EasyStep Interview Window—Select Your Industry Page

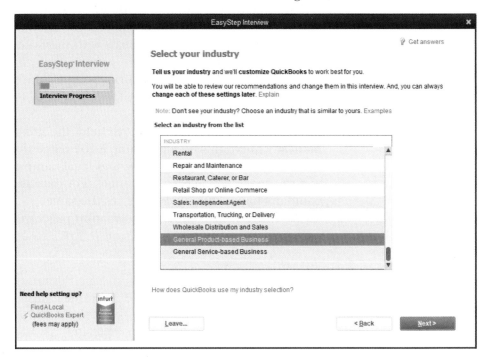

FIGURE 6–C
EasyStep Interview Window—Select Your Industry Page

HINT

When you are in the EasyStep Interview window, all the choices at the main menu bar are inactive.

HINT

If you do not enter a password here and leave the company file, the next time you open the new company file, you will need to enter a password, a challenge question, and an answer before you will be able to open the new company file. Refer to Chapter 7, "Company File Password" section, page 272, if you leave the company file without creating a password.

HINT

See Appendix J for information on how to set up users.

QuickBooks provides several sample-type industries to assist in creating your new company file. Based on the industry you select, QuickBooks inquires if you wish to use particular features or recommends that you use certain features. In addition, QuickBooks creates the Chart of Accounts List, which includes some accounts typical for the industry you chose. Later in the EasyStep Interview, you have the opportunity to review and edit the suggested revenue and expense accounts to be included in the Chart of Accounts List.

6. If the information is correct, click Next.
7. At the How is your company organized? page, click *Sole Proprietorship* and then click Next.
8. At the Select the first month of your fiscal year page, at the *My fiscal year starts in* field, click *January* and then click Next.
9. At the Set up your administrator password page, in the *Administrator password* text box and the *Retype password* text box, type Student1 (or a password of your choosing).

In business, it is advisable to protect access to financial records with a password. QuickBooks has the ability to password protect not only the entire company file but also specific sections of the company file. This allows a company to limit employees' access to their respective areas of responsibility. For instance, the accounts receivable bookkeeper may be permitted to access only the information pertaining to the customers' accounts, the payroll bookkeeper may be permitted to access only the payroll information, and so on.

10. Click Next.

In the *File name* text box, use the arrow keys to scroll through the entire name.

HINT

11. At the Create your company file page, click Next. The Filename for New Company dialog box appears.

12. Choose your subfolder in the *Save in* text box, and accept the file name **CH6** *[Your Name]* **Kristin Raina Interior Designs.QBW**.

13. If the information is correct, click Save. The new company file has been created and saved.

    At this point, the company file has been saved. It is now safe to use the Leave button at any time from this point on. If you do leave the EasyStep Interview at this point, QuickBooks closes the company file. The next time you open QuickBooks and the company file, you are returned to the EasyStep Interview window and the last page you opened.

14. At the Customizing QuickBooks for your business page, read the page and then click Next.

15. At the What do you sell? page, click *Both services and products* and then click Next.

16. At the Do you charge sales tax? page, click *Yes* and then click Next.

17. At the Do you want to create estimates in QuickBooks? page, click *No* and then click Next.

18. At the Tracking customer orders in QuickBooks page, click *No* and then click Next.

19. At the Using statements in QuickBooks page, click *No* and then click Next.

20. At the Using invoices in QuickBooks page, click *Yes* and then click Next.

21. At the Using progress invoicing page, click *No* and then click Next.

22. At the Managing bills you owe page, click *Yes* and then click Next.

23. At the Tracking inventory in QuickBooks page, click *Yes* and then click Next.

24. At the Tracking time in QuickBooks page, click *No* and then click Next.

25. At the Do you have employees? page, click *No* and then click Next.

26. At the Using accounts in QuickBooks page, read the page and then click Next.

27. At the Select a date to start tracking your finances page, click *Use today's date or the first day of the quarter or month* and then choose *04/01/2021*.

    This identifies the date the company began to use QuickBooks. For our sample company, Kristin Raina Interior Designs, the fiscal start date is January 1, 2021. The QuickBooks start date is April 1, 2021. You will enter the balances as of April 1, which represent January 1 to March 31 activities, in the new company file as part of the New Company Setup. See Figure 6–D.

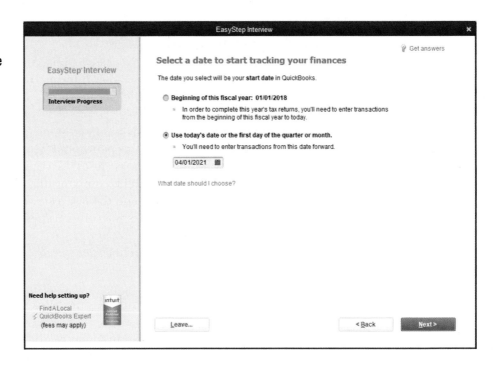

28. If the information is correct, click Next.

    The Review income and expense accounts page appears. See
Figure 6–E.

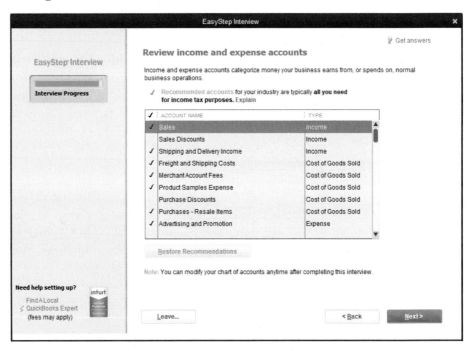

    This page lists common Chart of Accounts income and expense
accounts names. Each account with a check mark to the left of the
account name is an account that QuickBooks recommends for your
company based on the industry type you selected earlier in the
EasyStep Interview window. You can remove the check mark for any
account your company does not use, and you can insert a check mark
for any account your company does use. At any time, you can click

the Restore Recommendations button to replace the original check marks inserted by QuickBooks.

Any account checked is created in the Chart of Accounts List by QuickBooks. After you finish the EasyStep Interview window, you can add, delete, and modify any account on the Chart of Accounts List using the procedures presented in Chapter 4.

29. Remove the check mark from each of the following accounts by clicking the check mark, since Kristin Raina Interior Designs does not use these accounts:
    Shipping and Delivery Income
    Freight and Shipping Costs
    Merchant Account Fees
    Product Samples Expense
    Purchases - Resale Items
    Automobile Expense
    Bank Service Charges
    Computer and Internet Expenses
    Dues and Subscriptions
    Meals and Entertainment
    Postage and Delivery
    Professional Fees
    Repairs and Maintenance
    Travel Expense

30. Insert a check mark to the left of each of the following accounts, as these are accounts Kristin Raina Interior Designs uses:
    Sales Discounts
    Janitorial Expense

31. Click Next. The EasyStep Interview is complete. The Congratulations! page appears.

32. Click Go to Setup.
    After completing the EasyStep Interview window, you are returned to the QuickBooks Desktop Setup window with the Get all the details into QuickBooks Desktop page displayed. See Figure 6–F.

FIGURE 6–F
QuickBooks Desktop Setup Window—Get All the Details into QuickBooks Desktop Page

HINT
The Add button may change to Add More.

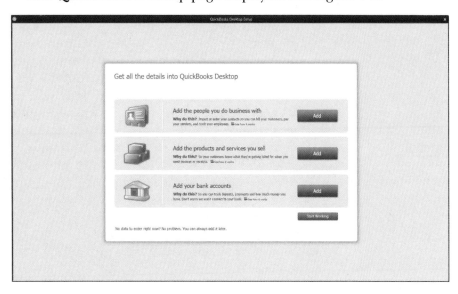

→ # QuickBooks Desktop Setup Window

You can use the QuickBooks Desktop Setup window—Get all the details into QuickBooks Desktop page to enter your customers (Customer Center), vendors (Vendor Center), service items and inventory items (Item List), and banking (Cash - Operating) information, or you can go directly into QuickBooks (Start Working).

For Kristin Raina Interior Designs, you will use the QuickBooks Desktop Setup window to continue setting up the new company file and to create the Customer Center, create the Vendor Center, and add to the Item List that begins in EasyStep Interview.

If you wish to leave the QuickBooks Desktop Setup window, click the X. You will enter QuickBooks in the new company file. To return to the QuickBooks Desktop Setup window, click Company at the main menu bar and then click *Bulk Enter Business Details.*

Setting Up the Customer Center

The Customer Center records the information for all the customers with whom the company does business. Kristin Raina has 10 customers. Two of the customers have outstanding balances. When you record the outstanding balance, QuickBooks creates the accounts receivable for that customer.

To add customers to the Customer Center using the QuickBooks Desktop Setup window:

1. At the QuickBooks Desktop Setup window, at the Get all the details into QuickBooks Desktop page, in the Add the people you do business with section, click the Add button.
2. At the next Add the people you do business with page, click the Paste from Excel or enter manually button and then click Continue.
3. At the next Add the people you do business with page, in the *Customer* column, click *Select all* and all the circles are filled in the *Customer* column.
4. At the *Name* field in the first row, type Alomar Company. Press the Tab key to move to the next field.
5. Enter the following information in the appropriate columns:

Company Name:	Alomar Company
First Name:	Oliver
Last Name:	Alomar
Phone:	612-555-5757
Address:	1001 Oak Lake Ave.
City, State, Zip:	Minneapolis, MN 55401
Contact Name:	Oliver Alomar

   See Figure 6–G.

HINT

See Appendix F for a summary of using the QuickBooks Desktop Setup window to enter data in New Company Setup.

HINT

If you leave the Quick-Books Desktop Setup window and the New Feature Tour window appears, click the X to close it. You can remove the Left Icon bar by clicking View and then clicking *Hide Icon Bar.* You can close the Home page by clicking the X.

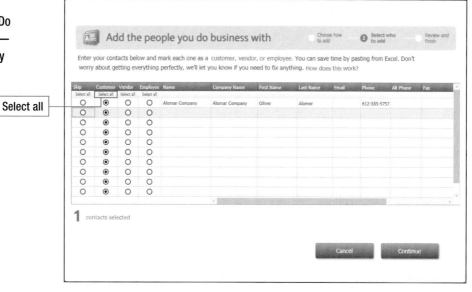

Select all

6. Add the remaining customers using the information in Table 6–1.

TABLE 6–1
Customers

Customer/ Company Name	Name/Contact	Phone	Address/ City, State, Zip
Barrera Bagel Barn	Belinda Barrera	612-555-1233	148 46th Ave. N Plymouth, MN 53406
Berger Bakery Company	Barry Berger	612-555-2240	18 N. Grand Ave. Minneapolis, MN 55403
Cook Caterers	Stephen Cook	612-555-7896	275 Oak Lake Ave. Minneapolis, MN 55401
Franco Films Co.	Fred Franco	612-555-4566	100 Pleasant Ave. S. Minneapolis, MN 55409
Guthrie, Jennie	Jennie Guthrie	651-555-1515	165 Terrace Ct. St. Paul, MN 55101
Hamilton Hotels	Hilda Hamilton	651-555-1050	1000 York Ave. St. Paul, MN 55101
Jones, Beverly	Beverly Jones	612-555-7778	333 York Circle Bloomington, MN 54603
Omari, Maria	Maria Omari	612-555-9999	210 NE Lowry Ave. Minneapolis, MN 54204
Plaza Pizza Palace	Mikey Plaza	612-555-9000	360 Border Ave. N Minneapolis, MN 46877

HINT

If you have information in an Excel spreadsheet, you can copy an entire column and paste it into the Add the people you do business with page. If you have difficulty pasting, press CTRL + V to paste.

After entering the information in Table 6–1, your screen should look like Figure 6–H.

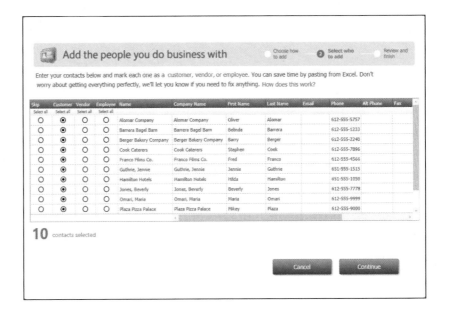

7. If the information is correct, click Continue. At the next Add the people you do business with page, it should indicate that 10 contacts are ready to be added. If that is incorrect, you will have an opportunity to make corrections later. See Figure 6–I.

FIGURE 6–I

Add the People You Do
Business With Page—
Enter Opening Balances
Link

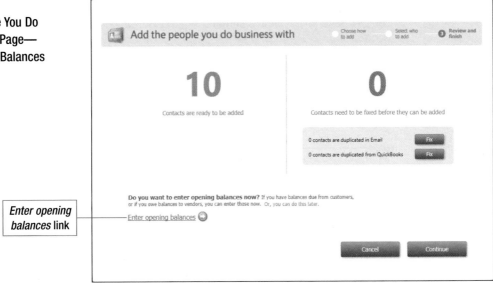

Enter opening
balances link

HINT

Exercise care in clicking the *Enter opening balances* link. If you do not click the *Enter opening balances* link here, then you will subsequently have to reenter the customers with balances.

8. Click the *Enter opening balances* link. At the Enter opening balances for your customers and vendors page, enter the balances for the following customers and change all the dates to 04/01/2021:

Berger Bakery Company $600
Franco Films Co.   940

See Figure 6–J.

FIGURE 6–J

Enter Opening Balances
for Your Customers
and Vendors Page—
Customers—Completed

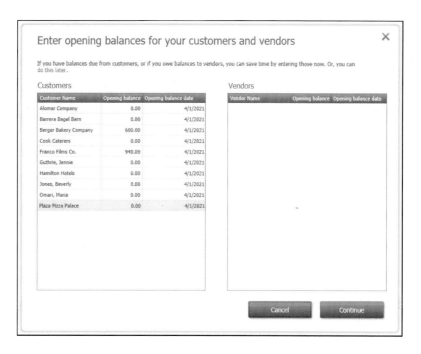

Enter opening balances for your customers and vendors   ×

If you have balances due from customers, or if you owe balances to vendors, you can save time by entering those now. Or, you can do this later.

Customers

Customer Name	Opening balance	Opening balance date
Alomar Company	0.00	4/1/2021
Barrera Bagel Barn	0.00	4/1/2021
Berger Bakery Company	600.00	4/1/2021
Cook Caterers	0.00	4/1/2021
Franco Films Co.	940.00	4/1/2021
Guthrie, Jennie	0.00	4/1/2021
Hamilton Hotels	0.00	4/1/2021
Jones, Beverly	0.00	4/1/2021
Omari, Maria	0.00	4/1/2021
Plaza Pizza Palace	0.00	4/1/2021

Vendors

Vendor Name	Opening balance	Opening balance date

Cancel   Continue

HINT

If a System Runtime error occurs after entering the opening balances for customers, click OK at the error message. You are returned to the Get all the details into QuickBooks Desktop page. Following the steps on pages 191–201, reenter the names for only two customers: Berger Bakery Company and Franco Films Co. Enter their opening balances of $600 and $940, respectively, for April 1, 2021. It may take a few tries. If you continue to have difficulty with this step, refer to your instructor.

9. If the information is correct, click Continue. You are returned to the Add the people you do business with page.
10. Click Continue. If you don't click Continue here, none of the customers and opening balances will be saved.
11. You are returned to the QuickBooks Desktop Setup window—Get all the details into QuickBooks page.

ACCOUNTING CONCEPT

1200 Accounts Receivable		49900 Uncategorized Income	
Dr	Cr	Dr	Cr
600			600
940			940
Bal 1,540			Bal 1,540

Setting Up the Vendor Center

The Vendor Center records the information for all the vendors with whom the company does business. Kristin Raina has 17 vendors. Seven of the vendors have outstanding balances. When you record the outstanding balance, QuickBooks creates the accounts payable for that vendor.

To add vendors to the Vendor Center using the QuickBooks Desktop Setup window:

1. At the QuickBooks Desktop Setup window, at the Get all the details into QuickBooks Desktop page, in the Add the people you do business with section, click the Add More button.
2. At the Add the people you do business with page, click the Paste from Excel or enter manually button and then click Continue.
3. At the next Add the people you do business with page, in the *Vendor* column, click *Select all*, and all the circles are filled in the *Vendor* column

on the displayed page. You may need to check the *Vendor* column again if you add more vendors than fit on this first page.

4. At the *Name* field in the first row, type Ace Glass Works. Press the Tab key to move to the next field.

5. Enter the following information in the appropriate columns:

Company Name:	Ace Glass Works
First Name:	Archie
Last Name:	Ace
Phone:	612-555-9812
Address:	25 SE Como Ave.
City, State, Zip:	Minneapolis, MN 53602
Contact:	Archie Ace

See Figure 6–K.

FIGURE 6–K
Add the People You Do Business With Page— Vendors—Partially Completed

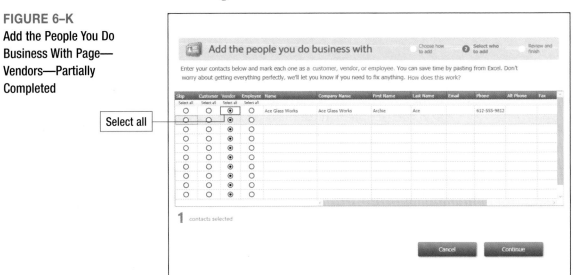

6. Add the remaining vendors using the information in Table 6–2.

TABLE 6–2
Vendors

Vendor/ Company Name	Name/Contact	Phone	Address/ City, State, Zip
Bell Carpet Design	Bill Bell	651-555-8823	55 North Main Ave. St. Paul, MN 54603
Cuza and Carl Associates	Carrie Cuza	651-555-8855	23 W. University Ave. St. Paul, MN 54603
Darren Tapestry	Donna Darren	612-555-2221	10 W. Larpenteur Ave. Minneapolis, MN 52604
Galeway Computers	Roger Rivera	617-555-4747	33 Route 10 Springfield, MA 24105
Grayson Graphics	Gregg Grayson	612-555-0002	56 Amity Way Bloomington, MN 53608
Jeter Janitorial Services	Jason Jeter	612-555-4444	233 Lilac Rd. Minneapolis, MN 54302
Kristin Raina	Kristin Raina		
Lumiare Lighting Company	Larry Lyght	612-555-4790	123 Glenwood Ave. Minneapolis, MN 53609

...continues

TABLE 6–2

Vendors...*continued*

Vendor/ Company Name	Name/Contact	Phone	Address/ City, State, Zip
Midwest Mutual Insurance Co.	Mike Mills	805-555-4545	3566 Broadway Chicago, IL 58303
Minn. Dept. of Revenue			
Minneapolis Electric & Gas Co.	Jack Watts	651-555-4949	150 Douglas Ave. St. Paul, MN 55303
Nordic Realty	Melanie Marx	612-555-3232	23 N. 12th St. Minneapolis, MN 53604
TwinCityTelCo	Terry Ameche	651-555-6667	3223 River Dr. St. Paul, MN 53908
Weaver Fabrics	Jon Weaver	612-555-8777	355 W. 70th St. Minneapolis, MN 53604
Williams Office Supply Company	Bernard Williams	612-555-2240	15 Grand Ave. S Minneapolis, MN 55404
[Your Name] Accounting Service	[Your Name]	612-555-2222	One Main Plaza St. Paul, MN 53602

Note: In the event that you do not have a person's name but instead have a department as a contact, you can still enter the information on the Address Info tab in the FULL NAME *field. For example, if the contact is* Customer Service, *you can enter* Customer *in the* First Name *field and* Service *in the* Last Name *field.*

After entering the information in Table 6–2, your screen should look like Figure 6–L.

FIGURE 6–L

Add the People You Do Business With Page— Vendors—Completed

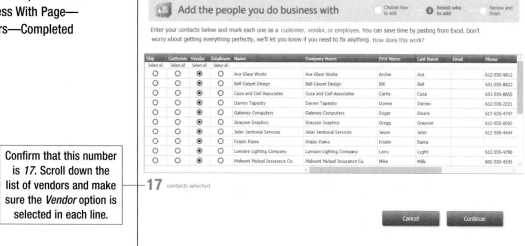

Confirm that this number is *17*. Scroll down the list of vendors and make sure the *Vendor* option is selected in each line.

7. Scroll down the list of vendors and make sure the *Vendor* option is selected in each line. If the information is correct, click Continue. At the next Add the people you do business with page, it should indicate that 17 contacts are ready to be added. If that is incorrect, you will have an opportunity to make corrections later.

HINT

Exercise care in clicking the *Enter opening balances* link. If you do not click the *Enter opening balances* link here, you will subsequently have to reenter the vendors with balances.

8. Click the *Enter opening balances* link. At the Enter opening balances for customers and vendors page, enter the balances for the following vendors and change all of the dates to 04/01/2021:

Ace Glass Works	$1,500
Bell Carpet Design	2,000
Cuza and Carl Associates	400
Galeway Computers	2,600
Midwest Mutual Insurance Co.	2,400
Minneapolis Electric & Gas Co.	450
Williams Office Supply Company	400

See Figure 6–M.

FIGURE 6–M

Enter Opening Balances for Your Customers and Vendors Page—Vendors—Completed

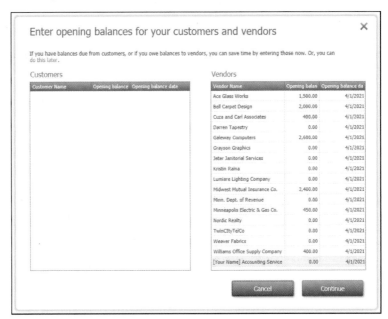

9. If the information is correct, click Continue. You are returned to the Add the people you do business with page.
10. Click Continue. If you don't click Continue here, none of the vendors and opening balances will be saved.
11. You are returned to the QuickBooks Desktop Setup window—Get all the details into QuickBooks Desktop page.

ACCOUNTING CONCEPT

69800 Uncategorized Expenses		2010 Accounts Payable	
Dr	Cr	Dr	Cr
1,500			1,500
2,000			2,000
400			400
2,600			2,600
2,400			2,400
450			450
400			400
Bal 9,750			Bal 9,750

Adding to the Item List

The Item List stores information about the service items, the inventory part items, and the sales tax. As transactions are recorded in the Activities windows, QuickBooks uses information in the Item List to record the transaction in the correct accounts. Kristin Raina has two service items and four inventory part items. When you record the quantity on hand for an inventory part, QuickBooks creates the inventory asset for that inventory part.

To add service items to the Item List using the QuickBooks Desktop Setup window:

1. At the QuickBooks Desktop Setup window, at the Get all the details into QuickBooks Desktop page, in the Add the products and services you sell section, click the Add button.
2. At the Add the products and services you sell page, click the *Service* option and then click Continue.
3. At the *Name* field in the first row, type Design Services.
4. At the *Description* field, type Design Services.
5. At the *Price* field, type 60.
6. Enter the following information for the next service item:

Name:	Decorating Services
Description:	Decorating Services
Price:	50

   See Figure 6–N.

FIGURE 6-N
Add the Products and Services You Sell Page—Services Items—Completed

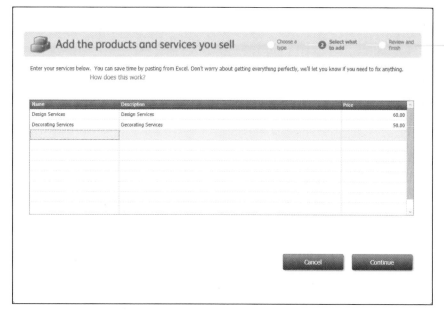

7. If the information is correct, click Continue. You are returned to the Add the products and services you sell page, which should indicate 2 Items are ready to be added. If that is incorrect, you will have an opportunity to make corrections later.
8. Click Continue. If you don't click Continue here, none of the service items will be saved. You are returned to the QuickBooks Desktop Setup window—Get all the details into QuickBooks Desktop page.

To add inventory part items to the Item List using the QuickBooks Desktop Setup window:

1. At the QuickBooks Desktop Setup window, at the Get all the details into QuickBooks Desktop page, in the Add the products and services you sell section, click the Add More button.
2. At the Add the products and services you sell page, click the Inventory part button and then click Continue.
3. At the *Name* field in the first row, type Carpets.
4. At the *Description* field, type Carpets.
5. At the *Price* field, type 400.
6. At the *Cost* field, type 200.
7. At the *On Hand* field, type 4. When you move to the next field, the amount in the *Total Value* field is computed automatically based on cost multiplied by quantity.
8. At the *As of date* field, choose *04/01/2021*.
9. Add the remaining inventory part items using the information in Table 6–3.

TABLE 6–3
Inventory Part Items

Name and Description	Price	Cost	On Hand	Total Value
Draperies	$250	$125	8	$1,000
Lamps	200	100	10	1,000
Mirrors	300	150	6	900

After entering the information in Table 6–3, your screen should look like Figure 6–O.

FIGURE 6–O

Add the Products and Services You Sell Page—Inventory Parts—Completed

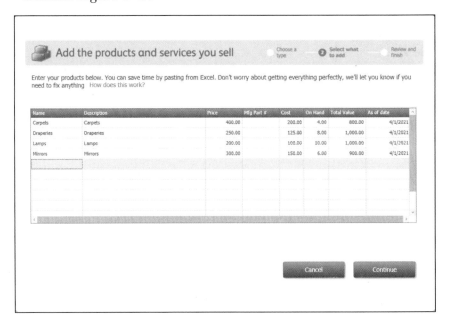

10. If the information is correct, click Continue. You are returned to the Add the products and services you sell page, which should indicate 4 Items are ready to be added. If that is incorrect, you will have an opportunity to make corrections later.

11. Click Continue. If you don't click Continue here, none of the inventory part items and opening balances will be saved. You are returned to the QuickBooks Desktop Setup window—Get all the details into QuickBooks Desktop page.

ACCOUNTING CONCEPT

Inventory Asset		Opening Balance Equity	
Dr	Cr	Dr	Cr
800			800
1,000			1,000
1,000			1,000
900			900

HINT

Recall that you can change the default so the Home page does not appear when opening a company file. Click Edit at the main menu bar and then click *Preferences*. In the left panel, click the Desktop View icon. Choose the My Preferences tab. Remove the check mark to the left of *Show Home page when opening a company file* and then click OK.

12. Exit the QuickBooks Desktop Setup window by clicking the X. You enter QuickBooks in the new company file. If the New Feature Tour window appears, click the X to close it. The QuickBooks Home page and the Left Icon bar appear. Close the Home page by clicking the X, and remove the Left Icon bar by clicking View and then clicking *Hide Icon Bar.*

Reviewing EasyStep Interview and QuickBooks Desktop Setup Information

The EasyStep Interview created the Chart of Accounts List and the Item List. It also established preferences that enabled certain features in QuickBooks. The activated preferences provide for choices to be listed on the drop-down menus and the Home page, and they allow for accessing activity windows. The QuickBooks Desktop Setup created the Customer Center and Vendor Center and added the service items and inventory part items to the Item List.

Chart of Accounts List

Reviewing the Chart of Accounts List allows you to see the accounts set up as part of the EasyStep Interview and QuickBooks Desktop Setup.

To view the Chart of Accounts List:
1. At the main menu bar, click Lists and then click *Chart of Accounts*. The Chart of Accounts List appears. See Figure 6–P.

FIGURE 6–P
Chart of Accounts List
Window

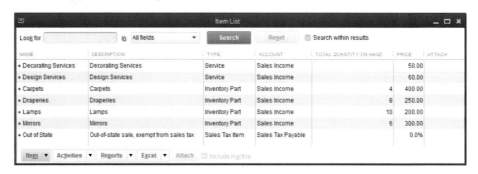

system default accounts
created by QuickBooks
as part of the EasyStep
Interview and QuickBooks
Desktop Setup

You can correct any errors by adding, deleting, or editing an account, as illustrated in Chapter 4.

Upon reviewing the Chart of Accounts List, observe that Kristin Raina Interior Designs uses many more accounts that are not included in the Chart of Accounts List created by the EasyStep Interview and QuickBooks Desktop Setup or uses different account names. Notice also that an account number was not assigned to each account.

2. Close the Chart of Accounts List.

Item List

Reviewing the Item List allows you to see the items set up as part of the EasyStep Interview and QuickBooks Desktop Setup.

To view the Item List:

1. At the main menu bar, click Lists and then click *Item List*. The Item List appears. See Figure 6–Q.

FIGURE 6–Q
Item List Window

At the QuickBooks Desktop Setup window, at the Add new products and services page, when you added service items and inventory part items, these items were added to the Item List.

2. Double-click the *Decorating Services* service item. The Edit Item window appears. See Figure 6–R.

FIGURE 6–R
Edit Item Window—
Service Item

When this service item was created, QuickBooks Desktop Setup recorded *Sales Income* in the *Account* field. If you double-click *Design Services* at the Item List window, you will see that QuickBooks Desktop Setup also uses Sales Income as the account for Design Services.

3. Close the Edit Item window.
4. At the Item List window, double-click the *Carpets* inventory part item. The Edit Item window appears. See Figure 6–S.

FIGURE 6–S
Edit Item Window—
Inventory Part Item

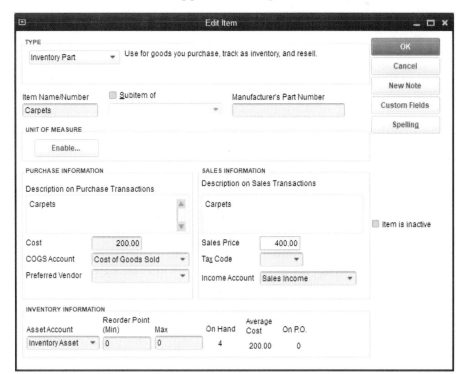

When this inventory part item was created, QuickBooks Desktop Setup recorded the COGS Account as *Cost of Goods Sold*, the Income Account as *Sales Income*, and the Asset Account as *Inventory Asset*. If you double-click each of the other inventory part items—*Draperies, Lamps,* and *Mirrors*—you will see that QuickBooks Desktop Setup also used Cost of Goods Sold, Sales Income, and Inventory Asset as the accounts for these inventory part items.

5. Close the Edit Item window.

At the EasyStep Interview window, when you indicated *Yes*, you do charge sales tax, the Item List was created with this sales tax item.

6. At the Item List window, double-click the Out of State Sales Tax item. The Edit Item window appears. See Figure 6–T.

FIGURE 6–T
Edit Item Window—
Sales Tax Item

The EasyStep Interview created this item in the Item List, but it does not include an appropriate name for the Kristin Raina Interior Designs tax item, a tax rate, or a tax agency. These will be added later.

7. Close the Edit Item and Item List windows.

There are different ways to correct the errors in the Item List. If there is an error in the type, name, cost, or price amounts in any of the service items, inventory part items, or sales tax, you can correct it in the Edit Item window. If there is an error in the quantity on hand, you can correct it when viewing journal entries. If there is no quantity on hand for an inventory part item, delete the inventory part item and then go back to the QuickBooks Desktop Setup—Add the products and services you sell page.

To return to the QuickBooks Desktop Setup, click Company and then click *Bulk Enter Business Details.* At the Add the products and services you sell section, click Add More and then reenter the inventory part item with the correct quantity on hand and the correct date, as previously illustrated.

Customer Center

Reviewing the Customer Center allows you to see the customers set up as part of the QuickBooks Desktop Setup.

To review the Customer Center:

1. At the main menu bar, click Customers and then click *Customer Center.* The Customer Center appears. See Figure 6–U.

FIGURE 6–U
Customer Center Window

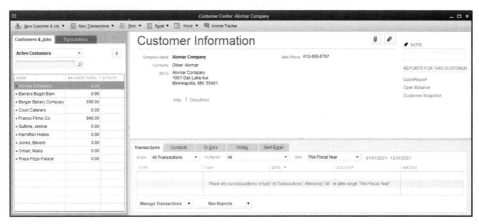

2. Double-click *Berger Bakery Company.* The Edit Customer window appears. See Figure 6–V.

FIGURE 6–V
Edit Customer Window

QuickBooks created this customer based on the information entered in QuickBooks Desktop Setup—Add the people you do business with pages. If you entered an opening balance, the balance is displayed in the *CURRENT BALANCE* field. If you did not enter an opening balance, the *CURRENT BALANCE* field indicates a zero. You can correct all the information in the Edit Customer window except the current balance.

3. Close the Edit Customer window and the Customer Center window.

There are different ways to correct the errors in the Customer Center. If there is an error in the name, address, or phone number for any of the customers, you can correct it in the Edit Customer window. If there is an error in the current balance, you can correct it when viewing journal entries. If there is no current balance for a customer with an outstanding balance, delete the customer and then go back to the QuickBooks Desktop Setup—Add people you do business with pages.

To return to the QuickBooks Desktop Setup, click Company and then click *Bulk Enter Business Details.* At the Add the people you do business with section, click Add More and then reenter the customer. Continue to the Enter opening balances page and enter the correct balance and the correct date, as previously illustrated. Be sure to click the Continue button to save the customers and opening balances.

Vendor Center

Reviewing the Vendor Center allows you to see the vendors set up as part of the QuickBooks Desktop Setup.

To review the Vendor Center:

1. At the main menu bar, click Vendors and then click *Vendor Center.* The Vendor Center appears. See Figure 6–W.

FIGURE 6–W
Vendor Center Window

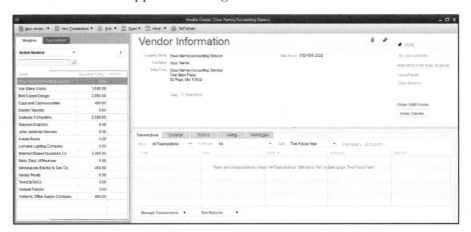

2. Double-click *Ace Glass Works Company.* The Edit Vendor window appears. See Figure 6–X.

FIGURE 6–X
Edit Vendor Window

QuickBooks created this vendor based on the information entered in QuickBooks Desktop Setup—Add the people you do business with pages. If you entered an opening balance, the balance is displayed in the *CURRENT BALANCE* field. If you did not enter an opening balance, the *CURRENT BALANCE* field indicates a zero. You can correct all the information in the Edit Vendor window except the current balance.

3. Close the Edit Vendor window and the Vendor Center window.

There are different ways to correct an error in the Vendor Center. If there is an error in the company name, address, or phone number for any of the vendors, you can correct it in the Edit Vendor window. If there is an error in the current balance, you can correct it when viewing journal entries. If there is no current balance for a vendor with an outstanding balance, delete the vendor and then go back to the QuickBooks Desktop Setup—Add people you do business with pages.

To return to the QuickBooks Desktop Setup, click Company and then click *Bulk Enter Business Details*. At the Add the people you do business with section, click Add More and then reenter the vendor. Continue to the Enter opening balances page and enter the correct balance and the correct date, as previously illustrated. Be sure to click the Continue button to save the vendors and opening balances.

Journal Report

Reviewing the *Journal* report allows you to see the journal entries created as part of the QuickBooks Desktop Setup.

To view and print the *Journal* report:
1. At the main menu bar, click Reports and then click *Accountant & Taxes*.
2. At the Accountant & Taxes submenu, click *Journal*. If the Collapsing and Expanding Transactions message appears, read the message, insert a check mark in the box to the left of *Do not display this message in the future*, and then click OK.
3. At the *From* and *To* fields, choose *04/01/2021* and *04/01/2021* and then click the Refresh button at the top of the report.
4. Print the report. Your printout should look like Figure 6–Y.

- The amount in the Inventory Asset account equals the amount in the Opening Balance Equity account.
- The amount in the Accounts Payable account equals the amount in the Uncategorized Expenses account.

4. Close the report.

Figure 6–AA shows the Trial Balance from **EX5** *[Your Name]* **Kristin Raina Interior Designs**. It reflects the activities of January 1 to March 31, 2021, which were recorded in Chapters 2 through 5. Compare the Trial Balance of April 1, 2021 (Figure 6–Z, page 215) with the Trial Balance of March 31, 2021 (Figure 6–AA).

FIGURE 6–AA
Trial Balance
March 31, 2021
(from Chapter 5)

EX5 [Your Name] Kristin Raina Interior Designs
Trial Balance

Accrual Basis — As of March 31, 2021

	Mar 31, 21	
	Debit	Credit
1010 · Cash - Operating	50,855.38	
1200 · Accounts Receivable	1,540.00	
1250 · Undeposited Funds	0.00	
1260 · Inventory of Carpets	800.00	
1265 · Inventory of Draperies	1,000.00	
1270 · Inventory of Lamps	1,000.00	
1275 · Inventory of Mirrors	900.00	
1300 · Design Supplies	200.00	
1305 · Office Supplies	250.00	
1410 · Prepaid Advertising	500.00	
1420 · Prepaid Insurance	2,200.00	
1700 · Furniture:1725 · Furniture, Cost	12,000.00	
1700 · Furniture:1750 · Accum. Dep., Furniture		100.00
1800 · Computers:1825 · Computers, Cost	3,600.00	
1800 · Computers:1850 · Accum. Dep., Computers		60.00
2010 · Accounts Payable		9,750.00
2020 · Notes Payable		7,000.00
2030 · Interest Payable		50.00
2200 · Sales Tax Payable	0.00	
3010 · Kristin Raina, Capital		50,000.00
3020 · Kristin Raina, Drawings	400.00	
4010 · Design Services		4,980.00
4020 · Decorating Services		3,400.00
4060 · Sale of Carpets		2,400.00
4065 · Sale of Draperies		1,000.00
4070 · Sale of Lamps		1,200.00
4075 · Sale of Mirrors		900.00
4100 · Sales Discounts	84.62	
5060 · Cost of Carpets Sold	1,200.00	
5065 · Cost of Draperies Sold	500.00	
5070 · Cost of Lamps Sold	600.00	
5075 · Cost of Mirrors Sold	450.00	
5900 · Inventory Adjustment	150.00	
6020 · Accounting Expense	300.00	
6050 · Advertising Expense	100.00	
6175 · Deprec. Exp., Furniture	100.00	
6185 · Deprec. Exp., Computers	60.00	
6200 · Insurance Expense	200.00	
6300 · Janitorial Expenses	125.00	
6325 · Office Supplies Expense	150.00	
6400 · Rent Expense	800.00	
6450 · Telephone Expense	275.00	
6500 · Utilities Expense	450.00	
7000 · Interest Expense	50.00	
TOTAL	**80,840.00**	**80,840.00**

Although the EasyStep Interview and QuickBooks Desktop Setup guide you in creating a new company file, they do not enter all the information for a company. Upon completion of the next parts of New Company Setup—customizing and updating the new company file and preparing for the accrual basis of accounting—the trial balance of April 1 in this chapter will be the same as the trial balance of March 31 from Chapter 5.

Profit & Loss Standard (Income Statement) Report

Reviewing the *Profit & Loss Standard* report allows you to see the balances created as part of the QuickBooks Desktop Setup that flow into the *Profit & Loss Standard* report.

To view the *Profit & Loss Standard* report:

1. At the main menu bar, click Reports and then click *Company & Financial.*
2. At the Company & Financial submenu, click *Profit & Loss Standard.*
3. At the *From* and *To* fields, choose *01/01/2021* and *04/01/2021* and then click the Refresh button at the top of the report. See Figure 6–BB.

FIGURE 6–BB

Profit & Loss Standard
Report

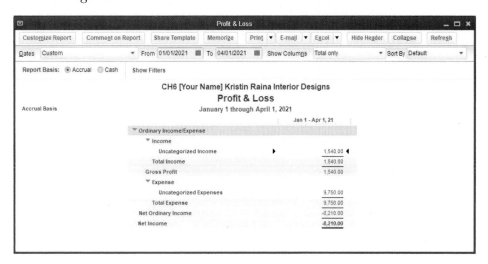

The *Profit & Loss Standard* report indicates only Uncategorized Income and Uncategorized Expenses. These amounts are off-setting amounts of the Accounts Receivable and Accounts Payable accounts, respectively. This is not a proper representation of the income and expenses of this company.

4. Close the report.

Balance Sheet Standard Report

Reviewing the *Balance Sheet Standard* report allows you to see the balances created as part of the QuickBooks Desktop Setup that flow into the *Balance Sheet Standard* report.

To display the *Balance Sheet Standard* report:

1. At the main menu bar, click Reports and then click *Company & Financial.*
2. At the Company & Financial submenu, click *Balance Sheet Standard.*
3. At the *As of* field, choose *04/01/2021* and then click the Refresh button at the top of the report. See Figure 6–CC.

FIGURE 6–CC
Balance Sheet Standard Report

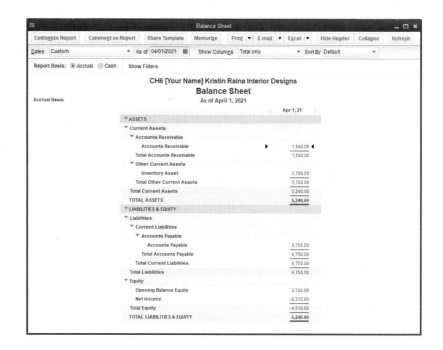

Note the following on the balance sheet:
- The only assets recorded so far are Accounts Receivable and Inventory Asset.
- The only liability recorded so far is Accounts Payable.
- The balance in the Opening Balance Equity account is the amount in Inventory Asset.
- The net income is incorrect as seen in the Income Statement (*Profit & Loss* report) because of incomplete information.

4. Close the report.

New Company Setup

Customizing the New Company File

When you use the EasyStep Interview and QuickBooks Desktop Setup windows, only part of the New Company Setup is completed. The EasyStep Interview window is used to create the new company file; enable or disable some preferences; record a sales tax item, which begins the Item List; and begin the setup of the Chart of Accounts List. When you enter information in the QuickBooks Desktop Setup window, you create the Customer Center, create the Vendor Center, and update the Item List to include service items and inventory part items. At the same time, the information entered in the QuickBooks Desktop Setup window records opening balances for Accounts Receivable, Accounts Payable, and Inventory Asset.

The next part of the process is to continue with the information set up in the EasyStep Interview and QuickBooks Desktop Setup windows to customize the new company file according to your company's preferences, update the Lists/Centers as needed, and prepare the company file for the accrual basis of accounting by recording three journal entries.

Customizing the Chart of Accounts List

You will customize the Chart of Accounts for Kristin Raina by enabling the account numbers feature and then editing the account numbers and names assigned by QuickBooks.

Adding Account Numbers

By default, QuickBooks does not use account numbers. This can be seen in the Chart of Accounts List and in the individual accounts.

To view an account in Edit mode:
1. At the main menu bar, click Lists and then click *Chart of Accounts.*
2. At the Chart of Accounts window, select the *Accounts Receivable* account.
3. Click the Account menu button.
4. At the Account button drop-down menu, click *Edit Account.* Notice that there is no field in which to place an account number.
5. Close the Edit account and Chart of Accounts List windows.

   To add account numbers to the Chart of Accounts List, you must activate the account numbers feature in the Preferences window.

To activate the account numbers feature:
1. At the main menu bar, click Edit and then click *Preferences.* The Preferences window appears.

   In the left panel of the window are 23 icons, which represent the different categories of features. For each category, there is a My Preferences tab and a Company Preferences tab. The Company Preferences tab is used for most customizations when setting up a new company file. The My Preferences tab records the preferences for each user on his or her own personal computer. When using the EasyStep Interview window, most preferences are established based on the responses to the questions in the EasyStep Interview.
2. In the left panel of the Preferences window, click the Accounting icon.
3. Click the Company Preferences tab.
4. In the ACCOUNTS section, insert a check mark in the box to the left of *Use account numbers* to turn on the account numbers feature. See Figure 6–DD.

FIGURE 6–DD
Preferences Window—
Accounting—Company
Preferences Tab

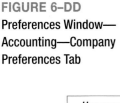

Use account numbers option

warning options

5. If the information is correct, click OK. The account *Number* field now appears in the New Account and Edit Account windows in the Chart of Accounts List.

Editing Account Numbers and Names

When you activate the account numbers feature, QuickBooks assigns account numbers to most accounts. You can change or delete these numbers.

To edit the account numbers and names:

1. At the main menu bar, click Lists and then click *Chart of Accounts.*
2. At the Chart of Accounts window, select the *Furniture and Equipment* account.
3. Click the Account menu button.
4. At the Account button drop-down menu, click *Edit Account.* Notice that a *Number* field has been added.
5. At the *Number* field, type 1700, and at the *Account Name* field, delete the text *and Equipment.* See Figure 6–EE.

FIGURE 6–EE
Edit Account Window—
Furniture—Number
Added and Account
Name Edited

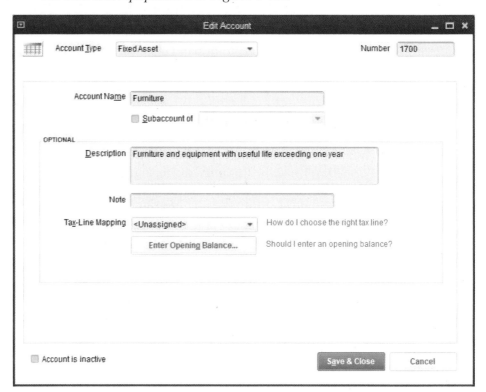

6. If the information is correct, click the Save & Close button.
7. Edit each of the accounts created by QuickBooks, changing the account number and name as listed on the next page. If an edited name is not listed, keep the name assigned by QuickBooks.

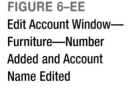

HINT

To edit an account in the Chart of Accounts List window, select the account, click the Account button, and then click the Edit button. Do not double-click the account.

QuickBooks		Edited	
Number	Account Name	Number	Account Name
17000	Accumulated Depreciation	1750	Accum. Dep., Furniture [Subaccount of 1700 Furniture]
30800	Owners Draw	3020	Kristin Raina, Drawings
	Sales Income	4060	Sale of Carpets
48300	Sales Discounts	4100	
60000	Advertising and Promotion	6050	Advertising Expense
62400	Depreciation Expense	6175	Deprec. Exp., Furniture
63300	Insurance Expense	6200	
63400	Interest Expense	7000	[Account Type: Other Expense]
63500	Janitorial Expense	6300	
64900	Office Supplies	6325	Office Supplies Expense
67100	Rent Expense	6400	
68100	Telephone Expense	6450	
68600	Utilities	6500	Utilities Expense
80000	Ask My Accountant	6020	Accounting Expense [Account Type: Expense]

HINT

As an alternative to selecting an account and then clicking the Account button, you can right-click an account and then choose *Edit Account* from the short-cut menu.

8. Close the Chart of Accounts List.

Deleting an Account

As part of the EasyStep Interview and QuickBooks Desktop Setup, QuickBooks created two sales accounts: Sales Income and 47900 Sales. The Sales Income account was not assigned an account number by QuickBooks but was the revenue account QuickBooks used in the Item List whenever an income account was needed. This account now has the number *4060,* and the name has been changed to *Sale of Carpets.* Kristin Raina does not need the 47900 Sales account and will delete it.

To delete an account:
1. At the main menu bar, click Lists and then click *Chart of Accounts.*
2. At the Chart of Accounts window, select the *47900 Sales* account.
3. Click the Account menu button.
4. At the Account button drop-down menu, click *Delete Account.*
5. At the Delete Account warning, click OK. The account is now deleted from the Chart of Accounts.

The customized Chart of Accounts List appears in Figure 6–FF.

FIGURE 6–FF
Chart of Accounts List—
Customized with Account
Numbers and Names

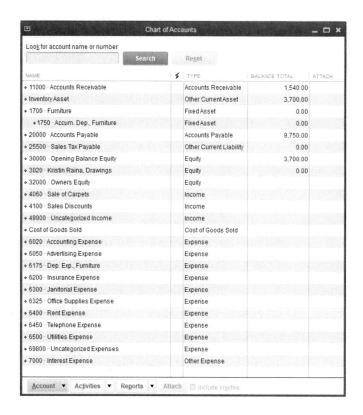

6. Close the Chart of Accounts List window.

Customizing System Default Accounts

As you saw in prior chapters, QuickBooks establishes default accounts and uses those accounts when recording transactions in the Activities windows. QuickBooks looks for these accounts in the Chart of Accounts List; if it cannot find an account, it creates one. Some system default accounts you have learned so far are Accounts Receivable, Undeposited Funds, Accounts Payable, Sales Tax Payable, Inventory Asset, and Cost of Goods Sold. Other system default accounts include the equity accounts (capital and accumulated earnings).

When you created the company file using the EasyStep Interview and QuickBooks Desktop Setup, QuickBooks created some of the system default accounts (Accounts Receivable, Accounts Payable, Sales Tax Payable, and the equity accounts) as part of the Chart of Accounts, as shown in Figure 6–P on page 208. You will customize the system default accounts that were created as part of the EasyStep Interview (Sales Tax Payable and the equity accounts) and QuickBooks Desktop Setup (Accounts Receivable and Accounts Payable) by editing the account names and numbers to follow the company's pattern for naming and numbering accounts on the Chart of Accounts List. You will then learn how to force QuickBooks to create additional system default accounts that were not created as part of the EasyStep Interview or QuickBooks Desktop Setup (Undeposited Funds, Inventory Asset, and Cost of Goods Sold). After QuickBooks creates the additional system default accounts, you will then customize these account names and numbers.

Customizing System Default Accounts
Created in a New Company File

When you created the company file and indicated the company was a sole proprietorship, QuickBooks automatically created three equity accounts: Opening Balance Equity, Owners Draw, and Owners Equity. When you activated the sales tax feature in the EasyStep Interview window, QuickBooks created a Sales Tax Payable account. When you added each customer in QuickBooks Desktop Setup, QuickBooks created the Accounts Receivable account. When you added each vendor in QuickBooks Desktop Setup, QuickBooks created the Accounts Payable account. When you added each inventory part in QuickBooks Desktop Setup, QuickBooks created the Inventory Asset and Cost of Goods Sold accounts. The numbers and names for all these accounts can be edited. The Opening Balance Equity account will be renamed as *Kristin Raina, Capital,* and the Owners Draw account was already renamed *Kristin Raina, Drawings.* QuickBooks uses the Opening Balance Equity account as an offsetting account when certain opening balances are entered in the accounts. The Owners Equity account is created to capture net income at the end of the fiscal year. In Chapter 12, you will see how QuickBooks uses the Owner's Equity account in a company file. This account will be renamed *Accumulated Earnings.*

As you will soon see, QuickBooks recognizes the Accounts Receivable; Accounts Payable; Sales Tax Payable; Kristin Raina, Capital (Opening Balance Equity); and Accumulated Earnings (Owners Equity) accounts as system default accounts, but QuickBooks does not recognize the Inventory Asset and Cost of Goods Sold accounts as system default accounts. QuickBooks usually identifies a system default account by graying, or dimming, the account type. As you edit each account, notice that the account type is dimmed.

To edit system default account numbers and account names:
1. At the main menu bar, click Lists and then click *Chart of Accounts.*
2. At the Chart of Accounts window, select *30000 Opening Balance Equity.*
3. Click the Account menu button.
4. At the Account button drop-down menu, click *Edit Account.* In the Edit Account window, notice that the Account Type drop-down list is dimmed.
5. At the *Number* field, delete *30000* and then type 3010.
6. At the *Account Name* field, delete the text *Opening Balance Equity* and then type Kristin Raina, Capital. See Figure 6–GG.

FIGURE 6–GG

Edit Account Window—
System Default Account

The Account Type drop-down list is dimmed because this is a system default account.

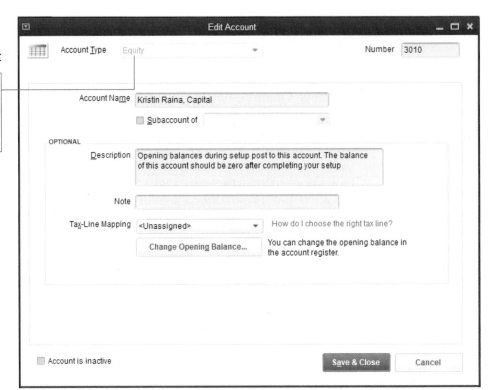

7. If the information is correct, click the Save & Close button.
8. Edit the other system default accounts created by the EasyStep Interview and QuickBooks Desktop Setup as follows:

QuickBooks		Edited	
Number	Account Name	Number	Account Name
11000	Accounts Receivable	1200	
20000	Accounts Payable	2010	
25500	Sales Tax Payable	2200	
32000	Owners Equity	3030	Accumulated Earnings

Notice that for the Accounts Receivable account, *Accounts Receivable* is both the account name and the account type. Similarly, notice that for the Accounts Payable account, *Accounts Payable* is both the account name and the account type. When QuickBooks looks for a system default account, it looks for the account type, not the account name.

9. Close the Chart of Accounts List window.

Customizing System Default Accounts
Created for Use in Activities Windows

Recall that in the Create Invoices window, the system default account is a debit to Accounts Receivable; in the Enter Bills window, the system default is a credit to Accounts Payable. When you chose an inventory item in any of the activity windows, QuickBooks knew—from the Item List—which inventory asset account, cost of goods sold account, and sale of inventory account was the system default account to use for properly recording the transaction. You also know that you can create accounts in the Chart of Accounts List. However, sometimes QuickBooks does not find an account

HINT

Upon completion of New Company Setup, the account 3010 Kristin Raina, Capital will show a balance of $50,000, which is the amount Kristin Raina originally invested in the company.

already created; you must let QuickBooks create the account for the software to identify it as a system default account.

To illustrate how QuickBooks creates its own system default accounts, you will first add an account to the Chart of Accounts List and then open some activity windows and the Item List. You will see that QuickBooks cannot locate the account you created and some accounts created in QuickBooks Desktop Setup and that it creates its own accounts.

To add a new account:

1. Click Lists and then click *Chart of Accounts*.
2. At the Chart of Accounts window, click the Account menu button and then click *New*. The Add New Account: Choose Account Type window appears.
3. Click *Other Account Types*. The drop-down list appears. See Figure 6–HH.

FIGURE 6–HH

Add New Account:
Choose Account Type
Window

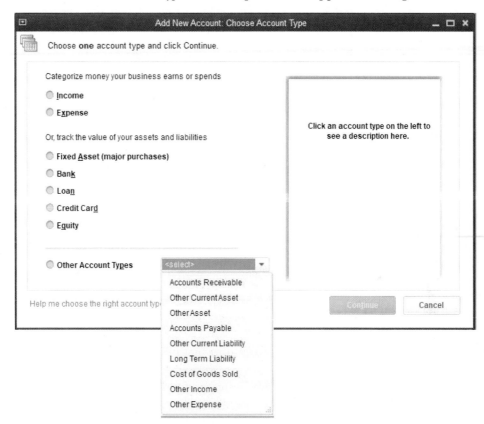

4. At the Other Account Types drop-down list, click *Other Current Asset*.
5. Click Continue. The Add New Account window appears.
6. At the *Number* field, type 1250.
7. At the *Account Name* field, type Undeposited Funds. See Figure 6–II.

FIGURE 6–II
Add New Account
Window—Completed

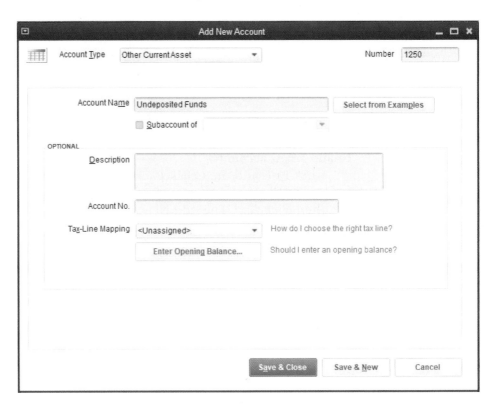

8. If the information is correct, click Save & Close. The Undeposited Funds account is added to the Chart of Accounts List.
9. Close the Chart of Accounts List window.

To allow QuickBooks to create system default accounts:
1. At the main menu bar, click Customers and then click *Create Invoices*. Close the Create Invoices window.
2. At the main menu bar, click Customers and then click *Enter Sales Receipts*. Close the Enter Sales Receipts window.
3. At the main menu bar, click Vendors and then click *Enter Bills*. Close the window.
4. At the main menu bar, click Lists and then click *Item List*.
5. At the Item List window, click the Item menu button.
6. At the Item button drop-down menu, click *New*.
7. At the New Item window, at the *TYPE* field, click *Inventory Part*.
8. Close the New Item window. If a Save or Name cannot be blank message appears, click No. Close the Item List.

As you opened each window, QuickBooks looked for certain system default accounts; when they could not be identified, QuickBooks created new system default accounts. Review the Chart of Accounts List and observe that QuickBooks created the following accounts, as shown in Figure 6–JJ: 12000 *Undeposited Funds, 12100 *Inventory Asset, and 50000 *Cost of Goods Sold.

FIGURE 6–JJ
Chart of Accounts
List—Additional System
Default Accounts Created
by QuickBooks

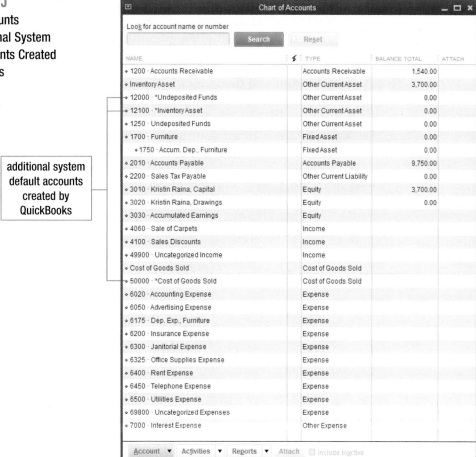

additional system default accounts created by QuickBooks

NAME	⚡	TYPE	BALANCE TOTAL	ATTACH
◦ 1200 · Accounts Receivable		Accounts Receivable	1,540.00	
◦ Inventory Asset		Other Current Asset	3,700.00	
◦ 12000 · *Undeposited Funds		Other Current Asset	0.00	
◦ 12100 · *Inventory Asset		Other Current Asset	0.00	
◦ 1250 · Undeposited Funds		Other Current Asset	0.00	
◦ 1700 · Furniture		Fixed Asset	0.00	
◦ 1750 · Accum. Dep., Furniture		Fixed Asset	0.00	
◦ 2010 · Accounts Payable		Accounts Payable	9,750.00	
◦ 2200 · Sales Tax Payable		Other Current Liability	0.00	
◦ 3010 · Kristin Raina, Capital		Equity	3,700.00	
◦ 3020 · Kristin Raina, Drawings		Equity	0.00	
◦ 3030 · Accumulated Earnings		Equity		
◦ 4060 · Sale of Carpets		Income		
◦ 4100 · Sales Discounts		Income		
◦ 49900 · Uncategorized Income		Income		
◦ Cost of Goods Sold		Cost of Goods Sold		
◦ 50000 · *Cost of Goods Sold		Cost of Goods Sold		
◦ 6020 · Accounting Expense		Expense		
◦ 6050 · Advertising Expense		Expense		
◦ 6175 · Dep. Exp., Furniture		Expense		
◦ 6200 · Insurance Expense		Expense		
◦ 6300 · Janitorial Expense		Expense		
◦ 6325 · Office Supplies Expense		Expense		
◦ 6400 · Rent Expense		Expense		
◦ 6450 · Telephone Expense		Expense		
◦ 6500 · Utilities Expense		Expense		
◦ 69800 · Uncategorized Expenses		Expense		
◦ 7000 · Interest Expense		Other Expense		

When you opened the Create Invoices window, QuickBooks looked for the Accounts Receivable account and was able to locate it because of the accounts receivable account type in that account. Similarly, when you opened the Enter Bills window, QuickBooks looked for the Accounts Payable account and was able to locate it because of the accounts payable account type.

But when you opened the Enter Sales Receipts window, QuickBooks looked for an Undeposited Funds account; even though you created this account, QuickBooks could not locate it and created the new account 12000 *Undeposited Funds. Likewise, when you chose the new inventory part type in the Item List, QuickBooks looked for an inventory asset account and cost of goods sold account. Even though an Inventory Asset account and Cost of Goods Sold account were created when you entered inventory part items in the QuickBooks Desktop Setup window, QuickBooks did not identify these accounts as system default accounts and therefore did not locate them; thus, it created a new account 12100 *Inventory Asset account and a new account 50000 *Cost of Goods Sold. In situations like these, you must allow QuickBooks to create its own accounts; then you can edit them to your liking. In all cases, the system default accounts created by QuickBooks will have dimmed account types; you cannot change the account types, but you can change the account numbers and account names.

Before you can edit the accounts that QuickBooks created, delete the 1250 Undeposited Funds account that you created. This account name and number can then be used when editing the accounts created by QuickBooks.

To delete an account and then edit the accounts created by QuickBooks:
1. At the main menu bar, click Lists and then click *Chart of Accounts.*
2. At the Chart of Accounts window, select *1250 Undeposited Funds.*
3. Click the Account menu button and then click *Delete Account.*
4. At the warning, click OK.

   At this time, you cannot delete the Inventory Asset account and Cost of Goods Sold account (the accounts without numbers) created in QuickBooks Desktop Setup because they are used in the Item List and in the *Journal* report. In the upcoming section on updating the Item List with the updated Chart of Accounts, you will be able to delete these two duplicated accounts.
5. Edit the accounts created by QuickBooks, noting that the account types are dimmed:

QuickBooks		Edited	
Number	Account Name	Number	Account Name
12000	*Undeposited Funds	1250	Undeposited Funds
12100	*Inventory Asset	1260	Inventory of Carpets
50000	*Cost of Goods Sold	5060	Cost of Carpets Sold

   After QuickBooks creates an Inventory account and a Cost of Goods Sold account, you can create as many additional inventory and cost of goods sold accounts as desired. You will do this in the upcoming section "Updating the Chart of Accounts List."
6. Close the Chart of Accounts List window.

Customizing Payment Terms

In QuickBooks, a list with payment terms is accessed in customer files, vendor files, and activities windows when needed. As shown in prior chapters, payment terms such as Net 30 Days and 2/10, Net 30 Days can be identified in both the customer and vendor files if they relate to a particular customer or vendor.

When you create a new company file, QuickBooks automatically creates a list of payment terms. As with all other Lists in QuickBooks, you can add, delete, or edit the Terms List to customize it for your company.

To add a payment term:
1. At the main menu bar, click Lists and then click *Customer & Vendor Profile Lists.*
2. At the Customer & Vendor Profile Lists submenu, click *Terms List.* The Terms List window appears with the terms of payment that were created by QuickBooks. See Figure 6–KK.

FIGURE 6–KK

Terms List Created by
QuickBooks

3. At the Terms List window, click the Terms menu button.
4. At the Terms menu, click *New.* The New Terms window appears.
5. At the *Terms* field, type Net 10 Days.
6. At the *Net due in days* field, type 10. See Figure 6–LL.

FIGURE 6–LL

New Terms Window—
Net 10 Days—Completed

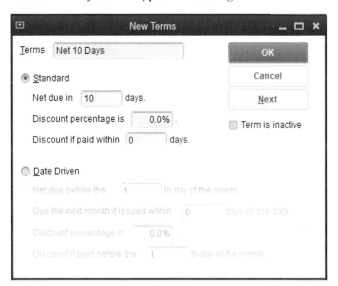

7. If the information is correct, click OK.

To delete a payment term:
1. At the Terms List, select *1% 10 Net 30,* but do not open it.
2. Click the Terms menu button. At the Terms menu, click *Delete Terms.*
3. A Delete Terms warning screen appears. Click OK. The payment term
   is deleted.
4. Delete the following terms of payment:
      Consignment
      Due on receipt
      Net 60

FIGURE 6–OO
Chart of Accounts List—
Updated

If you incorrectly labeled
an account as a parent
account or subaccount,
you can edit the account
or move the entry. To
move the entry, click
the diamond to the left
of the account number.
If you drag the diamond
to the left, a subac-
count becomes a parent
account. If you drag the
diamond to the right, a
parent account becomes
a subaccount. You can
also click and drag up
or down to reorganize
the list.

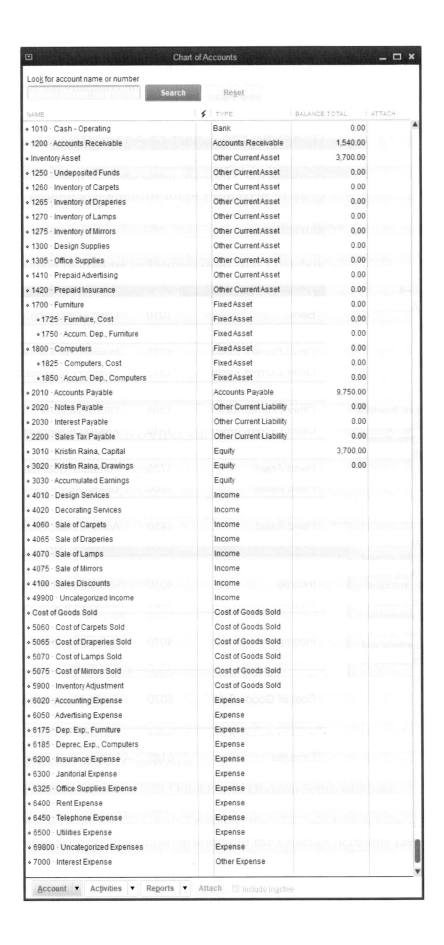

NAME	TYPE	BALANCE TOTAL	ATTACH
1010 · Cash - Operating	Bank	0.00	
1200 · Accounts Receivable	Accounts Receivable	1,540.00	
Inventory Asset	Other Current Asset	3,700.00	
1250 · Undeposited Funds	Other Current Asset	0.00	
1260 · Inventory of Carpets	Other Current Asset	0.00	
1265 · Inventory of Draperies	Other Current Asset	0.00	
1270 · Inventory of Lamps	Other Current Asset	0.00	
1275 · Inventory of Mirrors	Other Current Asset	0.00	
1300 · Design Supplies	Other Current Asset	0.00	
1305 · Office Supplies	Other Current Asset	0.00	
1410 · Prepaid Advertising	Other Current Asset	0.00	
1420 · Prepaid Insurance	Other Current Asset	0.00	
1700 · Furniture	Fixed Asset	0.00	
1725 · Furniture, Cost	Fixed Asset	0.00	
1750 · Accum. Dep., Furniture	Fixed Asset	0.00	
1800 · Computers	Fixed Asset	0.00	
1825 · Computers, Cost	Fixed Asset	0.00	
1850 · Accum. Dep., Computers	Fixed Asset	0.00	
2010 · Accounts Payable	Accounts Payable	9,750.00	
2020 · Notes Payable	Other Current Liability	0.00	
2030 · Interest Payable	Other Current Liability	0.00	
2200 · Sales Tax Payable	Other Current Liability	0.00	
3010 · Kristin Raina, Capital	Equity	3,700.00	
3020 · Kristin Raina, Drawings	Equity	0.00	
3030 · Accumulated Earnings	Equity		
4010 · Design Services	Income		
4020 · Decorating Services	Income		
4060 · Sale of Carpets	Income		
4065 · Sale of Draperies	Income		
4070 · Sale of Lamps	Income		
4075 · Sale of Mirrors	Income		
4100 · Sales Discounts	Income		
49900 · Uncategorized Income	Income		
Cost of Goods Sold	Cost of Goods Sold		
5060 · Cost of Carpets Sold	Cost of Goods Sold		
5065 · Cost of Draperies Sold	Cost of Goods Sold		
5070 · Cost of Lamps Sold	Cost of Goods Sold		
5075 · Cost of Mirrors Sold	Cost of Goods Sold		
5900 · Inventory Adjustment	Cost of Goods Sold		
6020 · Accounting Expense	Expense		
6050 · Advertising Expense	Expense		
6175 · Dep. Exp., Furniture	Expense		
6185 · Deprec. Exp., Computers	Expense		
6200 · Insurance Expense	Expense		
6300 · Janitorial Expense	Expense		
6325 · Office Supplies Expense	Expense		
6400 · Rent Expense	Expense		
6450 · Telephone Expense	Expense		
6500 · Utilities Expense	Expense		
69800 · Uncategorized Expenses	Expense		
7000 · Interest Expense	Other Expense		

Updating the Item List

In QuickBooks, the Item List stores information about the service items, the inventory part items, and the sales tax. As each transaction is recorded in an Activity window, QuickBooks uses information in the Item List to record the transaction in the correct accounts.

Open and review the Item List. In the EasyStep Interview, when you responded *Yes* to the question of whether sales tax is used, QuickBooks created a sales tax item. In the QuickBooks Desktop Setup, service and inventory part items were added on the Add products and services you sell pages. As this information was entered in the EasyStep Interview and QuickBooks Desktop Setup windows, QuickBooks recorded the information in the Item List. Earlier in the chapter, you reviewed the Item List (Figure 6–Q, page 208) and saw that for the service items and inventory part items (Figure 6–R and Figure 6–S, page 209), QuickBooks used the same Sales Income account as the income account for each item. In addition, for each inventory part item (Figure 6–S), QuickBooks used the same Cost of Goods Sold account and Inventory Asset account. When customizing the system default accounts, some of the account names and numbers were changed. *Sales Income* was changed to *4060 Sale of Carpets*, *12100 Inventory Asset* was changed to *1260 Inventory of Carpets*, and *50000 Cost of Goods Sold* was changed to *5060 Cost of Carpets Sold*. In addition, when updating the Chart of Accounts List, you added additional inventory accounts, income accounts, and cost of goods sold accounts. When you changed the account names and numbers of the system default accounts, these changes flowed into the Item List. You will now edit the service items and inventory part items to reflect the accounts used by Kristin Raina Interior Designs.

When you entered each service item and inventory part item in the QuickBooks Desktop Setup window, you were not allowed to indicate if the item was taxable or nontaxable. When you edit each service and inventory part item for the correct accounts, you will also indicate if the item is taxable or nontaxable. In addition, the sales tax item (see Figure 6–T on page 210) does not have the necessary information for Kristin Raina Interior Designs sales tax and must be edited.

To edit a service item:
1. At the main menu bar, click Lists and then click *Item List*.
2. At the Item List window, double-click the *Decorating Services* service item. The Edit Item window appears.
3. At the *Tax Code* field, click *Non Non-Taxable Sales*.
4. At the *Account* field, click *4020 Decorating Services*. See Figure 6–PP.

FIGURE 6–PP
Edit Item Window—
Service—Completed

5. If the information is correct, click OK. At the warning, click Yes.
6. Double-click the *Design Services* service item.
7. At the *Tax Code* field, click *Non Non-Taxable*, and at the *Account* field, click *4010 Design Services.*
8. Click OK, and then at the warning, click Yes.

To edit an inventory part item:
1. At the Item List window, double-click the *Carpets* inventory part item. The Edit Item window appears.
2. At the *COGS Account* field, click *5060 Cost of Carpets Sold.*
3. At the *Tax Code* field, click *Tax Taxable Sales.*
4. At the *Income Account* field, click *4060 Sale of Carpets*, if necessary.
5. At the *Asset Account* field, click *1260 Inventory of Carpets.* See Figure 6–QQ.

FIGURE 6–QQ
Edit Item Window—
Inventory Part—
Completed

HINT

If a warning appears about the minimum quantity, click OK at the warning and then delete the zero in the *Reorder Point (min)* field.

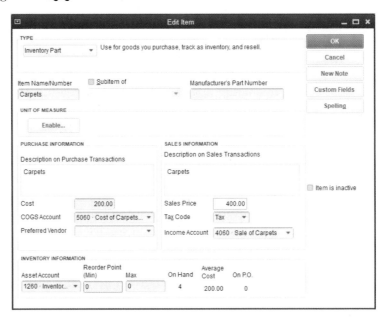

6. If the information is correct, click OK. At the warning, click Yes.
7. Using the information in Table 6–5, update the remainder of the inventory part items. All inventory part items are taxable.

TABLE 6–5
Update Inventory
Part Items

Inventory Part Item	COGS Account	Income Account	Asset Account
Draperies	5065	4065	1265
Lamps	5070	4070	1270
Mirrors	5075	4075	1275

After the updating of the accounts for the inventory part items has been completed, the Inventory Asset account and Cost of Goods Sold account (the accounts without numbers) can be deleted from the Chart of Accounts List. Accounts 1260 Inventory of Carpets and 5060 Cost of Carpets Sold are the system default accounts created by QuickBooks, as indicated by the dimmed account types. Inventory accounts and cost of goods sold accounts can be added or deleted, since QuickBooks will always find the two system default accounts.

To edit the sales tax item:

1. Double-click the *Sales Tax* item. The Edit Item window appears.
2. At the *Sales Tax Name* field, delete the text *Out of State* and type Minn. Sales Tax.
3. At the *Description* field, delete the description and type Sales Tax.
4. At the *Tax Rate (%)* field, type 7.
5. At the Tax Agency drop-down list, click *Minn. Dept. of Revenue.* The Edit Item window is complete. See Figure 6–RR.

FIGURE 6–RR

Edit Item Window—Sales Tax Item—Completed

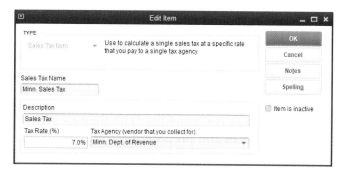

6. If the information is correct, click OK.

   The updated Item List appears in Figure 6–SS. Compare it with the list shown in Figure 6–Q on page 208.

FIGURE 6–SS

Item List—Updated

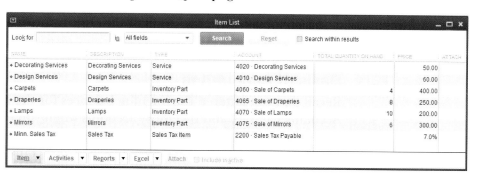

7. Close the Item List window.

ACCOUNTING CONCEPT

1260 Inventory of Carpets		1265 Inventory of Draperies		3010 Kristin Raina, Capital	
Dr	Cr	Dr	Cr	Dr	Cr
800		1,000			800

1270 Inventory of Lamps		1275 Inventory of Mirrors			
					1,000
					1,000
Dr	Cr	Dr	Cr		900
1,000		900			

...continued

Number	Account Name	Balance
2030	Interest Payable	50.00
4010	Design Services	4,980.00
4020	Decorating Services	3,400.00
4060	Sale of Carpets	2,400.00
4065	Sale of Draperies	1,000.00
4070	Sale of Lamps	1,200.00
4075	Sale of Mirrors	900.00

QuickCheck: $54,510.00

7. Record the credit balance of $54,510.00 as a credit to account 3010 Kristin Raina, Capital. See Figure 6–TT.

FIGURE 6–TT
Make General Journal
Entries Window—
Opening Balances

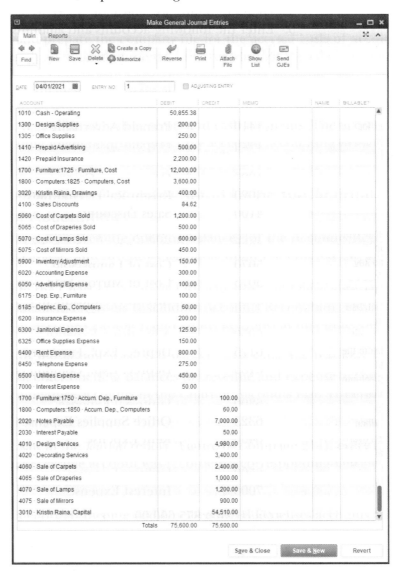

HINT

If the Future Transactions message appears, click Yes. To change this preference, click Edit at the main menu bar and then click *Preferences*. In the left panel of the Preferences window, click the Accounting icon. Choose the Company Preferences tab. Remove the check marks in the warning options and then click OK.

8. If the information is correct, click the Save & New button. If a message appears about Tracking fixed assets, insert a check mark in the box to the left of *Do not display this message in the future* and then click OK.

The effects of recording the opening balances are as follows:

1010-1825 Assets		
Dr		**Cr**
Cash - Operating	50,855.38	
Design Supplies	200.00	
Office Supplies	250.00	
Prepaid Advertising	500.00	
Prepaid Insurance	2,200.00	
Furniture	12,000.00	
Computers	3,600.00	
	69,605.38	

1750-1850 Accum Dep	
Dr	**Cr**
	100.00
	60.00
	160.00

2020-2030 Payables		
Dr	**Cr**	
	7,000.00	Notes
	50.00	Interest
	7,050.00	

3010 Kristin Raina, Capital	
Dr	**Cr**
	54,510.00

3020 Kristin Raina, Drawings	
Dr	**Cr**
400.00	

4010-4020 Service Revenue		
Dr	**Cr**	
	Design	4,980.00
	Decor	3,400.00
		8,380.00

4060-4075 Sale of Inventory		
Dr	**Cr**	
	Carpets	2,400.00
	Draperies	1,000.00
	Lamps	1,200.00
	Mirrors	900.00
		5,500.00

4100 Sales Discounts	
Dr	**Cr**
84.62	

5060-5075,5900 Cost of Goods Sold		
Dr		**Cr**
Carpets	1,200.00	
Draperies	500.00	
Lamps	600.00	
Mirrors	450.00	
Invent Adj	150.00	
	2,900.00	

6020-6500 Expenses		
Dr		**Cr**
Accounting	300.00	
Advertising	100.00	
Dep Exp, Furniture	100.00	
Dep Exp, Computers	60.00	
Insurance	200.00	
Janitorial	125.00	
Office Supplies	150.00	
Rent	800.00	
Telephone	275.00	
Utilities	450.00	
	2,560.00	

7000 Interest Exp	
Dr	**Cr**
50.00	

Reversing the Uncategorized Income Account

Recall that in the *Journal* report in Figure 6–Y on page 214, two journal entries are recorded that debit Accounts Receivable and credit Uncategorized Income for two customers as follows:

Berger Bakery Company	$ 600
Franco Films Co.	940
	$1,540

The debit entries to the Accounts Receivable account are correct and will stay in that account. The credits to the Uncategorized Income account will be reversed by debiting Uncategorized Income for the total of $1,540 and crediting the account 3010 Kristin Raina, Capital (formerly the Opening Balance Equity account) for $1,540.

HINT

As part of customizing the Chart of Accounts, the account Opening Balance Equity, created by QuickBooks, was renamed *3010 Kristin Raina, Capital.*

To reverse the Uncategorized Income account:
1. At the Make General Journal Entries window, choose the date *04/01/2021*, and at the *ENTRY NO.* field, accept *2*.
2. Remove the check mark next to *ADJUSTING ENTRY*, if necessary.
3. Debit account 49900 Uncategorized Income for 1,540 and credit account 3010 Kristin Raina, Capital, for 1,540. See Figure 6–UU.

FIGURE 6–UU
Make General Journal
Entries Window—
Reverse Uncategorized
Income

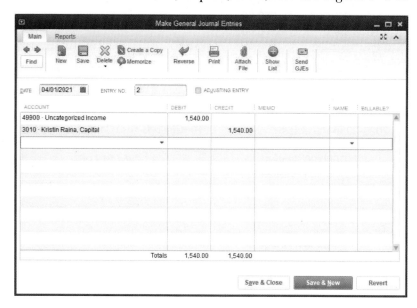

4. If the information is correct, click the Save & New button.

ACCOUNTING CONCEPT

49900 Uncategorized Income		3010 Kristin Raina, Capital	
Dr	Cr	Dr	Cr
Rev 1,540	1,540		1,540
	0		

Reversing the Uncategorized Expenses Account

In the *Journal* report shown in Figure 6–Y on page 214, there are seven journal entries that credit Accounts Payable and debit Uncategorized Expenses for seven vendor balances as follows:

Ace Glass Works	$1,500
Bell Carpet Design	2,000
Cuza and Carl Associates	400
Galeway Computers	2,600
Midwest Mutual Insurance Co.	2,400
Minneapolis Electric & Gas Co.	450
Williams Office Supply Company	400
	$9,750

The credit entries to the Accounts Payable account are correct and will stay in that account. The debits to the Uncategorized Expenses, however, have to be reversed by crediting Uncategorized Expenses for the total of $9,750 and debiting the 3010 Kristin Raina, Capital, account for $9,750.

To reverse the Uncategorized Expenses account:

1. At the Make General Journal Entries window, choose the date *04/01/2021*, and at the *ENTRY NO.* field, accept *3*.
2. Remove the check mark next to *ADJUSTING ENTRY*, if necessary.
3. Debit account 3010 Kristin Raina, Capital, for 9,750 and credit account 69800 Uncategorized Expenses for 9,750. See Figure 6–VV.

FIGURE 6–VV
Make General Journal Entries Window—Reverse Uncategorized Expenses

4. If the information is correct, click the Save & Close button.

ACCOUNTING CONCEPT

69800 Uncategorized Expenses		3010 Kristin Raina, Capital	
Dr	Cr	Dr	Cr
9,750	Rev 9,750	9,750	
0			

Reports

Accounting Reports and Financial Statements

Upon completing the New Company Setup, you should display and print the accounting reports and financial statements.

Accounting Reports

HINT

To display only the last three journal entries in the *Journal* report, click the Customize Report button and then click the Filters tab. In the *FILTER* field, click *Transaction Type*. In the *Transaction Type* field, click *Journal* and then click OK.

The accounting reports you need to print and review consist of the *Journal* and the *Trial Balance*.

Journal Report

You displayed and printed the *Journal* report after the EasyStep Interview and QuickBooks Desktop Setup windows were completed (Figure 6–Y on page 214). After recording the opening balances and reversing the Uncategorized Income and Uncategorized Expenses accounts, you added three more journal entries to the *Journal* report. View and print all the journal entries for April 1, 2021. The total debits and credits is $101,880. Figure 6–WW displays only the additional three journal entries.

FIGURE 6–WW Additional Journal Entries

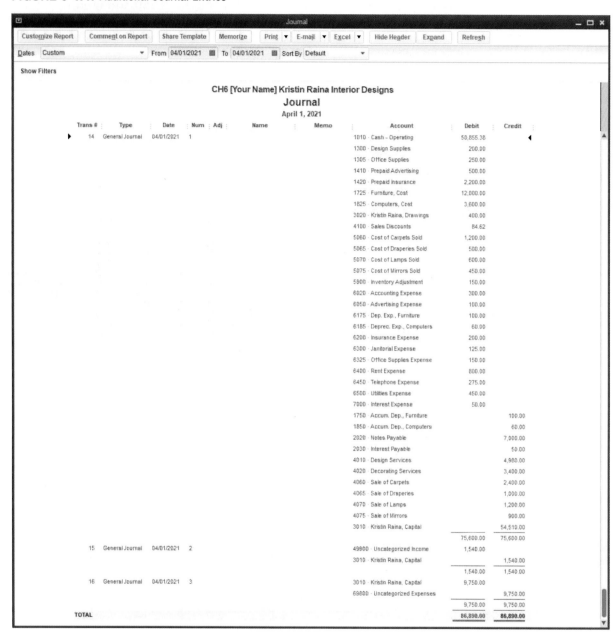

Trial Balance Report

Next, view and print the *Trial Balance* report for April 1, 2021. See Figure 6–XX.

FIGURE 6–XX Trial Balance Report

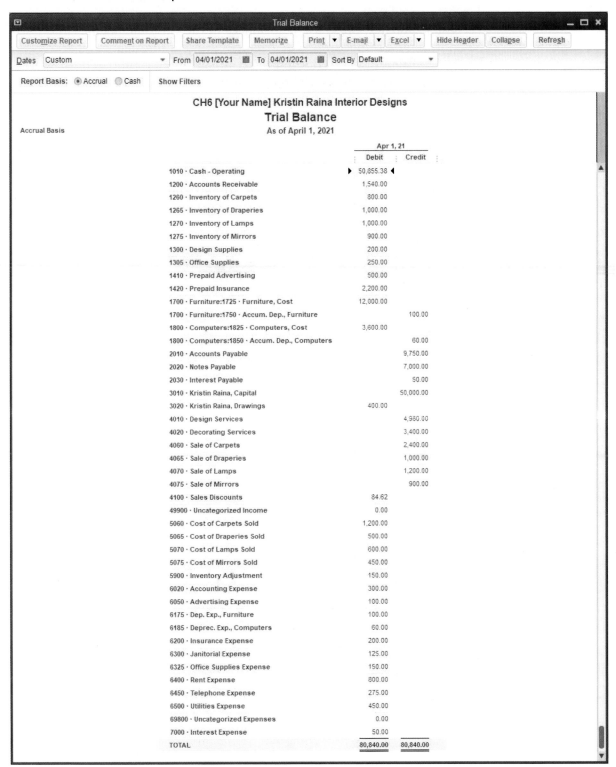

The accounts and balances on this trial balance should match the trial balance of March 31, 2021 (Figure 6–AA on page 216), after transactions were recorded in Chapters 2 through 5.

Recall that QuickBooks created the Uncategorized Income and Uncategorized Expenses accounts when you entered outstanding accounts receivable and accounts payable balances in the Customer Center and Vendor Center, respectively. The balances in these uncategorized accounts were subsequently reversed when the company file was prepared for the accrual basis of accounting. These accounts are no longer needed and can be marked inactive in the Chart of Accounts List.

Financial Statements

The financial statements consist of the *Profit & Loss Standard* report (see Figure 6–YY) and the *Balance Sheet Standard* report (see Figure 6–ZZ). Upon completion of the New Company Setup, these reports should be the same as the financial statements printed at the end of Chapter 5.

FIGURE 6–YY Profit & Loss Standard Report

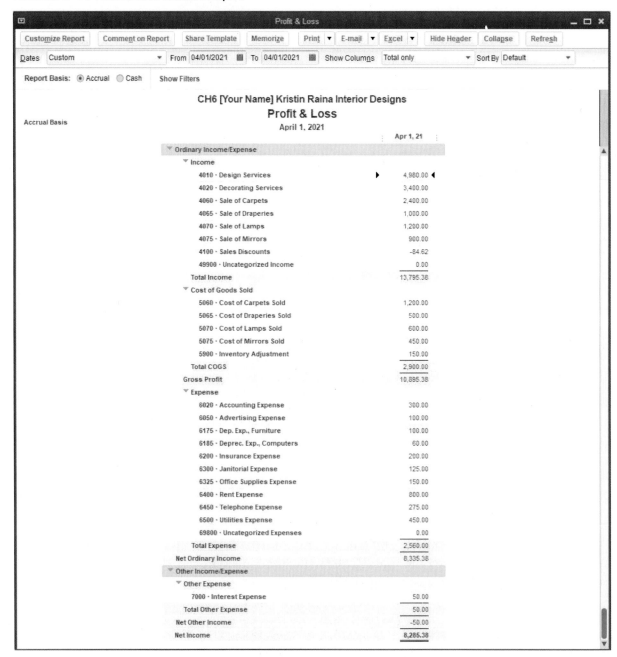

FIGURE 6–ZZ
Balance Sheet Standard Report

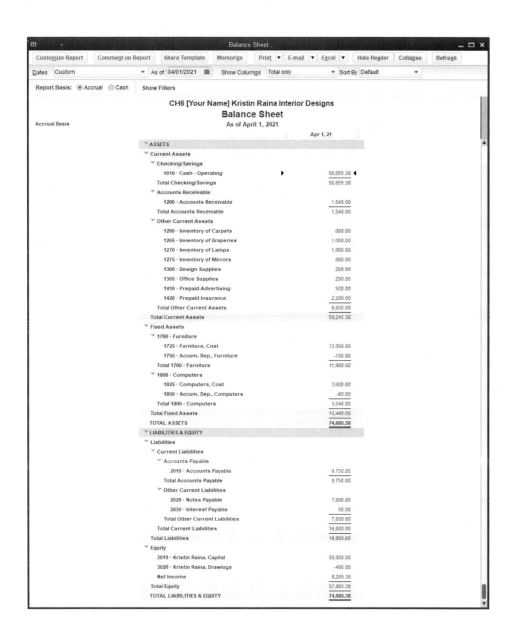

Backing Up the New Company File and Exiting QuickBooks

You should make a backup copy of the new company file in the event there is damage to the file or the computer or you work on a different computer at some point. Using the procedures learned in previous chapters, make a backup copy of the new company file to your subfolder and/or a removable storage device and name it **EX6** *[Your Name]* **Kristin Raina Interior Designs**. Restore the backup copy and change the company name to **EX6** *[Your Name]* **Kristin Raina Interior Designs**.

Upon completing the New Company Setup level of operation, customizing and updating the Lists/Centers, recording the appropriate journal entries, viewing and printing Reports, and making a backup copy of the new company file, your accounting records are now ready for recording daily activities. Activities should be recorded in the new company file using the procedures illustrated in prior chapters.

Close the company file and then exit QuickBooks.

Chapter Review and Assessment

Procedure Review

To begin the New Company Setup and create a new company file using the Detailed Start method and the EasyStep Interview window:

1. Open QuickBooks.
2. At the No Company Open window, click *Create a new company*, or click File and then click *New Company*. The QuickBooks Desktop Setup window appears with the Let's get your business set up quickly! page displayed. This is the page where you select the method of New Company Setup.
3. At the QuickBooks Desktop Setup window, at the Let's get your business set up quickly! page, click the Detailed Start button. The EasyStep Interview window appears.
4. At the EasyStep Interview window, read and complete each page. Click Next after completing each page.
5. At the Congratulations! window, click Go to Setup. Continue the New Company Setup using the QuickBooks Desktop Setup window, or exit the QuickBooks Desktop Setup window and go directly into the new company file.

To leave the EasyStep Interview window:

1. Click the Leave button.
2. Click OK at the EasyStep Interview message.
   You should not leave the EasyStep Interview window until the new company file has been saved.

To reenter the EasyStep Interview window:

1. At the No Company Open window, click *Open or Restore an existing company* or click File and then click *Open Company*.
2. Open the new company file.
3. Enter the password at the QuickBooks Desktop Login window.
4. Click OK at the QuickBooks Desktop Information message.
   When you open the company file, you are returned to the page you used last.

To enter the QuickBooks Desktop Setup window:

1. At the main menu bar, click Company and then click *Bulk Enter Business Details*.

To add customers to the Customer Center using the QuickBooks Desktop Setup window:

1. At the QuickBooks Desktop Setup window, at the Get all the details into QuickBooks Desktop page, in the Add the people you do business with section, click the Add button.
2. At the next Add the people you do business with page, click the Paste from Excel or enter manually button and then click Continue.
3. At the next Add the people you do business with page, in the *Customer* column, click *Select all* to fill in all the circles in the *Customer* column.
4. Enter the information for the customers in the appropriate columns.
5. After entering all the customer information, click Continue.

6. At the next Add the people you do business with page, click the *Enter opening balances* link.

7. At the Enter opening balances for customers and vendors page, enter the balances for the customers and enter the correct date.

8. Click Continue. You are returned to the Add the people you do business with page.

9. Click Continue. If you do not click Continue, the customers and opening balances will not be saved. You are returned to the QuickBooks Desktop Setup window—Get all the details into QuickBooks Desktop page.

10. Click Add More to enter additional customers, vendors, or items, or close the QuickBooks Desktop Setup window.

To add vendors to the Vendor Center using the QuickBooks Desktop Setup window:

1. At the QuickBooks Desktop Setup window, at the Get all the details into QuickBooks Desktop page, in the Add the people you do business with section, click the Add or Add More button.

2. At the next Add the people you do business with page, click the Paste from Excel or enter manually button and then click Continue.

3. At the next Add the people you do business with page, in the *Vendor* column, click *Select all* to fill in all the circles in the *Vendor* column.

4. Enter the information for the vendors in the appropriate columns.

5. After entering all the vendor information, click Continue.

6. At the next Add the people you do business with page, click the *Enter opening balances* link.

7. At the Enter opening balances for customers and vendors page, enter the balances for the vendors and enter the correct date.

8. Click Continue. You are returned to the Add the people you do business with page.

9. Click Continue. If you do not click Continue, the vendors and opening balances will not be saved. You are returned to the QuickBooks Desktop Setup window—Get all the details into QuickBooks Desktop page.

10. Click Add More to enter additional vendors, customers, or items, or close the QuickBooks Desktop Setup window.

To add service items to the Item List using the QuickBooks Desktop Setup window:

1. At the QuickBooks Desktop Setup window, at the Get all the details into QuickBooks Desktop page, in the Add the products and services you sell section, click the Add button.

2. At the Add the products and services you sell page, click the Service button and then click Continue.

3. Enter the information for the service items in the appropriate columns.

4. After entering all the service items information, click Continue. You are returned to the Add the products and services you sell page.

5. Click Continue. If you do not click Continue, the service items will not be saved. You are returned to the QuickBooks Desktop Setup window—Get all the details into QuickBooks Desktop page.

6. Click Add More to enter additional items, customers, or vendors, or close the QuickBooks Desktop Setup window.

To add inventory part items to the Item List using QuickBooks Desktop Setup:

1. At the QuickBooks Desktop Setup window, at the Get all the details into QuickBooks Desktop page, in the Add the products and services you sell section, click the Add or Add More button.
2. At the Add the products and services you sell page, click the Inventory part button and then click Continue.
3. Enter the information for the inventory part items in the appropriate columns and choose the correct date.
4. After entering all the inventory part items information, click Continue. You are returned to the Add the products and services you sell page.
5. Click Continue. If you do not click Continue, the inventory part items and opening balances will not be saved. You are returned to the QuickBooks Desktop Setup window—Get all the details into QuickBooks Desktop page.
6. Click Add More to enter additional items, customers, or vendors, or close the QuickBooks Desktop Setup window.

To correct an error in the *Journal* report:

1. In the *Journal* report, double-click the transaction with the error. The Invoice type will bring you to the Create Invoices window. The Bill type will bring you to the Enter Bills window. The Inventory Adjust type will bring you to the Adjust Quantity/Value on Hand window.
2. Make the correction in the appropriate window and then click Save & Close.
3. At the warning, click Yes.

To activate the account numbers feature:

1. At the main menu bar, click Edit and then click *Preferences*.
2. In the left panel of the Preferences window, click the Accounting icon.
3. Click the Company Preferences tab.
4. In the ACCOUNTS section, insert a check mark in the box to the left of *Use account numbers* to turn on the account numbers feature.
5. Click OK.

To customize the accounts on the Chart of Accounts List created in the EasyStep Interview and QuickBooks Desktop Setup windows and change account numbers and names:

1. At the main menu bar, click Lists and then click *Chart of Accounts*.
2. Select the account to edit.
3. Click the Account menu button.
4. At the Account button drop-down menu, click *Edit Account*.
5. Make any necessary changes to the account and then click Save & Close.

To allow QuickBooks to create system default accounts:
1. Open and close Activities windows, such as the Create Invoices, Enter Sales Receipts, and Enter Bills windows. Also open the Item List and the New Item window and then select *Inventory Part.*

   This process creates the system default accounts Undeposited Funds, Inventory Asset, and Cost of Goods Sold. After QuickBooks creates these accounts, you can edit each account number and name. If you created an accounts receivable–type account and an accounts payable–type account, QuickBooks will accept the accounts. If you did not previously create them, when you open and close the Create Invoices and Enter Bills windows, QuickBooks will create the accounts receivable and accounts payable accounts, respectively.
2. Follow the steps to customize the Chart of Accounts List and to customize the numbers and names of the system default accounts created by QuickBooks.

To customize the payment terms created in the EasyStep window:
1. At the main menu bar, click Lists and then click *Customer & Vendor Profile Lists.*
2. At the Customer & Vendor Profile Lists submenu, click *Terms List.*
3. At the Terms List window, click the Terms menu button.
4. At the Terms button drop-down menu, click *New.*
5. At the New Terms window, type the appropriate information for any terms QuickBooks did not create that you wish to create.
6. Click Next or OK.
7. At the Terms List window, select the terms created by QuickBooks that you wish to delete.
8. Click the Terms menu button and then click *Delete Terms.* Click OK at the warning.
9. At the Terms List window, select the terms created by QuickBooks that you wish to edit.
10. Click the Terms menu button and then click *Edit Terms.*
11. Change the appropriate information and then click OK.

To update the Chart of Accounts List:
1. At the main menu bar, click Lists and then click *Chart of Accounts.*
2. Click the Account menu button.
3. At the Account button drop-down menu, click *New.*
4. At the Add New Account: Choose Account Type window, choose the type and then click Continue.
5. At the Add New Account window, type in the information and then click Save & New or Save & Close.

To edit the Item List for service items created in the QuickBooks Desktop Setup window:
1. At the main menu bar, click Lists and then click *Item List.*
2. At the Item List window, double-click the service item. The Edit Item window appears.
3. At the *Tax Code* field, click *Non Non-Taxable Sales.*
4. At the *Account* field, click the correct account.
5. If the information is correct, click OK.
6. At the warning, click Yes.

To edit an inventory part item created in the QuickBooks Desktop Setup window:

1. At the main menu bar, click Lists and then click *Item List*.
2. At the Item List window, double-click the inventory part item. The Edit Item window appears.
3. At the *COGS Account* field, click the correct account.
4. At the *Tax Code* field, click *Tax Taxable Sales*.
5. At the *Income Account* field, click the correct account.
6. At the *Asset Account* field, click the correct account.
7. If the information is correct, click OK.
8. At the warning, click Yes.

To edit the Item List for sales tax created in EasyStep Interview:

1. At the main menu bar, click Lists and then click *Item List*.
2. At the Item List window, double-click the sales tax item to display the Edit window for that item.
3. Review the sales tax information and make any necessary changes.
4. Click OK.

To enter opening balances in the Make General Journal Entries window:

1. At the main menu bar, click Company and then click *Make General Journal Entries*.
2. Choose the date and make or accept the entry in the *ENTRY NO.* field.
3. Remove the check mark next to *ADJUSTING ENTRY*.
4. Enter the accounts and amounts to be debited.
5. Enter the accounts and amounts to be credited.
6. Record the balancing amount as a credit (or debit) to the capital account.
7. Click the Save & Close button.

To reverse the Uncategorized Income account:

1. At the main menu bar, click Company and then click *Make General Journal Entries*.
2. Choose the date and check the entry in the *ENTRY NO.* field.
3. Remove the check mark next to *ADJUSTING ENTRY*.
4. Debit the Uncategorized Income account for the full amount in that account and credit the Capital account for the same amount.
5. Click the Save & Close button.

To reverse the Uncategorized Expenses account:

1. At the main menu bar, click Company and then click *Make General Journal Entries*.
2. Choose the date and check the entry in the *ENTRY NO.* field.
3. Remove the check mark next to *ADJUSTING ENTRY*.
4. Debit the Capital account for the full amount in the Uncategorized Expenses account and credit the Uncategorized Expenses account for the same amount.
5. Click the Save & Close button.

To view and print accounting reports from the Reports menu:

1. At the main menu bar, click Reports and then click *Accountant & Taxes*.
2. At the Accountant & Taxes submenu, choose a report.

3. Indicate the start and end dates for the report.
4. Print the report.
5. Close the report.

To view and print financial statements from the Reports menu:
1. At the main menu bar, click Reports and then click *Company & Financial.*
2. At the Company & Financial submenu, choose a financial report.
3. Indicate the start and end dates for the report.
4. Print the report.
5. Close the report.

Key Concepts

Select the letter of the item that best matches each definition.

a. System default accounts
b. EasyStep Interview
c. Account numbers
d. Uncategorized Expenses
e. Customizing the Chart of Accounts List
f. Inventory Asset and Cost of Goods Sold

g. Lists - Customer & Vendor Profile Lists - Terms
h. Uncategorized Income
i. Edit - Preferences
j. Dimmed account type

_____ 1. The way QuickBooks identifies system default accounts.
_____ 2. A feature in a company file to identify accounts; must be activated in the Preferences window.
_____ 3. Menu choice used to customize payment terms.
_____ 4. Window where a new company file is created when using the Detailed Start method of New Company Setup.
_____ 5. Account created by QuickBooks as an offsetting amount for Accounts Receivable.
_____ 6. Accounts created by QuickBooks to be used in the Activities windows and journal entries.
_____ 7. Menu choice used to make account numbers active.
_____ 8. Adding and editing account numbers and names.
_____ 9. Accounts created by QuickBooks as an offsetting amount of Accounts Payable.
_____ 10. System default accounts QuickBooks looks for when an inventory part item is set up.

Procedure Check

1. What is New Company Setup? What is one method of New Company Setup?
2. You have switched your company accounting records to QuickBooks using the EasyStep Interview window and QuickBooks Desktop Setup window. What would you do to customize the Chart of Accounts List created by QuickBooks?
3. How and why would you adjust the Uncategorized Income and Uncategorized Expenses accounts?

4. You are reviewing the new company file you created in QuickBooks using EasyStep Interview and QuickBooks Desktop Setup, and you notice that there are no balances in the revenue and expense accounts. Why is this, and how would you correct it?

5. You have created an Inventory account and a Cost of Goods Sold account, but every time you add a new inventory part item to the Item List, QuickBooks creates an Inventory Asset account and Cost of Goods Sold account. Why does this happen, and how can you correct it?

6. Your manager is just learning QuickBooks. She has asked you to explain EasyStep Interview and QuickBooks Desktop Setup. Provide the manager with a written explanation of the EasyStep Interview and QuickBooks Desktop Setup windows. Be sure to explain what is included in the EasyStep Interview window and QuickBooks Desktop Setup window, and describe the additional procedures necessary to complete the New Company Setup after completing the EasyStep Interview and QuickBooks Desktop Setup windows.

Case Problems

Demonstrate your knowledge of the QuickBooks features discussed in this chapter by completing the following case problems.

Case Problem 6–1

On April 1, 2021, Lynn Garcia began her business, Lynn's Music Studio. In the first month of business, Lynn set up the music studio, provided guitar and piano lessons, and recorded month-end activity. In May, the second month of business, Lynn started purchasing and selling inventory items of guitars, keyboards, music stands, and sheet music. In April and May, Lynn recorded the financial activities using a manual accounting system. On June 1, 2021, Lynn decides to switch her accounting method to QuickBooks. Lynn has organized the information about the company but has hired you to convert the accounting records to QuickBooks.

1. Use the following information to create the company file and record the information for the company using the Detailed Start method and the EasyStep Interview window. Where no specific information is given, accept the EasyStep Interview window default setting.

Company Name:	CH6 *[Your Name]* Lynn's Music Studio
Tax ID:	45-6123789
Address:	228 Pearl Street Scranton, PA 18501
Country:	U.S.
Phone:	570-555-0400
Fax:	570-555-0500
E-mail:	LYNN@ppi-edu.net
Industry:	General Product-based Business
Company:	Sole Proprietorship
Fiscal Year Start:	January
Password:	Student1

Save As:	CH6 *[Your Name]* Lynn's Music Studio
Sell:	Both services and products
Sales Tax:	Yes
Estimates:	No
Tracking Customer Orders:	No
Statements:	No
Invoices:	Yes
Progress Invoicing:	No
Bills You Owe:	Yes
Tracking Inventory:	Yes
Tracking Time:	No
Employees:	No
Start Tracking:	06/01/2021

Remove the check mark from each of the following accounts:
  Shipping and Delivery Income
  Freight and Shipping Costs
  Merchant Account Fees
  Product Samples Expense
  Purchases - Resale Items
  Advertising and Promotion
  Automobile Expense
  Bank Service Charges
  Computer and Internet Expenses
  Dues and Subscriptions
  Meals and Entertainment
  Postage and Delivery
  Professional Fees
  Repairs and Maintenance
  Travel Expense
  Ask My Accountant

Insert a check mark to the left of the following account:
  Sales Discounts

2. Use the information in Table LMS—Customers to create and update the Customer Center using the QuickBooks Desktop Setup window. Be sure to use the date *June 1, 2021.*

TABLE LMS Customers

Customer/Company Name	Name/Contact	Phone	Address/ City, State, Zip	Balance
Douglaston Senior Center	Herbie Richardson	570-555-7749	574 S Beech Street Scranton, PA 18506	$175.00
Highland School	Asst. Principal Office	570-555-6963	115 Forrest Street Waymart, PA 18472	
Jefferson High School	Music Department	570-555-9600	500 Apple Street Dunmore, PA 18512	

...continues

TABLE LMS Customers...*continued*

Customer/Company Name	Name/Contact	Phone	Address/ City, State, Zip	Balance
Mulligan Residence	Adam Smith	570-555-3325	299 Hickory Lane Scranton, PA 18504	$1,575.90
Musical Youth Group	Dana Thompson	570-555-6642	550 Marion Lane Scranton, PA 18504	
Patel Family	Ari Patel	570-555-1132	574 Kenwood Drive Dickson City, PA 18519	
Patterson Family	Jonathan Patterson	570-555-6321	650 Memory Lane Dickson City, PA 18519	
Schroeder Family	Betty Schroeder	570-555-1897	98 Belmont Rd. Carbondale, PA 18407	
Twin Lakes Elementary	Miss Brooks	570-555-4474	515 Hobson Street Honesdale, PA 18431	

3. Use the information in Table LMS—Vendors to create and update the Vendor Center using the QuickBooks Desktop Setup window. Be sure to use the date *June 1, 2021*.

TABLE LMS Vendors

Vendor/Company Name	Name/Contact	Phone	Address/ City, State, Zip	Balance
Computer Town	Customer Service	570-555-1500	1000 Carbondale Highway Scranton, PA 18502	$2,000.00
Katie's Keyboards	Katie Shea	570-555-7777	158 Clay Road Scranton, PA 18505	1,500.00
Lynn Garcia				
Melody Music Equipment	Melody Arhmand	570-555-1120	780 Roselyn Ave. Scranton, PA 18505	
Mills Family Furniture	Edna Mills	570-555-7144	150 Amelia Street Scranton, PA 18503	1,500.00
Music Instruments, Inc.	Matilda Molloy	570-555-9630	25 Monroe Ave. Scranton, PA 18505	
Mutual Insurance Company	Bob Maxwell	570-555-5600	1 Main Street Honesdale, PA 18431	1,200.00
PA Dept. of Revenue				
Paper, Clips, and More	Justin Daves	570-555-8558	157 Waymart Lane Waymart, PA 18472	350.00
Pioneer Phone	Customer Service	570-555-6000	1000 Route 6 Carbondale, PA 18407	
Steamtown Electric	Customer Service	570-555-2500	150 Vine Lane Scranton, PA 18501	
Strings, Sheets & Such	Manuela Perez	570-555-3636	250 Lincoln St. Scranton, PA 18505	
Tune Tones	Tony Tune	570-555-1111	500 Monroe Ave. Dunmore, PA 18512	
Viewhill Realty	Matt Snyder	570-555-1000	100 Commerce Blvd. Scranton, PA 18501	

4. Use the information in Table LMS—Items to update the Item List using the QuickBooks Desktop Setup window. Be sure to use the date *June 1, 2021*.

TABLE LMS
Items

Item Name and Description	Price	Cost	On Hand	Total Value
Service Items:				
Guitar Lessons	$ 30			
Piano Lessons	35			
Inventory Part Items:				
Guitars	100	$50	6	$ 300
Keyboards	150	75	17	1,275
Music Stands	40	20	17	340
Sheet Music	6	3	165	495

5. Activate the account numbers feature. Use the following information to customize the Chart of Accounts List:

	QuickBooks		Edited	
Number	Account Name	Number	Account Name	
15000	Furniture and Equipment	1700	Music Instruments	
17000	Accumulated Depreciation	1750	Accum. Dep., Music Instruments [Subaccount of 1700 Music Instruments]	
30800	Owners Draw	3020	Lynn Garcia, Drawings	
	Sales Income	4060	Sale of Guitars	
48300	Sales Discounts	4100		
62400	Depreciation Expenses	6075	Deprec. Exp., Music Instruments	
63300	Insurance Expense	6200		
63400	Interest Expense	7000	[Account Type: Other Expense]	
64900	Office Supplies	6325	Office Supplies Expense	
67100	Rent Expense	6400		
68100	Telephone Expense	6450		
68600	Utilities	6500	Utilities Expense	

6. Delete the following account:
   47900 Sales

7. Open and close the following windows to allow QuickBooks to create default accounts:
   Create Invoices
   Enter Sales Receipts
   Enter Bills
   Item List: New Item: Inventory Part

8. Customize the system default accounts:

	QuickBooks			Edited	
Number	Account Name		Number	Account Name	
11000	Accounts Receivable		1200		
12000	Undeposited Funds		1250		
12100	*Inventory Asset		1260	Inventory of Guitars	
20000	Accounts Payable		2010		
25500	Sales Tax Payable		2200		
30000	Opening Balance Equity		3010	Lynn Garcia, Capital	
32000	Owners Equity		3030	Accumulated Earnings	
50000	*Cost of Goods Sold		5060	Cost of Guitars Sold	

9. Customize the payment Terms List to list only the following:
   2/10, Net 30 Days
   Net 10 Days
   Net 15 Days
   Net 30 Days

10. Use the information in Table LMS—New Accounts to update the Chart of Accounts List.

TABLE LMS
New Accounts

Account Type	Number	Account Name
Bank	1010	Cash - Operating
Other Current Asset	1265	Inventory of Keyboards
Other Current Asset	1270	Inventory of Music Stands
Other Current Asset	1275	Inventory of Sheet Music
Other Current Asset	1300	Music Supplies
Other Current Asset	1305	Office Supplies
Other Current Asset	1410	Prepaid Advertising
Other Current Asset	1420	Prepaid Insurance
Fixed Asset	1725	Music Instruments, Cost [Subaccount of 1700]
Fixed Asset	1800	Furniture
Fixed Asset	1825	Furniture, Cost [Subaccount of 1800]
Fixed Asset	1850	Accum. Dep., Furniture [Subaccount of 1800]
Fixed Asset	1900	Computers
Fixed Asset	1925	Computers, Cost [Subaccount of 1900]
Fixed Asset	1950	Accum. Dep., Computers [Subaccount of 1900]
Other Current Liability	2020	Notes Payable
Other Current Liability	2030	Interest Payable
Income	4010	Piano Lessons
Income	4020	Guitar Lessons
Income	4065	Sale of Keyboards
Income	4070	Sale of Music Stands
Income	4075	Sale of Sheet Music

...continues

Account Type	Number	Account Name
Cost of Goods Sold	5065	Cost of Keyboards Sold
Cost of Goods Sold	5070	Cost of Music Stands Sold
Cost of Goods Sold	5075	Cost of Sheet Music Sold
Cost of Goods Sold	5900	Inventory Adjustment
Expense	6085	Deprec. Exp., Furniture
Expense	6095	Deprec. Exp., Computers
Expense	6150	Instrument Tuning Expense
Expense	6300	Music Supplies Expense

11. Use the information in Table LMS—Update Item List to update the Item List for items created as part of the QuickBooks Desktop Setup.

**TABLE LMS
Update Item List**

Item Name and Description	COGS Account	Income Account	Asset Account
Service Items (nontaxable):			
Guitar Lessons		4020	
Piano Lessons		4010	
Inventory Part Items (taxable):			
Guitars	5060	4060	1260
Keyboards	5065	4065	1265
Music Stands	5070	4070	1270
Sheet Music	5075	4075	1275

After updating the Item List, you can delete the Inventory Asset account and Cost of Goods Sold account (the accounts with no numbers).

12. Edit the Item List for the sales tax item created in the EasyStep Interview:

Sales Tax Name:	PA Sales Tax
Description:	Sales Tax
Tax Rate:	7%
Tax Agency:	PA Dept. of Revenue

13. Make three journal entries on June 1, 2021 (accept the default Entry Nos.):
    a. Enter the opening balances listed below. Enter the following accounts and amounts as debits:

Number	Account Name	Balance
1010	Cash - Operating	$14,615.18
1300	Music Supplies	430.00
1305	Office Supplies	300.00
1420	Prepaid Insurance	1,100.00
1725	Music Instruments, Cost	4,000.00
1825	Furniture, Cost	2,500.00
1925	Computers, Cost	3,000.00

...continues

...continued

Number	Account Name	Balance
3020	Lynn Garcia, Drawings	1,000.00
4100	Sales Discounts	188.92
5060	Cost of Guitars Sold	1,150.00
5065	Cost of Keyboards Sold	2,475.00
5070	Cost of Music Stands Sold	460.00
5075	Cost of Sheet Music Sold	1,305.00
5900	Inventory Adjustment	50.00
6075	Deprec. Exp., Music Instruments	60.00
6085	Deprec. Exp., Furniture	40.00
6095	Deprec. Exp., Computers	35.00
6150	Instrument Tuning Expense	100.00
6200	Insurance Expense	100.00
6300	Music Supplies Expense	70.00
6325	Office Supplies Expense	50.00
6400	Rent Expense	600.00
6450	Telephone Expense	50.00
6500	Utilities Expense	70.00
7000	Interest Expense	15.00

Enter the following accounts and amounts as credits:

Number	Account Name	Balance
1750	Accum. Dep., Music Instruments	$ 60.00
1850	Accum. Dep., Furniture	40.00
1950	Accum. Dep., Computers	35.00
2020	Notes Payable	2,000.00
2030	Interest Payable	15.00
4010	Piano Lessons	3,535.00
4020	Guitar Lessons	2,910.00
4060	Sale of Guitars	2,300.00
4065	Sale of Keyboards	4,950.00
4070	Sale of Music Stands	920.00
4075	Sale of Sheet Music	2,610.00

  b. Make a journal entry to reverse the Uncategorized Income account.

  c. Make a journal entry to reverse the Uncategorized Expenses account.

14. Display and print the following reports for June 1, 2021:
  a. *Journal*
  b. *Trial Balance*
  c. *Profit & Loss Standard* (04/01/2021–06/01/2021)
  d. *Balance Sheet Standard*
  e. *Item Listing*
  f. *Customer Contact List*
  g. *Vendor Contact List*

15. Make a backup copy of the new company file. Use the name **LMS6 *[Your Name]* Lynn's Music Studio**. Restore the backup copy and change the company name to **LMS6 *[Your Name]* Lynn's Music Studio**.

Case Problem 6–2

On June 1, 2021, Olivia Chen began her business, Olivia's Web Solutions. In the first month of business, Olivia set up the office, provided web page design and internet consulting services, and recorded month-end activity. In July, the second month of business, Olivia began to purchase and sell inventory items of computer hardware and software. In June and July, Olivia recorded the financial activities using a manual accounting system. On August 1, 2021, Olivia decides to switch her accounting method to QuickBooks. Olivia has organized the information about the company but has hired you to convert the accounting records to QuickBooks.

1. Use the information below to create the company file and record the information for the company using the Detailed Start method and the EasyStep Interview window. Where no specific information is given, accept the EasyStep Interview window default setting.

Company Name:	CH6 *[Your Name]* Olivia's Web Solutions
Tax ID:	55-5656566
Address:	547 Miller Place
	Westport, NY 11858
Country:	U.S.
Phone:	516-555-5000
Fax:	516-555-6000
E-mail:	LIV@ppi-edu.net
Industry:	General Product-based Business
Company:	Sole Proprietorship
Fiscal Year Start:	January
Password:	Student1
Save As:	CH6 *[Your Name]* Olivia's Web Solutions
Sell:	Both services and products
Sales Tax:	Yes
Estimates:	No
Tracking Customer Orders:	No
Statements:	No
Invoices:	Yes
Progress Invoicing:	No
Bills You Owe:	Yes
Tracking Inventory:	Yes
Tracking Time:	No
Employees:	No
Start Tracking:	08/01/2021

Remove the check mark from each of the following accounts:
    Shipping and Delivery Income
    Freight and Shipping Costs
    Merchant Account Fees
    Product Samples Expense
    Purchases - Resale Items
    Automobile Expense
    Bank Service Charges

...continues

...continued

> Computer and Internet Expenses
> Dues and Subscriptions
> Meals and Entertainment
> Postage and Delivery
> Professional Fees
> Repairs and Maintenance
> Travel Expense
> Ask My Accountant

Insert a check mark to the left of the following account:
> Sales Discounts

2. Use the information in Table OWS—Customers to create and update the Customer Center using the QuickBooks Desktop Setup window. Be sure to use the date *August 1, 2021*.

TABLE OWS Customers

Customer/ Company Name	Name/Contact	Phone	Address/ City, State, Zip	Balance
Artie's Auto Repair	Leon Artie	516-555-1221	32 W. 11th Street New Hyde Park, NY 11523	$ 800.00
Breathe Easy A/C Contractors	Allen Scott	516-555-6868	556 Atlantic Ave. Freeport, NY 11634	
Long Island Water Works	Customer Service	516-555-4747	87-54 Bayview Ave. Glen Cove, NY 11536	
Miguel's Restaurant	Miguel Perez	516-555-3236	30 Willis Ave. Roslyn, NY 11541	
Schneider Family	Johnny Schneider	516-555-8989	363 Farmers Rd. Syosset, NY 11547	1,000.00
Sehorn & Smith Attorneys	Jerry Sehorn	212-555-3339	510 Fifth Ave. New York, NY 10022	800.00
Singh Family	David Singh	718-555-3233	363 Marathon Parkway Little Neck, NY 11566	
South Shore School District	Joseph Porter	516-555-4545	3666 Ocean Ave. South Beach, NY 11365	12,056.00
Thrifty Stores	William Way	718-555-2445	23 Boston Ave. Bronx, NY 11693	1,500.00

3. Use the information in Table OWS—Vendors to create and update the Vendor Center using the QuickBooks Desktop Setup window. Be sure to use the date *August 1, 2021*.

TABLE OWS Vendors

Vendor/Company Name	Name/Contact	Phone	Address/ City, State, Zip	Balance
ARC Management	Alvin R. Clinton	516-555-6363	668 Lakeville Ave. Garden City, NY 11678	
Chrbet Advertising	Chris Chrbet	212-555-8777	201 E. 10th Street New York, NY 10012	$1,200.00

...continues

TABLE OWS Vendors...*continued*

Vendor/Company Name	Name/Contact	Phone	Address/ City, State, Zip	Balance
Comet Computer Supplies	Customer Service	631-555-4444	657 Motor Parkway Center Island, NY 11488	
Computec Computers	Customer Service	702-555-6564	3631 Gate Blvd. Greenboro, NC 27407	$10,000.00
Eastel	Customer Service	212-555-6565	655 Fifth Ave. New York, NY 10012	350.00
Eastern Mutual Insurance	Customer Service	212-555-6363	55 Broadway Room 55 New York, NY 10001	
InterSoft Development Co.	Customer Service	361-555-3634	556 Route 347 Hauppauge, NY 11654	
Lewis Furniture Co.	Manny Lewis	631-555-6161	1225 Route 110 Farmingdale, NY 11898	1,700.00
LI Power Company	Customer Service	516-555-8888	5444 Northern Ave. Plainview, NY 11544	
Martin Computer Repairs	Ken Martin	516-555-7777	366 N. Franklin St. Garden City, NY 11568	
Netsoft Development Co.	Customer Service	974-555-7873	684 Mountain View Rd Portland, OR 68774	1,600.00
NYS Tax Dept.				
Office Plus	Customer Service	516-555-3214	45 Jericho Tpke. Jericho, NY 11654	375.00
Olivia Chen				
Scanntronix	Customer Service	617-555-8778	2554 Bedford Rd. Boston, MA 02164	
Systems Service	Jeremy Jones	516-555-2525	36 Sunrise Lane Hempstead, NY 11004	
Textpro Software, Inc.	Customer Service	615-555-4545	877 Route 5 Ft. Lauderdale, FL 70089	

4. Use the information in Table OWS—Items to update the Item List using the QuickBooks Desktop Setup window. Be sure to use the date *August 1, 2021*.

TABLE OWS Items

Item Name and Description	Price	Cost	On Hand	Total Value
Service Items:				
Internet Consulting Services	$100			
Web Page Design Services	125			
Inventory Part Items:				
Computers	2,000	$1,000	10	$10,000
Scanners	600	300	12	3,600
HTML Software	150	75	18	1,350
Desktop Pub. Software	200	100	10	1,000

5. Activate the account numbers feature. Use the following information to customize the Chart of Accounts List:

QuickBooks		Edited	
Number	Account Name	Number	Account Name
15000	Furniture and Equipment	1700	Computers
17000	Accumulated Depreciation	1750	Accum. Dep., Computers Subaccount of 1700]
30800	Owners Draw	3020	Olivia Chen, Drawings
	Sales Income	4060	Sale of Computers
48300	Sales Discounts	4100	
60000	Advertising and Promotion	6050	Advertising Expense
62400	Depreciation Expense	6075	Deprec. Exp., Computers
63300	Insurance Expense	6100	
63400	Interest Expense	7000	[Account Type: Other Expense]
64900	Office Supplies	6325	Office Supplies Expense
67100	Rent Expense	6400	
68100	Telephone Expense	6450	
68600	Utilities	6500	Utilities Expense

6. Delete the following account:
   47900 Sales

7. Open and close the following windows to allow QuickBooks to create default accounts:
   Create Invoices
   Enter Sales Receipts
   Enter Bills
   Item List: New Item: Inventory Part

8. Customize the system default accounts:

QuickBooks		Edited	
Number	Account Name	Number	Account Name
11000	Accounts Receivable	1200	
12000	Undeposited Funds	1250	
12100	*Inventory Asset	1260	Inventory of Computers
20000	Accounts Payable	2010	
25500	Sales Tax Payable	2200	
30000	Opening Balance Equity	3010	Olivia Chen, Capital
32000	Owners Equity	3030	Accumulated Earnings
50000	*Cost of Goods Sold	5060	Cost of Computers Sold

9. Customize the payment Terms List to list only the following:
   2/10, Net 30 Days
   Net 10 Days
   Net 15 Days
   Net 30 Days

10. Use the information in Table OWS—New Accounts to update the Chart of Accounts List.

Account Type	Number	Account Name
Bank	1010	Cash - Operating
Other Current Asset	1265	Inventory of Scanners
Other Current Asset	1270	Inventory of HTML Software
Other Current Asset	1275	Inventory of Desktop Pub. Soft.
Other Current Asset	1300	Computer Supplies
Other Current Asset	1305	Office Supplies
Other Current Asset	1410	Prepaid Advertising
Other Current Asset	1420	Prepaid Insurance
Fixed Asset	1725	Computers, Cost [Subaccount of 1700]
Fixed Asset	1800	Furniture
Fixed Asset	1825	Furniture, Cost [Subaccount of 1800]
Fixed Asset	1850	Accum. Dep., Furniture [Subaccount of 1800]
Fixed Asset	1900	Software
Fixed Asset	1925	Software, Cost [Subaccount of 1900]
Fixed Asset	1950	Accum. Dep., Software [Subaccount of 1900]
Other Current Liability	2020	Notes Payable
Other Current Liability	2030	Interest Payable
Income	4010	Web Page Design Fees
Income	4020	Internet Consulting Fees
Income	4065	Sale of Scanners
Income	4070	Sale of HTML Software
Income	4075	Sale of Desktop Pub. Software
Cost of Goods Sold	5065	Cost of Scanners Sold
Cost of Goods Sold	5070	Cost of HTML Software Sold
Cost of Goods Sold	5075	Cost of Desktop Pub. Soft. Sold
Cost of Goods Sold	5900	Inventory Adjustment
Expense	6085	Deprec. Exp., Furniture
Expense	6095	Deprec. Exp., Software
Expense	6300	Computer Supplies Expense
Expense	6350	Online Service Expense

11. Use the information in Table OWS—Update Item List to update the Item List for items created as part of QuickBooks Desktop Setup.

TABLE OWS
Update Item List

Item Name and Description	COGS Account	Income Account	Asset Account
Service Items (nontaxable):			
Internet Consulting Services		4020	
Web Page Design Services		4010	
Inventory Part Items (taxable):			
Computers	5060	4060	1260
Scanners	5065	4065	1265
HTML Software	5070	4070	1270
Desktop Pub. Software	5075	4075	1275

After updating the Item List, you can delete the Inventory Asset account and Cost of Goods Sold account (the accounts with no numbers).

12. Edit the Item List for the sales tax item created in the EasyStep Interview:

Sales Tax Name:	NY Sales Tax
Description:	Sales Tax
Tax Rate:	8%
Tax Agency:	NYS Tax Dept.

13. Make three journal entries on August 1, 2021 (accept the default Entry Nos.):
    a. Enter the opening balances listed below. Enter the following accounts and amounts as debits:

Number	Account Name	Balance
1010	Cash - Operating	$24,489.16
1300	Computer Supplies	350.00
1305	Office Supplies	325.00
1410	Prepaid Advertising	1,000.00
1420	Prepaid Insurance	1,650.00
1725	Computers, Cost	5,000.00
1825	Furniture, Cost	3,200.00
1925	Software, Cost	3,600.00
3020	Olivia Chen, Drawings	500.00
4100	Sales Discounts	179.84
5060	Cost of Computers Sold	10,000.00
5065	Cost of Scanners Sold	2,400.00
5070	Cost of HTML Software Sold	75.00
5075	Cost of Desktop Pub. Soft. Sold	500.00
5900	Inventory Adjustment	75.00
6050	Advertising Expense	200.00
6075	Deprec. Exp., Computers	75.00
6085	Deprec. Exp., Furniture	50.00
6095	Deprec. Exp., Software	100.00
6100	Insurance Expense	150.00

...continues

...continued

Number	Account Name	Balance
6300	Computer Supplies Expense	250.00
6325	Office Supplies Expense	50.00
6350	Online Service Expense	150.00
6400	Rent Expense	800.00
6450	Telephone Expense	350.00
6500	Utilities Expense	125.00
7000	Interest Expense	25.00

Enter the following accounts and amounts as credits:

Number	Account Name	Balance
1750	Accum. Dep., Computers	$ 75.00
1850	Accum. Dep., Furniture	50.00
1950	Accum. Dep., Software	100.00
2020	Notes Payable	2,500.00
2030	Interest Payable	25.00
4010	Web Page Design Fees	9,750.00
4020	Internet Consulting Fees	6,600.00
4060	Sale of Computers	20,000.00
4065	Sale of Scanners	4,800.00
4070	Sale of HTML Software	150.00
4075	Sale of Desktop Pub. Software	1,000.00

  b. Make a journal entry to reverse the Uncategorized Income account.
  c. Make a journal entry to reverse the Uncategorized Expenses account.

14. Display and print the following reports for August 1, 2021:
  a. *Journal*
  b. *Trial Balance*
  c. *Profit & Loss Standard (06/01/2021–08/01/2021)*
  d. *Balance Sheet Standard*
  e. *Item Listing*
  f. *Customer Contact List*
  g. *Vendor Contact List*

15. Make a backup copy of the new company file. Use the name **OWS6 *[Your Name]* Olivia's Web Solutions**. Restore the backup copy and change the company name to **OWS6 *[Your Name]* Olivia's Web Solutions**.

CHAPTER 7

New Company Setup— Express Start

Setting Up Company Preferences

Objectives

- Create a new company file using the QuickBooks Express Start method

- Set up a company file password

- Establish preferences

- Update the Chart of Accounts List

- Customize the system default accounts and Terms List

- Update the Item List

- Update the Customer and Vendor Centers

- Adjust the new company file to follow the accrual basis of accounting

- Display and print accounting reports and financial statements

In this chapter, you will learn an alternative method for creating a new company file in QuickBooks. As you know, the four levels of operation for QuickBooks are New Company Setup, Lists/Centers, Activities, and Reports. In Chapters 2 through 5, the Lists, Activities, and Reports levels were presented for both a service company and a merchandise company. In those chapters, you opened an existing company file, updated the Lists/Centers, recorded Activities in the various windows, and viewed and printed Reports. You will now learn another method for the first level of operation for QuickBooks: New Company Setup.

QuickBooks provides two methods of New Company Setup: Detailed Start and Express Start. In Chapter 6, the New Company Setup level of operation was presented using the Detailed Start method, which moves you to the EasyStep Interview window. In addition, you used the QuickBooks Desktop Setup window to continue with the New Company Setup.

In Chapter 7, you will learn how to conduct the New Company Setup using the Express Start method. With this method, you do not use the EasyStep Interview window; instead, you will set up a company file password and then directly enable the features you desire. In addition, you will not use the QuickBooks Desktop Setup window to enter information. Instead, you will use many of the procedures you learned earlier for updating the Lists/Centers to enter information in the new company file. Finally, the new company file will be prepared for the accrual basis of accounting.

In this chapter, you will again create and set up a new company file for our sample company, Kristin Raina Interior Designs. It is assumed that Kristin Raina Interior Designs has been recording accounting activities using a manual accounting system and will convert the company's accounting records to QuickBooks.

QuickBooks versus Manual Accounting: New Company Setup

In a manual accounting system, a company's records are set up by creating the Chart of Accounts and a general ledger. The Chart of Accounts is the list of accounts (assets, liabilities, equity, revenues, and expenses) the company intends to use. The general ledger is the book of all accounts, with the beginning balance for each account. If desired, subsidiary ledgers can also be created and beginning balances recorded. The subsidiary ledgers typically include accounts receivable and accounts payable. If the perpetual inventory system is used, an inventory subsidiary ledger is also created.

In QuickBooks, a company's records are set up by creating a new company file and establishing the Chart of Accounts List. As the opening balances are entered, QuickBooks simultaneously sets up the general ledger. The Customer Center and Vendor Center are set up; these centers are equivalent to the accounts receivable and accounts payable subsidiary ledgers. The Item List, which is equivalent to an inventory subsidiary ledger, is set up. However, in QuickBooks, the Item List includes service revenue items and sales tax items in addition to inventory items.

When you set up a new company file using the Express Start method—that is, without using the EasyStep Interview window—you first set up a company file password, and then you identify certain company preferences. After that, you customize parts of the company file. You can use the QuickBooks Desktop Setup window to enter the information for customers, vendors, and items, as illustrated in Chapter 6, but doing so is not required. If you choose not to use the QuickBooks Desktop Setup window to enter information, you will then use the Lists/Centers windows to continue with the setup of the new company file. Entering information in the Lists/Centers is similar to creating a Chart of Accounts, general ledger, and subsidiary ledgers in a manual accounting system. Finally, you need to make three journal entries to complete the New Company Setup. One journal entry records the opening balances in the accounts that were not included when you set up the Lists/Centers; the other two journal entries reverse accounts set up by QuickBooks during the New Company Setup that are not used in the accrual basis of accounting.

Chapter Problem

In this chapter, there is no prepared company file to open from the company files. Instead, you will create and set up the company file for Kristin Raina Interior Designs.

Assume that Kristin Raina began her interior design business in January 2021 and has maintained accounting records with a manual accounting system for January through March. Effective April 1, 2021, Kristin Raina will convert the company's accounting records to QuickBooks using the Express Start method.

Before you create a new company file, gather all the information you need, including company information (name, address, tax identification numbers); password information (password, challenge question, answer); general ledger account names and account numbers; customer information (name, address, telephone numbers, and so on) and outstanding balances; vendor information (name, address, telephone numbers, and so on) and outstanding balances; service items and billing amounts; inventory part items (name, cost, selling price, and quantity on hand); and sales tax information. You will enter this information into QuickBooks as you create and set up the new company file.

To begin the New Company Setup:
1. Open QuickBooks.
2. At the No Company Open window, click Create a new company or click File and then click *New Company*. The QuickBooks Desktop Setup window appears with the Let's get your business set up quickly! page displayed. This is the page where you select the method of New Company Setup. See Figure 7–A.

FIGURE 7–A
QuickBooks Desktop Setup Window—Let's Get Your Business Set Up Quickly! Page

Express Start

In the New Company Setup, the first level of operation in QuickBooks, you will enter the information needed to create and set up a company file for Kristin Raina Interior Designs using the Express Start method. With the Express Start method of New Company Setup, you will enter some information about the company and identify the type of industry for the business. You will then save the company file.

To create a new company file using the Express Start method:

1. At the QuickBooks Desktop Setup window, at the Let's get your business set up quickly! page, click the Express Start button. The Glad you're here! page appears.
2. At the Glad you're here! page, at the *Business Name* field, type CH7 *[Your Name]* Kristin Raina Interior Designs.
3. At the *Industry* field, click *Help me choose.* The Select Your Industry page appears.
4. At the Select Your Industry page, at the *Industry* field, scroll to the bottom and select *Other/None.* See Figure 7–B.

FIGURE 7–B
Select Your Industry Page

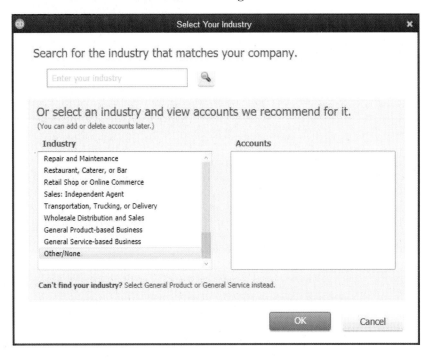

5. If the information is correct, click OK. You are returned to the Glad you're here! page.
6. At the *Business Type* field, choose *Sole Proprietorship* from the drop-down menu.
7. At the *Employer Identification Number (EIN)* field, type 33-4777781.
8. Enter the following business contact information:

Business Address:	25 NE Johnson Street
City:	Minneapolis
State:	MN
ZIP:	53402
Country:	U.S.
Phone:	651-555-1000

When you are finished, your screen should look like Figure 7–C.

FIGURE 7–C

Glad You're Here! Page—
Completed

Glad you're here!

Tell us about your business so we can give you the right tools for what you do.

* Business Name	CH7 [Your Name] Kristin Raina Interior Designs
* Industry	Other/None Help me choose
* Business Type	Sole Proprietorship Help me choose
Employer Identification Number (EIN)	33-4777781
Business Address	25 NE Johnson Street
City	Minneapolis
State	MN ZIP 53402
Country	U.S.
Phone	651-555-1000

* Required

Intuit's Privacy Statement

Back   Preview Your Settings   Create Company

HINT

If you click the Create Company button before clicking the Preview Your Settings button, QuickBooks will save your file in the most recent folder you used or in the default path C:\Users\Public\(Public) Documents\Intuit\ QuickBooks\Company Files.

9. If the information is correct, click the Preview Your Settings button.

10. At the Preview Your Company Settings page, click the Company File Location tab.

11. On the Company File Location tab, click the Change Location button. You are moved to the Browse For Folder window.

12. At the Browse For Folder window, scroll through the list, choose the folder where you save your files, and then click OK. You are returned to the Company File Location tab with the path and folder displayed.

13. If the path and folder are correct, click OK. You are returned to the Glad you're here! page.

14. Click the Create Company button. The company file **CH7 [Your Name] Kristin Raina Interior Designs** is saved in the path and folder you indicated in Step 12.

    The QuickBooks Desktop Setup window appears with the Get all the details into QuickBooks Desktop Setup page displayed. The QuickBooks Desktop Setup window could now be used to enter information for customers, vendors, service items, and inventory part items, as was illustrated in Chapter 6. However, in this chapter, you will not use the QuickBooks Desktop Setup window. Instead, you will enter information directly into Lists and Centers.

15. Close the QuickBooks Desktop Setup window. If the New Feature Tour window appears, click the X to close it. The Home page and Left Icon bar appear. Close the Home page. To remove the Left Icon bar, click View and then click *Hide Icon Bar*.

To continue the New Company Setup using the Express Start method and not the QuickBooks Desktop Setup window to enter information, you must take the following steps: set up a company file password; establish Preferences; update the Chart of Accounts List; customize the system default accounts and the Terms List; update the Item List, Customer Center, and Vendor Center with beginning balances; and adjust for the accrual basis of accounting by entering opening balances in accounts by journal entry and recording two journal entries to offset two accounts created by QuickBooks that are not used in the accrual basis of accounting.

New Company Setup → ## Company File Password

In business, it is advisable to protect access to financial records with a password. QuickBooks has the ability to password protect not only the entire company file but also specific sections of the company file. This allows a company to limit employees' access to their respective areas of responsibility. For instance, the accounts receivable bookkeeper may be permitted to access only the information pertaining to customers' accounts; the payroll bookkeeper may be permitted to access only the payroll information; and so on.

Originally, it was optional for the user to password protect a company file. But in recent versions of QuickBooks, password protection has become mandatory. There are a few instances when a password can be optional (such as when a business identification number has not been entered), but in most situations, a password is now required to open a company file.

In Chapter 6, when you created a new company file using the EasyStep Interview window, you were asked if you wanted to set up a password. In Chapter 6, you set up a password. However, if you chose to leave the new company file before setting up a password, the next time you open the company file, you will be asked to set up a password before the company file can be opened. In Chapter 7, when you create a new company file using the Express method, you are not asked to set up a password. In both Chapter 6 and Chapter 7, when you leave the new company file without setting up a password, the next time you open the new company file, you will need to enter a password, a challenge question, and an answer before the company file can be opened.

You do not have to exit the new company file and then reopen the new company file to set up the password. You can set up a company file password before you leave the new company file.

To create a company file password:
1. At the main menu bar, click Company and then click *Setup Users and Passwords*.
2. At the Setup Users and Passwords submenu, click *Change Your Password*. The Change Your Password window appears. See Figure 7–D.

FIGURE 7–D
Change Your Password
Window

3. In the *New Password* and *Confirm New Password* text boxes, type
   Student1 or a password of your choosing.
4. At the Challenge Question drop-down list, select *First college roommate's
   name* or a question of your choosing.
5. In the *Answer* text box, type Friend or an answer of your choosing.
   See Figure 7–E.

FIGURE 7–E
Change Your Password
Window—Completed

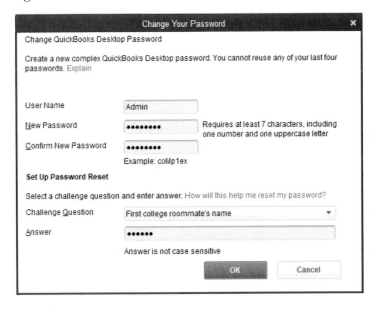

6. If the information is correct, click OK. At the QuickBooks Desktop
   Information message, click OK. Close the Home page if it appears.
   The password is now created for the new company file, and you will
   need to enter the password each time you open the company file.

   If you closed the company file before creating a password, the next time
you open the company file, a window labeled Sensitive Data Protection
Setup appears instead of the Change Your Password window. However, the
fields of information in both windows are the same, and the steps in both
windows are the same for entering the password, challenge question, and
answer.

Establishing Preferences

When you use the EasyStep Interview window in the Detailed Start method of New Company Setup, as seen in Chapter 6, QuickBooks asks questions and, based on your responses, establishes preferences for your company. When you use the Express Start method of New Company Setup, you do not use the EasyStep Interview window. Therefore, you must establish the preferences for the new company file yourself. Company preferences enable or disable features available in QuickBooks. When a feature is enabled, it allows for choices to be listed on the drop-down menus and the Home page. If a feature is disabled, some choices will not be listed on the drop-down menus and the Home page.

You set these preferences in the Preferences window. You will use the Preferences window to activate the account *Number* field in the Chart of Accounts List window, activate the inventory feature, activate sales tax, and disable the payroll feature.

Account Numbers

By default, QuickBooks does not use account numbers. You must activate the account numbers feature to add them.

To activate the account numbers feature:
1. At the main menu bar, click Edit and then click *Preferences*. The Preferences window appears.

   In the left panel of the window are 23 icons that represent the different categories of features. For each category, there is a My Preferences tab and a Company Preferences tab. The Company Preferences tab is used for most preferences when setting up a new company file. The My Preferences tab is used to record the preferences for each user on his or her personal computer.
2. In the left panel of the Preferences window, click the Accounting icon.
3. Click the Company Preferences tab.
4. In the Accounts section, insert a check mark in the box to the left of *Use account numbers* to turn on the account numbers feature. See Figure 7–F.

FIGURE 7–F
Preferences Window—
Accounting—Company
Preferences Tab

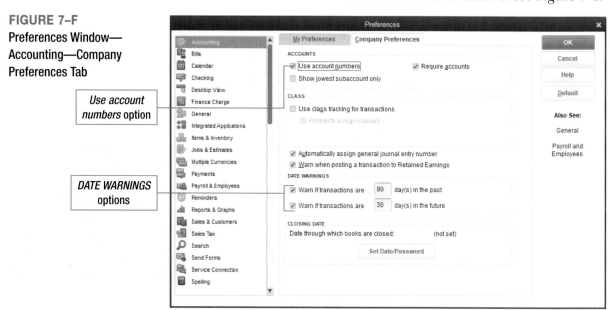

HINT

If you receive warnings about dates, remove the check marks from the DATE WARNINGS section.

5. If the information is correct, click OK. The account *Number* field now appears in the New Account and Edit Account windows in the Chart of Accounts List.

Inventory

QuickBooks provides you with the ability to maintain inventory records, but the inventory feature must be activated.

To activate the inventory feature:
1. At the main menu bar, click Edit and then click *Preferences*. The Preferences window appears.
2. In the left panel of the Preferences window, click the Items & Inventory icon.
3. Click the Company Preferences tab.
4. In the PURCHASE ORDERS AND INVENTORY section, insert a check mark in the box to the left of *Inventory and purchase orders are active* to turn on the inventory feature. See Figure 7–G.

FIGURE 7–G
Preferences Window—
Items & Inventory—
Company Preferences
Tab

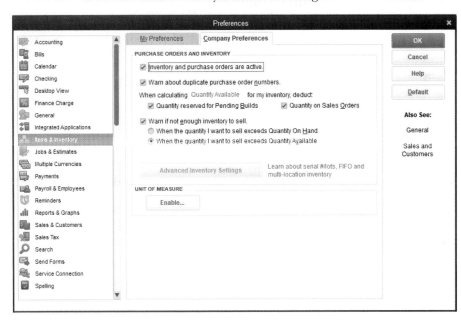

5. If the information is correct, click OK. The inventory feature is now activated, and fields of information relevant to inventory appear in the Activities windows.

Sales Tax

QuickBooks also provides you with the ability to charge and maintain sales tax information, but the sales tax feature must be activated.

To activate the sales tax feature:
1. At the main menu bar, click Edit and then click *Preferences.*
2. In the left panel of the Preferences window, click the Sales Tax icon.
3. Click the Company Preferences tab.
4. At the *Do you charge sales tax?* field, click *Yes.* The other fields of information that were dimmed are now activated.
   You must complete the *Your most common sales tax item* field.

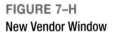
HINT

You could also click the Add sales tax item button.

5. At the *Your most common sales tax item* field, click the drop-down arrow. Because this is a new company, there is no information regarding sales tax. You will add it in this window.

6. Click *< Add New >*.

The New Item window appears. This allows you to add sales tax to the Item List.

7. Enter the following sales tax item information:

TYPE:	Sales Tax Item
Sales Tax Name:	Minn. Sales Tax
Description:	Sales Tax
Tax Rate (%):	7

8. At the *Tax Agency (vendor that you collect for)* field, click the drop-down arrow. Again, because this is a new company file, vendors have not yet been entered into the file.

9. At the Tax Agency drop-down list, click *< Add New >*. The New Vendor window appears.

10. At both the *VENDOR NAME* and *COMPANY NAME* fields, type Minn. Dept. of Revenue. Press the Tab key. This adds Minn. Dept. of Revenue to the *BILLED FROM* field. See Figure 7–H.

FIGURE 7–H
New Vendor Window

11. If the information is correct, click OK. The Minn. Dept. of Revenue has been added to the Vendor Center, and the New Item window is complete. See Figure 7–I.

FIGURE 7–I
New Item Window— Completed

12. If the information is correct, click OK. The Preferences window for sales tax is complete. See Figure 7–J.

13. If the information is correct, click OK. The Updating Sales Tax dialog box appears. In this dialog box, QuickBooks is inquiring if all existing customers and all non-inventory and inventory parts should be made taxable. See Figure 7–K.

14. In the Updating Sales Tax dialog box, click OK. The sales tax item is established and added to the Item List.

Payroll

When you create a new company file using the Express Start method, QuickBooks assumes you will be using the Payroll feature and activates it by default. When QuickBooks activates the payroll feature, it automatically creates a Payroll Liabilities account and Payroll Expenses account in the Chart of Accounts List. Our sample company, Kristin Raina Interior Designs, has not yet used the payroll feature and does not need it activated.

To disable the payroll feature:
1. At the main menu bar, click Edit and then click *Preferences*.
2. In the left panel of the Preferences window, click the Payroll & Employees icon.

TABLE 7–1
Chart of Accounts List

Account Type	Number	Account Name
Accounts Receivable	1200	Accounts Receivable
Other Current Asset	1250	Undeposited Funds
Other Current Asset	1265	Inventory of Draperies
Other Current Asset	1270	Inventory of Lamps
Other Current Asset	1275	Inventory of Mirrors
Other Current Asset	1300	Design Supplies
Other Current Asset	1305	Office Supplies
Other Current Asset	1410	Prepaid Advertising
Other Current Asset	1420	Prepaid Insurance
Fixed Asset	1700	Furniture
Fixed Asset	1725	Furniture, Cost [Subaccount of 1700]
Fixed Asset	1750	Accum. Dep., Furniture [Subaccount of 1700]
Fixed Asset	1800	Computers
Fixed Asset	1825	Computers, Cost [Subaccount of 1800]
Fixed Asset	1850	Accum. Dep., Computers [Subaccount of 1800]
Accounts Payable	2010	Accounts Payable
Other Current Liability	2020	Notes Payable
Other Current Liability	2030	Interest Payable
Income	4010	Design Services
Income	4020	Decorating Services
Income	4060	Sale of Carpets
Income	4065	Sale of Draperies
Income	4070	Sale of Lamps
Income	4075	Sale of Mirrors
Income	4100	Sales Discounts
Cost of Goods Sold	5065	Cost of Draperies Sold
Cost of Goods Sold	5070	Cost of Lamps Sold
Cost of Goods Sold	5075	Cost of Mirrors Sold
Cost of Goods Sold	5900	Inventory Adjustment
Expense	6020	Accounting Expense
Expense	6050	Advertising Expense
Expense	6175	Deprec. Exp., Furniture
Expense	6185	Deprec. Exp., Computers
Expense	6200	Insurance Expense
Expense	6300	Janitorial Expense
Expense	6325	Office Supplies Expense
Expense	6400	Rent Expense
Expense	6450	Telephone Expense
Expense	6500	Utilities Expense
Other Expense	7000	Interest Expense

HINT

In the *Account Type* field, instead of looking for the type in the drop-down list, type the first letter of the type name.

HINT

The Inventory of Carpets and Cost of Carpets Sold accounts will be added in the next section of this chapter.

The updated Chart of Accounts List appears in Figure 7–O.

FIGURE 7–O
Chart of Accounts List—
Updated

NAME	TYPE	BALANCE TOTAL	ATTACH
1010 · Cash - Operating	Bank	0.00	
1200 · Accounts Receivable	Accounts Receivable	0.00	
1250 · Undeposited Funds	Other Current Asset	0.00	
1265 · Inventory of Draperies	Other Current Asset	0.00	
1270 · Inventory of Lamps	Other Current Asset	0.00	
1275 · Inventory of Mirrors	Other Current Asset	0.00	
1300 · Design Supplies	Other Current Asset	0.00	
1305 · Office Supplies	Other Current Asset	0.00	
1410 · Prepaid Advertising	Other Current Asset	0.00	
1420 · Prepaid Insurance	Other Current Asset	0.00	
1700 · Furniture	Fixed Asset	0.00	
1725 · Furniture, Cost	Fixed Asset	0.00	
1750 · Accum. Dep., Furniture	Fixed Asset	0.00	
1800 · Computers	Fixed Asset	0.00	
1825 · Computers, Cost	Fixed Asset	0.00	
1850 · Accum. Dep., Computers	Fixed Asset	0.00	
2010 · Accounts Payable	Accounts Payable	0.00	
2020 · Notes Payable	Other Current Liability	0.00	
2030 · Interest Payable	Other Current Liability	0.00	
24000 · Payroll Liabilities	Other Current Liability	0.00	
25500 · Sales Tax Payable	Other Current Liability	0.00	
30000 · Opening Balance Equity	Equity	0.00	
30800 · Owners Draw	Equity	0.00	
32000 · Owners Equity	Equity		
4010 · Design Services	Income		
4020 · Decorating Services	Income		
4060 · Sale of Carpets	Income		
4065 · Sale of Draperies	Income		
4070 · Sale of Lamps	Income		
4075 · Sale of Mirrors	Income		
4100 · Sales Discounts	Income		
5065 · Cost of Draperies Sold	Cost of Goods Sold		
5070 · Cost of Lamps Sold	Cost of Goods Sold		
5075 · Cost of Mirrors Sold	Cost of Goods Sold		
5900 · Inventory Adjustment	Cost of Goods Sold		
6020 · Accounting Expense	Expense		
6050 · Advertising Expense	Expense		
6175 · Deprec. Exp., Furniture	Expense		
6185 · Deprec. Exp., Computers	Expense		
6200 · Insurance Expense	Expense		
6300 · Janitorial Expense	Expense		
6325 · Office Supplies Expense	Expense		
6400 · Rent Expense	Expense		
6450 · Telephone Expense	Expense		
6500 · Utilities Expense	Expense		
66000 · Payroll Expenses	Expense		
7000 · Interest Expense	Other Expense		

HINT

If you incorrectly labeled an account as a parent account or subaccount, you can edit the account or move the entry. To move the entry, click the diamond to the left of the account number. If you drag the diamond to the left, a subaccount becomes a parent account. If you drag the diamond to the right, a parent account becomes a subaccount. You can also click and drag up or down to reorganize the list.

HINT

If the account 90000 Estimates is displayed, click Edit and then click *Preferences.* At the Preferences window, click the Jobs & Estimates icon and then click the Company Preferences tab. At the *DO YOU CREATE ESTIMATES?* field, click No and then click OK. In the Chart of Accounts List, delete the account 90000 Estimates.

7. Close the Add New Account and Chart of Accounts windows.

New Company Setup

Customizing the New Company File

As previously stated, when creating a new company file using the Express Start method of New Company Setup, you first set up the preferences for the company file. As you do this, accounts are set up on the Chart of Accounts List. Then the Chart of Accounts List is updated to add more of the accounts the company uses. The next step is to customize the new company file. This consists of customizing the system default accounts and payment terms created by QuickBooks.

Customizing System Default Accounts

As you learned in prior chapters, QuickBooks establishes default accounts and uses those accounts when recording transactions in the Activities windows. QuickBooks looks for these system default accounts in the Chart of Accounts List; if it cannot find an account, it will create one. Some of the system default accounts you have learned so far are Accounts Receivable, Undeposited Funds, Accounts Payable, Sales Tax Payable, Inventory Asset, and Cost of Goods Sold. Other system default accounts include the equity accounts (capital and accumulated earnings) and payroll accounts (payroll liabilities and payroll expenses).

When you created the company file and established some of the company preferences, QuickBooks created some of the system default accounts, as you saw in Figure 7–M on page 278.

You will now customize the system default accounts that were created by QuickBooks (sales tax payable and equity accounts) by editing the account names and numbers to follow the company's pattern for naming and numbering accounts on the Chart of Accounts List. The payroll accounts that QuickBooks creates cannot be deleted, but since they will not be used in our sample company file, they can be marked as inactive to hide them on the Chart of Accounts List. Then you will learn how to force QuickBooks to create additional system default accounts that were not created when you created the company file and established the preferences (undeposited funds, inventory asset, and cost of goods sold). After QuickBooks creates the additional system default accounts, you will then customize these account names and numbers.

Customizing System Default Accounts Created in a New Company File and Company Preferences

When you created the company file and indicated the company was a sole proprietorship, QuickBooks automatically created three equity accounts: Opening Balance Equity, Owners Draw, and Owners Equity. When you activated the sales tax feature in the Preferences window, QuickBooks created a Sales Tax Payable account. The numbers and names for each of these accounts can be edited. The Opening Balance Equity account will be renamed as *Kristin Raina, Capital,* and the Owners Draw account will be renamed *Kristin Raina, Drawings.* The Opening Balance Equity account is used by QuickBooks as an offsetting account when certain opening balances are entered in the accounts. The Owners Equity account is created to capture net income at the end of the fiscal year. In Chapter 12, you will see how QuickBooks uses the Owner's Equity account in a company file. This account will be renamed *Accumulated Earnings.*

As you will soon see, QuickBooks recognizes the Accounts Receivable; Accounts Payable; Sales Tax Payable; Kristin Raina, Capital (Opening Balance Equity); and Accumulated Earnings (Owners Equity) accounts as system default accounts, but QuickBooks does not recognize the Undeposited Funds, Inventory Asset, and Cost of Goods Sold accounts as system default accounts. QuickBooks usually identifies a system default account by graying, or dimming, the account type. As you edit each of these accounts, notice that the account type is dimmed.

To edit account numbers and account names:

1. At the main menu bar, click Lists and then click *Chart of Accounts.*
2. At the Chart of Accounts window, select *30000 Opening Balance Equity* but do not open the account.
3. Click the Account menu button.
4. At the Account button drop-down menu, click *Edit Account.*
5. At the *Number* field, delete *30000* and then type 3010.
6. At the *Account Name* field, delete the text *Opening Balance Equity* and then type Kristin Raina, Capital. See Figure 7–P.

FIGURE 7–P
Edit Account Window—
System Default Account

account type dimmed

7. If the information is correct, click the Save & Close button.
8. Edit the two other equity accounts and the Sales Tax Payable account as follows:

QuickBooks		Edited	
Number	Account Name	Number	Account Name
30800	Owners Draw	3020	Kristin Raina, Drawings
32000	Owners Equity	3030	Accumulated Earnings
25500	Sales Tax Payable	2200	

Hiding Inactive System Default Accounts Created in a New Company File

When you create a new company file using the Express Start method, QuickBooks assumes by default that you will be using the payroll feature and automatically creates a Payroll Liabilities account and a Payroll Expenses account. Even though you subsequently turned off the payroll feature in the Preferences window, once you have created the payroll accounts in QuickBooks, you cannot delete them.

In addition, once you turned on the account numbers feature, QuickBooks assigned the account numbers *24000* to the Payroll Liabilities account and

Profit & Loss Standard (Income Statement) Report

To view the *Profit & Loss Standard* report:

1. At the main menu bar, click Reports and then click *Company & Financial.*
2. At the Company & Financial submenu, click *Profit & Loss Standard.*
3. At the *From* and *To* fields, choose *01/01/2021* and *04/01/2021* and then click the Refresh button at the top of the report. See Figure 7–EE.

FIGURE 7–EE

Profit & Loss Standard Report

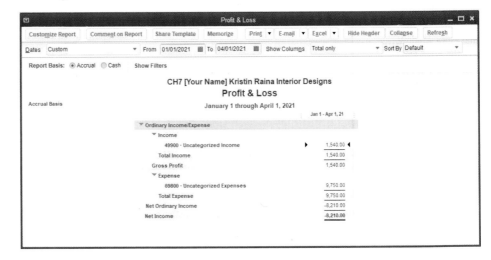

The *Profit & Loss Standard* report indicates only Uncategorized Income and Uncategorized Expenses. These amounts are offsetting amounts of the Accounts Receivable and Accounts Payable accounts. This is not a proper representation of the income and expenses of this company.

4. Close the report.

Balance Sheet Standard Report

To display the *Balance Sheet Standard* report:

1. At the main menu bar, click Reports and then click *Company & Financial.*
2. At the Company & Financial submenu, click *Balance Sheet Standard.*
3. At the *As of* field, choose *04/01/2021* and then click the Refresh button at the top of the report. See Figure 7–FF.

   A review of the balance sheet indicates the following:
   - The only assets recorded so far are Accounts Receivable and the Inventory accounts.
   - The only liabilities recorded so far are the Accounts Payable.
   - The balance in the Kristin Raina, Capital (Opening Balance Equity) account is the same as the sum of the total inventory.
   - The net income is incorrect as seen in the *Profit & Loss Standard* report.
4. Close the report.

FIGURE 7-FF

Balance Sheet Standard Report

Adjusting for the Accrual Basis of Accounting

You have now created the new company file, set up a company file password, established preferences, and updated and customized the Lists and Centers. The final step is to enter the remaining opening balances and prepare the company file for the accrual basis of accounting.

accrual basis of accounting
an accounting method that requires the recording of revenue when it is earned and the recording of expenses when they are incurred, regardless of cash receipts and cash payments

You may have noticed the label *accrual basis* in the upper left corner of many reports. In QuickBooks, by default, the accounting reports and financial statements are prepared using the accrual basis of accounting, which records revenue when earned and expenses when incurred regardless of cash receipts and cash payments. The accrual basis of accounting follows GAAP—generally accepted accounting principles—and is the basis used in this text.

Completing the New Company Setup Using the Accrual Basis of Accounting

Recall that you entered the opening balances for the Inventory accounts, Accounts Receivable, and Accounts Payable accounts when you set up and updated the Lists/Centers. When you set up the Chart of Accounts List, you also could have entered the opening balances for assets (excluding Accounts Receivable and Inventory), liabilities (excluding Accounts Payable), and equity accounts at that time. But you cannot enter opening balances for some system default accounts (such as Accounts Receivable, Accounts Payable, and Sales Tax Payable), and you cannot enter opening balances for revenue and expense accounts when creating new accounts in the Chart of Accounts List. Therefore, all the opening balances (excluding inventory, accounts receivable, and accounts payable) will be entered in one journal entry.

As you saw in the *Journal* report (Figure 7–DD on page 297), every time an Accounts Receivable account was recorded, a corresponding Uncategorized Income account was recorded, and every time an Accounts Payable account was recorded, a corresponding Uncategorized Expenses account was

Reversing the Uncategorized Expenses Account

In the *Journal* report shown in Figure 7–DD on page 297, there are seven journal entries that credit Accounts Payable and debit Uncategorized Expenses for seven vendors as follows:

Ace Glass Works	$1,500
Bell Carpet Design	2,000
Cuza and Carl Associates	400
Galeway Computers	2,600
Midwest Mutual Insurance Co.	2,400
Minneapolis Electric & Gas Co.	450
Williams Office Supply Company	400
	$9,750

The credit entries to the Accounts Payable account are correct and will stay in that account. The debits to the Uncategorized Expenses, however, have to be reversed by crediting Uncategorized Expenses for $9,750 and debiting the 3010 Kristin Raina, Capital account for $9,750.

To reverse the Uncategorized Expenses account:

1. At the Make General Journal Entries window, choose the date *04/01/2021*, and at the *ENTRY NO.* field, accept *3*.
2. Remove the check mark next to *ADJUSTING ENTRY*, if necessary.
3. Debit account 3010 Kristin Raina, Capital for 9,750 and credit account 69800 Uncategorized Expenses for 9,750. See Figure 7–II.

FIGURE 7–II
Make General Journal Entries Window— Reverse Uncategorized Expenses

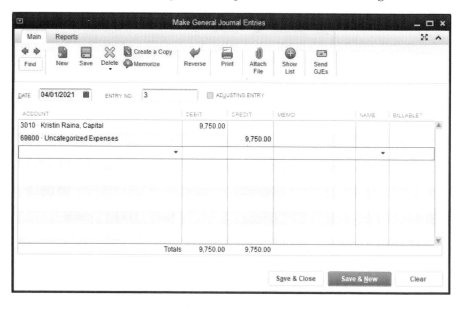

4. If the information is correct, click the Save & Close button.

ACCOUNTING CONCEPT

69800 Uncategorized Expenses			3010 Kristin Raina, Capital	
Dr	Cr		Dr	Cr
9,750	Rev 9,750		9,750	
0				

Accounting Reports and Financial Statements

Upon completing the New Company Setup, you should display and print the accounting reports and financial statements.

Accounting Reports

The accounting reports you need to print and review include the *Journal* and the *Trial Balance.*

Journal Report

You displayed and printed the *Journal* report after the initial company setup was completed (Figure 7–DD, page 297). After recording the opening balances and reversing the Uncategorized Income and Uncategorized Expenses accounts, you added three more journal entries to the *Journal* report. You can view and print all the journal entries for April 1, 2021. Figure 7–JJ displays only the additional three journal entries.

FIGURE 7–JJ
Additional Journal Entries

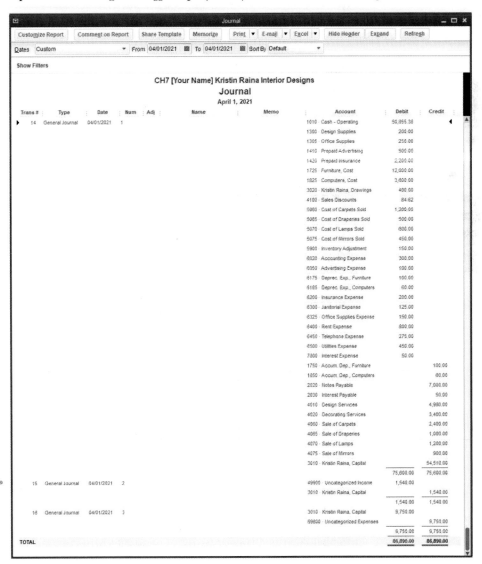

Trial Balance **Report**

Review and print the *Trial Balance* report for April 1, 2021. (It should look like Figure 7–KK.) The accounts and balances on this trial balance should match those on the trial balance of March 31, 2021, after transactions were recorded in Chapters 2 through 5.

FIGURE 7–KK
Trial Balance Report

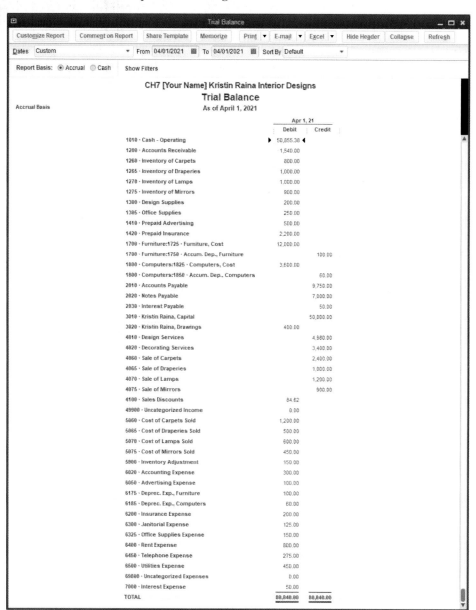

Recall that QuickBooks created the Uncategorized Income and Uncategorized Expenses accounts when you entered outstanding accounts receivable and accounts payable balances in the Customer Center and Vendor Center, respectively. The balances in these uncategorized accounts were subsequently reversed when the company file was prepared for the accrual basis of accounting. These accounts are no longer needed and can be marked inactive in the Chart of Accounts List.

Financial Statements

The financial statements consist of the *Profit & Loss Standard* report (see Figure 7–LL) and the *Balance Sheet Standard* report (see Figure 7–MM). Upon completion of the New Company Setup, these reports should be the same as the financial reports printed at the end of Chapter 5.

FIGURE 7-LL

Profit & Loss Standard Report

To reverse the Uncategorized Expenses account:
1. At the main menu bar, click Company and then click *Make General Journal Entries.*
2. Choose the date and check the entry at the *ENTRY NO.* field.
3. Remove the check mark next to *ADJUSTING ENTRY.*
4. Debit the Capital account for the full amount in the Uncategorized Expenses account and credit the Uncategorized Expenses account for the same amount.
5. Click the Save & Close button.

To view and print accounting reports from the Reports menu:
1. At the main menu bar, click Reports and then click *Accountant & Taxes.*
2. At the Accountant & Taxes submenu, choose a report.
3. Indicate the start and end dates for the report.
4. Print the report.
5. Close the report.

To view and print financial statements from the Reports menu:
1. At the main menu bar, click Reports and then click *Company & Financial.*
2. At the Company & Financial submenu, choose a financial report.
3. Indicate the start and end dates for the report.
4. Print the report.
5. Close the report.

Key Concepts

Select the letter of the item that best matches each definition.

a. Most common sales tax
b. Make account inactive
c. Uncategorized Income
d. Preferences - Accounting
e. Inventory Asset and Cost of Goods Sold
f. Preferences - Items & Inventory
g. Express Start
h. System default accounts
i. Uncategorized Expenses
j. Customer & Vendor Profile Lists

_____ 1. An alternative method of New Company Setup.
_____ 2. Accounts automatically created by QuickBooks when you choose an inventory item part in the New Item window.
_____ 3. An option you can choose so accounts not in use are not displayed in the reports.
_____ 4. The window used to activate account numbers.
_____ 5. Accounts automatically created by QuickBooks.
_____ 6. The account created by QuickBooks as an offsetting amount of Accounts Receivable.
_____ 7. The window used to activate the inventory feature.
_____ 8. The submenu used to open the Terms List window.
_____ 9. The field that must be completed to activate the sales tax feature.
_____ 10. The account created by QuickBooks as an offsetting amount of Accounts Payable.

Procedure Check

1. You are setting up a new company file and wish to use the Express Start method. Should you set up a password? Which preferences should you establish before recording data?
2. When you first choose *Inventory Part* in the *TYPE* field in the New Item window of the Item List, which two accounts does QuickBooks look for on the Chart of Accounts List? Can you customize these accounts? If so, explain how.
3. What is the Opening Balance Equity account? Can you customize this account? If so, explain how.
4. Why would you mark an account inactive, and how would you do it? What would you do to display inactive accounts in the Chart of Accounts List?
5. If you set up a new company file using the Express Start method, which journal entries would you normally record to complete the New Company Setup process?
6. Your manager is just learning QuickBooks. She has asked you if it is necessary to use the Detailed Start method with the EasyStep Interview window or the QuickBooks Desktop Setup window for New Company Setup. Provide the manager with a written explanation of how she could set up the new company file using the Express Start method instead of using the EasyStep Interview and QuickBooks Desktop Setup windows.

Case Problems

Demonstrate your knowledge of the QuickBooks features discussed in this chapter by completing the following case problems.

Case Problem 7–1

On April 1, 2021, Lynn Garcia began her business, Lynn's Music Studio. In the first month of business, Lynn set up the music studio, provided guitar and piano lessons, and recorded month-end activity. In May, the second month of business, Lynn started purchasing and selling inventory items of guitars, keyboards, music stands, and sheet music. In April and May, Lynn recorded the financial activities using a manual accounting system. On June 1, 2021, Lynn decided to switch her accounting method to QuickBooks. Lynn has organized the information about the company but has hired you to convert the accounting records to QuickBooks.

1. Use the information below to create and set up the company file using the Express Start method. (Skip the QuickBooks Desktop Setup window after the new company file is created.)

Business Name:	CH7 *[Your Name]* Lynn's Music Studio
Industry:	Other/None
Business Type:	Sole Proprietorship
Employer Identification Number (EIN):	45-6123789
Business Address:	228 Pearl Street

City:	Scranton
State:	PA
ZIP:	18501
Country:	U.S.
Phone:	570-555-0400

2. Set up the company file password.

New Password:	Student1
Confirm New Password:	Student1
Challenge Question:	First college roommate's name
Answer:	Friend

3. Activate the account numbers, inventory, and sales tax features. For sales tax, use the following information:

TYPE:	Sales Tax Item
Sales Tax Name:	PA Sales Tax
Description:	Sales Tax
Tax Rate (%):	7
Tax Agency:	PA Dept. of Revenue

4. Disable the payroll.
5. Open and close the following windows to allow QuickBooks to create system default accounts:
    Create Invoices
    Enter Sales Receipts
    Enter Bills
    Item List: New Item: Inventory Part

6. Use the following information to customize the system default accounts:

QuickBooks		Edited	
Number	Account Name	Number	Account Name
11000	Accounts Receivable	1200	
12000	Undeposited Funds	1250	
12100	Inventory Asset	1260	Inventory of Guitars
20000	Accounts Payable	2010	
25500	Sales Tax Payable	2200	
30000	Opening Balance Equity	3010	Lynn Garcia, Capital
30800	Owners Draw	3020	Lynn Garcia, Drawings
32000	Owners Equity	3030	Accumulated Earnings
50000	Cost of Goods Sold	5060	Cost of Guitars Sold

7. Mark the Payroll Liabilities and Payroll Expenses accounts as inactive.
8. Customize the payment Terms List to list only the following:
    2/10, Net 30 Days
    Net 10 Days
    Net 15 Days
    Net 30 Days

9. Use the information in Table LMS—Accounts to update the Chart of Accounts List.

TABLE LMS
Accounts

Account Type	Number	Account Name
Bank	1010	Cash - Operating
Other Current Asset	1265	Inventory of Keyboards
Other Current Asset	1270	Inventory of Music Stands
Other Current Asset	1275	Inventory of Sheet Music
Other Current Asset	1300	Music Supplies
Other Current Asset	1305	Office Supplies
Other Current Asset	1410	Prepaid Advertising
Other Current Asset	1420	Prepaid Insurance
Fixed Asset	1700	Music Instruments
Fixed Asset	1725	Music Instruments, Cost [Subaccount of 1700]
Fixed Asset	1750	Accum. Dep., Music Instruments [Subaccount of 1700]
Fixed Asset	1800	Furniture
Fixed Asset	1825	Furniture, Cost [Subaccount of 1800]
Fixed Asset	1850	Accum. Dep., Furniture [Subaccount of 1800]
Fixed Asset	1900	Computers
Fixed Asset	1925	Computers, Cost [Subaccount of 1900]
Fixed Asset	1950	Accum. Dep., Computers [Subaccount of 1900]
Other Current Liability	2020	Notes Payable
Other Current Liability	2030	Interest Payable
Income	4010	Piano Lessons
Income	4020	Guitar Lessons
Income	4060	Sale of Guitars
Income	4065	Sale of Keyboards
Income	4070	Sale of Music Stands
Income	4075	Sale of Sheet Music
Income	4100	Sales Discounts
Cost of Goods Sold	5065	Cost of Keyboards Sold
Cost of Goods Sold	5070	Cost of Music Stands Sold
Cost of Goods Sold	5075	Cost of Sheet Music Sold
Cost of Goods Sold	5900	Inventory Adjustment
Expense	6075	Deprec. Exp., Music Instruments
Expense	6085	Deprec. Exp., Furniture
Expense	6095	Deprec. Exp., Computers
Expense	6150	Instrument Tuning Expense
Expense	6200	Insurance Expense
Expense	6300	Music Supplies Expense
Expense	6325	Office Supplies Expense
Expense	6400	Rent Expense
Expense	6450	Telephone Expense
Expense	6500	Utilities Expense
Other Expense	7000	Interest Expense

…continued

Number	Account Name	Balance
4100	Sales Discounts	188.92
5060	Cost of Guitars Sold	1,150.00
5065	Cost of Keyboards Sold	2,475.00
5070	Cost of Music Stands Sold	460.00
5075	Cost of Sheet Music Sold	1,305.00
5900	Inventory Adjustment	50.00
6075	Deprec. Exp., Music Instruments	60.00
6085	Deprec. Exp., Furniture	40.00
6095	Deprec. Exp., Computers	35.00
6150	Instrument Tuning	100.00
6200	Insurance Expense	100.00
6300	Music Supplies Expense	70.00
6325	Office Supplies Expense	50.00
6400	Rent Expense	600.00
6450	Telephone Expense	50.00
6500	Utilities Expense	70.00
7000	Interest Expense	15.00

Enter the following accounts and amounts as credits:

Number	Account Name	Balance
1750	Accum. Dep., Music Instruments	$ 60.00
1850	Accum. Dep., Furniture	40.00
1950	Accum. Dep., Computers	35.00
2020	Notes Payable	2,000.00
2030	Interest Payable	15.00
4010	Piano Lessons	3,535.00
4020	Guitar Lessons	2,910.00
4060	Sale of Guitars	2,300.00
4065	Sale of Keyboards	4,950.00
4070	Sale of Music Stands	920.00
4075	Sale of Sheet Music	2,610.00

b. Make a journal entry to reverse the Uncategorized Income account.

c. Make a journal entry to reverse the Uncategorized Expenses account.

14. Display and print the following reports for June 1, 2021:
    a. *Journal*
    b. *Trial Balance*
    c. *Profit & Loss Standard* (04/01/2021–06/01/2021)
    d. *Balance Sheet Standard*
    e. *Item Listing*
    f. *Customer Contact List*
    g. *Vendor Contact List*

15. Make a backup copy of the new company file and name it **LMS7 *[Your Name]* Lynn's Music Studio**. Restore the backup copy and change the company name to **LMS7 *[Your Name]* Lynn's Music Studio**.

Case Problem 7–2

On June 1, 2021, Olivia Chen began her business, Olivia's Web Solutions. In the first month of business, Olivia set up the office, provided web page design and internet consulting services, and recorded month-end activity. In July, the second month of business, Olivia began to purchase and sell inventory items of computer hardware and software. In June and July, Olivia recorded the financial activities using a manual accounting system. On August 1, 2021, Olivia decides to switch her accounting method to QuickBooks. Olivia has organized the information about the company but has hired you to convert the accounting records to QuickBooks.

1. Use the information below to create and set up the company file using the Express Start method. (Skip the Quickbooks Desktop Setup window after the new company file is created.)

Business Name:	CH7 *[Your Name]* Olivia's Web Solutions
Industry:	Other/None
Business Type:	Sole Proprietorship
Employer Identification Number (EIN):	55-5656566
Business Address:	547 Miller Place
City:	Westport
State:	NY
ZIP:	11858
Country:	U.S.
Phone:	516-555-5000

2. Set up the company file password.

New Password:	Student1
Confirm New Password:	Student1
Challenge Question:	First college roommate's name
Answer:	Friend

3. Activate the account numbers, inventory, and sales tax features. For sales tax, use the following information:

TYPE:	Sales Tax Item
Tax Name:	NYS Sales Tax
Description:	Sales Tax
Tax Rate (%):	8
Tax Agency:	NYS Tax Dept.

4. Disable the payroll.
5. Open and close the following windows to allow QuickBooks to create system default accounts:
   Create Invoices
   Enter Sales Receipts
   Enter Bills
   Item List: New Item: Inventory Part

6. Use the following information to customize the system default accounts:

	QuickBooks			Edited	
Number	Account Name		Number	Account Name	
11000	Accounts Receivable		1200		
12000	Undeposited Funds		1250		
12100	Inventory Asset		1260	Inventory of Computers	
20000	Accounts Payable		2010		
25500	Sales Tax Payable		2200		
30000	Opening Balance Equity		3010	Olivia Chen, Capital	
30800	Owners Draw		3020	Olivia Chen, Drawings	
32000	Owners Equity		3030	Accumulated Earnings	
50000	Cost of Goods Sold		5060	Cost of Computers Sold	

7. Mark the Payroll Liabilities and Payroll Expenses accounts as inactive.
8. Customize the payment Terms List to list only the following:
   2/10, Net 30 Days
   Net 10 Days
   Net 15 Days
   Net 30 Days

9. Use the information in Table OWS—Accounts to update the Chart of Accounts List.

TABLE OWS
Accounts

Account Type	Number	Account Name
Bank	1010	Cash - Operating
Other Current Asset	1265	Inventory of Scanners
Other Current Asset	1270	Inventory of HTML Software
Other Current Asset	1275	Inventory of Desktop Pub. Soft.
Other Current Asset	1300	Computer Supplies
Other Current Asset	1305	Office Supplies
Other Current Asset	1410	Prepaid Advertising
Other Current Asset	1420	Prepaid Insurance
Fixed Asset	1700	Computers
Fixed Asset	1725	Computers, Cost [Subaccount of 1700]
Fixed Asset	1750	Accum. Dep., Computers [Subaccount of 1700]
Fixed Asset	1800	Furniture
Fixed Asset	1825	Furniture, Cost [Subaccount of 1800]
Fixed Asset	1850	Accum. Dep., Furniture [Subaccount of 1800]
Fixed Asset	1900	Software
Fixed Asset	1925	Software, Cost[Subaccount of 1900]

continues...

TABLE OWS

Accounts...*continued*

Account Type	Number	Account Name
Fixed Asset	1950	Accum. Dep., Software [Subaccount of 1900]
Other Current Liability	2020	Notes Payable
Other Current Liability	2030	Interest Payable
Income	4010	Web Page Design Fees
Income	4020	Internet Consulting Fees
Income	4060	Sale of Computers
Income	4065	Sale of Scanners
Income	4070	Sale of HTML Software
Income	4075	Sale of Desktop Pub. Software
Income	4100	Sales Discounts
Cost of Goods Sold	5065	Cost of Scanners Sold
Cost of Goods Sold	5070	Cost of HTML Software Sold
Cost of Goods Sold	5075	Cost of Desktop Pub. Soft. Sold
Cost of Goods Sold	5900	Inventory Adjustment
Expense	6050	Advertising Expense
Expense	6075	Deprec. Exp., Computers
Expense	6085	Deprec. Exp., Furniture
Expense	6095	Deprec. Exp., Software
Expense	6100	Insurance Expense
Expense	6300	Computer Supplies Expense
Expense	6325	Office Supplies Expense
Expense	6350	Online Service Expense
Expense	6400	Rent Expense
Expense	6450	Telephone Expense
Expense	6500	Utilities Expense
Other Expense	7000	Interest Expense

10. Use the information in Table OWS—Items to update the Item List. For the Inventory Part Items, be sure to use the date *August 1, 2021.*

TABLE OWS Items

Item Name and Description on Purchase and Sales Transactions	Cost	COGS Account	Rate/ Sales Price	Income Account	Asset Account	On Hand	Total Value
Service Items (nontaxable):							
Internet Consulting Services			$ 100	4020			
Web Page Design Services			125	4010			
Inventory Part Items (taxable):							
Computers	$1,000	5060	2,000	4060	1260	10	$10,000
Scanners	300	5065	600	4065	1265	12	3,600
HTML Software	75	5070	150	4070	1270	18	1,350
Desktop Pub. Software	100	5075	200	4075	1275	10	1,000

11. Use the information in Table OWS—Customers to update the Customer Center. Be sure to use the date *August 1, 2021*, for each customer with an opening balance.

TABLE OWS Customers

Customer/ Company Name	Opening Balance	Full Name	Main Phone/ Mobile	Invoice/Bill To	Payment Terms
Artie's Auto Repair	$800.00	Leon Artie	516-555-1221 516-555-1231	32 W. 11th Street New Hyde Park, NY 11523	Net 30 Days
Breathe Easy A/C Contractors		Allen Scott	516-555-6868 516-555-6869	556 Atlantic Ave. Freeport, NY 11634	Net 30 Days
Long Island Water Works		Customer Service	516-555-4747 516-555-4748	87-54 Bayview Ave. Glen Cove, NY 11563	2/10, Net 30 Days
Miguel's Restaurant		Miguel Perez	516-555-3236 516-555-3237	30 Willis Ave. Roslyn, NY 11541	2/10, Net 30 Days
Schneider Family	1,000.00	Johnny Schneider	516-555-8989 516-555-8990	363 Farmers Rd. Syosset, NY 11547	Net 15 Days
Sehorn & Smith Attorneys	800.00	Jerry Sehorn	212-555-3339 212-555-3338	510 Fifth Ave. New York, NY 10022	Net 30 Days
Singh Family		David Singh	718-555-3233 718-555-3239	363 Marathon Parkway Little Neck, NY 11566	Net 15 Days
South Shore School District	12,056.00	Joseph Porter	516-555-4545 516-555-4546	3666 Ocean Ave. South Beach, NY 11365	2/10, Net 30 Days
Thrifty Stores	1,500.00	William Way	718-555-2445 718-555-2446	23 Boston Ave. Bronx, NY 11693	Net 30 Days

12. Use the information in Table OWS—Vendors to update the Vendor Center. Be sure to use the date of *August 1, 2021*, for each vendor with an opening balance.

TABLE OWS Vendors

Vendor/Company Name	Opening Balance	Full Name	Main Phone/ Mobile	Billed To	Payment Terms
ARC Management		Alvin R. Clinton	516-555-6363 516-555-6364	668 Lakeville Ave. Garden City, NY 11678	Net 30 Days
Chrbet Advertising	$1,200.00	Chris Chrbet	212-555-8777 212-555-8778	201 E. 10th Street New York, NY 10012	Net 30 Days
Comet Computer Supplies		Customer Service	631-555-4444 631-555-4455	657 Motor Parkway Center Island, NY 11488	Net 15 Days
Computec Computers	10,000.00	Customer Service	702-555-6564 702-555-6563	3631 Gate Blvd. Greenboro, NC 27407	Net 30 Days
Eastel	350.00	Customer Service	212-555-6565 212-555-6566	655 Fifth Ave. New York, NY 10012	Net 30 Days
Eastern Mutual Insurance		Customer Service	212-555-6363 212-555-6364	55 Broadway Room 55 New York, NY 10001	Net 30 Days
InterSoft Development Co.		Customer Service	631-555-3634 631-555-3635	556 Route 347 Hauppauge, NY 11654	Net 30 Days

continues...

TABLE OWS Vendors...*continued*

Vendor/Company Name	Opening Balance	Full Name	Main Phone/ Mobile	Billed To	Payment Terms
Lewis Furniture Co.	1,700.00	Manny Lewis	631-555-6161 631-555-6162	1225 Route 110 Farmingdale, NY 11898	Net 30 Days
LI Power Company		Customer Service	516-555-8888 516-555-8889	5444 Northern Ave. Plainview, NY 11544	Net 15 Days
Martin Computer Repairs		Ken Martin	516-555-7777 516-555-7778	366 N. Franklin St. Garden City, NY 11568	Net 30 Days
Netsoft Development Co.	1,600.00	Customer Service	974-555-7873 974-555-7874	684 Mountain View Rd. Portland, OR 68774	Net 30 Days
Office Plus	375.00	Customer Service	516-555-3214 516-555-3213	45 Jericho Tpke. Jericho, NY 11654	Net 30 Days
Olivia Chen					
Scanntronix		Customer Service	617-555-8778 617-555-8776	2554 Bedford Rd. Boston, MA 02164	Net 30 Days
Systems Service		Jeremy Jones	516-555-2525 516-555-2526	36 Sunrise Lane Hempstead, NY 11004	Net 30 Days
Textpro Software, Inc.		Customer Service	615-555-4545 615-555-4546	877 Route 5 Ft. Lauderdale, FL 70089	Net 30 Days

13. Make three journal entries on August 1, 2021 (accept the default Entry Nos.):

   a. Enter the opening balances listed below. Enter the following accounts and amounts as debits:

Number	Account Name	Balance
1010	Cash - Operating	$24,489.16
1300	Computer Supplies	350.00
1305	Office Supplies	325.00
1410	Prepaid Advertising	1,000.00
1420	Prepaid Insurance	1,650.00
1725	Computers, Cost	5,000.00
1825	Furniture, Cost	3,200.00
1925	Software, Cost	3,600.00
3020	Olivia Chen, Drawings	500.00
4100	Sales Discounts	179.84
5060	Cost of Computers Sold	10,000.00
5065	Cost of Scanners Sold	2,400.00
5070	Cost of HTML Software Sold	75.00
5075	Cost of Desktop Pub. Soft. Sold	500.00
5900	Inventory Adjustment	75.00
6050	Advertising Expense	200.00
6075	Deprec. Exp., Computers	75.00
6085	Deprec. Exp., Furniture	50.00
6095	Deprec. Exp., Software	100.00
6100	Insurance Expense	150.00
6300	Computer Supplies Expense	250.00

...continues

...continued

Number	Account Name	Balance
6325	Office Supplies Expense	50.00
6350	Online Service Expense	150.00
6400	Rent Expense	800.00
6450	Telephone Expense	350.00
6500	Utilities Expense	125.00
7000	Interest Expense	25.00

Enter the following accounts and amounts as credits:

Number	Account Name	Balance
1750	Accum. Dep., Computers	$ 75.00
1850	Accum. Dep., Furniture	50.00
1950	Accum. Dep., Software	100.00
2020	Notes Payable	2,500.00
2030	Interest Payable	25.00
4010	Web Page Design Fees	9,750.00
4020	Internet Consulting Fees	6,600.00
4060	Sale of Computers	20,000.00
4065	Sale of Scanners	4,800.00
4070	Sale of HTML Software	150.00
4075	Sale of Desktop Pub. Software	1,000.00

   b. Make a journal entry to reverse the Uncategorized Income account.

   c. Make a journal entry to reverse the Uncategorized Expenses account.

14. Display and print the following reports for August 1, 2021:
   a. *Journal*
   b. *Trial Balance*
   c. *Profit & Loss Standard* (06/01/2021–08/01/2021)
   d. *Balance Sheet Standard*
   e. *Item Listing*
   f. *Customer Contact List*
   g. *Vendor Contact List*

15. Make a backup copy of the new company file and name it **OWS7 *[Your Name]* Olivia's Web Solutions**. Restore the backup copy and change the company name to **OWS7 *[Your Name]* Olivia's Web Solutions**.

CHAPTER 8

Payroll Setup

Customizing Payroll Setup

Objectives

- Review payroll terminology
- Activate the payroll preference
- Customize payroll system default accounts
- Customize and update the Chart of Accounts List for payroll
- Set up payroll to accept manual entries
- Customize the Payroll Item List for payroll items created by QuickBooks
- Update the Payroll Item List
- Display and print the *Payroll Item Listing* report

QuickBooks allows you to process payroll and track payroll information for your company's employees. The company that hires the workers is called the **employer**. The person hired by a company who will receive salary or wages on a regular basis is called the **employee**. **Payroll** involves computing each employee's gross earnings, determining each employee's **withholdings** and **deductions**, and calculating each employee's net pay. It also involves preparing employees' paychecks or setting up direct deposits, properly recording payroll-related transactions (journal entries), submitting payroll withholdings and deductions to the appropriate tax agency or other entity, and preparing payroll compliance reports.

To process payroll in QuickBooks, it must first be set up. Payroll setup involves enabling the payroll feature, customizing and adding payroll accounts to the Chart of Accounts List, choosing a QuickBooks payroll service or activating the manual entries feature, customizing pre-established payroll items, and establishing payroll items such as compensation and payroll taxes or payroll deductions. These payroll items comprise the Payroll Item List.

In this chapter, our sample company, Kristin Raina Interior Designs, will set up the payroll in anticipation of hiring two employees beginning April 1, 2021. After the payroll setup is complete and the employees are hired, the payroll transactions for Kristin Raina Interior Designs will then be illustrated in Chapter 9.

QuickBooks versus Manual Accounting: Payroll

In a manual accounting system, the process of preparing a payroll is laborious and time consuming. For each employee, the company has to tally the hours worked in a pay period, compute the gross pay for the pay period, and then determine all the withholdings and deductions from that employee's pay. After completing these computations, the company has to prepare a paycheck or direct deposit, along with a pay stub showing all the earnings, withholdings, and deductions for the pay period, as well as all the year-to-date earnings, withholdings, and deductions. When computers are not used, payroll withholdings are calculated manually using preprinted withholding tables. The gross pay, withholdings, and deductions for all employees then have to be totaled to record the payroll in a payroll journal, which subsequently is posted to the general ledger accounts. In addition, year-to-date earnings and withholdings need to be accumulated and used in preparing government-required quarterly and year-end reports. In dealing with such a quantity and variety of computations, it is easy to make a mistake.

Payroll was one of the first accounting tasks to be available on computers. Payroll preparation firms were formed for this sole purpose. A company simply prepares a list of each employee's name and the hours that person worked during a pay period. This information is submitted to the payroll processing firm and—usually overnight—the payroll is prepared; the company receives its properly completed paychecks or list of direct deposits and a summary report the next morning. The paychecks are distributed to the employees or the direct deposits are processed, and the summary report is used to record the appropriate journal entries for the payroll. The payroll processing firm also accumulates the necessary

employer the company that hires the workers

employee the person hired by a company who will receive salary or wages on a regular basis

payroll involves computing each employee's gross earnings, withholdings and deductions, and net pay; preparing employees' paychecks or setting up direct deposits; properly recording payroll-related transactions; submitting payroll withholdings and deductions to the appropriate agencies; and preparing payroll compliance reports

withholdings generally refer to the payroll taxes the employer is required to take out of the employee's paycheck and submit to the appropriate government agency

deductions generally refer to amounts taken out of the employee's paycheck for various fringe benefits, such as insurance, pension, and so on information for preparing government compliance reports. As personal computers and accounting software packages became available, companies were able to process their payroll in-house as part of their routine accounting tasks without needing to use an outside payroll preparation firm.

QuickBooks includes a payroll feature that, once activated, allows processing a payroll with employees' gross earnings, withholdings, deductions, and net pay both quickly and easily. Simultaneously, the payroll transactions are recorded in the journal. In addition, the paychecks can be immediately printed when the printer is set up to do so, or the direct deposit can be set up and immediately processed. QuickBooks also simultaneously prepares reports that summarize all quarterly and annual information needed for required filings and for required payments of employee withholdings to the appropriate agencies.

Part of what makes payroll processing easier in QuickBooks than in a manual system is the use of Lists/Centers, which you will recall function as a database. Typical gross earnings, withholdings, and deductions are detailed in the Payroll Item List. In addition, exact payroll taxes are maintained within the payroll feature and QuickBooks payroll services. When employees are to be paid, QuickBooks calls on the information in the Payroll Item List, along with information about the employee (discussed in Chapter 9), and quickly does all the computations and prepares all the related reports. But because QuickBooks computes the employee's pay by accessing information from the Payroll Item List, it is important that the Payroll Item List be accurate and complete. Any errors in the Payroll Item List will result in inaccurate computations in the payroll and the subsequent recording of incorrect entries in the general journal.

Payroll Definitions and Terms

Whether payroll is processed manually or with a software package, the laws, procedures, filing requirements, definitions, and terminology remain the same. The following is a brief review of the more common payroll definitions.

Employee Payroll Information

To properly determine an employee's gross pay, tax withholdings, deductions, and net pay and to meet federal and state record-keeping requirements, the employer needs specific information about the employee. This information includes but is not limited to the following:

- Name
- Address
- Social Security number
- Marital status
- Gross pay amount or hourly rate
- Tax withholding allowances
- Voluntary deductions (pension, 401(k), insurance, and so on)

The employer uses this information along with the applicable tax rates to compute the employee's paycheck and track the employee's pay information.

Gross Pay

Gross pay, also known as *gross earnings*, is the total earnings for the employee for a specific pay period before any withholdings and deductions. Compensation can be in the form of a salary, hourly wages, tips, commissions, bonus, and overtime earned during a pay period. If the

gross pay total earnings for an employee for a specific pay period before withholdings and deductions employee is paid based on an annual salary, the annual amount is divided over the number of pay periods in the year. Gross pay for an hourly worker is determined based on the number of hours worked during the pay period multiplied by the employee's hourly pay rate. The gross pay will be subject to payroll taxes for both the employer and the employee.

FICA Tax (Social Security) and Medicare Tax

The Federal Insurance Contribution Act (FICA) tax, also known as Social Security, is a tax imposed on both the employer and the employee at a rate of 6.2% of the first $128,400 (year 2018) of wages for each employee. Medicare tax is also imposed on both the employer and the employee at a rate of 1.45% each; there is no wage maximum for the Medicare tax. Beginning in 2013, an Additional Medicare Tax of 0.9% (0.009) was imposed, which has different thresholds for different taxpayers ($250,000/$200,000). The employer periodically remits both the employer and the employee portions of the tax to the federal government.

Federal Income Tax (FIT)

Employers are required to withhold from each employee's pay the appropriate amount of federal income tax (FIT). The Internal Revenue Service (IRS) publishes tables and instructions to assist employers in determining the proper withholding amount for each employee. The withholding amount is determined based on the employee's gross pay, marital status, and exemption allowances claimed. The employer periodically forwards the tax withheld to the federal government along with the Social Security and Medicare taxes.

State Income Tax (SIT)

Many states impose an income tax and require employers to withhold the tax from employees' pay in a manner similar to that used for FIT. The employer will remit this tax periodically to the appropriate state taxing authority. Some local governments (city, county) may also impose income taxes. Rules for withholding local taxes for local governments are similar to those used by federal and state governments.

Federal Unemployment Tax Act (FUTA)

The Federal Unemployment Tax Act (FUTA) imposes a tax on the employer only. The tax is used to fund unemployment insurance programs administered by the federal government. The effective rate of the tax is 0.6% of the first $7,000 of each employee's wages.

State Unemployment Insurance (SUI)

In addition to paying the FUTA tax, employers are required by all states to contribute to a state unemployment insurance (SUI) fund. Rates and regulations vary from state to state. However, most states impose the tax only on the employer. The rate can vary from 1% to 11% based on the employer's location and unemployment experience, and the taxable amount varies from state to state.

State Disability Insurance (SDI)

Most states require employers to purchase an insurance policy, sometimes called *state disability insurance* (SDI), that compensates employees if they are unable to work for an extended period due to illness or injury. Some states allow the employer to withhold a small amount from each employee's pay to defray the employer's insurance premium cost.

Company Deductions

Many employers sponsor various fringe benefit programs and deduct amounts from an employee's pay to fund or offset the costs of the benefits. Programs such as 401(k) plans, medical and dental insurance, pension and profit-sharing plans, long-term disability, life insurance, and so on may be partially funded by a deduction made by the company from an employee's paycheck.

Net Pay

net pay total gross earnings for an employee minus all employee withholdings and deductions

Net pay is the amount of the employee's gross pay less all employee withholdings and deductions. As anyone who has worked knows, net pay is only a fraction of the gross pay earned.

United States Treasury

The United States Treasury is the tax-collecting agency of the federal government. The United States Treasury is responsible for collecting the FICA tax, Medicare tax, FIT, and FUTA tax. Most states have a similar department for collecting SIT, SUI, and SDI.

Chapter Problem

In this chapter, Kristin Raina Interior Designs will set up the payroll in anticipation of hiring two employees during April 2021. The April 1 beginning balances for the company are contained in the company file **CH8 Kristin Raina Interior Designs**.

Before you begin, open the company file **CH8 Kristin Raina Interior Designs.QBW**. Enter the password, *Student1*. Make a backup copy of the file, name it **EX8 *[Your Name]* Kristin Raina Interior Designs**, and then restore the file. Enter the password, *Student1*. Finally, change the company name in the file to **EX8 *[Your Name]* Kristin Raina Interior Designs**.

New Company Setup

Payroll Setup—Activate the Payroll Feature

To set up payroll in QuickBooks, you must first activate the payroll feature. If you set up a new company file using the Detailed Start method—by using the EasyStep Interview window (Chapter 6)—you have the choice of disabling the payroll feature. However, if you set up a new company file using the Express Start method (Chapter 7), QuickBooks automatically activates the payroll feature. In the company file for this chapter problem, the payroll feature was disabled and needs to be activated at the Preferences window on the Edit menu.

To activate the QuickBooks payroll feature:
1. At the main menu bar, click Edit and then click *Preferences*.
2. In the left panel of the Preferences window, click the Payroll & Employees icon.
3. Click the Company Preferences tab. If the payroll processing feature is not activated, the *No payroll* option is selected.
4. Click the *Full payroll* option. See Figure 8–A.

FIGURE 8–A

Preferences Window—
Payroll & Employees—
Company Preferences

Full payroll option

5. Accept the defaults and click OK.

Once you have activated the payroll feature, QuickBooks automatically creates two default general ledger accounts: Payroll Liabilities and Payroll Expenses.

Lists/Centers

Updating the Chart of Accounts List for Payroll

When the payroll feature is activated, QuickBooks establishes one default general ledger liability posting account for *all* payroll-related liabilities and one expense account for *all* payroll expenses. Open and review the Chart of Accounts List. The accounts created by QuickBooks are 24000 Payroll Liabilities and 66000 Payroll Expenses. When these accounts are created, each account type is dimmed in the Edit Account window to indicate that QuickBooks has created each account and that each account is a system default account. Recall that you must allow QuickBooks to create its own accounts in some situations, but then you can edit the account names and account numbers.

HINT

Notice that on the Chart of Accounts List, there is a Cash - Payroll account. Many companies use a separate checking account for payroll transactions. Periodically, funds are transferred into this account from the Cash - Operating account. Transfer of funds between cash accounts is covered in Chapter 10.

QuickBooks creates one payroll liability account and one payroll expense account to be used in the payroll processing transactions (Chapter 9). However, most companies usually create separate payroll liability accounts for FIT, SIT, Social Security, Medicare, and so on. Similarly, most companies usually create separate payroll expense accounts for Social Security, Medicare, FUTA, SUI, and so on. For our sample company, Kristin Raina Interior Designs, you will create separate payroll liability accounts that will be subaccounts of the system default Payroll Liabilities account created by QuickBooks. Similarly, you will create separate payroll expense accounts that will be subaccounts of the system default Payroll Expenses account created by QuickBooks. Before creating the additional payroll accounts, you will customize the system default accounts to change the account numbers to follow the company pattern for numbering accounts on the Chart of Accounts List.

Customize the Payroll System Default Accounts

Using the procedures illustrated in Chapter 4, customize the payroll system default accounts in the Chart of Accounts List as follows:

	QuickBooks		Edited
Number	Account Name		Number
24000	Payroll Liabilities		2100
66000	Payroll Expenses		6560

Adding Payroll Accounts

HINT

To add an account, click the Account menu button in the Chart of Accounts List window and then click *New*.

Using the procedures illustrated in Chapter 4, add the payroll accounts listed below to the Chart of Accounts List.

Other Current Liability account type:

2110	Social Sec/Medicare Tax Payable	Subaccount of 2100 Payroll Liabilities
2115	FIT Payable	Subaccount of 2100 Payroll Liabilities
2120	SIT Payable	Subaccount of 2100 Payroll Liabilities
2125	FUTA Payable	Subaccount of 2100 Payroll Liabilities
2130	SUI Payable	Subaccount of 2100 Payroll Liabilities

HINT

Use *Edit* from the Account menu in the Chart of Accounts List window to correct any errors.

Expense account type:

6565	Salaries and Wages Expense	Subaccount of 6560 Payroll Expenses
6610	Social Sec/Medicare Tax Expense	Subaccount of 6560 Payroll Expenses
6625	FUTA Expense	Subaccount of 6560 Payroll Expenses
6630	SUI Expense	Subaccount of 6560 Payroll Expenses

QuickCheck: The updated Chart of Accounts List appears in Figure 8–B.

FIGURE 8-B
Updated Chart of
Accounts List

NAME	TYPE	BALANCE TOTAL	ATTACH
1010 · Cash - Operating	Bank	43,355.38	
1020 · Cash - Payroll	Bank	7,500.00	
1200 · Accounts Receivable	Accounts Receivable	1,540.00	
1250 · Undeposited Funds	Other Current Asset	0.00	
1260 · Inventory of Carpets	Other Current Asset	800.00	
1265 · Inventory of Draperies	Other Current Asset	1,000.00	
1270 · Inventory of Lamps	Other Current Asset	1,000.00	
1275 · Inventory of Mirrors	Other Current Asset	900.00	
1300 · Design Supplies	Other Current Asset	200.00	
1305 · Office Supplies	Other Current Asset	250.00	
1410 · Prepaid Advertising	Other Current Asset	500.00	
1420 · Prepaid Insurance	Other Current Asset	2,200.00	
1700 · Furniture	Fixed Asset	11,900.00	
1725 · Furniture, Cost	Fixed Asset	12,000.00	
1750 · Accum. Dep., Furniture	Fixed Asset	-100.00	
1800 · Computers	Fixed Asset	3,540.00	
1825 · Computers, Cost	Fixed Asset	3,600.00	
1850 · Accum. Dep., Computers	Fixed Asset	-60.00	
2010 · Accounts Payable	Accounts Payable	9,750.00	
2020 · Notes Payable	Other Current Liability	7,000.00	
2030 · Interest Payable	Other Current Liability	50.00	
2100 · Payroll Liabilities	Other Current Liability	0.00	
2110 · Social Sec/Medicare Tax Payable	Other Current Liability	0.00	
2115 · FIT Payable	Other Current Liability	0.00	
2120 · SIT Payable	Other Current Liability	0.00	
2125 · FUTA Payable	Other Current Liability	0.00	
2130 · SUI Payable	Other Current Liability	0.00	
2200 · Sales Tax Payable	Other Current Liability	0.00	
3010 · Kristin Raina, Capital	Equity	50,000.00	
3020 · Kristin Raina, Drawings	Equity	-400.00	
3030 · Accumulated Earnings	Equity		
4010 · Design Services	Income		
4020 · Decorating Services	Income		
4060 · Sale of Carpets	Income		
4065 · Sale of Draperies	Income		
4070 · Sale of Lamps	Income		
4075 · Sale of Mirrors	Income		
4100 · Sales Discounts	Income		
5060 · Cost of Carpets Sold	Cost of Goods Sold		
5065 · Cost of Draperies Sold	Cost of Goods Sold		
5070 · Cost of Lamps Sold	Cost of Goods Sold		
5075 · Cost of Mirrors Sold	Cost of Goods Sold		
5900 · Inventory Adjustment	Cost of Goods Sold		
6020 · Accounting Expense	Expense		
6050 · Advertising Expense	Expense		
6175 · Deprec. Exp., Furniture	Expense		
6185 · Deprec. Exp., Computers	Expense		
6200 · Insurance Expense	Expense		
6300 · Janitorial Expenses	Expense		
6325 · Office Supplies Expense	Expense		
6400 · Rent Expense	Expense		
6450 · Telephone Expense	Expense		
6500 · Utilities Expense	Expense		
6560 · Payroll Expenses	Expense		
6565 · Salaries and Wages Expense	Expense		
6610 · Social Sec/Medicare Tax Expense	Expense		
6625 · FUTA Expense	Expense		
6630 · SUI Expense	Expense		
7000 · Interest Expense	Other Expense		

Payroll Liabilities—
parent account and
subaccounts

Payroll Expenses—
parent account and
subaccounts

Chart of Accounts

Look for account name or number

Search   Reset

Account ▼   Activities ▼   Reports ▼   Attach   ☐ Include inactive

Using QuickBooks Payroll Services versus Calculating Payroll Manually

Like most computerized accounting packages, QuickBooks offers several desktop payroll services: QuickBooks Basic Payroll, QuickBooks Enhanced Payroll, and QuickBooks Assisted Payroll. A company would choose the service that best fits its needs, from the Basic service, which allows the company to prepare and issue paychecks or direct deposits, to the Enhanced service, which also prepares the federal and state tax reporting information. If a company prefers, it could use the Assisted Payroll, which does the payroll setup and then does the same as the Enhanced service but also files and pays the taxes. If a company chooses to use one of the QuickBooks payroll services, it subscribes to the service and pays a monthly fee, and then the taxes imposed on the employer and the employees' withholdings are automatically computed based on the information in the Payroll Item List, the employee's file (Chapter 9), and the QuickBooks payroll service. If a company has not subscribed to a QuickBooks payroll service, then the firm's payroll withholdings, deductions, and payroll taxes must be entered by typing the amounts into QuickBooks.

Part of the payroll setup is to indicate either that a specific QuickBooks payroll service will be used or that the payroll will be processed manually. In business, it is commonly advisable to subscribe to a payroll service. However, in the classroom environment, the payroll withholdings, deductions, and payroll taxes will be entered manually. The payroll for manual processing is set up using the Help menu.

To set up payroll for manual processing using the Help menu:

1. At the main menu bar, click Help and then click *QuickBooks Desktop Help*. The Have a Question? window appears. If the Help Article window appears, click the X to close it.
2. At the Have a Question? window, in the *Search* text box, type payroll and then press the Enter key or click the Search icon. Some payroll topics are displayed.
3. In the Answers in Help section, click *Show more answers*. Additional payroll topics are displayed. See Figure 8–C.

FIGURE 8–C
Have a Question? Window—Payroll Topics Listed

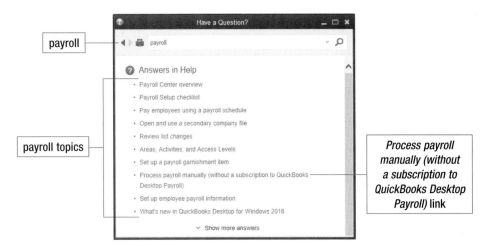

4. Click the *Process payroll manually (without a subscription to QuickBooks Desktop Payroll)* link. The Process payroll manually (without a subscription to QuickBooks Desktop Payroll) information appears in the Have a Question? window. See Figure 8–D.

FIGURE 8–D

Have a Question? Window—Process Payroll Manually (without a Subscription to QuickBooks Desktop Payroll) Information

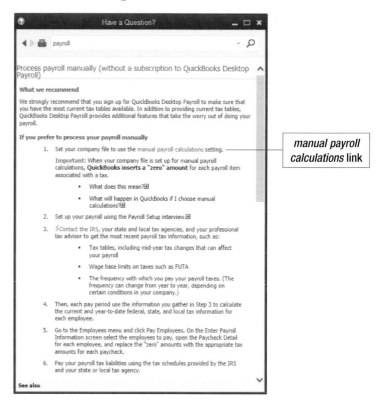

5. At the Have a Question? window, in the If you prefer to process your payroll manually section, click the *manual payroll calculations* link. You are moved to the Are you sure you want to set your company file to use manual calculations? information. See Figure 8–E.

FIGURE 8–E

Have a Question? Window—Are You Sure You Want to Set Your Company File to Use Manual Calculations? Information

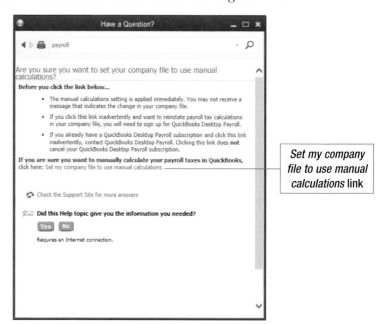

6. Click the *Set my company file to use manual calculations* link.
7. Close the Have a Question? window and then click OK at the QuickBooks Desktop Information message.

Lists/Centers

The Payroll Item List

HINT

The Payroll Item List was not a choice on the Lists menu in earlier chapters because the payroll and manual calculations features had not been activated.

Once you have activated the payroll feature and the manual calculations feature, QuickBooks automatically sets up a Payroll Item List, which you may now access. The Payroll Item List contains a file for each type of payroll item that affects both the company and the employees. QuickBooks automatically creates several standard payroll items, including Social Security Company (FICA tax), Social Security Employee, Medicare Company (Medicare tax), Medicare Employee, federal withholding, and so on. Typically, you must modify the Payroll Item List based on your company's geographic location, company deductions, and pay policies.

As you know, the second level of operation in QuickBooks is to update the background information in the Lists/Centers. In earlier chapters, you added, deleted, or edited vendor files, customer files, accounts, and inventory item files to keep the Lists/Centers current for your company. Now you will customize and update the Payroll Item List to match the payroll information unique to your company.

To review the Payroll Item List created by QuickBooks:
1. At the main menu bar, click Lists and then click *Payroll Item List*. The Payroll Item List appears. See Figure 8–F.

FIGURE 8–F Payroll Item List

ITEM NAME	TYPE	AMOUNT	LIMIT	TAX TRACKING	PAYABLE TO	ACCOUNT ID
Advance Earned Income Credit	Federal Tax			Advance EIC Payment		33-4777781
Federal Unemployment	Federal Tax	0.6%	7,000.00	FUTA		33-4777781
Federal Withholding	Federal Tax			Federal		33-4777781
Medicare Company	Federal Tax	1.45%		Comp. Medicare		33-4777781
Medicare Employee	Federal Tax	1.45%		Medicare		33-4777781
Social Security Company	Federal Tax	6.2%	128,400.00	Comp. SS Tax		33-4777781
Social Security Employee	Federal Tax	6.2%	-128,400.00	SS Tax		33-4777781

Payroll Item ▼   Activities ▼   Reports ▼   ☐ Include inactive

Notice that the payroll items initially created by QuickBooks are the ones generally applicable to all payroll situations, such as Social Security tax, Medicare tax, Federal Withholding tax, and Federal Unemployment tax.

The tax rates (amounts) and limits displayed on the Payroll Item List are those that were in effect when this book was prepared. As the government revises tax rates and limits, QuickBooks should update them in the Payroll Item List accordingly. The tax rates and limits in the Payroll Item List and subsequent windows illustrated in this chapter may be different from what appears on your computer screen. In general, accept the tax rates and limits on your computer screen.

To view a specific payroll item, such as Federal Withholding:

1. Double-click *Federal Withholding*. The Edit payroll item (Federal Withholding) window appears. See Figure 8–G.

FIGURE 8–G

Edit Payroll Item (Federal Withholding) Window— Name Used in Paychecks and Payroll Reports Page

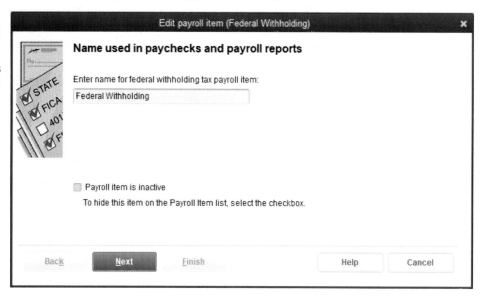

This window displays the name used in paychecks and payroll reports. The Edit payroll item window for each payroll item file displays several pages of information that are displayed each time you click Next.

2. Click Next and the Agency for employee-paid liability page appears. See Figure 8–H. (This information will be filled in later.)

FIGURE 8–H

Edit Payroll Item (Federal Withholding) Window— Agency for Employee-Paid Liability Page

HINT

An alternative method is to select (highlight) the payroll item, click the Payroll Item button, and then click *Edit Payroll Item.*

This page displays the government agency to which payment should be forwarded as well as the general ledger account for the tax liability. Remember that federal income tax withheld from the employee's paycheck is counted as a liability to the employer that must at some time be paid to the appropriate tax agency. The Edit payroll item (Federal Withholding) window—Agency for employee-paid liability page identifies that agency. This page also identifies the general ledger liability account that will be used for this payroll item. The 2100 Payroll Liabilities system default account is automatically listed as the liability account. This account will be customized for Kristin Raina Interior Designs.

3. Click Next to move to the next page, Taxable compensation. This page indicates all items subject to federal income tax withholdings. As Taxable Compensation payroll items are added to the Payroll Item List, this page is automatically updated.
4. Click Finish. You are returned to the Payroll Item List window.
5. Close the Payroll Item List.

Lists/Centers ──→ ## Customizing the Payroll Item List

When you activated the payroll feature and the manual calculations feature, QuickBooks created several payroll items that are required of all companies, as shown in Figure 8–F on page 337. You will customize these items for Kristin Raina Interior Designs to include identifying the government agency to which payment will be directed, the appropriate liability account, and the appropriate expense account for each pre-established payroll item.

Kristin Raina wishes to enter the vendor for Social Security Company tax payments. She also wants to change the general ledger posting accounts for the liability and the expense for this payroll item.

Recall that Social Security tax is withheld from the employee's paycheck and that the employer must also pay an equal amount, which is an expense to the company. QuickBooks creates two payroll items: Social Security Company and Social Security Employee. When you edit one of these payroll items, the changes you make carry over to the other payroll item.

To customize the Social Security Company payroll item:
1. At the main menu bar, click Lists and then click *Payroll Item List*.
2. Double-click the *Social Security Company* payroll item. The payroll item opens in Edit mode. See Figure 8–I.

FIGURE 8–I
Edit Payroll Item
(Social Security Taxes)
Window—Name Used in
Paychecks and Payroll
Reports Page

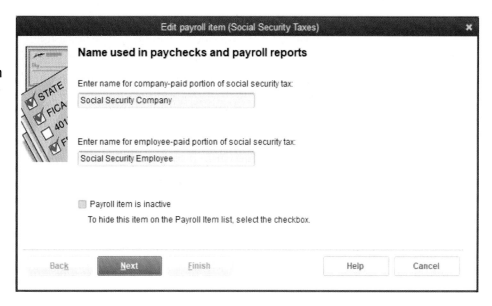

3. Accept the default names and then click Next. The Liability agency page appears.

   This payroll item, Social Security Company, represents the Social Security tax that the employer must pay. This tax—both the employee's withholding and the employer's portion—is subsequently paid to the United States Treasury. Since the company will write a check to this government agency, QuickBooks considers it a vendor of the company; thus, it must be included in the Vendor Center. Once the agency is included in the Vendor Center, it can be selected from this drop-down list.

4. At the *Enter name of agency to which liability is paid* field, click *United States Treasury* at the drop-down list.

   For each payroll item, you will need to indicate general ledger accounts. For some payroll items, you will select a liability account, for some you will select an expense account, and for some you will select both a liability account and an expense account. When selecting accounts, be careful to choose the correct liability account or expense account, and then be careful to choose the proper subaccount. QuickBooks eventually uses the general ledger accounts in the Payroll Item List to record the payroll journal entries. If an incorrect general ledger account is recorded in the Payroll Item List, the payroll journal entries will be incorrect.

   The Liability agency page also asks for the liability account that will be used for both the amount to be paid by the employer and the amount withheld from the employees' paychecks. These can be different liability accounts, but Kristin Raina uses the same liability account for both the employer and the employee. Notice that you must enter two liability accounts on this page.

HINT
If the vendor is not on the Vendor List, click
< *Add New* > to add the new vendor.

5. At both the *Liability account (company-paid)* field and the *Liability account (employee-paid)* field, click *2110 Social Sec/Medicare Tax Payable.* Both the parent account 2100 Payroll Liabilities and the subaccount 2110 Social Sec/Medicare Payable are displayed. See Figure 8–J.

FIGURE 8–J
Edit Payroll Item
(Social Security Taxes)
Window—Liability
Agency Page

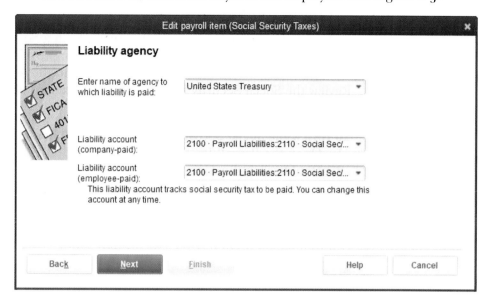

6. If the information is correct, click Next. The Expense account page appears.

   Only the employer's portion of Social Security and Medicare is considered an expense for the company. The portion withheld from the employee's paycheck is not.
7. At the *Enter the account for tracking this expense* field, click *6610 Social Sec/Medicare Tax Expense.* Both the parent account 6560 Payroll Expenses and the subaccount 6610 Social Sec/Medicare Expense are displayed. See Figure 8–K.

FIGURE 8–K
Edit Payroll Item
(Social Security Taxes)
Window—Expense
Account Page

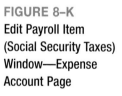

8. If the information is correct, click Next. The Company and employee tax rates page appears, displaying the current tax rates. Notice that

Adding a Salary and Wage Payroll Item

Kristin Raina wishes to add Salary to the Payroll Item List.

To add Salary to the Payroll Item List:

1. At the main menu bar, click Lists and then click *Payroll Item List.*
2. At the Payroll Item List window, click the Payroll Item menu button.
3. At the Payroll Item button drop-down menu, click *New.* The Add new payroll item window with the Select setup method page appears.
4. At the Select setup method page, click the *Custom Setup* option. See Figure 8–M.

FIGURE 8-M

Add New Payroll Item Window—Select Setup Method Page

5. Click Next.

    Similar to what happens in editing a payroll item when you create a new payroll item, a new page of information displays each time you click Next.

    The second page in the Add new payroll item window—the Payroll item type page—lists the types of payroll items you can create. There are seven payroll item types: Wage, Addition, Deduction, Company Contribution, Federal Tax, State Tax, and Other Tax. For each type, several subtypes are listed in parentheses next to it. When adding a new payroll item, you will first select the payroll item type on this page; then, on the next page, you will select the subtype.

6. At the Payroll item type page, click *Wage (Hourly Wages, Annual Salary, Commission, Bonus).* See Figure 8–N.

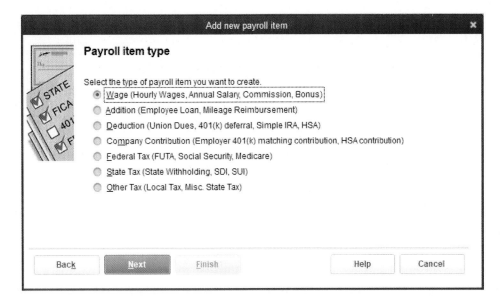

7. Click Next. The Wages page appears with the subtypes listed. Observe that the subtypes on this page are the choices noted in parentheses on the previous Payroll item type page (refer to Figure 8–N).
8. Choose the *Annual Salary* subtype. See Figure 8–O.

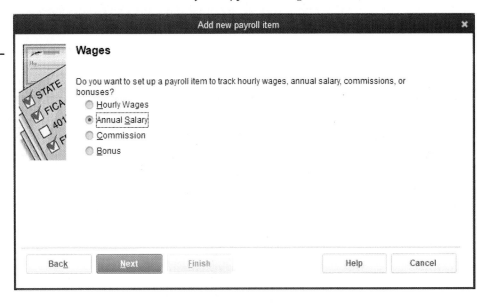

9. Click Next. The next page lets you indicate the form of pay: regular, sick, or vacation.
10. Choose the *Regular Pay* option. See Figure 8–P.

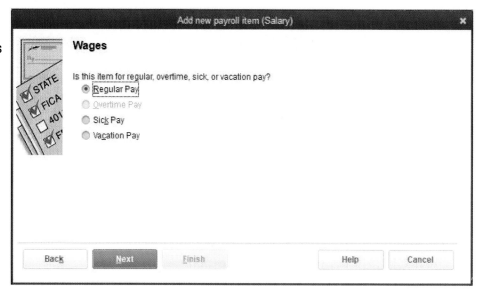

11. Click Next. The Name used in paychecks and payroll reports page appears. This step is where you assign a name for the item on paychecks and reports.

12. At the *Enter name for salary item* field, type Salary and then click Next. The Expense account page appears. This step is where you assign the general ledger account for Salary expense.

13. At the *Enter the account for tracking this expense* field, click *6565 Salaries and Wages Expense* at the drop-down list. Both the parent account 6560 Payroll Expenses and the subaccount 6565 Salaries and Wages are displayed. See Figure 8–Q.

FIGURE 8–Q

Add New Payroll Item
(Salary:Salary) Window—
Expense Account Page

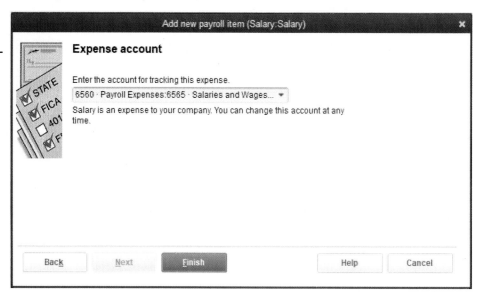

14. If the information is correct, click Finish. You are returned to the Payroll Item List window with the new payroll item included. See Figure 8–R.

FIGURE 8-R Payroll Item List Window with New Payroll Item

ITEM NAME	TYPE	AMOUNT	LIMIT	TAX TRACKING	PAYABLE TO	ACCOUNT ID
Salary	Yearly Salary			Compensation		
Advance Earned Income Credit	Federal Tax			Advance EIC Payment	United States Treasury	33-4777781
Federal Unemployment	Federal Tax	0.6%	7,000.00	FUTA	United States Treasury	33-4777781
Federal Withholding	Federal Tax			Federal	United States Treasury	33-4777781
Medicare Company	Federal Tax	1.45%		Comp. Medicare	United States Treasury	33-4777781
Medicare Employee	Federal Tax	1.45%		Medicare	United States Treasury	33-4777781
Social Security Company	Federal Tax	6.2%	128,400.00	Comp. SS Tax	United States Treasury	33-4777781
Social Security Employee	Federal Tax	6.2%	-128,400.00	SS Tax	United States Treasury	33-4777781

Payroll Item ▼   Activities ▼   Reports ▼   ☐ Include inactive

new payroll item

15. Close the Payroll Item List.

Adding a Payroll Withholding Payroll Item

Kristin Raina wishes to add Minnesota state income tax to the Payroll Item List.

To add Minnesota state income tax to the Payroll Item List:
1. At the main menu bar, click Lists and then click *Payroll Item List.*
2. At the Payroll Item List window, click the Payroll Item menu button.
3. At the Payroll Item button drop-down menu, click *New.* The Add new payroll item window with the Select setup method page appears.
4. At the Select a setup method page, click the *Custom Setup* option and then click Next. The Payroll item type page appears.
5. At the Payroll item type page, click the *State Tax (State Withholding, SDI, SUI)* type and then click Next. The State tax page appears.
6. At the Enter the state drop-down list, click *MN.* After you select a state, the subtypes that apply to that state become active.
7. At the *Select the type of tax you want to create* field, click the *State Withholding* subtype. See Figure 8-S.

HINT
To choose the state, use the drop-down list or type **M.** Keep typing **M** until *MN* appears.

FIGURE 8-S
Add New Payroll Item Window—State Tax Page— State Withholding Subtype Selected

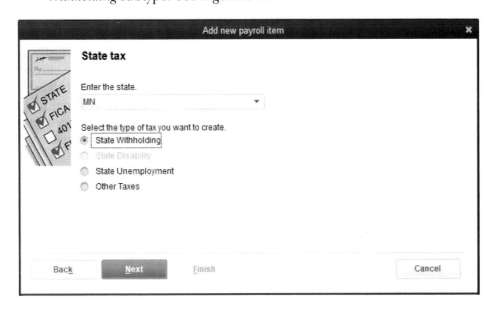

State tax

Enter the state.

MN

Select the type of tax you want to create.
- ⦿ State Withholding
- ○ State Disability
- ○ State Unemployment
- ○ Other Taxes

Back   Next   Finish   Cancel

To add a salary or wages payroll item:
1. At the main menu bar, click Lists and then click *Payroll Item List.*
2. At the Payroll Item List window, click the Payroll Item menu button.
3. At the Payroll Item button drop-down menu, click *New.*
4. At the Select setup method page, click the *Custom Setup* option and then click Next.
5. At the Payroll item type page, click the *Wage (Hourly Wages, Annual Salary, Commission, Bonus)* type and then click Next.
6. At the Wages page, choose the *Annual Salary* or *Hourly Wages* subtype and then click Next.
7. Choose *Regular Pay* and then click Next.
8. At the Name used in paychecks and payroll reports page, at the *Enter name for salary item* field, type Salary or Hourly Wages and then click Next.
9. At the Expense account page, choose the expense account to track this item and then click Finish.
10. Close the Payroll Item List.

To add a state withholding or tax payroll item:
1. At the main menu bar, click Lists and then click *Payroll Item List.*
2. At the Payroll Item List window, click the Payroll Item menu button.
3. At the Payroll Item button drop-down menu, click *New.*
4. At the Select setup method page, click the *Custom Setup* option and then click Next.
5. At the Payroll item type page, choose the *State Tax (State Withholding, SDI, SUI)* type and then click Next.
6. At the State page, enter the state. After you select a state, the subtypes that apply to that state become active.
7. At the *Select the type of tax you want to create* field, click the appropriate withholding or tax subtype and then click Next.
8. At the Name used in paychecks and payroll reports page, at the *Enter name for state withholding tax* field, accept the default and then click Next.
9. At the Agency for employee-paid liability page, at the *Enter name of agency* field, click the tax agency at the drop-down list.
10. Type the tax ID number.
11. At the *Liability account* field, choose the liability account for the tax. If it is a tax payroll item, choose the expense account and then click Next.
12. If it is a tax payroll item, accept the default tax rates and then click Next.
13. The Taxable compensation page shows which types of income are subject to tax. Click Finish to accept.
14. Close the Payroll Item List.

To view and print the *Payroll Item Listing* report from the Reports menu:
1. At the main menu bar, click Reports and then click *Employees & Payroll.*
2. At the Employees & Payroll submenu, click *Payroll Item Listing.* The *Payroll Item Listing* report is displayed.
3. Print the report.
4. Close the report.

Key Concepts

Select the letter of the item that best matches each definition.

a. Payroll
b. Social Security tax, Medicare tax, FUTA, and SUI
c. Manual payroll calculations
d. Payroll Item List
e. Social Security tax, Medicare tax, federal withholding, and state withholding
f. Payroll items
g. Payroll Liabilities and Payroll Expenses
h. Government agency
i. Social Security and Medicare
j. QuickBooks Payroll Services

_____ 1. Payroll taxes imposed on the employer.

_____ 2. A variety of services offered by QuickBooks; includes automatic processing of payroll and requires a monthly service fee.

_____ 3. Two default general ledger accounts created by QuickBooks when the payroll feature is activated.

_____ 4. Payroll taxes imposed on the employee and collected by the employer.

_____ 5. Contains a file for each type of payroll item that affects the payroll computation.

_____ 6. Included in the Vendor Center and selected when creating a new payroll item identifying the entity to which the payroll liability is paid.

_____ 7. An option that must be activated to access the Payroll Item List when a company does not subscribe to QuickBooks Payroll Services.

_____ 8. Payroll items that require identifying two liability accounts and one expense account in the Payroll Item List.

_____ 9. Compensation, payroll taxes, and payroll withholdings created by QuickBooks that you can customize or add to; each requires identifying the related liability accounts, expense accounts, and government agency.

_____ 10. Involves computing each employee's gross earnings, withholdings and deductions, and net pay; preparing paychecks or setting up direct deposits; recording payroll journal entries; and submitting payroll withholdings to the appropriate agency.

Procedure Check

1. You have decided to use the payroll feature of QuickBooks. How do you activate the payroll feature in an existing company file, and what does QuickBooks automatically set up?
2. After activating the payroll feature, what must you do to access the Payroll Item List?

3. What items on the Payroll Item List are automatically created by QuickBooks, and how would you customize them for your company?
4. What types of payroll items does QuickBooks allow to be created, and which types and subtypes would a company be interested in adding to the Payroll Item List?
5. Which payroll items have two liability accounts and one expense account, and which payroll items have one liability account and one expense account? How many pages are used to enter the liability accounts and expense accounts?
6. Your company has been using the services of an outside payroll processing firm. You, as a junior accountant, know that QuickBooks has a payroll feature; you wish to recommend to your manager that your company process payroll within the company. Prepare a summary of the steps involved in setting up payroll in QuickBooks.

Case Problems

Demonstrate your knowledge of the QuickBooks features discussed in this chapter by completing the following case problems.

Case Problem 8–1

In June, the third month of business for Lynn's Music Studio, Lynn Garcia has decided to hire two employees. To prepare for this, Lynn wishes to set up the payroll feature. The company file includes information for Lynn's Music Studio as of June 1, 2021.

1. Open the company file **CH8 Lynn's Music Studio.QBW**.
2. At the QuickBooks Desktop Login window, in the *Password* text box, type Student1 and then click OK.
3. Make a backup copy of the company file and name it **LMS8 *[Your Name]* Lynn's Music Studio**.
4. Restore the backup copy of the company file. In both the Open Backup Copy and Save Company File as dialog boxes, use the file name **LMS8 *[Your Name]* Lynn's Music Studio** and enter the password.
5. Change the company name to **LMS8 *[Your Name]* Lynn's Music Studio**.
6. Activate the payroll feature for Lynn's Music Studio.
7. Customize the system default accounts:

QuickBooks		Edited
Number	Account Name	Number
24000	Payroll Liabilities	2100
66000	Payroll Expenses	6560

8. Add the following accounts to the Chart of Accounts List:

2110	Social Sec/Medicare Tax Payable	Subaccount of 2100 Payroll Liabilities
2115	FIT Payable	Subaccount of 2100 Payroll Liabilities

2120	SIT Payable	Subaccount of 2100 Payroll Liabilities
2125	FUTA Payable	Subaccount of 2100 Payroll Liabilities
2130	SUI Payable	Subaccount of 2100 Payroll Liabilities
6565	Salaries and Wages Expense	Subaccount of 6560 Payroll Expenses
6611	Social Sec/Medicare Tax Expense	Subaccount of 6560 Payroll Expenses
6625	FUTA Expense	Subaccount of 6560 Payroll Expenses
6630	SUI Expense	Subaccount of 6560 Payroll Expenses

9. Select the *manual payroll calculations* option.
10. Customize each of the payroll items listed below. For each item, proceed as follows:
    - Accept the name listed.
    - Choose *United States Treasury* as the agency to which the liability will be paid.
    - Select the liability and expense accounts indicated below.
    - Accept all tax rates.
    - Accept all taxable compensation defaults.

Payroll Item	Liability Account	Expense Account
Federal Unemployment	2125 FUTA Payable	6625 FUTA Expense
Federal Withholding	2115 FIT Payable	
Medicare Company	2110 Social Sec/ Medicare Tax Payable	6611 Social Sec/ Medicare Tax Expense
Medicare Employee	2110 Social Sec/ Medicare Tax Payable	6611 Social Sec/ Medicare Tax Expense
Social Security Company	2110 Social Sec/ Medicare Tax Payable	6611 Social Sec/ Medicare Tax Expense
Social Security Employee	2110 Social Sec/ Medicare Tax Payable	6611 Social Sec/ Medicare Tax Expense

11. Add the following payroll items:

Salary

Payroll Item Type:	Wage (Hourly Wages, Annual Salary, Commission, Bonus)
Payroll Item Subtype—Wages:	Annual Salary
Wages:	Regular Pay
Name:	Salary
Expense Account:	6565 Salaries and Wages Expense

Wages

Payroll Item Type:	Wage (Hourly Wages, Annual Salary, Commission, Bonus)
Payroll Item Subtype—Wages:	Hourly Wages
Wages:	Regular Pay

Name:	Hourly Wages
Expense Account:	6565 Salaries and Wages Expense

State Tax Withholding

Payroll Item Type:	State Tax (State withholding, SDI, SUI)
State:	PA
Payroll Item Subtype—State Tax:	State Withholding
Name Used in Paychecks:	PA – Withholding
Agency for Liabilities:	PA Dept. of Revenue
Identifying Number:	45-6123789
Liability Account:	2120 SIT Payable
Taxable Compensation:	Accept defaults

SUI

Payroll Item Type:	State Tax (State withholding, SDI, SUI)
State:	PA
Payroll Item Subtype—State Tax:	State Unemployment
Names Used in Paychecks:	PA – Unemployment Company/ Employee
Agency for Liabilities:	PA Dept. of Revenue
Identifying Number:	ER-76558
Liability Accounts:	2130 SUI Payable
Expense Account:	6630 SUI Expense
Company Tax Rate:	3.689% each quarter (or accept the default)
Employee Tax Rate:	.06% each quarter
Taxable Compensation:	Accept defaults

12. Display and print the *Payroll Item Listing* report.

Case Problem 8–2

In August, the third month of business for Olivia's Web Solutions, Olivia Chen has decided to hire two employees. To prepare for this, Olivia wishes to set up the payroll feature. The company file includes information for Olivia's Web Solutions as of August 1, 2021.

1. Open the company file **CH8 Olivia's Web Solutions.QBW**.
2. At the QuickBooks Desktop Login window, in the *Password* text box, type Student1 and then click OK.
3. Make a backup copy of the company file and name it **OWS8 *[Your Name]* Olivia's Web Solutions**.
4. Restore the backup copy of the company file. In both the Open Backup Copy and Save Company File as dialog boxes, use the file name **OWS8 *[Your Name]* Olivia's Web Solutions** and enter the password.
5. Change the company name to **OWS8 *[Your Name]* Olivia's Web Solutions**.
6. Activate the payroll feature for Olivia's Web Solutions.

7. Customize the system default accounts:

	QuickBooks	Edited
Number	Account Name	Number
24000	Payroll Liabilities	2100
66000	Payroll Expenses	6560

8. Add the following accounts to the Chart of Accounts List:

2110	Social Sec/Medicare Tax Payable	Subaccount of 2100 Payroll Liabilities
2115	FIT Payable	Subaccount of 2100 Payroll Liabilities
2120	SIT Payable	Subaccount of 2100 Payroll Liabilities
2125	FUTA Payable	Subaccount of 2100 Payroll Liabilities
2130	SUI Payable	Subaccount of 2100 Payroll Liabilities
6565	Salaries and Wages Expense	Subaccount of 6560 Payroll Expenses
6611	Social Sec/Medicare Tax Expense	Subaccount of 6560 Payroll Expenses
6625	FUTA Expense	Subaccount of 6560 Payroll Expenses
6630	SUI Expense	Subaccount of 6560 Payroll Expenses

9. Select the *manual payroll calculations* option.
10. Customize each of the payroll items listed below. For each item, proceed as follows:
    - Accept the name listed.
    - Choose *United States Treasury* as the agency to which the liability will be paid.
    - Select the liability and expense accounts indicated below.
    - Accept all tax rates.
    - Accept all taxable compensation defaults.

Payroll Item	Liability Account	Expense Account
Federal Unemployment	2125 FUTA Payable	6625 FUTA Expense
Federal Withholding	2115 FIT Payable	
Medicare Company	2110 Social Sec/ Medicare Tax Payable	6611 Social Sec/ Medicare Tax Expense
Medicare Employee	2110 Social Sec/ Medicare Tax Payable	6611 Social Sec/ Medicare Tax Expense
Social Security Company	2110 Social Sec/ Medicare Tax Payable	6611 Social Sec/ Medicare Tax Expense
Social Security Employee	2110 Social Sec/ Medicare Tax Payable	6611 Social Sec/ Medicare Tax Expense

In Chapter 8, you learned to activate the payroll feature, customize and update the Chart of Accounts List to include the appropriate payroll accounts required for payroll processing, set up the payroll to accept manual entries, and customize and add various payroll items to the Payroll Item List. Once payroll has been activated and set up, QuickBooks allows you to process payroll and track payroll information for your company's employees. You can establish a file for each employee and then process payroll transactions. These employee files comprise the Employee Center.

Once you have established an employee file, you can enter transactions for payroll (Activities) in the Pay Employees and Pay Liabilities windows. Every time your company processes payroll for employees in the activities windows, QuickBooks simultaneously updates the information in the Employee Center. In addition, QuickBooks changes balance sheet and income statement accounts based on payroll transactions entered in the payroll activities windows.

In this chapter, our sample company, Kristin Raina Interior Designs, will hire and pay two employees beginning April 1, 2021. Kristin Raina will have to establish an employee file for each employee in the Employee List.

QuickBooks versus Manual Accounting: Payroll Transactions

In a manual accounting system, employee pay transactions are usually recorded in a **payroll journal** or **register**. The employee's gross pay, tax withholdings, and other payroll deductions are calculated in the journal using the employee's background information (pay rate, marital status, state of residency, and so on) along with the applicable tax schedules. Payroll checks and tax remittance checks are usually recorded in a cash payments journal.

payroll journal (register) a journal used to calculate payroll and record payroll entries for each employee

In QuickBooks, the Employee Center contains background information for each employee, such as name, address, Social Security number, pay rate, and applicable tax deductions. The Payroll Item List contains a file for all the payroll items, such as taxes and withholdings, that affect pay computations for the company (Chapter 8).

When the company processes payroll, the transactions are recorded in the Pay Employees windows. QuickBooks uses the information entered in the Employee Center, along with the items on the Payroll Item List applicable to the employee, to determine gross pay, payroll deductions, and net pay in the Pay Employees windows.

When payroll tax liabilities are paid, the Pay Liabilities window is used to record the transaction. These transactions update the Chart of Accounts List (general ledger) and at the same time update the employee's file.

In both manual and computerized systems, payroll reports are generated and forwarded periodically to the appropriate federal and state tax authorities. In QuickBooks, these payroll forms are prepared using the Process Payroll Forms window if you subscribe to a QuickBooks payroll service.

Accounting for Payroll Transactions

When a company generates a paycheck, the transaction affects a number of expense and liability accounts.

The employee's gross pay is an expense the company records at the payroll date. Additional expenses for the company include the various taxes imposed on the employer, including but not limited to Social Security tax (FICA), Medicare tax, Federal Unemployment Tax Act (FUTA) tax, and state unemployment insurance (SUI). All of these taxes are recorded in the appropriate expense accounts at the payroll date.

The employee, at a minimum, will have amounts for FICA, Medicare, federal income tax (FIT), and state income tax (SIT) (if applicable) deducted from his or her paycheck by the employer. These withheld taxes, along with the taxes imposed on the employer, are recorded as liabilities on the company books, because the company is responsible for remitting these taxes to the appropriate government tax-collecting agency at a later date.

The gross pay less the employee deductions results in a net payroll check to the employee. The following example illustrates the effect that issuing one paycheck has on the general ledger:

> Company A has one employee who earns an annual salary of $48,000. The company pays its employees semimonthly on the 15th and last day of the month. Therefore, there are 24 pay periods in the year. Consequently, that employee will earn $2,000 of salary income for each pay period. The employee is subject to FICA (6.2% of $2,000 = $124), Medicare tax (1.45% of $2,000 = $29), FIT ($300), and SIT ($100)—with a resulting net pay of $1,447. The employer is also subject to the matching FICA tax and Medicare tax along with FUTA (0.6% of $2,000 = $12) and SUI (3% of $2,000 = $60).

The journal entry to record the employee's earnings, deductions, and net pay is as follows:

		Salaries Expense	2 0 0 0		
		Social Sec/Medicare Tax Payable		1 5 3
		($124 + $29)		
		FIT Payable		3 0 0
		SIT Payable		1 0 0
		Cash – Payroll		1 4 4 7

Many companies use a separate checking account for payroll transactions. Periodically, funds are transferred into this account from the operating account. Having a separate checking account helps track payroll transactions.

In addition, the journal entry of the employer's payroll tax expenses is recorded on the paycheck date as follows:

		Social Sec/Medicare Tax Expense	1 5 3		
		FUTA Expense (.006 × $2,000)	1 2		
		SUI Expense (.03 × $2,000)	6 0		
		Social Sec/Medicare Tax Payable		1 5 3
		FUTA Payable		1 2
		SUI Payable		6 0

When the company remits the employer and employee taxes to the federal and local governments, it records several journal entries. Payment for the employer and employee Social Security tax and Medicare tax, the employee federal withholding, and the FUTA tax will be forwarded to the federal government. The journal entry is as follows:

		Social Sec/Medicare Tax Payable	3 0 6			
		($153 + $153)				
		FIT Payable	3 0 0			
		FUTA Payable	1 2			
		Cash – Payroll			6 1 8	

Payment for the state withholding tax and the SUI is usually made with one check payable to the state taxing authority responsible for these taxes. In some states, two checks have to be sent because two different tax agencies are responsible. The journal entry is as follows:

		SIT Payable	1 0 0			
		SUI Payable	6 0			
		Cash – Payroll			1 6 0	

As you can see, the journal entries for the foregoing transactions can be complex, as several general ledger accounts are affected. In addition, federal and state payroll and compliance laws are detailed and burdensome, with costly penalties for noncompliance. As a result, payroll accounting is a time-consuming process that can result in costly errors and omissions.

Before the availability of low-cost, off-the-shelf accounting software, most small companies either processed payroll manually or used outside computerized payroll services that charged per check. With the coming of QuickBooks and other general ledger software packages, small companies can now process payroll; determine gross pay, tax expenses, and tax liabilities; and prepare employee paychecks and payroll data in compliance with federal and state payroll regulations.

Chapter Problem

In this chapter, Kristin Raina Interior Designs will hire two employees and begin to process payroll during the month of April 2021. You will enter information for each employee in the Employee Center. The April 1 beginning balances for the company are contained in the company file **CH9 Kristin Raina Interior Designs**.

Before you begin, open the company file **CH9 Kristin Raina Interior Designs.QBW**. Make a backup copy of the file, name it **EX9** *[Your Name]* **Kristin Raina Interior Designs**, and restore the file. Enter the password, *Student1*. Finally, change the company name in the file to **EX9** *[Your Name]* **Kristin Raina Interior Designs**.

Lists/Centers

The Employee Center

The Employee Center contains a file for each employee of the company. Information such as name, address, Social Security number, hire date, pay rate, and applicable payroll taxes are indicated for each employee. QuickBooks uses the information contained in each employee's file, along with the information in the Payroll Item List, to calculate the employee's gross pay, deductions, and net paycheck.

Like all the other Lists and Centers, in QuickBooks, the Employee Center needs to be updated as new employees are hired, employees leave the company, or information about an employee changes and needs to be revised.

HINT

See Appendix G for the steps to set up the payroll, including the Employee Center, using the alternative method of the QuickBooks Payroll Setup window.

To view the Employee Center:

1. Click Employees and then click *Employee Center.* The Employee Center appears. See Figure 9–A.

FIGURE 9–A Employee Center

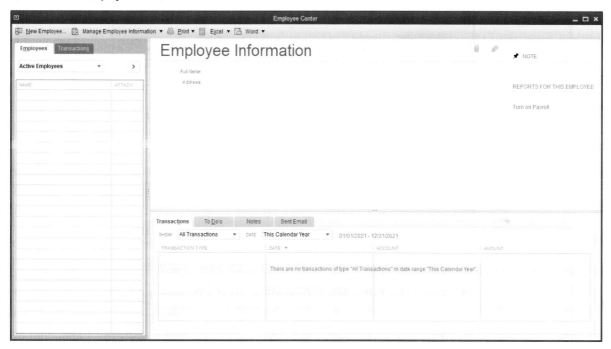

Table 9–1 describes the various parts of the Employee Center.

TABLE 9–1
Employee Center

Part	Description
Employees tab	Lists all current employees. You can display active employees, all employees, or only released employees.
Transactions tab	Lists all transactions for selected employees.
New Employee button	Used to add a new employee.
Employee Information section	Displays background and transaction information for the employee selected on the Employees tab.
Edit icon	Used to edit background information for the employee selected on the Employees tab.
Notes tab	Used to include narrative information specific to an employee.

Add the following employee:

Personal tab	*First Name:*	Richard
	Last Name:	Henderson
	PRINT ON CHECKS AS:	Richard Henderson
	SOCIAL SECURITY NO.:	333-44-5555
	GENDER:	Male
	DATE OF BIRTH:	8/1/95
Address & Contact tab	*ADDRESS:*	23 Ashland Rd.
		St. Paul, MN 54120
	MAIN PHONE:	651-555-6868
	Mobile:	651-555-2541
Payroll Info tab	*PAY FREQUENCY:*	Semimonthly
	EARNINGS-ITEM NAME:	Hourly Wages
	HOURLY/ANNUAL RATE:	20
Taxes	*Federal Filing Status:*	Married
	Federal Allowances:	2
	State Worked/Subject to Withholding:	MN
	SUI (Company Paid):	(Insert a check mark, if necessary.)
	State Filing Status:	Married
	State Allowances:	2

Delete the taxes added by QuickBooks on the Other tab and confirm No when prompted.

QuickCheck: The updated Employee Center appears in Figure 9–H.

FIGURE 9–H
Updated Employee Center

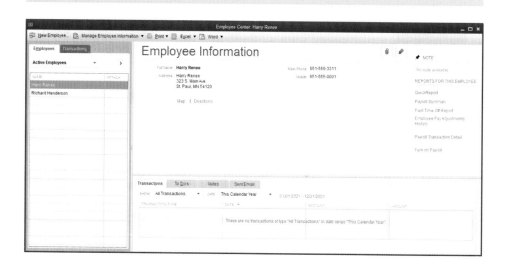

The Pay Employees Windows

You use the Pay Employees windows to calculate gross pay, taxes, and net payroll for employees—a daily business activity that is part of the third order of operations in QuickBooks. As you would in a manual accounting system, when you process payroll through the Pay Employees windows, a number of general ledger accounts are affected by the transaction.

As illustrated earlier in the chapter, it is common in a manual accounting system to record payroll using two journal entries. One journal entry records the salaries/wages expense, the employees' withholdings as liabilities, and the net pay. The second journal entry usually records the employer's related tax expense and related liabilities.

In QuickBooks, the transaction is recorded as one compound journal entry instead of two separate journal entries. The transaction is recorded as follows:

	Salaries Expense (Gross pay)	XXX	
	Social Sec/Medicare Tax Expense	XXX	
	FUTA Expense	XXX	
	SUI Expense	XXX	
	Social Sec/Medicare Tax Payable		XXX
	Federal Withholding Tax Payable		XXX
	State Withholding Tax Payable		XXX
	FUTA Payable		XXX
	SUI Payable		XXX
	Cash – Payroll		XXX

At the same time the transaction is recorded, QuickBooks updates the Employee Center and payroll reports to reflect the pay earned to date and taxes withheld.

There are three Pay Employees windows: Enter Payroll Information, Preview Paycheck, and Review and Create Paychecks. The Enter Payroll Information window is used to select the employee(s) to be paid at the current pay date. See Figure 9–I.

FIGURE 9–I
Enter Payroll Information Window

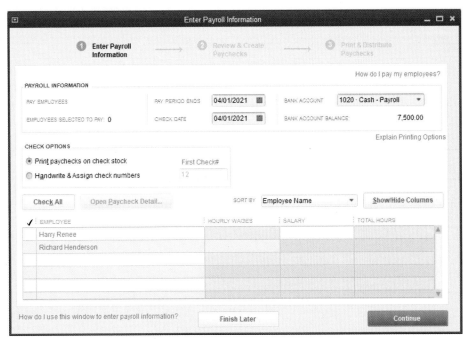

After selecting an employee, you move to the Preview Paycheck window. See Figure 9–J.

FIGURE 9–J
Preview Paycheck Window

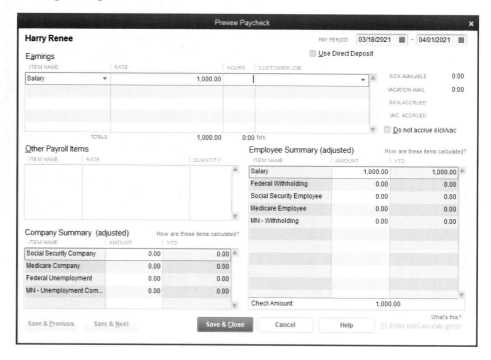

If the company has subscribed to a QuickBooks payroll service, tax figures and deductions will be calculated and displayed automatically in the taxes and deductions columns. If you do not subscribe to a payroll service, which is assumed in this text, you will need to type in the amount for the taxes in the Preview Paycheck window. Once all the payroll information has been entered, you will move to the Review and Create Paychecks window. See Figure 9–K.

FIGURE 9–K
Review and Create Paychecks Window

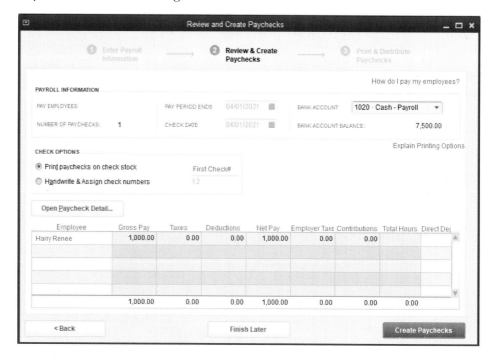

Paying an Employee

On April 15, 2021, Kristin Raina will pay the company's two employees. Harry Renee will be paid first. When Harry Renee was entered in the Employee Center, an annual salary of $24,000 was entered and the semi-monthly pay period was indicated. Semimonthly pay periods result in 24 paychecks per year. Based on this information, QuickBooks determines that Harry Renee is to be paid $1,000 ($24,000/24 pay periods) per pay period.

To pay an employee:

HINT

Remember that many companies set up a separate checking account dedicated to payroll transactions.

1. At the main menu bar, click Employees and then click *Pay Employees.* The Enter Payroll Information window appears.
2. At the *PAY PERIOD ENDS* and *CHECK DATE* fields, choose *04/15/2021.*
3. At the *BANK ACCOUNT* field, click *1020 Cash - Payroll.*
4. In the CHECK OPTIONS section, choose the *Handwrite & Assign check numbers* option and then type 1, if necessary, in the *First Check#* field.
5. Select *Harry Renee* by inserting a check mark next to the name. See Figure 9–L.

FIGURE 9–L

Enter Payroll Information Window—Completed

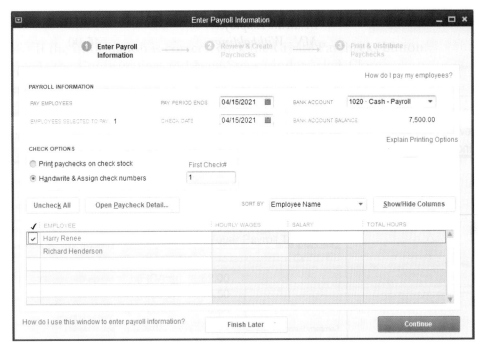

6. If the information is correct, click the Open Paycheck Detail button. The Preview Paycheck window appears.
7. Confirm that the *ITEM NAME* field in the EARNINGS section lists *Salary,* that the *RATE* field shows *1,000,* and that the *PAY PERIOD* fields display *04/01/2021* and *04/15/2021.*
8. Move to the Company Summary (adjusted) section.

    In the Company Summary (adjusted) section, you enter the employer's payroll-related tax expenses. When you type information in this section, use the mouse or press the Tab key, *not* the Enter key, to move to each field. If you press the Enter key, QuickBooks will assume the pay information is complete and close the window. Click the Open Paycheck Detail button to reenter the window, if necessary.

4. Confirm that the *To be printed* box is unchecked, that the *Review liability check to enter expenses/penalties* option is selected, and that the correct date range appears.
5. At the Bank Account drop-down list, click *1020 Cash - Payroll.*
6. At the *Check Date* field, choose *04/30/2021.*
7. Insert a check mark next to each of the following liabilities, all of which are payable to the United States Treasury:

   Federal Unemployment
   Federal Withholding
   Medicare Company
   Medicare Employee
   Social Security Company
   Social Security Employee

   The *AMT. TO PAY* column should total $1,344.24. See Figure 9–R.

FIGURE 9–R

Pay Liabilities Window—Completed

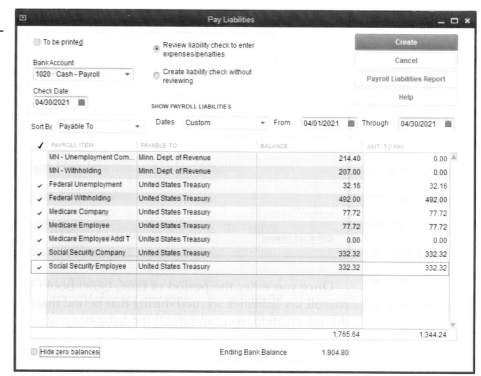

8. If all the information is correct, click the Create button. The Liability Check - Cash - Payroll window is displayed. See Figure 9–S.
9. If the information on the check is correct, click the Save & Close button.

   As in the other Write Check windows in QuickBooks, even though a check is not printed, the liability is considered paid and a check is recorded in the system.

FIGURE 9–S
Liability Check - Cash -
Payroll Window

HINT

If you make an error in the Pay Liabilities window, you cannot correct it in that window once you have saved the information. You must use the Liability Check - Cash - Payroll window *(Write Checks)* in the Banking menu. Click the Cash - Payroll account and then click the Previous arrow until the check with the error is displayed. Make any corrections or delete the entire check using the Edit menu.

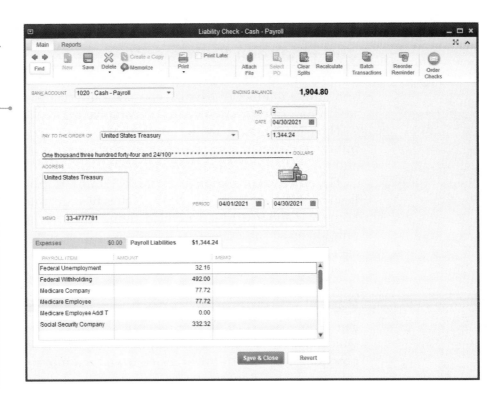

ACCOUNTING CONCEPT

For a payment of payroll liabilities, the general ledger posting is as follows:

2110 Social Security/Medicare Taxes Payable

Dr	Cr
Pmt 820.08	820.08
	Bal 0

2115 FIT Payable

Dr	Cr
Pmt 492.00	492.00
	Bal 0

2125 FUTA Payable

Dr	Cr
Pmt 32.16	32.16
	Bal 0

1020 Cash in Bank - Payroll

Dr	Cr
	1,354.96

Practice Exercise   9–3

On April 30, 2021, pay the payroll tax liabilities for MN - Unemployment Company and MN-Withholding.

QuickCheck: The amount due and to pay is $421.40.

Payroll Reports, Accounting Reports, and Financial Statements

Reports, the fourth level of operation in QuickBooks, allows you to display and print a number of payroll reports for internal payroll management as well as government and payroll tax compliance.

The payroll management reports provide the company with valuable information concerning payroll costs, such as gross pay, payroll liabilities and withholding, and employer payroll taxes.

The government compliance reports (Forms 941, W-2, and 940) are replications of the federal Form 941, which is filed quarterly, and the federal Forms W-2 and 940, which are filed annually. These reports are available only when you subscribe to a QuickBooks payroll service, but payroll management reports can provide the information needed to complete state and local compliance reports that the company may be required to submit.

Payroll Management Reports

The reports described in the following sections are available in QuickBooks to assist the company in managing and tracking the payroll process. These reports are accessed from the Employees & Payroll submenu of the Reports menu. They are not required by law and therefore are not forwarded to a government agency. However, the information contained in these reports is sometimes used to complete government-mandated payroll reports, especially at the state or local level.

Payroll Summary Report

The *Payroll Summary* report lists the earnings, deductions, and employer payroll taxes for each employee for a specified period of time.

To view and print the *Payroll Summary* report:

HINT

You can also view payroll management reports from the Reports menu of the Payroll Item List or the Employee Center window.

1. At the main menu bar, click Reports and then click *Employees & Payroll.*
2. At the Employees & Payroll submenu, click *Payroll Summary.*
3. At the *From* and *To* fields, choose *04/01/2021* and *04/30/2021* and then click Refresh. The report is displayed for the period.
4. Print the report. Your report should look like Figure 9–T.
5. Close the report.

FIGURE 9–T

Payroll Summary Report

EX9 [Your Name] Kristin Raina Interior Designs
Payroll Summary
April 2021

	Harry Renee			Richard Henderson			TOTAL		
	Hours	Rate	Apr 21	Hours	Rate	Apr 21	Hours	Rate	Apr 21
Employee Wages, Taxes and Adjustments									
Gross Pay									
Salary			2,000.00			0.00			2,000.00
Hourly Wages			0.00	168	20.00	3,360.00	168.00		3,360.00
Total Gross Pay			2,000.00	168		3,360.00	168.00		5,360.00
Adjusted Gross Pay			2,000.00	168		3,360.00	168.00		5,360.00
Taxes Withheld									
Federal Withholding			-240.00			-252.00			-492.00
Medicare Employee			-29.00			-48.72			-77.72
Social Security Employee			-124.00			-208.32			-332.32
MN - Withholding			-92.00			-115.00			-207.00
Medicare Employee Addl Tax			0.00			0.00			0.00
Total Taxes Withheld			-485.00			-624.04			-1,109.04
Net Pay			1,515.00	168		2,735.96	168.00		4,250.96
Employer Taxes and Contributions									
Federal Unemployment			12.00			20.16			32.16
Medicare Company			29.00			48.72			77.72
Social Security Company			124.00			208.32			332.32
MN - Unemployment Company			80.00			134.40			214.40
Total Employer Taxes and Contributions			245.00			411.60			656.60

Payroll Liability Balances **Report**

The *Payroll Liability Balances* report lists all the payroll liabilities owed and unpaid for a specified period of time. If liabilities have been accrued and paid, a zero will appear for that liability.

To view and print the *Payroll Liability Balances* report:
1. At the main menu bar, click Reports and then click *Employees & Payroll.*
2. At the Employees & Payroll submenu, click *Payroll Liability Balances.*
3. At the *From* and *To* fields, choose *04/01/2021* and *04/30/2021* and then click Refresh. The report is displayed for the period. See Figure 9–U.

FIGURE 9–U Payroll Liability Balances Report

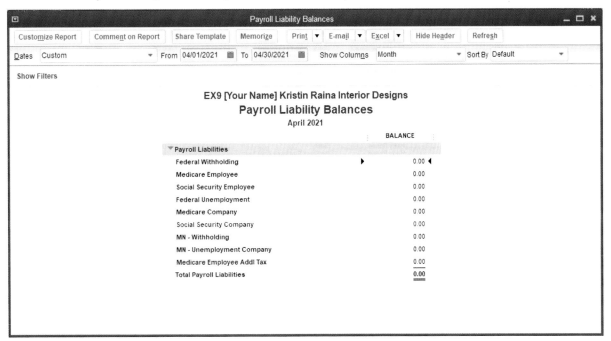

4. Print the report.
5. Close the report.

Payroll Transaction Detail **Report**

The *Payroll Transaction Detail* report provides detailed information for each payroll transaction (paychecks and payroll liability payments) recorded during the period. Information such as employee salary per paycheck, tax withholdings, net pay, employer-paid taxes, and taxes remitted are presented in this report.

To view and print the *Payroll Transaction Detail* report:
1. At the main menu bar, click Reports and then click *Employees & Payroll.*
2. At the Employees & Payroll submenu, click *Payroll Transaction Detail.*
3. At the *From* and *To* fields, choose *04/01/2021* and *04/30/2021* and then click Refresh. The report displays all the payroll transactions recorded during the specified period.
4. Print the report. See Figure 9–V.

Form 940

Form 940—Employer's Annual Federal Unemployment (FUTA) Tax Return is filed annually with the Internal Revenue Service. This form computes the FUTA tax liability for the company for the year and reconciles the amount to the tax payments made by the company toward the tax during the year.

Form W-2

Form W-2—Wage and Tax Statement is prepared annually and furnished to each employee. This report totals the employee's earnings and tax withholdings for the year. The employee uses this form to complete his or her personal income tax return. A copy of this form is also forwarded to the federal government to be reconciled with the quarterly Form 941 filings and the employee's tax return.

Accounting Reports and Financial Statements

At the end of the month, the *Journal* report, *Profit & Loss Standard* report, and *Balance Sheet Standard* report should be displayed and printed. See Figures 9–X through 9–Z.

FIGURE 9–X Journal Report—April 1, 2021–April 30, 2021

EX9 [Your Name] Kristin Raina Interior Designs
Journal
April 2021

Trans #	Type	Date	Num	Name	Memo	Account	Debit	Credit
52	Transfer	04/01/2021			Funds Transfer	1010 · Cash - Operating		7,500.00
					Funds Transfer	1020 · Cash - Payroll	7,500.00	
							7,500.00	7,500.00
53	Paycheck	04/15/2021	1	Harry Renee		1020 · Cash - Payroll		757.50
				Harry Renee		6565 · Salaries and Wages Expense	1,000.00	
				Harry Renee		2100 · Payroll Liabilities	0.00	
				Harry Renee		2115 · FIT Payable		120.00
				Harry Renee		6610 · Social Sec/Medicare Tax Expense	76.50	
				Harry Renee		2110 · Social Sec/Medicare Tax Payable		153.00
				Harry Renee		6625 · FUTA Expense	6.00	
				Harry Renee		2125 · FUTA Payable		6.00
				Harry Renee		2120 · SIT Payable		46.00
				Harry Renee		6630 · SUI Expense	40.00	
				Harry Renee		2130 · SUI Payable		40.00
							1,122.50	1,122.50
54	Paycheck	04/15/2021	2	Richard Henderson		1020 · Cash - Payroll		1,303.60
				Richard Henderson		6565 · Salaries and Wages Expense	1,600.00	
				Richard Henderson		2115 · FIT Payable		120.00
				Richard Henderson		6610 · Social Sec/Medicare Tax Expense	122.40	
				Richard Henderson		2110 · Social Sec/Medicare Tax Payable		244.80
				Richard Henderson		6625 · FUTA Expense	9.60	
				Richard Henderson		2125 · FUTA Payable		9.60
				Richard Henderson		2120 · SIT Payable		54.00
				Richard Henderson		6630 · SUI Expense	64.00	
				Richard Henderson		2130 · SUI Payable		64.00
							1,796.00	1,796.00
55	Paycheck	04/30/2021	3	Harry Renee		1020 · Cash - Payroll		757.50
				Harry Renee		6565 · Salaries and Wages Expense	1,000.00	
				Harry Renee		2100 · Payroll Liabilities	0.00	
				Harry Renee		2115 · FIT Payable		120.00
				Harry Renee		6610 · Social Sec/Medicare Tax Expense	76.50	
				Harry Renee		2110 · Social Sec/Medicare Tax Payable		153.00
				Harry Renee		6625 · FUTA Expense	6.00	
				Harry Renee		2125 · FUTA Payable		6.00
				Harry Renee		2120 · SIT Payable		46.00
				Harry Renee		6630 · SUI Expense	40.00	
				Harry Renee		2130 · SUI Payable		40.00
							1,122.50	1,122.50
56	Paycheck	04/30/2021	4	Richard Henderson		1020 · Cash - Payroll		1,432.36
				Richard Henderson		6565 · Salaries and Wages Expense	1,760.00	
				Richard Henderson		2100 · Payroll Liabilities	0.00	
				Richard Henderson		2115 · FIT Payable		132.00
				Richard Henderson		6610 · Social Sec/Medicare Tax Expense	134.64	
				Richard Henderson		2110 · Social Sec/Medicare Tax Payable		269.28
				Richard Henderson		6625 · FUTA Expense	10.56	
				Richard Henderson		2125 · FUTA Payable		10.56
				Richard Henderson		2120 · SIT Payable		61.00
				Richard Henderson		6630 · SUI Expense	70.40	
				Richard Henderson		2130 · SUI Payable		70.40
							1,975.60	1,975.60
57	Liability Check	04/30/2021	5	United States Treas...	33-4777781	1020 · Cash - Payroll		1,344.24
				United States Treas...	33-4777781	2125 · FUTA Payable	32.16	
				United States Treas...	33-4777781	2115 · FIT Payable	492.00	
				United States Treas...	33-4777781	2110 · Social Sec/Medicare Tax Payable	820.08	
				United States Treas...	33-4777781	2100 · Payroll Liabilities	0.00	
							1,344.24	1,344.24
58	Liability Check	04/30/2021	6	Minn. Dept. of Reve...	ER-12343, 33...	1020 · Cash - Payroll		421.40
				Minn. Dept. of Reve...	ER-12343, 33...	2130 · SUI Payable	214.40	
				Minn. Dept. of Reve...	ER-12343, 33...	2120 · SIT Payable	207.00	
							421.40	421.40
TOTAL							**15,282.24**	**15,282.24**

EX9 [Your Name] Kristin Raina Interior Designs
Profit & Loss
January through April 2021

Accrual Basis

	Jan - Apr 21
Ordinary Income/Expense	
Income	
4010 · Design Services	4,980.00
4020 · Decorating Services	3,400.00
4060 · Sale of Carpets	2,400.00
4065 · Sale of Draperies	1,000.00
4070 · Sale of Lamps	1,200.00
4075 · Sale of Mirrors	900.00
4100 · Sales Discounts	-84.62
Total Income	13,795.38
Cost of Goods Sold	
5060 · Cost of Carpets Sold	1,200.00
5065 · Cost of Draperies Sold	500.00
5070 · Cost of Lamps Sold	600.00
5075 · Cost of Mirrors Sold	450.00
5900 · Inventory Adjustment	150.00
Total COGS	2,900.00
Gross Profit	10,895.38
Expense	
6020 · Accounting Expense	300.00
6050 · Advertising Expense	100.00
6175 · Deprec. Exp., Furniture	100.00
6185 · Deprec. Exp., Computers	60.00
6200 · Insurance Expense	200.00
6300 · Janitorial Expenses	125.00
6325 · Office Supplies Expense	150.00
6400 · Rent Expense	800.00
6450 · Telephone Expense	275.00
6500 · Utilities Expense	450.00
6560 · Payroll Expenses	
6565 · Salaries and Wages Expense	5,360.00
6610 · Social Sec/Medicare Tax Expense	410.04
6625 · FUTA Expense	32.16
6630 · SUI Expense	214.40
Total 6560 · Payroll Expenses	6,016.60
Total Expense	8,576.60
Net Ordinary Income	2,318.78
Other Income/Expense	
Other Expense	
7000 · Interest Expense	50.00
Total Other Expense	50.00
Net Other Income	-50.00
Net Income	**2,268.78**

FIGURE 9–Z Balance Sheet Standard Report April 30, 2021

EX9 [Your Name] Kristin Raina Interior Designs
Balance Sheet

Accrual Basis   As of April 30, 2021

	Apr 30, 21
ASSETS	
Current Assets	
Checking/Savings	
1010 · Cash - Operating	43,355.38
1020 · Cash - Payroll	1,483.40
Total Checking/Savings	44,838.78
Accounts Receivable	
1200 · Accounts Receivable	1,540.00
Total Accounts Receivable	1,540.00
Other Current Assets	
1260 · Inventory of Carpets	800.00
1265 · Inventory of Draperies	1,000.00
1270 · Inventory of Lamps	1,000.00
1275 · Inventory of Mirrors	900.00
1300 · Design Supplies	200.00
1305 · Office Supplies	250.00
1410 · Prepaid Advertising	500.00
1420 · Prepaid Insurance	2,200.00
Total Other Current Assets	6,850.00
Total Current Assets	53,228.78
Fixed Assets	
1700 · Furniture	
1725 · Furniture, Cost	12,000.00
1750 · Accum. Dep., Furniture	-100.00
Total 1700 · Furniture	11,900.00
1800 · Computers	
1825 · Computers, Cost	3,600.00
1850 · Accum. Dep., Computers	-60.00
Total 1800 · Computers	3,540.00
Total Fixed Assets	15,440.00
TOTAL ASSETS	**68,668.78**
LIABILITIES & EQUITY	
Liabilities	
Current Liabilities	
Accounts Payable	
2010 · Accounts Payable	9,750.00
Total Accounts Payable	9,750.00
Other Current Liabilities	
2020 · Notes Payable	7,000.00
2030 · Interest Payable	50.00
Total Other Current Liabilities	7,050.00
Total Current Liabilities	16,800.00
Total Liabilities	16,800.00
Equity	
3010 · Kristin Raina, Capital	50,000.00
3020 · Kristin Raina, Drawings	-400.00
Net Income	2,268.78
Total Equity	51,868.78
TOTAL LIABILITIES & EQUITY	**68,668.78**

Exiting QuickBooks

Upon completing this session, make a backup copy of your practice exercise company file to a removable storage device using the Back Up command. Be sure to change the *Save in* field to the removable storage device and then carefully type the correct file name. Close the company file and then exit QuickBooks.

Chapter Review and Assessment

Procedure Review

To add an employee:
1. At the main menu bar, click Employees and then click *Employee Center*.
2. At the Employee Center window, click the New Employee button.
3. Enter the information on the Personal tab.
4. Click the Address & Contact tab. Enter the information.
5. Click the Payroll Info tab.
6. On the Payroll Info tab, enter the information at the *ITEM NAME, HOURLY/ANNUAL RATE*, and *PAY FREQUENCY* fields.
7. Click the Taxes button. The Taxes window is displayed.
8. On the Federal tab, enter the information for federal withholding tax.
9. Click the State tab and enter the state withholding tax information.
10. Click OK. If the Information window appears, click OK to close it, and click the Delete button to remove the tax added by the program.
11. Click OK.
12. At the question box, click No.
13. Click OK.
14. Click Leave As Is.
15. Close the Employee Center.

To pay an employee:
1. At the main menu bar, click Employees and then click *Pay Employees*. Click *No* at the QuickBooks Payroll Services message if it appears. The Enter Payroll Information window appears.
2. Enter the correct dates at the *PAY PERIOD ENDS* and *CHECK DATE* fields.
3. At the *BANK ACCOUNT* field, click *1020 Cash - Payroll*.
4. In the CHECK OPTIONS section, choose the *Handwrite & Assign check numbers* option and then type the check number in the *First Check#* field.
5. Select the employee to be paid by inserting a check mark next to the name.
6. If the information is correct, click the Open Paycheck Detail button. The Preview Paycheck window appears.
7. Enter the needed information in the EARNINGS section.
8. In the Company Summary (adjusted) section, enter the company tax information.
9. In the Employee Summary (adjusted) section, enter the employee taxes.
10. If the information is correct, click the Save & Close button. You are returned to the Enter Payroll Information window.
11. Click Continue. The Review and Create Paychecks window appears with the taxes columns completed.
12. If the information is correct, click the Create Paychecks button.

To pay payroll liabilities:
1. At the main menu bar, click Employees and then click *Payroll Taxes and Liabilities*.
2. At the Payroll Taxes and Liabilities submenu, click *Pay Payroll Liabilities*.

3. In the Select Date Range For Liabilities dialog box, choose the date range and then click OK.
4. Confirm that the *To be printed* box is unchecked, the *Review liability check to enter expenses/penalties* option is selected, and the correct date range appears.
5. At the Bank Account drop-down list, click *1020 Cash - Payroll.*
6. Enter the payment date.
7. Insert a check mark next to each liability you wish to pay.
8. If the information is correct, click the Create button. The liability check is displayed.
9. If the information on the check is correct, click the Save & Close button.

To view and print reports from the Reports menu:
1. At the Reports menu, click *Employees & Payroll.*
2. At the Employees & Payroll submenu, click a report.
3. Indicate the appropriate dates.
4. Print the report.
5. Close the report.

Key Concepts

Select the letter of the item that best matches each definition.

a. Pay Employee windows
b. Payroll Info tab
c. Employee Center
d. Preview Paycheck window
e. New Employee button

f. *Payroll Summary* report
g. Form 941
h. *Employee State Taxes Detail* report
i. *Payroll Liability Balances* report
j. Pay Liabilities window

_____ 1. The tab in the New Employee window on which pay information is entered.
_____ 2. Quarterly payroll report forwarded to the Internal Revenue Service.
_____ 3. The series of three windows used to calculate gross pay, taxes, and net pay for an employee.
_____ 4. The button in the Employee Center used to access the New Employee window.
_____ 5. The Pay Employee window used to enter pay and tax information to calculate net pay.
_____ 6. Report that lists all the payroll liabilities unpaid as of a specified date.
_____ 7. Contains a file with each employee's payroll background information.
_____ 8. Report that displays information concerning state taxes imposed on the employer and employee.
_____ 9. Window used to pay payroll liabilities accumulated when pay is processed.
_____ 10. Report that displays the earnings, deductions, and employer payroll taxes for each employee.

Procedure Check

1. Your company plans to convert from a manual payroll process to a computerized payroll processing system. What information must be assembled before you can process the first payroll check?
2. Your company has hired a new employee. Describe the steps to add this employee to the Employee Center.
3. After setting up a new employee in the Employee Center, you want to prepare a paycheck for the employee. Describe the steps to pay an employee.
4. Your company's management wishes to have a report that shows the amount of each local payroll tax to which the company is subject. How would you use QuickBooks to gather this information?
5. Your company wishes to have a report that displays the earnings, deductions, and employer payroll taxes paid for each employee for a specific period of time. Describe how you would use QuickBooks to obtain this information.
6. Your company's newly hired college intern has just received her first paycheck. She is disappointed that her net check is only a fraction of what she thought she was earning. Prepare a brief memo describing the taxes that must be withheld from her check.

Case Problems

Demonstrate your knowledge of the QuickBooks features discussed in this chapter by completing the following case problems.

Case Problem 9–1

In June, the third month of business for Lynn's Music Studio, Lynn Garcia decides to hire two employees. One employee will be the studio manager, who will be paid a salary. The other employee, an assistant instructor, will be paid on an hourly basis. The company file includes information for Lynn's Music Studio as of June 1, 2021.

1. Open the company file **CH9 Lynn's Music Studio.QBW**.
2. At the QuickBooks Desktop Login window, in the *Password* text box, type Student1 and then click OK.
3. Make a backup copy of the company file and name it **LMS9 *[Your Name]* Lynn's Music Studio**.
4. Restore the backup copy of the company file. In both the Open Backup Copy and Save Company File as dialog boxes, use the file name **LMS9 *[Your Name]* Lynn's Music Studio** and enter the password.

5. Change the company name to **LMS9** *[Your Name]* **Lynn's Music Studio**.

6. Add the following employees:

First Name:	Wei
Last Name:	Chan
PRINT ON CHECKS AS:	Wei Chan
SOCIAL SECURITY NO.:	159-89-2527
GENDER:	Female
DATE OF BIRTH:	3/23/80
ADDRESS:	417 Willow Street
	Scranton, PA 18505
MAIN PHONE:	570-555-3980
Mobile:	570-555-9898
PAY FREQUENCY:	Semimonthly
ITEM NAME:	Salary
HOURLY/ANNUAL RATE:	$18,000
Federal Filing Status:	Married
Federal Allowances:	1
State Worked/	
Subject to Withholding:	PA
SUI (Company Paid):	Yes
State Filing Status:	Withhold
State Allowances:	1
Not Subject to Other Taxes	

First Name:	Michelle
Last Name:	Auletta
PRINT ON CHECKS AS:	Michelle Auletta
SOCIAL SECURITY NO.:	291-08-7433
GENDER:	Female
DATE OF BIRTH:	8/9/85
ADDRESS:	23 Grand Ave.
	Scranton, PA 18505
MAIN PHONE:	570-555-4872
Mobile:	570-555-4949
PAY FREQUENCY:	Semimonthly
ITEM NAME:	Hourly Wages
HOURLY/ANNUAL RATE:	15
Federal Filing Status:	Single
Federal Allowances:	1
State Worked/	
Subject to Withholding:	PA
SUI (Company Paid):	Yes
State Filing Status:	Withhold
State Allowances:	1
Not Subject to Other Taxes	

7. Process pay for June 15, 2021, using the following information:

Check No.:	1
Check Date:	06/15/2021
Pay Period Ends:	06/15/2021
Employee:	Michelle Auletta
Item Name:	Hourly Wages
Rate:	15
Hours:	30
Company Taxes:	
Social Security Company:	27.90
Medicare Company:	6.52
Federal Unemployment:	2.70
PA - Unemployment Company:	18.00
Employee Taxes:	
Federal Withholding:	32.40
Social Security Employee:	27.90
Medicare Employee:	6.52
PA - Withholding:	10.80
PA - Unemployment Employee:	0
Check No.:	2
Check Date:	06/15/2021
Pay Period Ends:	06/15/2021
Employee:	Wei Chan
Item Name:	Salary
Rate:	750.00
Company Taxes:	
Social Security Company:	46.50
Medicare Company:	10.88
Federal Unemployment:	4.50
PA - Unemployment Company:	30.00
Employee Taxes:	
Federal Withholding:	82.50
Social Security Employee:	46.50
Medicare Employee:	10.88
PA - Withholding:	22.50
PA - Unemployment Employee:	0

8. Process pay for June 30, 2021, using the following information:

Check No.:	3
Check Date:	06/30/2021
Pay Period Ends:	06/30/2021
Employee:	Michelle Auletta
Item Name:	Hourly Wages
Rate:	15
Hours:	45

Company Taxes:

Social Security Company:	41.85
Medicare Company:	9.79
Federal Unemployment:	4.05
PA - Unemployment Company:	27.00

Employee Taxes:

Federal Withholding:	60.75
Social Security Employee:	41.85
Medicare Employee:	9.79
PA - Withholding:	20.25
PA - Unemployment Employee:	0

Check No.:	4
Check Date:	06/30/2021
Pay Period Ends:	06/30/2021
Employee:	Wei Chan
Item Name:	Salary
Rate:	750.00

Company Taxes:

Social Security Company:	46.50
Medicare Company:	10.88
Federal Unemployment:	4.50
PA - Unemployment Company:	30.00

Employee Taxes:

Federal Withholding:	82.50
Social Security Employee:	46.50
Medicare Employee:	10.88
PA - Withholding:	22.50
PA - Unemployment Employee:	0

9. On June 30, 2021, pay all payroll tax liabilities owed to the United States Treasury for the period June 1, 2021, to June 30, 2021, Check No. 5.

10. Display and print the following reports for June 1, 2021, to June 30, 2021:
    a. *Payroll Summary*
    b. *Payroll Transaction Detail*
    c. *Journal*
    d. *Employee State Taxes Detail*

Case Problem 9–2

In August, the third month of business for Olivia's Web Solutions, Olivia Chen decides to hire two employees. One employee will be a web page designer, who will be paid hourly. The other employee, an administrative assistant, will be paid on a salary. The company file includes information for Olivia's Web Solutions as of August 1, 2021.

1. Open the company file **CH9 Olivia's Web Solutions.QBW**.
2. At the QuickBooks Desktop Login window, in the *Password* text box, type Student1 and then click OK.
3. Make a backup copy of the company file and name it **OWS9 *[Your Name]* Olivia's Web Solutions**.
4. Restore the backup copy of the company file. In both the Open Backup Copy and Save Company File as dialog boxes, use the file name **OWS9 *[Your Name]* Olivia's Web Solutions** and enter the password.
5. Change the company name to **OWS9 *[Your Name]* Olivia's Web Solutions**.
6. Add the following employees:

First Name:	Fiona
Last Name:	Ferguson
PRINT ON CHECKS AS:	Fiona Ferguson
SOCIAL SECURITY NO.:	449-99-3333
GENDER:	Female
DATE OF BIRTH:	8/8/81
ADDRESS:	23 E. 14th Street
	Westport, NY 11858
MAIN PHONE:	631-555-1020
Mobile:	631-555-3814
PAY FREQUENCY:	Semimonthly
ITEM NAME:	Salary
HOURLY/ANNUAL RATE:	19,200
Federal Filing Status:	Single
Federal Allowances:	1
State Worked/	
Subject to Withholding:	NY
SUI (Company Paid):	Yes
SDI:	(Remove check mark.)
	(Click Continue at the potential setup error window.)
State Filing Status:	Single
State Allowances:	1
Not Subject to Other Taxes	(Click the Delete button six times to remove other taxes.)

First Name:	Gary
Last Name:	Glenn
PRINT ON CHECKS AS:	Gary Glenn
SOCIAL SECURITY NO.:	101-55-3333
GENDER:	Male
DATE OF BIRTH:	12/23/95
ADDRESS:	1050 York Ave.
	Westport, NY 11858
MAIN PHONE:	631-555-5447
Mobile:	631-555-7111
PAY FREQUENCY:	Semimonthly
ITEM NAME:	Hourly Wages
HOURLY ANNUAL RATE:	25

Federal Filing Status:	Married
Federal Allowances:	2
State Worked/	
Subject to Withholding:	NY
SUI (Company Paid):	Yes
SDI:	(Remove check mark.)
State Filing Status:	Married
State Allowances:	2
Not Subject to Other Taxes	(Click the Delete button six times to remove other taxes.)

7. Process pay for August 15, 2021, using the following information:

Check No.:	1
Check Date:	08/15/2021
Pay Period Ends:	08/15/2021
Employee:	Fiona Ferguson
Item Name:	Salary
Rate:	800
Company Taxes:	
Social Security Company:	49.60
Medicare Company:	11.60
Federal Unemployment:	4.80
NY - Unemployment Company:	32.00
Employee Taxes:	
Federal Withholding:	110.00
Social Security Employee:	49.60
Medicare Employee:	11.60
NY - Withholding:	40.00

Check No.:	2
Check Date:	08/15/2021
Pay Period Ends:	08/15/2021
Employee:	Gary Glenn
Item Name:	Hourly Wages
Rate:	25
Hours:	80
Company Taxes:	
Social Security Company:	124.00
Medicare Company:	29.00
Federal Unemployment:	12.00
NY - Unemployment Company:	80.00
Employee Taxes:	
Federal Withholding:	360.00
Social Security Employee:	124.00
Medicare Employee:	29.00
NY - Withholding:	98.00

8. Process pay for August 31, 2021, using the following information:

Check No.:	3
Check Date:	08/31/2021
Pay Period Ends:	08/31/2021
Employee:	Fiona Ferguson
Item Name:	Salary
Rate:	800
Company Taxes:	
Social Security Company:	49.60
Medicare Company:	11.60
Federal Unemployment:	4.80
NY - Unemployment Company:	32.00
Employee Taxes:	
Federal Withholding:	110.00
Social Security Employee:	49.60
Medicare Employee:	11.60
NY - Withholding:	40.00

Check No.:	4
Check Date:	08/31/2021
Pay Period Ends:	08/31/2021
Employee:	Gary Glenn
Item Name:	Hourly Wages
Rate:	25
Hours:	88
Company Taxes:	
Social Security Company:	136.40
Medicare Company:	31.90
Federal Unemployment:	13.20
NY - Unemployment Company:	88.00
Employee Taxes:	
Federal Withholding:	400.00
Social Security Employee:	136.40
Medicare Employee:	31.90
NY - Withholding:	105.00

9. On August 31, 2021, pay all payroll tax liabilities owed to the United States Treasury for the period August 1, 2021, to August 31, 2021, Check No. 5.

10. Display and print the following reports for August 1, 2021, to August 31, 2021:
    a. *Payroll Summary*
    b. *Payroll Transaction Detail*
    c. *Journal*
    d. *Employee State Taxes Detail*

An integral part of operating any business is effectively managing cash. This usually involves maintaining cash in one or more bank accounts. In addition, it involves transferring funds among the bank accounts, reconciling account balances, using credit cards for business purchases, and making credit card payments. QuickBooks allows you to transfer funds from one bank account to another, process the month-end bank reconciliation, and enter and pay credit card charges using the Banking menu at the main menu bar.

Many companies have more than one checking account. The regular checking account, commonly known as the *operating account*, is used to pay bills and collect and deposit receivables and other funds. Usually, a company maintains a separate checking account solely for payroll transactions. Periodically, funds from the operating checking account are transferred to the payroll checking account to pay employees and payroll taxes.

As a business grows in complexity, the need for special-purpose accounts grows correspondingly. For example, many companies have interest-bearing money market accounts that are designed to hold excess funds temporarily. These funds earn interest until they are needed for an operating activity, at which time they are transferred to a checking account.

transfer funds to move money from one account to another account

Companies can **transfer funds** as needed among the different accounts, often via online banking connections. With QuickBooks, you can use the Transfer Funds Between Accounts window to record and monitor the transfer of funds between accounts.

A company typically receives a statement from the bank at the end of the month detailing the activity the bank has recorded in the company's checking account, along with a month-end balance. Often, this balance does not agree with the company's records. Differences in the account balance usually occur because the bank has recorded transactions that the company does not know about. **Bank reconciliation** is a procedure used to determine the correct cash balance by accounting for these differences and ensuring that they are not a result of errors, either by the bank or the company, or from theft of funds. In addition, if the bank makes changes to the company's account, the company will have to record transactions in the general ledger accounts to reflect these changes. In QuickBooks, the Reconcile window is used to reconcile the balance per the bank statement to the balance per the accounting records.

bank reconciliation a procedure used to determine the correct cash balance in an account by comparing the activity recorded in the account with the activity recorded on the bank statement

credit card charges expenditures charged to a credit card to be paid at a later date

Many companies use credit cards to pay bills. These **credit card charges** allow the company to track expenses of a specific nature, such as travel and entertainment expenses, and to defer payment of expenses as needed. In QuickBooks, the Enter Credit Card Charges window is used to record credit card expenditures.

In this chapter, our sample company, Kristin Raina Interior Designs, will transfer funds between accounts, process bank reconciliations, and use a credit card to pay for expenses.

QuickBooks versus Manual Accounting: Banking

Banking activities in both manual and computerized accounting systems require a company to record transfers of funds among bank accounts, reconcile each bank account balance to the company's balances, and track charges and payments by credit card.

Transfer Funds

In a manual accounting system, when funds are transferred to or from one cash account to another, the transaction can be handled in several ways. Transfers from the company's operating account can be recorded in the cash payments journal or the general journal. If the cash payments journal is used for transfers out of the cash accounts, the cash receipts journal will be used for transfers into the cash accounts. Similarly, if the general journal is used to record transfers out of the cash accounts, it also will be used to record transfers into the cash accounts. A cash payments journal procedure is used when a check is drawn from a cash account to accomplish the transfer. If the transfer is accomplished via a bank credit and debit memo, electronic transfer, or phone transfer, the general journal procedure is used.

In QuickBooks, transfers among bank accounts that are not done by check are recorded in the Transfer Funds Between Accounts activity window. This window indicates the cash accounts involved in the transfer and the amount of the transfer.

Bank Reconciliation

The steps to completing a bank reconciliation in QuickBooks are similar to those in a manual accounting system. The company receives a statement from the bank detailing the activity in the account for the month. The statement shows the deposits (or other additions) to the account along with the checks that have cleared (were paid by) the bank. If the account has earned interest, the amount is added to the balance by the bank. If the bank has charged any fees, called *service charges*, they will be deducted from the account. Other items that may appear are non-sufficient funds (NSF) checks, credit memos (additions), and debit memos (subtractions).

The bank statement is compared with the company's accounting records, and any differences are identified. Generally, these differences, called **reconciling items**, fall into three categories: timing differences, such as **deposits in transit** and **outstanding checks**; omissions, such as the interest recorded by the bank not yet recorded by the company; and errors by either party. The first two are normal differences that are expected as part of the reconciliation process. If all the timing differences and omissions are accounted for and there are no errors, the adjusted bank balances will agree with the adjusted balance for the company's books. The account is then said to be *reconciled*. However, if there is an error, a difference will remain until the source of the mistake is found.

In QuickBooks, the bank reconciliation procedure is carried out using the Reconcile windows. Once a cash account has been identified, the windows display all activity to the account, including deposits or other additions (debits) and checks or other reductions (credits). This information is compared with that in the bank statement to reconcile the account.

---

reconciling items
differences between the bank statement and the company's records that have to be reconciled so that the cash balance in the company's accounting records agrees with the balance in its bank statement

deposit in transit
a deposit recorded on the company's books, usually at the end of the month, yet deposited too late to be on the current month's bank statement

outstanding check
a check written and recorded by the company that has not yet been paid by the bank

Credit Card Charges

In a manual accounting system, a credit card charge is usually recorded when the bill is paid by the company or tracked as part of accounts payable. Doing so often results in expenses being recorded in periods after they are actually incurred. In QuickBooks, a credit card charge can be recorded immediately when it is incurred by using the Enter Credit Card Charges window. The program also tracks the resulting credit card liability, which will be paid at a later date and separate from accounts payable. Using this method ensures that assets and/or expenses are recorded in the proper time period and that the credit card liability is tracked.

Chapter Problem

In this chapter, Kristin Raina Interior Designs will transfer funds among the company's bank accounts, prepare a reconciliation of the cash accounts, and enter credit card transactions. The balances as of April 30, 2021, are contained in the company file **CH10 Kristin Raina Interior Designs**. Open that file, make a backup copy, name it **EX10** *[Your Name]* **Kristin Raina Interior Designs**, restore the backup copy, and then enter the password. Change the company name to **EX10** *[Your Name]* **Kristin Raina Interior Designs**.

Lists/Centers ⟶ ## Updating the Chart of Accounts List

Kristin Raina has decided to open and fund a money market cash account, because the bank offers a higher rate of interest on money market funds than it offers on a Cash - Operating account. Typically, a company will have a separate general ledger account for each bank account to facilitate the bank reconciliation process. Kristin Raina needs to add another cash account as well as accounts that reflect the adjustments resulting from the bank reconciliation. Kristin also will begin using a credit card to pay for travel-related expenses, so accounts must be added for this additional expense and liability. You will need to update Kristin Raina's Chart of Accounts List to include the new accounts needed for the additional banking procedures.

Follow the procedures presented in Chapter 4 to add these accounts:

Type	Number	Account Name
Bank	1050	Cash - Money Market
Credit Card	2015	American Travel Card
Expense	6100	Bank Service Charges
Expense	6475	Travel Expense
Other Income	6900	Interest Income

The revised Account Listing appears in Figure 10–A.

FIGURE 10–A Updated Account Listing

EX10 [Your Name] Kristin Raina Interior Designs
Account Listing
April 30, 2021

Account	Type	Balance Total	Accnt. #	Tax Line
1010 · Cash - Operating	Bank	43,355.38	1010	<Unassigned>
1020 · Cash - Payroll	Bank	1,483.40	1020	<Unassigned>
1050 · Cash - Money Market	Bank	0.00	1050	<Unassigned>
1200 · Accounts Receivable	Accounts Receivable	1,540.00	1200	<Unassigned>
1250 · Undeposited Funds	Other Current Asset	0.00	1250	<Unassigned>
1260 · Inventory of Carpets	Other Current Asset	800.00	1260	<Unassigned>
1265 · Inventory of Draperies	Other Current Asset	1,000.00	1265	<Unassigned>
1270 · Inventory of Lamps	Other Current Asset	1,000.00	1270	<Unassigned>
1275 · Inventory of Mirrors	Other Current Asset	900.00	1275	<Unassigned>
1300 · Design Supplies	Other Current Asset	200.00	1300	<Unassigned>
1305 · Office Supplies	Other Current Asset	250.00	1305	<Unassigned>
1410 · Prepaid Advertising	Other Current Asset	500.00	1410	<Unassigned>
1420 · Prepaid Insurance	Other Current Asset	2,200.00	1420	<Unassigned>
1700 · Furniture	Fixed Asset	11,900.00	1700	<Unassigned>
1700 · Furniture:1725 · Furniture, Cost	Fixed Asset	12,000.00	1725	<Unassigned>
1700 · Furniture:1750 · Accum. Dep., Furniture	Fixed Asset	-100.00	1750	<Unassigned>
1800 · Computers	Fixed Asset	3,540.00	1800	<Unassigned>
1800 · Computers:1825 · Computers, Cost	Fixed Asset	3,600.00	1825	<Unassigned>
1800 · Computers:1850 · Accum. Dep., Computers	Fixed Asset	-60.00	1850	<Unassigned>
2010 · Accounts Payable	Accounts Payable	9,750.00	2010	<Unassigned>
2015 · American Travel Card	Credit Card	0.00	2015	<Unassigned>
2020 · Notes Payable	Other Current Liability	7,000.00	2020	<Unassigned>
2030 · Interest Payable	Other Current Liability	50.00	2030	<Unassigned>
2100 · Payroll Liabilities	Other Current Liability	0.00	2100	<Unassigned>
2100 · Payroll Liabilities:2110 · Social Sec/Medicare Tax Payable	Other Current Liability	0.00	2110	<Unassigned>
2100 · Payroll Liabilities:2115 · FIT Payable	Other Current Liability	0.00	2115	<Unassigned>
2100 · Payroll Liabilities:2120 · SIT Payable	Other Current Liability	0.00	2120	<Unassigned>
2100 · Payroll Liabilities:2125 · FUTA Payable	Other Current Liability	0.00	2125	<Unassigned>
2100 · Payroll Liabilities:2130 · SUI Payable	Other Current Liability	0.00	2130	<Unassigned>
2200 · Sales Tax Payable	Other Current Liability	0.00	2200	<Unassigned>
3010 · Kristin Raina, Capital	Equity	50,000.00	3010	<Unassigned>
3020 · Kristin Raina, Drawings	Equity	-400.00	3020	<Unassigned>
3030 · Accumulated Earnings	Equity		3030	<Unassigned>
4010 · Design Services	Income		4010	<Unassigned>
4020 · Decorating Services	Income		4020	<Unassigned>
4060 · Sale of Carpets	Income		4060	<Unassigned>
4065 · Sale of Draperies	Income		4065	<Unassigned>
4070 · Sale of Lamps	Income		4070	<Unassigned>
4075 · Sale of Mirrors	Income		4075	<Unassigned>
4100 · Sales Discounts	Income		4100	<Unassigned>
5060 · Cost of Carpets Sold	Cost of Goods Sold		5060	<Unassigned>
5065 · Cost of Draperies Sold	Cost of Goods Sold		5065	<Unassigned>
5070 · Cost of Lamps Sold	Cost of Goods Sold		5070	<Unassigned>
5075 · Cost of Mirrors Sold	Cost of Goods Sold		5075	<Unassigned>
5900 · Inventory Adjustment	Cost of Goods Sold		5900	<Unassigned>
6020 · Accounting Expense	Expense		6020	<Unassigned>
6050 · Advertising Expense	Expense		6050	<Unassigned>
6100 · Bank Service Charges	Expense		6100	<Unassigned>
6175 · Deprec. Exp., Furniture	Expense		6175	<Unassigned>
6185 · Deprec. Exp., Computers	Expense		6185	<Unassigned>
6200 · Insurance Expense	Expense		6200	<Unassigned>
6300 · Janitorial Expenses	Expense		6300	<Unassigned>
6325 · Office Supplies Expense	Expense		6325	<Unassigned>
6400 · Rent Expense	Expense		6400	<Unassigned>
6450 · Telephone Expense	Expense		6450	<Unassigned>
6475 · Travel Expense	Expense		6475	<Unassigned>
6500 · Utilities Expense	Expense		6500	<Unassigned>
6560 · Payroll Expenses	Expense		6560	<Unassigned>
6560 · Payroll Expenses:6565 · Salaries and Wages Expense	Expense		6565	<Unassigned>
6560 · Payroll Expenses:6610 · Social Sec/Medicare Tax Expense	Expense		6610	<Unassigned>
6560 · Payroll Expenses:6625 · FUTA Expense	Expense		6625	<Unassigned>
6560 · Payroll Expenses:6630 · SUI Expense	Expense		6630	<Unassigned>
6900 · Interest Income	Other Income		6900	<Unassigned>
7000 · Interest Expense	Other Expense		7000	<Unassigned>

The Transfer Funds Window

As you know, the third level of operations in QuickBooks is to record the daily transactions of the business. In QuickBooks, you use the Transfer Funds Between Accounts window (or Transfer Funds window, for short) to record the movement of funds among the cash accounts of the business. If you transfer funds by writing a check from one cash account to be deposited into another cash account, you can use the Write Checks window. However, when you transfer funds via bank memo, telephone, ATM, or online services, you use the Transfer Funds window to record the transaction. In this window, since there are no default accounts, you identify the source (transferor) cash account, the receiving account (transferee), and the amount to be transferred. The transaction is recorded as follows:

			Transferee Cash Account		XXX		
			Transferor Cash Account				XXX

The Transfer Funds window appears in Figure 10–B.

FIGURE 10–B

Transfer Funds Between Accounts Window

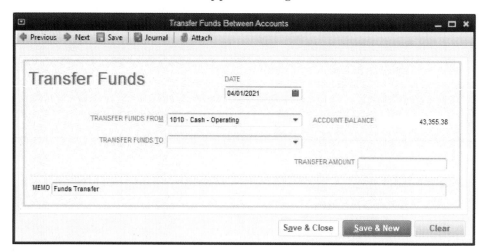

In addition to displaying the source and receiving cash accounts, the Transfer Funds window also displays the current balance of the source account, thus preventing you from overdrawing it. The Previous and Next arrows, as well as the Save & Close, Save & New, and Clear buttons, all have the same functions in this window as in other Activity windows.

On April 30, 2021, Kristin Raina wants you to transfer $7,000 from the company's Cash - Operating account to its Cash - Payroll account so there are sufficient funds in that account to pay the payroll and payroll tax liabilities for May.

<table>
<tr><td>**HINT**</td></tr>
</table>

Remember, all payroll and payroll taxes are paid from the Cash - Payroll account.

To transfer funds:

1. At the main menu bar, click Banking and then click *Transfer Funds.*
2. At the *DATE* field, choose *04/30/2021.*
3. At the TRANSFER FUNDS FROM drop-down list, click *1010 Cash - Operating.* The balance in the account is displayed.
4. At the TRANSFER FUNDS TO drop-down list, click *1020 Cash - Payroll.*
5. At the *TRANSFER AMOUNT* field, type *7000.* See Figure 10–C.

FIGURE 10–C
Transfer Funds Between Accounts Window— Completed

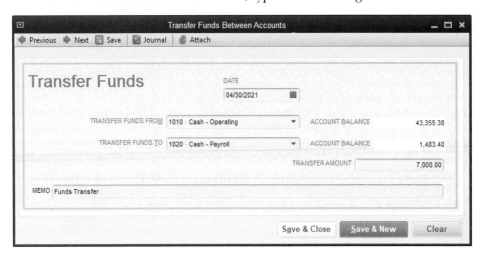

6. If the information is correct, click Save & New.

ACCOUNTING CONCEPT

For a transfer of funds between accounts, the general ledger posting is as follows:

1010 Cash - Operating				1020 Cash - Payroll			
	Dr		Cr		Dr		Cr
Bal	43,355.38	Trf	7,000	Bal	1,472.68		
				Trf	7,000.00		
Bal	36,355.38			Bal	8,472.68		

Practice Exercise   10–1

On April 30, 2021, transfer $10,000 from the Cash - Operating account to the Cash - Money Market account.

In QuickBooks, Activities identified as bank reconciliation are processed in the Reconcile windows. The reconciliation procedure in QuickBooks accomplishes two purposes. First, it ensures that the company's cash records are correct and agree with that of the bank. Second, transactions that are missing from the company's records and discovered during the reconciling process can be recorded at this time.

The Reconcile windows display all the additions to a given account, such as deposits and transfers in, and all reductions to the account, such as checks written and transfers out. Using these windows, you can compare the information for each account with that in the bank statement for that account. You can indicate the transactions that have cleared or have been paid by the bank by inserting check marks next to these transactions, and you can add transactions recorded on the bank statement that are not yet on the company's books.

As part of the reconciling process, you may need to make adjustments to the cash account. For example, the bank may have deducted service charges from the company's bank account during the month. This deduction is reflected on the bank statement but has not yet been recorded in the company's records. The same holds true for any interest income earned on the company's bank account. While performing the bank reconciliation in the Reconcile windows, you have the opportunity to identify and record these transactions and adjust the company's accounts accordingly.

When you add service charges, the default accounts are the Bank Service Charges account and the Cash account. QuickBooks records the transaction as follows:

			Bank Service Charges (expense)		XXX			
			Cash				XXX	

When you record interest income, the default accounts are the Cash account and the Interest Income account. QuickBooks records the transaction as follows:

			Cash		XXX			
			Interest Income				XXX	

If the bank records an NSF check from a customer, QuickBooks does not automatically record the transaction. Instead, you must record the transaction in the Create Invoices window to reestablish the accounts receivable for this customer and deduct the cash that was never actually collected.

Recall that the system default account in the Create Invoices window is a debit to Accounts Receivable. When you select an item, usually a service or inventory part item, the appropriate revenue account is credited. If you are using QuickBooks to reconcile accounts, you create an item for NSFs in the Item List. When you establish an NSF item, you will identify the default account as Cash. When you record an NSF item in the Create Invoices window, Accounts Receivable is debited for the amount of the NSF still due the company; the corresponding credit, based on the NSF item, will be to Cash.

The QuickBooks Reconcile window has two parts. The first window, the Begin Reconciliation window, allows you to select a bank account to reconcile, add transactions such as service charges and interest income, and enter the bank statement balance. See Figure 10–D.

FIGURE 10–D
Begin Reconciliation
Window

Table 10–1 describes the key parts of the Begin Reconciliation window.

TABLE 10–1
Begin Reconciliation
Window

Part	Description
Account	QuickBooks allows you to reconcile all the cash accounts set up by the company. Once you select an account at the drop-down list, all the activity for only that account is displayed.
Beginning Balance	Indicates the opening balance for the bank statement. If this is the first time you are reconciling the account, the figure will be zero. *You cannot edit this number.*
Ending Balance	Used to enter the ending balance that appears on the bank statement.
Service Charge	Used to enter the amount of the service charges on the bank statement. You also indicate the service charge general ledger posting account. When you click the Reconcile Now button at the Reconcile window, QuickBooks automatically posts the expense and reduces the Cash account.
Interest Earned	Used to enter the amount of interest shown on the bank statement along with the appropriate income account for interest. When you click the Reconcile Now button at the Reconcile window, QuickBooks automatically posts the increase to both Cash and Interest Income.
Locate Discrepancies button	Used to locate changes to previously cleared transactions.
Undo Last Reconciliation button	Used to undo the previous reconciliation to correct errors or omissions.

Once the information has been entered in the first window, the second window, the Reconcile window, will be used to indicate which transactions recorded on the company's books have cleared the bank. Once all the cleared and missing transactions have been accounted for, the *Difference* amount should be zero. See Figure 10–E.

FIGURE 10–E
Reconcile Window

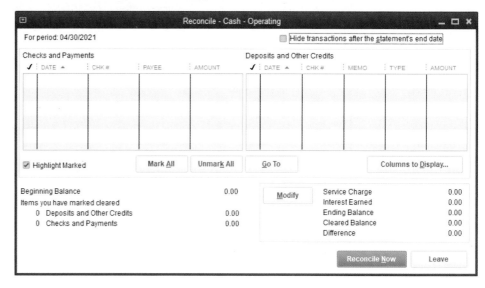

Table 10–2 describes the key parts of the Reconcile window.

TABLE 10–2
Reconcile Window

Part	Description
Difference amount	If all the reconciling items have been accounted for, the difference will be zero. If after the reconciliation process has been completed a difference remains, it is probably due to an error by either the bank or the company. You must identify the error and correct it before completing the reconciliation.
Reconcile Now button	Click this button if the *Difference* amount is zero. The account is now reconciled, and a *Reconciliation* report can be printed.

On April 30, 2021, Kristin Raina receives the bank statement for the Cash - Operating account. After reviewing the bank statement, you determine the following:

1. The cash balance per the bank statement is $20,675.00.
2. The cash balance per the company's books is $26,355.38.
   You can review the Chart of Accounts List, the trial balance, or the general ledger for the Cash - Operating account to determine the balance on the company's books.
3. The bank charged the account $35 for bank service charges.
4. The bank credited the account $10 for interest income.

5. All deposits except the deposit of March 31, 2021, have cleared the bank.
6. All checks and payments except Check Nos. 10 and 11 have cleared the bank.
7. A check for $600 from Berger Bakery Company, which was included in the deposit of February 28, 2021, was returned as NSF. The bank deducted the amount from the bank statement.

To reconcile the Cash - Operating account with the bank statement:

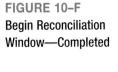

HINT
You cannot edit the *Beginning Balance* figure.

1. At the main menu bar, click Banking and then click *Reconcile*. The Begin Reconciliation window appears.
2. At the Account drop-down list, click *1010 Cash - Operating*.
3. At the *Statement Date* field, choose *04/30/2021*.
4. At the *Ending Balance* field, type *20,675*.
5. At the *Service Charge* field, type *35*.
6. At the *Service Charge Date* field, choose *04/30/2021*.
7. At the Service Charge Account drop-down list, click *6100 Bank Service Charges*.
8. At the *Interest Earned* field, type *10*.
9. At the *Interest Earned Date* field, choose *04/30/2021*.
10. At the Interest Earned Account drop-down list, click *6900 Interest Income*. See Figure 10–F.

FIGURE 10–F
Begin Reconciliation Window—Completed

11. If the information is correct, click Continue. The Reconcile - Cash - Operating window appears. The activity for that account is displayed.
12. Click to insert a check mark next to each deposit and credit, except the deposit of March 31 to indicate that they have cleared. See Figure 10–G.

FIGURE 10–G

Reconcile - Cash -
Operating Window with
Cleared Deposits

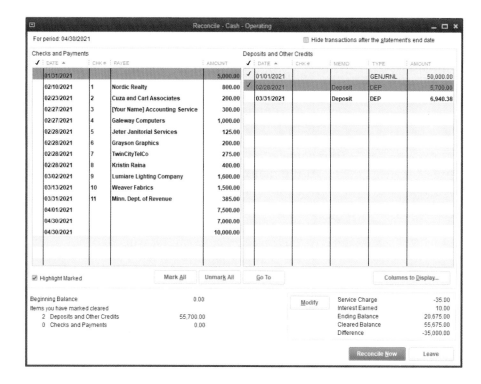

13. Click to insert a check mark next to each check and payment except Check Nos. 10 and 11, as they have not cleared the bank. The *Difference* amount is now *-600.00*, which is the amount of the NSF. See Figure 10–H.

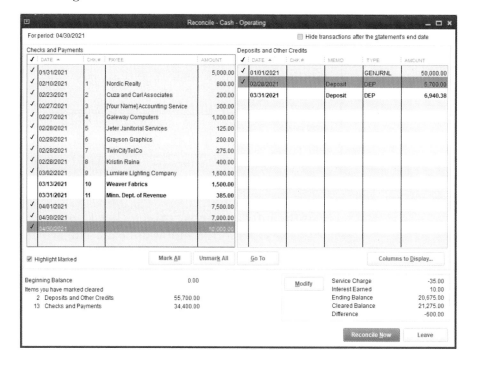

14. Click the *02/28/2021* deposit to select it and then click the Go To button. The Make Deposits window appears, listing the checks that were included in the deposit of February 28. Notice that the $600 check from Berger Bakery Company is included in the deposit. See Figure 10–I.

FIGURE 10–I
Make Deposits Window

Make Deposits

Previous | Next | Save | Print ▾ | Payments | History | Journal | Attach

Deposit To 1010 · Cash -... ▾ | Date 02/28/2021 | Memo Deposit

Click Payments to select customer payments that you have received. List any other amounts to deposit below.

RECEIVED FROM	FROM ACCOUNT	MEMO	CHK NO.	PMT METH.	AMOUNT
Jones, Beverly	1250 · Undeposited Funds		6544	Check	600.00
Franco Films Co.	1250 · Undeposited Funds		1255	Check	500.00
Hamilton Hotels	1250 · Undeposited Funds		25546	Check	480.00
Cook Caterers	1250 · Undeposited Funds		655	Check	2,560.00
Guthrie, Jennie	1250 · Undeposited Funds		674	Check	960.00
Berger Bakery Compa...	1250 · Undeposited Funds		12458	Check	600.00

Deposit Subtotal 5,700.00

To get cash back from this deposit, enter the amount below. Indicate the account where you want this money to go, such as your Petty Cash account.

Cash back goes to | Cash back memo | Cash back amount

Deposit Total 5,700.00

Save & Close | Save & New | Revert

When this deposit was made on February 28, the bank recorded the total deposit and increased the bank balance by $5,700. When the Berger Bakery Company check was returned due to NSFs, the bank then deducted the $600 from the bank balance. To reconcile with the bank account, the $600 must be deducted from the Cash - Operating account.

15. Close the Make Deposits window. If the check mark was removed from the February 28 deposit, click the deposit to replace the check mark.

16. With the Reconcile window open, at the main menu bar, click Customers and then click *Create Invoices*.

17. At the Create Invoices window, enter the following information:

CUSTOMER:JOB:	Berger Bakery Company
Date:	04/30/2021
Invoice #:	NSF1
ITEM CODE:	NSF
AMOUNT:	600
TAX:	Non

See Figure 10–J.

FIGURE 10–J

Create Invoices Window

18. If the information is correct, click the Save & Close button. You are returned to the Reconcile window.
19. Scroll in the Checks and Payments section until you locate the $600 adjustment to the Cash account for the NSF check.
20. Insert a check mark next to the 600 NSF check. The difference is now zero. See Figure 10–K.

FIGURE 10–K

Reconcile - Cash - Operating Window—Completed

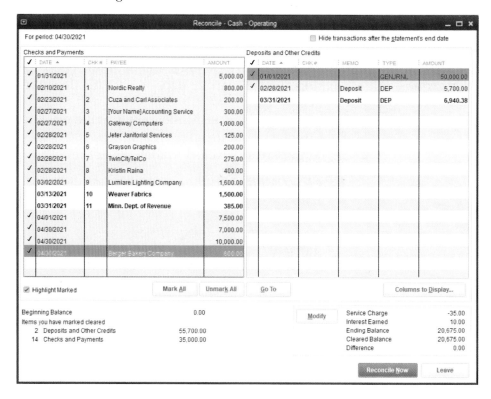

21. If the information is correct, click Reconcile Now. If the Information message appears, click OK. The account is now reconciled, and the missing transactions for service charges and interest are now posted to the appropriate accounts.

22. In the Select Reconciliation Report dialog box, click *Detail* and then click Print.

23. In the Print Lists dialog box, choose the *Portrait* orientation and then click Print. The report should look like Figure 10–L.

FIGURE 10–L Reconciliation Detail Report—Cash - Operating Account

EX10 [Your Name] Kristin Raina Interior Designs
Reconciliation Detail
1010 · Cash - Operating, Period Ending 04/30/2021

Type	Date	Num	Name	Clr	Amount	Balance
Beginning Balance						0.00
Cleared Transactions						
Checks and Payments - 15 items						
General Journal	01/31/2021			X	-5,000.00	-5,000.00
Bill Pmt -Check	02/10/2021	1	Nordic Realty	X	-800.00	-5,800.00
Bill Pmt -Check	02/23/2021	2	Cuza and Carl Associates	X	-200.00	-6,000.00
Bill Pmt -Check	02/27/2021	4	Galeway Computers	X	-1,000.00	-7,000.00
Bill Pmt -Check	02/27/2021	3	[Your Name] Accounting S...	X	-300.00	-7,300.00
Check	02/28/2021	8	Kristin Raina	X	-400.00	-7,700.00
Check	02/28/2021	7	TwinCityTelCo	X	-275.00	-7,975.00
Check	02/28/2021	6	Grayson Graphics	X	-200.00	-8,175.00
Check	02/28/2021	5	Jeter Janitorial Services	X	-125.00	-8,300.00
Check	03/02/2021	9	Lumiare Lighting Company	X	-1,600.00	-9,900.00
Transfer	04/01/2021			X	-7,500.00	-17,400.00
Transfer	04/30/2021			X	-10,000.00	-27,400.00
Transfer	04/30/2021			X	-7,000.00	-34,400.00
Invoice	04/30/2021	NSF1	Berger Bakery Company	X	-600.00	-35,000.00
Check	04/30/2021			X	-35.00	-35,035.00
Total Checks and Payments					-35,035.00	-35,035.00
Deposits and Credits - 3 items						
General Journal	01/01/2021			X	50,000.00	50,000.00
Deposit	02/28/2021			X	5,700.00	55,700.00
Deposit	04/30/2021			X	10.00	55,710.00
Total Deposits and Credits					55,710.00	55,710.00
Total Cleared Transactions					20,675.00	20,675.00
Cleared Balance					20,675.00	20,675.00
Uncleared Transactions						
Checks and Payments - 2 items						
Check	03/13/2021	10	Weaver Fabrics		-1,500.00	-1,500.00
Sales Tax Payment	03/31/2021	11	Minn. Dept. of Revenue		-385.00	-1,885.00
Total Checks and Payments					-1,885.00	-1,885.00
Deposits and Credits - 1 item						
Deposit	03/31/2021				6,940.38	6,940.38
Total Deposits and Credits					6,940.38	6,940.38
Total Uncleared Transactions					5,055.38	5,055.38
Register Balance as of 04/30/2021					25,730.38	25,730.38
Ending Balance					25,730.38	25,730.38

Page 1

You should print the report immediately. The *Reconciliation Detail* report is available from the Reports menu. However, this option is available only until you do the next reconciliation.

Paying a Credit Card Charge

On May 22, 2021, Kristin Raina wishes to pay the $600 credit card charge incurred on May 1, 2021, Check No. 12.

To pay a credit card charge:

HINT

Remember that since the vendor was paid via a credit card, the liability for the charge is now with the credit card company.

1. At the main menu bar, click Banking and then click *Write Checks*.
2. At the *BANK ACCOUNT* field, click *1010 Cash - Operating*. Confirm that the *NO.* field reads *12* and the *Pay Online* and *Print Later* options are not checked.
3. At the *DATE* field, choose *05/22/2021*.
4. At the PAY TO THE ORDER OF drop-down list, click *American Travel Card*.
5. At the *$* field, type 600.
6. On the Expenses tab, at the *ACCOUNT* field, click *2015 American Travel Card*. Do not choose the 6475 Travel Expense account on the Expenses tab, as that account was already debited when the charges were recorded. When paying a credit card bill, always choose the credit card liability account. See Figure 10–R.

FIGURE 10–R Write Checks Window—Completed

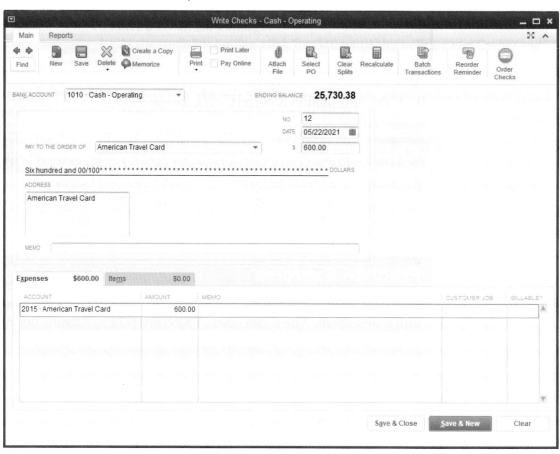

7. If the information is correct, click Save & New.

For a payment of a credit card charge, the general ledger posting is as follows:

2015 Credit Card Liability		1010 Cash - Operating	
Dr	Cr	Dr	Cr
Pmt 600	600		600
	Bal 0		

Practice Exercise   10–4

On May 31, 2021, pay the remaining credit card balance to American Travel, $350, Check No. 13.

Reports

Banking Reports, Accounting Reports, and Financial Statements

As you know, in QuickBooks, the fourth level of operation is to view and print reports. As described in prior chapters, the reports for an activity can be accessed from both the Reports menu and the Lists menu.

Banking Reports from the Reports Menu

The *Reconciliation Detail* report is printed as part of the reconciliation process. In addition to this report, the company uses the following reports:

Deposit Detail Report

The *Deposit Detail* report displays the components of each deposit to each cash account for a specified period of time. The report shows the payee's name, amount of payment, nature of payment, and date of payment and deposit. This report is helpful in tracing a collection from a customer to the actual bank deposit.

To view and print the *Deposit Detail* report:
1. At the main menu bar, click Reports and then click *Banking*.
2. At the Banking submenu, click *Deposit Detail*.
3. At the *From* and *To* fields, choose *02/01/2021* and *04/30/2021*.
4. Click Refresh. The report for the period is displayed. See Figure 10–S.
5. Close the report.

FIGURE 10–S Deposit Detail Report

EX10 [Your Name] Kristin Raina Interior Designs
Deposit Detail
February through April 2021

Type	Num	Date	Name	Account	Amount
Deposit		**02/28/2021**		**1010 · Cash - Operating**	**5,700.00**
Payment	6544	02/13/2021	Jones, Beverly	1250 · Undeposited Funds	-600.00
Payment	1255	02/20/2021	Franco Films Co.	1250 · Undeposited Funds	-500.00
Sales Receipt	1007	02/24/2021	Hamilton Hotels	1250 · Undeposited Funds	-480.00
Payment	655	02/27/2021	Cook Caterers	1250 · Undeposited Funds	-2,560.00
Payment	674	02/28/2021	Guthrie, Jennie	1250 · Undeposited Funds	-960.00
Payment	12458	02/28/2021	Berger Bakery Company	1250 · Undeposited Funds	-600.00
TOTAL					-5,700.00
Deposit		**03/31/2021**		**1010 · Cash - Operating**	**6,940.38**
Sales Receipt	1009	03/22/2021	Jones, Beverly	1250 · Undeposited Funds	-1,163.00
Payment	2453	03/23/2021	Guthrie, Jennie	1250 · Undeposited Funds	-2,384.34
Sales Receipt	1011	03/29/2021	Franco Films Co.	1250 · Undeposited Funds	-1,631.00
Payment	6555	03/30/2021	Hamilton Hotels	1250 · Undeposited Funds	-1,762.04
TOTAL					-6,940.38
Deposit		**04/30/2021**		**1010 · Cash - Operating**	**10.00**
				6900 · Interest Income	-10.00
TOTAL					-10.00

Missing Checks Report

The title of this report is somewhat misleading. The *Missing Checks* report actually displays detailed information for each check written from a specified cash account. The report includes the check number, date written, payee, and purpose (type) of check. Since the report lists each check, it is useful in finding missing and duplicate checks.

To view and print the *Missing Checks* report:
1. At the main menu bar, click Reports and then click *Banking*.
2. At the Banking submenu, click *Missing Checks*. The Missing Checks dialog box appears. See Figure 10–T.

FIGURE 10–T
Missing Checks
Dialog Box

3. At the Specify Account drop-down list, click *1010 Cash - Operating* and then click OK. The report displays all checks written since the account was opened. See Figure 10–U.
4. Close the report.

FIGURE 10–U Missing Checks Report

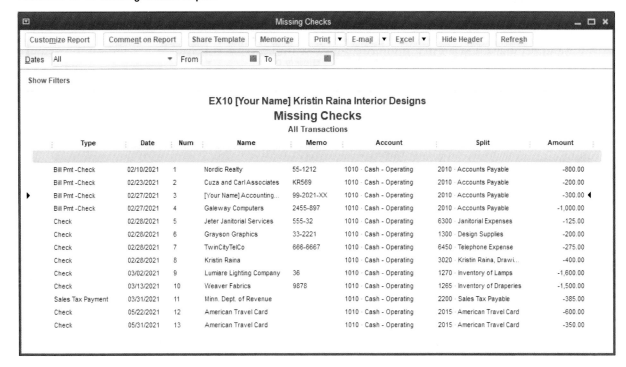

Banking Reports from the Lists Menu

QuickBooks allows you to view and print banking reports from the Lists windows. Once you access a List, you can view a list of available reports by clicking the Reports button in the List window.

HINT

An *Account QuickReport* can be displayed for any cash account and for any time period specified.

To view and print an *Account QuickReport* of the cash account:

1. At the main menu bar, click Lists and then click *Chart of Accounts.*
2. Select (highlight) *1010 Cash - Operating,* but do not open the account.
3. Click the Reports menu button.
4. At the Reports button drop-down menu, click *QuickReport: 1010 Cash - Operating.* The report is displayed. See Figure 10–V.

FIGURE 10-X Journal Report April 30, 2021–May 31, 2021

EX10 [Your Name] Kristin Raina Interior Designs
Journal
April 30 through May 31, 2021

Trans #	Type	Date	Num	Name	Memo	Account	Debit	Credit
55	Paycheck	04/30/2021	3	Harry Renee		1020 · Cash - Payroll		757.50
				Harry Renee		6565 · Salaries and Wages Expense	1,000.00	
				Harry Renee		2100 · Payroll Liabilities	0.00	
				Harry Renee		2115 · FIT Payable		120.00
				Harry Renee		6610 · Social Sec/Medicare Tax Expense	76.50	
				Harry Renee		2110 · Social Sec/Medicare Tax Payable		153.00
				Harry Renee		6625 · FUTA Expense	6.00	
				Harry Renee		2125 · FUTA Payable		6.00
				Harry Renee		2120 · SIT Payable		46.00
				Harry Renee		6630 · SUI Expense	40.00	
				Harry Renee		2130 · SUI Payable		40.00
							1,122.50	1,122.50
56	Paycheck	04/30/2021	4	Richard Henderson		1020 · Cash - Payroll		1,432.36
				Richard Henderson		6565 · Salaries and Wages Expense	1,760.00	
				Richard Henderson		2100 · Payroll Liabilities	0.00	
				Richard Henderson		2115 · FIT Payable		132.00
				Richard Henderson		6610 · Social Sec/Medicare Tax Expense	134.64	
				Richard Henderson		2110 · Social Sec/Medicare Tax Payable		269.28
				Richard Henderson		6625 · FUTA Expense	10.56	
				Richard Henderson		2125 · FUTA Payable		10.56
				Richard Henderson		2120 · SIT Payable		61.00
				Richard Henderson		6630 · SUI Expense	70.40	
				Richard Henderson		2130 · SUI Payable		70.40
							1,975.60	1,975.60
57	Liability Check	04/30/2021	5	United States Treas...	33-4777781	1020 · Cash - Payroll		1,344.24
				United States Treas...	33-4777781	2125 · FUTA Payable	32.16	
				United States Treas...	33-4777781	2115 · FIT Payable	492.00	
				United States Treas...	33-4777781	2110 · Social Sec/Medicare Tax Payable	820.08	
				United States Treas...	33-4777781	2100 · Payroll Liabilities	0.00	
							1,344.24	1,344.24
58	Liability Check	04/30/2021	6	Minn. Dept. of Reve...	ER-12343, 33-4...	1020 · Cash - Payroll		421.40
				Minn. Dept. of Reve...	ER-12343, 33-4...	2130 · SUI Payable	214.40	
				Minn. Dept. of Reve...	ER-12343, 33-4...	2120 · SIT Payable	207.00	
							421.40	421.40
59	Transfer	04/30/2021			Funds Transfer	1010 · Cash - Operating		7,000.00
					Funds Transfer	1020 · Cash - Payroll	7,000.00	
							7,000.00	7,000.00
60	Transfer	04/30/2021			Funds Transfer	1010 · Cash - Operating		10,000.00
					Funds Transfer	1050 · Cash - Money Market	10,000.00	
							10,000.00	10,000.00
61	Invoice	04/30/2021	NS...	Berger Bakery Com...		1200 · Accounts Receivable	600.00	
				Berger Bakery Com...	Returned check ...	1010 · Cash - Operating		600.00
				Minn. Dept. of Reve...	Sales Tax	2200 · Sales Tax Payable	0.00	
							600.00	600.00
62	Check	04/30/2021			Service Charge	1010 · Cash - Operating		35.00
					Service Charge	6100 · Bank Service Charges	35.00	
							35.00	35.00
63	Deposit	04/30/2021			Interest	1010 · Cash - Operating	10.00	
					Interest	6900 · Interest Income		10.00
							10.00	10.00
64	Check	04/30/2021			Service Charge	1020 · Cash - Payroll		25.00
					Service Charge	6100 · Bank Service Charges	25.00	
							25.00	25.00
65	Credit Card Ch...	05/01/2021	478...	Atlantis Business Tr...		2015 · American Travel Card		600.00
				Atlantis Business Tr...		6475 · Travel Expense	600.00	
							600.00	600.00
66	Credit Card Ch...	05/17/2021	844...	Atlantis Business Tr...		2015 · American Travel Card		350.00
				Atlantis Business Tr...		6475 · Travel Expense	350.00	
							350.00	350.00
67	Check	05/22/2021	12	American Travel Card		1010 · Cash - Operating		600.00
				American Travel Card		2015 · American Travel Card	600.00	
							600.00	600.00
68	Check	05/31/2021	13	American Travel Card		1010 · Cash - Operating		350.00
				American Travel Card		2015 · American Travel Card	350.00	
							350.00	350.00
TOTAL							**24,433.74**	**24,433.74**

FIGURE 10–Y Profit & Loss Standard Report January 1, 2021–May 31, 2021

EX10 [Your Name] Kristin Raina Interior Designs
Profit & Loss
Accrual Basis   January through May 2021

	Jan - May 21
Ordinary Income/Expense	
Income	
4010 · Design Services	4,980.00
4020 · Decorating Services	3,400.00
4060 · Sale of Carpets	2,400.00
4065 · Sale of Draperies	1,000.00
4070 · Sale of Lamps	1,200.00
4075 · Sale of Mirrors	900.00
4100 · Sales Discounts	-84.62
Total Income	13,795.38
Cost of Goods Sold	
5060 · Cost of Carpets Sold	1,200.00
5065 · Cost of Draperies Sold	500.00
5070 · Cost of Lamps Sold	600.00
5075 · Cost of Mirrors Sold	450.00
5900 · Inventory Adjustment	150.00
Total COGS	2,900.00
Gross Profit	10,895.38
Expense	
6020 · Accounting Expense	300.00
6050 · Advertising Expense	100.00
6100 · Bank Service Charges	60.00
6175 · Deprec. Exp., Furniture	100.00
6185 · Deprec. Exp., Computers	60.00
6200 · Insurance Expense	200.00
6300 · Janitorial Expenses	125.00
6325 · Office Supplies Expense	150.00
6400 · Rent Expense	800.00
6450 · Telephone Expense	275.00
6475 · Travel Expense	950.00
6500 · Utilities Expense	450.00
6560 · Payroll Expenses	
6565 · Salaries and Wages Expense	5,360.00
6610 · Social Sec/Medicare Tax Expense	410.04
6625 · FUTA Expense	32.16
6630 · SUI Expense	214.40
Total 6560 · Payroll Expenses	6,016.60
Total Expense	9,586.60
Net Ordinary Income	1,308.78
Other Income/Expense	
Other Income	
6900 · Interest Income	10.00
Total Other Income	10.00
Other Expense	
7000 · Interest Expense	50.00
Total Other Expense	50.00
Net Other Income	-40.00
Net Income	**1,268.78**

FIGURE 10–Z Balance Sheet Standard Report May 31, 2021

EX10 [Your Name] Kristin Raina Interior Designs
Balance Sheet
As of May 31, 2021

Accrual Basis

	May 31, 21
ASSETS	
Current Assets	
Checking/Savings	
1010 · Cash - Operating	24,780.38
1020 · Cash - Payroll	8,458.40
1050 · Cash - Money Market	10,000.00
Total Checking/Savings	43,238.78
Accounts Receivable	
1200 · Accounts Receivable	2,140.00
Total Accounts Receivable	2,140.00
Other Current Assets	
1260 · Inventory of Carpets	800.00
1265 · Inventory of Draperies	1,000.00
1270 · Inventory of Lamps	1,000.00
1275 · Inventory of Mirrors	900.00
1300 · Design Supplies	200.00
1305 · Office Supplies	250.00
1410 · Prepaid Advertising	500.00
1420 · Prepaid Insurance	2,200.00
Total Other Current Assets	6,850.00
Total Current Assets	52,228.78
Fixed Assets	
1700 · Furniture	
1725 · Furniture, Cost	12,000.00
1750 · Accum. Dep., Furniture	-100.00
Total 1700 · Furniture	11,900.00
1800 · Computers	
1825 · Computers, Cost	3,600.00
1850 · Accum. Dep., Computers	-60.00
Total 1800 · Computers	3,540.00
Total Fixed Assets	15,440.00
TOTAL ASSETS	**67,668.78**
LIABILITIES & EQUITY	
Liabilities	
Current Liabilities	
Accounts Payable	
2010 · Accounts Payable	9,750.00
Total Accounts Payable	9,750.00
Other Current Liabilities	
2020 · Notes Payable	7,000.00
2030 · Interest Payable	50.00
Total Other Current Liabilities	7,050.00
Total Current Liabilities	16,800.00
Total Liabilities	16,800.00
Equity	
3010 · Kristin Raina, Capital	50,000.00
3020 · Kristin Raina, Drawings	-400.00
Net Income	1,268.78
Total Equity	50,868.78
TOTAL LIABILITIES & EQUITY	**67,668.78**

Exiting QuickBooks

Upon completing this session, make a backup copy of your practice exercise company file to a removable storage device using the Back Up command. Be sure to change the *Save in* field to the removable storage device and then carefully type the correct file name. Close the company file and then exit QuickBooks.

Chapter Review and Assessment

Procedure Review

To transfer funds between accounts:

1. At the main menu bar, click Banking and then click *Transfer Funds.*
2. At the *DATE* field, enter the transfer date.
3. At the TRANSFER FUNDS FROM drop-down list, click the cash account from which the funds are transferring.
4. At the TRANSFER FUNDS TO drop-down list, click the cash account to which the funds are transferring.
5. Enter the transfer amount at the *TRANSFER AMOUNT* field.
6. Click the Save & Close button.

To reconcile a cash account:

1. At the main menu bar, click Banking and then click *Reconcile.*
2. At the Begin Reconciliation window, at the Account drop-down list, click the account to reconcile.
3. Enter the date at the *Statement Date* field.
4. Enter the bank statement ending balance at the *Ending Balance* field.
5. Enter the bank service charges at the *Service Charge* field.
6. Enter the reconciliation date at the *Service Charge Date* field.
7. Click the expense account for the service charges at the Service Charge Account drop-down list.
8. Enter the interest income at the *Interest Earned* field.
9. Enter the reconciliation date at the *Interest Earned Date* field.
10. Click the revenue account for interest income at the Interest Earned Account drop-down list.
11. If the information is correct, click Continue. The Reconcile window appears. The activity for that account is displayed.
12. Insert a check mark next to each deposit that has cleared the bank.
13. Insert a check mark next to each check and payment that has cleared the bank.
14. If there are any NSF checks, record them at the Create Invoices window while the Reconcile window is open.
15. At the Create Invoices window, click the Save & Close button and then return to the Reconcile window.
16. Insert a check mark next to any NSF amounts at the *Checks and Payments* field.
17. Confirm that the *Difference* amount reads zero.
18. If the information is complete and the difference is zero, click the Reconcile Now button.
19. In the Select Reconciliation Detail Report dialog box, click *Detail* and then click Print.
20. In the Print dialog box, click Print.

To enter a credit card charge:

1. At the main menu bar, click Banking and then click *Enter Credit Card Charges.*
2. At the CREDIT CARD drop-down list, click the appropriate credit card.
3. At the PURCHASED FROM drop-down list, click the vendor name.
4. Choose the charge date at the *DATE* field.

10. Using the Enter Credit Card Charges window, enter the following transaction:

Sep. 15   Travel and entertainment expenses of $750 to attend a sales convention in Florida were paid to Reliable Business Travel with the Travelers Express credit card. Ref. No. 6554.

11. Using the Write Checks window, enter the following transaction:

Sep. 28   Paid $400 toward the Travelers Express credit card charge incurred on September 15; Check No. 15.

12. Display and print the following reports:
    a. *Deposit Detail* for June 1, 2021, to August 31, 2021
    b. *Missing Checks* for the Cash - Operating account
    c. *Journal* for August 31, 2021, to September 30, 2021

CHAPTER 11

Jobs and Time Tracking

Recording Job Income and Job Payroll Expenses; Tracking Time for Employees and Jobs; and Creating Customer Statements

Objectives

- Add a job to the Customer Center

- Record and allocate payroll incurred for a specific job in the Pay Employees windows

- Record and allocate services rendered for a specific job in the Create Invoices windows

- Set up Time Tracking

- Track employee time for each job using the Weekly Timesheet window

- Pay employees using Time-Tracking data

- Create invoices using Time-Tracking data

- Create customer statements

- Display and print job and Time-Tracking reports, accounting reports, and financial statements

job a project, assignment, or any identifiable
segment of work for a
customer

QuickBooks allows you to allocate income and expenses for a specific job for a customer. A **job** is a project, assignment, or any identifiable segment of work for a customer. Identifying jobs allows the company to measure the profitability of individual customer projects and assignments. When you record revenue in windows such as the Create Invoices and Enter Sales Receipts windows, you can indicate the job for which the revenue was earned. When you record expenses such as payroll in the Pay Employees windows, you can also allocate employee pay and payroll tax expenses to a job.

Most service businesses track employee hours as part of the invoicing process. Customers are billed, usually at an hourly rate, for services provided by various company personnel. This is called *billable time* or *billable hours*. Time tracking mechanisms can vary from a simple manual system using handwritten timesheets to stand-alone time-and-billing software. The billable hours are used to allocate expenses to a job, determine the invoice to be billed for the job, and ultimately determine the profit (job revenue less job expenses) for the job.

To allocate the revenue and expenses to a specific job, you can either maintain the details manually or use the QuickBooks Time-Tracking feature. When activated, this feature allows you to record time spent by company personnel for customers and specific jobs by entering data in the Weekly Timesheet window. This data is then used to allocate payroll expenses to those jobs and to bill customers for work done.

QuickBooks versus Manual Accounting: Jobs and Time Tracking

In a manual accounting system, when revenue is recorded in a sales or cash receipts journal, an additional step must be taken to identify the job earning the revenue and to record that revenue in a jobs subsidiary ledger. Similarly, when job expenses are recorded in the purchases, cash payments, or payroll journals, they also must be posted to the jobs subsidiary ledger. These steps must be taken in addition to the customer and vendor subsidiary ledger posting.

In QuickBooks, the job file in the Customer Center serves as the jobs subsidiary ledger for the company. When it is desirable to track revenues and expenses for a particular job, that job is created as part of the customer's file in the Customer Center. Relevant information—such as job name, status, start date, and job description—is entered when the job file is created and updated as necessary.

When the company earns revenue from the job, the revenue is recorded in much the same manner as previously recorded in the Create Invoices window or the Enter Sales Receipts window. However, when the revenue is identified with a particular job in each window, it is automatically allocated to the job while the transaction is recorded. These transactions simultaneously update the general ledger for the revenue earned, the customer file for the account receivable (in the Create Invoices window), and the job file for the job revenue. If employees work on a specific job, the Pay Employees windows allow you to identify the time spent or salary expense related to the job.

In addition, QuickBooks has a Time-Tracking feature that is integrated into the existing accounting software. Time-Tracking is used to track the billable time allocated to the jobs. Billable time by job is recorded in the Weekly Timesheet window for each employee. This information is then carried to the Pay Employees window when payroll is processed; there, the payroll expense is allocated to the identified jobs. This information is also used in the Create Invoices and Enter Sales Receipts windows to bill customers by job based on the billable time.

Chapter Problem

In this chapter, our sample company, Kristin Raina Interior Designs, will track revenue and expenses for several jobs for a customer. As revenue is generated, you will identify the job earning the revenue and allocate the revenue to that job. You will also charge selected payroll to a specific job. Although not an employee, Kristin Raina also will track and allocate her time to specific jobs.

The Time-Tracking feature is an optional feature; you can track revenue and expenses with or without using it. For the first half of the month, you will allocate revenues and expenses to jobs without using the Time-Tracking feature. In the second half of the month, you will activate the Time-Tracking feature and then use it to allocate revenues and expenses to jobs. Additionally, at the end of the month, Kristin Raina will display and print a customer statement for the company that she is invoicing for the jobs.

Beginning balances for May 1, 2021, along with banking activity from Chapter 10, are contained in the company file **CH11 Kristin Raina Interior Designs**. Open that file, enter the password, make a backup copy, name it **EX11** *[Your Name]* **Kristin Raina Interior Designs**, restore the backup copy, and then enter the password. Change the company name to **EX11** *[Your Name]* **Kristin Raina Interior Designs**.

Lists/Centers → # The Customer Center

As you know, the Customer Center contains a file for each customer with which the company does business. If there are specific jobs for a customer or multiple jobs for that customer, you identify those jobs in the customer file. *A job must always be associated with a customer.* Once a job has been added, it will have its own file—separate but part of the customer's file. The job file carries over the customer information from the customer's file (name, address, telephone, and so on). In addition, the job file will contain important information such as the job name, description, start and expected completion dates, and status.

On May 1, 2021, Kristin Raina Interior Designs was awarded a contract to redesign the lobbies of three hotels owned by Hamilton Hotels. Kristin Raina wishes to track the revenue and payroll expenses for each of the three jobs by using the Job feature of QuickBooks.

HINT

To *select* is to highlight something by clicking once. To *choose* is to activate a command, usually by double-clicking.

To add a job:
1. At the main menu bar, click Customers and then click *Customer Center*.
2. At the Customer Center window, select (highlight) *Hamilton Hotels*, but do not open the file. See Figure 11–A.

FIGURE 11–A Hamilton Hotels File Selected

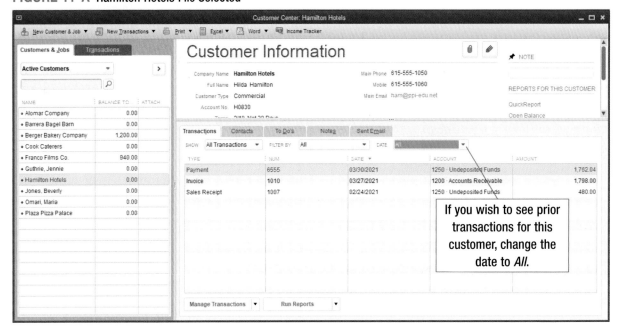

3. Click the New Customer & Job button.
4. At the New Customer & Job menu, click *Add Job.* The New Job window opens. Notice that the New Job window carries over information from the Hamilton Hotels file. See Figure 11–B.

FIGURE 11–B
New Job Window

5. At the *JOB NAME* field, type Lakeside Hotel.

6. On the Job Info tab, enter the following data:

JOB DESCRIPTION: Lakeside Hotel Lobby Redesign
JOB STATUS: Awarded
START DATE: 05/01/2021
PROJECTED END DATE: 08/31/2021

See Figure 11–C.

FIGURE 11–C
New Job Window—
Completed

7. If the information is correct, click OK. You are returned to the Customer Center. Notice that the Lakeside Hotel job is listed below the Hamilton Hotels file as a subfile and the job data is displayed on the Job Information page. See Figure 11–D.

FIGURE 11–D Customer Center

FIGURE 11–G Item List—Updated

NAME	DESCRIPTION	TYPE	ACCOUNT	TOTAL QUANTITY ON HAND	ON S	PRICE	ATTACH
◆ Decorating Services - Assistant	Decorating Services - Assistant	Service	4020 · Decorating Services			40.00	
◆ Decorating Services - Owner	Decorating Services - Owner	Service	4020 · Decorating Services			50.00	
◆ Design Services - Assistant	Design Services - Assistant	Service	4010 · Design Services			40.00	
◆ Design Services - Owner	Design Services - Owner	Service	4010 · Design Services			60.00	
◆ Carpets	Carpets	Inventory Part	4060 · Sale of Carpets	4	0	400.00	
◆ Draperies	Draperies	Inventory Part	4065 · Sale of Draperies	8	0	250.00	
◆ Lamps	Lamps	Inventory Part	4070 · Sale of Lamps	10	0	200.00	
◆ Mirrors	Decorative Mirrors	Inventory Part	4075 · Sale of Mirrors	6	0	300.00	
◆ NSF	Returned check - non-sufficient funds	Other Charge	1010 · Cash - Operating			0.00	
◆ Minn. Sales Tax	Sales Tax	Sales Tax Item	2200 · Sales Tax Payable			7.0%	

Item ▼   Activities ▼   Reports ▼   Excel ▼   Attach   ☐ Include inactive

Activities

Allocating Payroll Expenses to a Job

As you recall from Chapter 9 on payroll, Kristin Raina has two employees, Harry Renee and Richard Henderson. Harry Renee is an administrative assistant whose time is not billable. Richard Henderson is a design assistant who, along with the owner Kristin Raina, provides design and decorating services to customers. Both Richard Henderson and Kristin Raina, will spend billable time working on the Hamilton Hotels projects.

Kristin Raina wishes to charge the payroll expense to each project to measure the profitability of the project. For the first payroll in May, Kristin Raina has used a manual system to keep track of the hours spent on each job by both Richard Henderson and by herself.

On May 15, 2021, Kristin Raina pays Richard Henderson, who spent all of his time during the pay period working on the Hamilton Hotels jobs. He worked 25 hours at Lakeside Hotel, 35 hours at Mountainside Hotel, and 28 hours at Riverside Hotel, for a total of 88 hours. In preparing the payroll for May 15, 2021, allocate the 88 hours he worked to the different jobs. This will allow you to keep track of the payroll costs by job.

To pay an employee and allocate hours to jobs:

1. At the main menu bar, click Employees and then click *Pay Employees.* The Enter Payroll Information window appears.
2. At the *PAY PERIOD ENDS* and *CHECK DATE* fields, choose *05/15/2021.*
3. At the *BANK ACCOUNT* field, click *1020 Cash - Payroll.*
4. Confirm that the *First Check#* box reads *7.*
5. Select *Richard Henderson* by inserting a check mark next to the name.
6. If the information is correct, click the Open Paycheck Detail button. You move to the Preview Paycheck window.
7. Confirm that the item name is *Hourly Wages,* the rate is *20,* and the pay period is *05/01/2021* to *05/15/2021.*
8. At the first line of the *HOURS* field, type *25.*
9. At the CUSTOMER:JOB drop-down list, click *Lakeside Hotel.* See Figure 11–H.

FIGURE 11–H
Preview Paycheck
Window

10. Move to the second line of the *ITEM NAME* field and then click *Hourly Wages* at the drop-down list.
11. At the *HOURS* field, type 35.
12. At the CUSTOMER:JOB drop-down list, click *Mountainside Hotel*. Notice that there are now two hourly wages totals. See Figure 11–I.

FIGURE 11–I
Preview Paycheck
Window

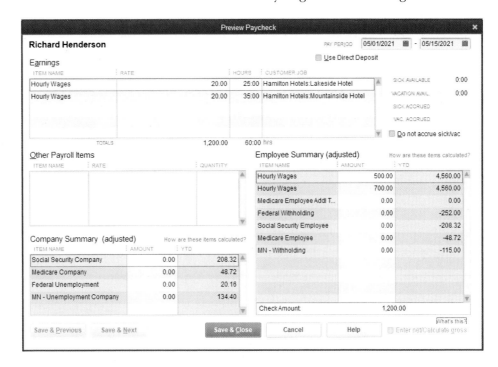

13. Move to the next line and complete the information for Riverside Hotel for 28 hours. Notice that there are three hourly wage amounts totaling $1,760 (88 hours @ $20 per hour). See Figure 11–J.

FIGURE 11–J
Preview Paycheck
Window—Completed

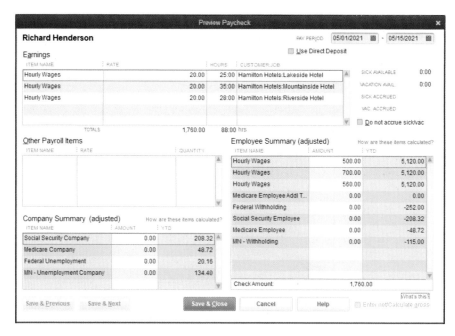

14. Complete the remainder of the window using the following information and the procedure learned in Chapter 9:

Company Taxes	Social Security Company:	109.12
	Medicare Company:	25.52
	Federal Unemployment:	10.56
	MN - Unemployment Company:	70.40
Employee Taxes	Federal Withholding:	132.00
	Social Security Employee:	109.12
	Medicare Employee:	25.52
	MN - Withholding:	61.00

QuickCheck: Check Amount $1,432.36.

See Figure 11–K.

FIGURE 11–K
Preview Paycheck
Window—Completed

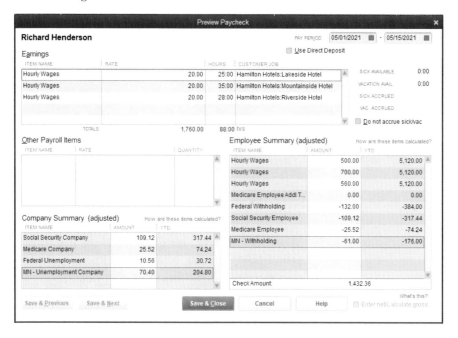

15. If the information is correct, click the Save & Close button. You are returned to the Enter Payroll Information window.
16. Click Continue. You move to the Review and Create Paychecks window, and the deductions and net pay columns are now completed.
17. If the information is correct, click the Create Paychecks button.
18. At the Confirmation and Next Steps window, click Close.

As a result of this transaction, payroll expense (including the employer payroll tax expense) is allocated to each job in proportion to the hours worked on it.

ACCOUNTING CONCEPT

For the processing of a paycheck, the general ledger posting is as shown below. (The taxes payable accounts consist of both the employee and employer taxes; *er* represents the employer's share, and *ee* represents the employee's share.)

6565 Salaries and Wages Expense		6610-6630 Employer Payroll Tax Expense	
Dr	Cr	Dr	Cr
(88 hrs @ $20) 1,760		(FICA er) 109.12	
		(Med er) 25.52	
		(FUTA) 10.56	
		(SUI) 70.40	
		Bal 215.60	

2210-2130 Payroll Taxes Payable		1020 Cash - Payroll	
Dr	Cr	Dr	Cr
	218.24 (FICA ee & er)		1,432.36
	51.04 (Med ee & er)		
	132.00 (FIT)		
	61.00 (SIT)		
	10.56 (FUTA)		
	70.40 (SUI)		
	Bal 543.24		

In addition, the job files keep track of the expenses as follows:

Lakeside		Mountainside	
Dr	Cr	Dr	Cr
(25 hrs @ $20) 500.00		(35 hrs @ $20) 700.00	
er taxes 61.25		er taxes 85.75	
Bal 561.25		Bal 785.75	

Riverside	
Dr	Cr
(28 hrs @ $20) 560.00	
er taxes 68.60	
Bal 628.60	

Employer taxes are allocated to the jobs as follows:

Lakeside:	25/88 × 215.60 =	$61.25
Mountainside:	35/88 × 215.60 =	85.75
Riverside:	28/88 × 215.60 =	68.60
		$215.60

FIGURE 11–R Weekly Timesheet Window—Completed

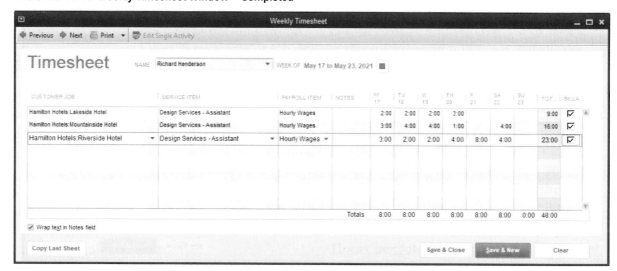

HINT

It is not necessary to enter a zero where no work is indicated for a job.

19. If the information is correct, click the Next arrow. You are moved to the next week for the same employee.

Note: If you click Save & New, you move to a new blank window.

20. Enter the information for May 24, 2021, through May 30, 2021, for all three jobs. See Figure 11–S.

FIGURE 11–S Weekly Timesheet Window—Completed

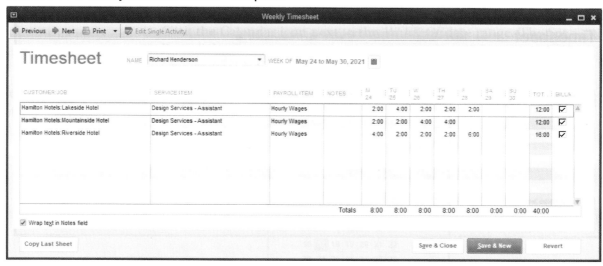

21. If the information is correct, click Save & Close.

The time records for Richard Henderson are now stored in the system for later use. When you bill Hamilton Hotels for the work done, QuickBooks will retrieve this information to assist in calculating billable time as part of creating an invoice for the work. In addition, this information will be part of the payroll processing and job allocation procedures. Since the time is billable, this information will be needed to create invoices for this customer.

Practice Exercise 11–4

May 31 — On May 31, 2021, Kristin Raina submitted the following data for Design Services time spent on each project. Enter the information in the Weekly Timesheet window. Since the *Mark all time entries as billable* box is checked in the Time & Expenses icon at the Preferences window, the *BILLABLE?* box will automatically fill.

Job	17	18	19	20	21	22	24	25	26	27	28	Totals
	\multicolumn{6}{Hours per Job for May by Date}						
Lakeside Hotel	2	1	2				4				2	11
Mountainside Hotel		1			1	1	3	2	2			10
Riverside Hotel	1		2	1	1	2	1	3	4	1	3	19

To review the data entered in the Weekly Timesheet, you can print the timesheets:

1. If necessary, open the Weekly Timesheet window and then click the Print button. The Select Timesheets to Print dialog box appears.
2. At the *Dated* fields, choose *05/24/2021* through *05/30/2021* and then move to the next field. All the personnel for whom time data has been entered are listed and selected.
3. Click OK. The Print Timesheets dialog box appears.
4. At the Print Timesheets dialog box, click the Print button. A timesheet is printed for each person for each week. One of the timesheets is shown in Figure 11–T.

FIGURE 11–T Timesheet - Page 1

Timesheet

Name: Richard Henderson

Customer:Job	Service Item	Payroll Item	Notes	M	Tu	W	Th	F	Sa	Su	Total	Bill*
Hamilton Hotels:Lakeside Hotel	Design Services - Assistant	Hourly Wages		2:00	4:00	2:00	2:00	2:00			12:00	B
Hamilton Hotels:Mountainside Hotel	Design Services - Assistant	Hourly Wages		2:00	2:00	4:00	4:00				12:00	B
Hamilton Hotels:Riverside Hotel	Design Services - Assistant	Hourly Wages		4:00	2:00	2:00	2:00	6:00			16:00	B
			Totals	8:00	8:00	8:00	8:00	8:00	0:00	0:00	40:00	

Signature _____

5. Close the Weekly Timesheet window.

Review the timesheets to make sure the hours are correct and the correct service item is listed for each employee. The data on these timesheets will flow through to the Pay Employees and Create Invoices windows. If there is an error, the payroll and invoices generated will be incorrect. Once you have recorded payroll and invoices, any subsequent changes you make to the timesheets will *not* flow through to correct them.

Activities

Paying an Employee and Allocating Payroll Expenses to a Job

On May 15, 2021, when Kristin Raina processed the pay for Richard Henderson, she manually entered the hours spent for each job at the Review Paycheck window. This was necessary because the QuickBooks Time-Tracking feature had not yet been set up. Now the Time-Tracking feature has been set up, and daily work activity has been entered at the Weekly Timesheet window. This information can now be used to assist in the payroll process and to allocate employee payroll costs to specific customer jobs.

On May 31, 2021, Kristin Raina will process the pay for Richard Henderson, who worked on all three jobs during the pay period.

To pay an employee and allocate payroll costs using Time-Tracking data:

1. At the main menu bar, click Employees and then click *Pay Employees.* The Enter Payroll Information window appears.
2. At the *PAY PERIOD ENDS* and *CHECK DATE* fields, choose *05/31/2021.* At the Pay Period Change message, click Yes to update the hours for the new pay period.
3. At the *BANK ACCOUNT* field, click *1020 Cash - Payroll* and confirm that the *First Check#* is *8.*
4. Select *Richard Henderson* by inserting a check mark next to the name.
5. If the information is correct, click the Open Paycheck Detail button. You move to the Preview Paycheck window. Notice that QuickBooks has automatically filled in the data for the hours worked on each job and for the amount paid. See Figure 11–U.

FIGURE 11–U
Preview Paycheck Window—Partially Completed

6. Complete the tax information with the following information and the procedures you learned in Chapter 9:

Company Taxes		
	Social Security Company:	109.12
	Medicare Company:	25.52
	Federal Unemployment:	10.56
	MN - Unemployment Company:	70.40
Employee Taxes	*Federal Withholding:*	132.00
	Social Security Employee:	109.12
	Medicare Employee:	25.52
	MN - Withholding:	61.00

QuickCheck: Check Amount $1,432.36.

See Figure 11–V.

8. Click OK and then click OK at the Invoicing for Vendor Time window. You are returned to the Create Invoices window with all the billable hours entered at the appropriate rates and times. See Figure 11–Y.

9. If the information is correct, click Save & New.

FIGURE 11–Y

Create Invoices Window—Completed

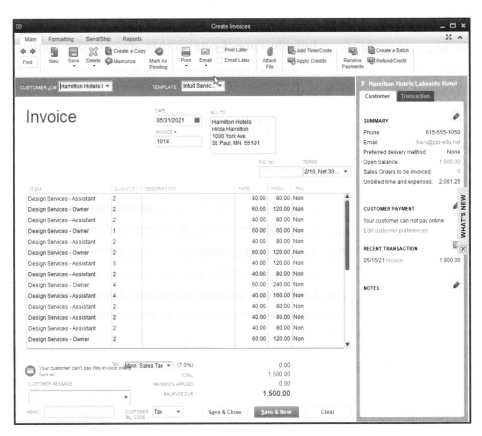

As a result of this transaction, $1,500 of Design Services revenue has been earned by the Lakeside Hotel job and will be credited to that job file.

Practice Exercise 11–5

May 31	Invoice Hamilton Hotels for all the work done on the Mountainside Hotel job. Invoice No. 1015. Terms 2/10, Net 30.
	QuickCheck: $1,720
May 31	Invoice Hamilton Hotels for all the work done on the Riverside Hotel job. Invoice No. 1016. Terms 2/10, Net 30.
	QuickCheck: $2,700

HINT

Use the Select All button on the Time tab to allocate all the time to a job.

Creating a Customer Statement

As part of the management of accounts receivable, it is often advisable to forward a statement of activity to a customer. The statement will list all the activity for that customer's account, such as sales on account or sales for cash, collections of receivables, and open balances, if any. This will act as a reminder to the customer if there is a balance due, especially if the balance is more than 30 days old. Often, the presentation of a statement will result in the payment of open invoices.

In QuickBooks, customer statements are prepared using the Create Statements window accessed from the Customers menu. Statements can be prepared for specific periods and for selected customers. Alternatively, statements can be prepared for all customers at one time, whether or not they have an open balance.

On May 31, 2021, Kristin Raina wishes to forward a statement to Hamilton Hotels, due to the increased activity with that customer during May.

To create a customer statement:

1. At the main menu bar, click Customers and then click *Create Statements.*
2. At the *Statement Date* field, choose *05/31/2021.*
3. At the *Statement Period From* and *To* fields, choose *02/01/2021* and *05/31/2021.*
4. In the SELECT CUSTOMERS section, click the *One Customer* option, and then at the drop-down list, click *Hamilton Hotels.* See Figure 11–Z.

FIGURE 11–Z
Create Statements Window—Hamilton Hotels Selected

5. In the SELECT ADDITIONAL OPTIONS section, confirm that *Intuit Standard Statement* is selected at the Template drop-down list and the *Print due date on transactions* box is checked.
6. If the information is correct, click the Preview button. The statement displays all the activity for this customer along with an aging of open receivables. See Figure 11–AA.

FIGURE 11–AA

Customer Statement—
Hamilton Hotels

Statement

EX11 [Your Name] Kristin Raina Interior Designs
25 NE Johnson Street
Minneapolis, MN 53402

Date
5/31/2021

To:
Hamilton Hotels Hilda Hamilton 1000 York Ave. St. Paul, MN 55101

Amount Due	Amount Enc.
$11,840.00	

Date	Transaction	Amount	Balance
01/31/2021	Balance forward		0.00
03/27/2021	INV #1010. Due 04/26/2021.	1,798.00	1,798.00
03/30/2021	PMT #6555.	-1,762.04	35.96
03/30/2021	Discount #6555.	-35.96	0.00
	Lakeside Hotel-		
05/15/2021	INV #1011. Due 06/14/2021.	1,900.00	1,900.00
05/31/2021	INV #1014. Due 06/30/2021.	1,500.00	3,400.00
	Mountainside Hotel-		
05/15/2021	INV #1012. Due 06/14/2021.	1,700.00	5,100.00
05/31/2021	INV #1015. Due 06/30/2021.	1,720.00	6,820.00
	Riverside Hotel-		
05/15/2021	INV #1013. Due 06/14/2021.	2,320.00	9,140.00
05/31/2021	INV #1016. Due 06/30/2021.	2,700.00	11,840.00

CURRENT	1-30 DAYS PAST DUE	31-60 DAYS PAST DUE	61-90 DAYS PAST DUE	OVER 90 DAYS PAST DUE	Amount Due
11,840.00	0.00	0.00	0.00	0.00	$11,840.00

7. Click Print to print the report. If the statement printed correctly, click *Yes* at the Did statement(s) print OK? window. If the Sending forms by e-mail window appears, insert a check mark in the box to the left of *Do not display this message in the future* and then click OK.
8. Close the report and the Create Statements window.

Job and Time-Tracking Reports, Accounting Reports, and Financial Statements

Both the Job and Time-Tracking features produce reports that companies find useful in measuring job profit and managing employee time. The job reports focus on profitability, while the Time-Tracking reports analyze time spent by each person or for each job.

Job and Time-Tracking Reports

Several reports can be accessed from the Reports menu that analyze information related to jobs. Two of these reports are the *Profit & Loss by Job* report and the *Time by Job Summary* report.

Profit & Loss by Job Report

The *Profit & Loss by Job* report provides information on the profitability of customer and job activity. The report shows the type of revenue earned and the expenses incurred for each job for a specified period of time.

To view and print the *Profit & Loss by Job* report:

1. At the main menu bar, click Reports and then click *Jobs, Time & Mileage*.
2. At the Jobs, Time & Mileage submenu, click *Profit & Loss by Job*.
3. At the *From* and *To* fields, choose *05/01/2021* and *05/31/2021* and then click Refresh. The report for the three jobs is displayed.
4. Print the report. See Figure 11–BB.

FIGURE 11–BB Profit & Loss by Job Report

EX11 [Student Name] Kristin Raina Interior Designs
Profit & Loss by Job

Accrual Basis | May 2021

	Lakeside Hotel (Hamilton Hotels)	Mountainside Hotel (Hamilton Hotels)	Riverside Hotel (Hamilton Hotels)	Total Hamilton Hotels	TOTAL
Ordinary Income/Expense					
Income					
4010 · Design Services	3,400.00	3,420.00	5,020.00	11,840.00	11,840.00
Total Income	3,400.00	3,420.00	5,020.00	11,840.00	11,840.00
Gross Profit	3,400.00	3,420.00	5,020.00	11,840.00	11,840.00
Expense					
6560 · Payroll Expenses					
6565 · Salaries and Wages Expense	920.00	1,260.00	1,340.00	3,520.00	3,520.00
6610 · Social Sec/Medicare Tax Expense	70.38	96.39	102.51	269.28	269.28
6625 · FUTA Expense	5.52	7.56	8.04	21.12	21.12
6630 · SUI Expense	36.80	50.40	53.60	140.80	140.80
Total 6560 · Payroll Expenses	1,032.70	1,414.35	1,504.15	3,951.20	3,951.20
Total Expense	1,032.70	1,414.35	1,504.15	3,951.20	3,951.20
Net Ordinary Income	2,367.30	2,005.65	3,515.85	7,888.80	7,888.80
Net Income	**2,367.30**	**2,005.65**	**3,515.85**	**7,888.80**	**7,888.80**

5. Close the report.

Time by Job Summary Report

The *Time by Job Summary* report lists hours spent by job for a specified period of time. The report lists the job and the time each employee devoted to each job.

To view and print the *Time by Job Summary* report:

1. At the main menu bar, click Reports and then click *Jobs, Time & Mileage*.
2. At the Jobs, Time & Mileage submenu, click *Time by Job Summary*.
3. At the *From* and *To* fields, choose *05/01/2021* and *05/31/2021* and then click Refresh. The report is displayed for the period. See Figure 11–CC.

FIGURE 11–CC

Time by Job Summary Report

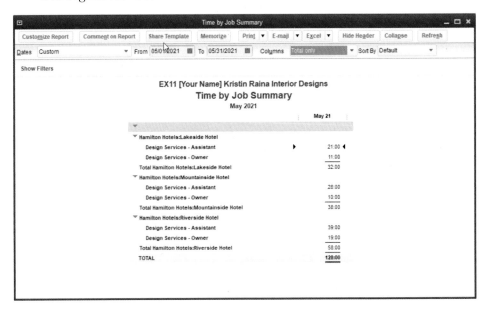

4. Print the report.
5. Close the report.

Accounting Reports and Financial Statements

At the end of the month, the *Journal* report, *Profit & Loss Standard* report, and *Balance Sheet Standard* report should be viewed and printed. The *Journal* report is displayed in Figure 11–DD, the *Profit & Loss Standard* report is displayed in Figure 11–EE, and the *Balance Sheet Standard* report is displayed in Figure 11–FF.

FIGURE 11–DD Journal Report May 1, 2021–May 31, 2021

EX11 [Your Name] Kristin Raina Interior Designs
Journal
May 2021

Trans #	Type	Date	Num	Name	Memo	Account	Debit	Credit
65	Credit Card Charge	05/01/2021	47887	Atlantis Business Travel		2015 · American Travel Card		600.00
				Atlantis Business Travel		6475 · Travel Expense	600.00	
							600.00	600.00
66	Credit Card Charge	05/17/2021	84441	Atlantis Business Travel		2015 · American Travel Card		350.00
				Atlantis Business Travel		6475 · Travel Expense	350.00	
							350.00	350.00
67	Check	05/22/2021	12	American Travel Card		1010 · Cash - Operating		600.00
				American Travel Card		2015 · American Travel Card	600.00	
							600.00	600.00
68	Check	05/31/2021	13	American Travel Card		1010 · Cash - Operating		350.00
				American Travel Card		2015 · American Travel Card	350.00	
							350.00	350.00
69	Paycheck	05/15/2021	7	Richard Henderson		1020 · Cash - Payroll		1,432.36
				-MULTIPLE-		6565 · Salaries and Wages Expense	1,760.00	
				Richard Henderson		2100 · Payroll Liabilities	0.00	
				Richard Henderson		2115 · FIT Payable		132.00
				-MULTIPLE-		6610 · Social Sec/Medicare Tax Exp...	134.64	
				Richard Henderson		2110 · Social Sec/Medicare Tax Pay...		269.28
				-MULTIPLE-		6625 · FUTA Expense	10.56	
				Richard Henderson		2125 · FUTA Payable		10.56
				Richard Henderson		2120 · SIT Payable		61.00
				-MULTIPLE-		6630 · SUI Expense	70.40	
				Richard Henderson		2130 · SUI Payable		70.40
							1,975.60	1,975.60
70	Invoice	05/15/2021	1011	Hamilton Hotels:Lakeside Hotel		1200 · Accounts Receivable	1,900.00	
				Hamilton Hotels:Lakeside Hotel	-MULTIPLE-	4010 · Design Services		1,900.00
				Minn. Dept. of Revenue	Sales Tax	2200 · Sales Tax Payable	0.00	
							1,900.00	1,900.00
71	Invoice	05/15/2021	1012	Hamilton Hotels:Mountainsid...		1200 · Accounts Receivable	1,700.00	
				Hamilton Hotels:Mountainsid...	-MULTIPLE-	4010 · Design Services		1,700.00
				Minn. Dept. of Revenue	Sales Tax	2200 · Sales Tax Payable	0.00	
							1,700.00	1,700.00
72	Invoice	05/15/2021	1013	Hamilton Hotels:Riverside Ho...		1200 · Accounts Receivable	2,320.00	
				Hamilton Hotels:Riverside Ho...	-MULTIPLE-	4010 · Design Services		2,320.00
				Minn. Dept. of Revenue	Sales Tax	2200 · Sales Tax Payable	0.00	
							2,320.00	2,320.00
73	Paycheck	05/31/2021	8	Richard Henderson		1020 · Cash - Payroll		1,432.36
				-MULTIPLE-		6565 · Salaries and Wages Expense	1,760.00	
				Richard Henderson		2100 · Payroll Liabilities	0.00	
				Richard Henderson		2115 · FIT Payable		132.00
				-MULTIPLE-		6610 · Social Sec/Medicare Tax Exp...	134.64	
				Richard Henderson		2110 · Social Sec/Medicare Tax Pay...		269.28
				-MULTIPLE-		6625 · FUTA Expense	10.56	
				Richard Henderson		2125 · FUTA Payable		10.56
				Richard Henderson		2120 · SIT Payable		61.00
				-MULTIPLE-		6630 · SUI Expense	70.40	
				Richard Henderson		2130 · SUI Payable		70.40
							1,975.60	1,975.60
74	Invoice	05/31/2021	1014	Hamilton Hotels:Lakeside Hotel		1200 · Accounts Receivable	1,500.00	
				Hamilton Hotels:Lakeside Hotel		4010 · Design Services		1,500.00
				Minn. Dept. of Revenue	Sales Tax	2200 · Sales Tax Payable	0.00	
							1,500.00	1,500.00
75	Invoice	05/31/2021	1015	Hamilton Hotels:Mountainsid...		1200 · Accounts Receivable	1,720.00	
				Hamilton Hotels:Mountainsid...		4010 · Design Services		1,720.00
				Minn. Dept. of Revenue	Sales Tax	2200 · Sales Tax Payable	0.00	
							1,720.00	1,720.00
76	Invoice	05/31/2021	1016	Hamilton Hotels:Riverside Ho...		1200 · Accounts Receivable	2,700.00	
				Hamilton Hotels:Riverside Ho...		4010 · Design Services		2,700.00
				Minn. Dept. of Revenue	Sales Tax	2200 · Sales Tax Payable	0.00	
							2,700.00	2,700.00
TOTAL							17,691.20	17,691.20

EX11 [Your Name] Kristin Raina Interior Designs
Profit & Loss
January through May 2021

Accrual Basis

	Jan - May 21
Ordinary Income/Expense	
Income	
4010 · Design Services	16,820.00
4020 · Decorating Services	3,400.00
4060 · Sale of Carpets	2,400.00
4065 · Sale of Draperies	1,000.00
4070 · Sale of Lamps	1,200.00
4075 · Sale of Mirrors	900.00
4100 · Sales Discounts	-84.62
Total Income	25,635.38
Cost of Goods Sold	
5060 · Cost of Carpets Sold	1,200.00
5065 · Cost of Draperies Sold	500.00
5070 · Cost of Lamps Sold	600.00
5075 · Cost of Mirrors Sold	450.00
5900 · Inventory Adjustment	150.00
Total COGS	2,900.00
Gross Profit	22,735.38
Expense	
6020 · Accounting Expense	300.00
6050 · Advertising Expense	100.00
6100 · Bank Service Charges	60.00
6175 · Deprec. Exp., Furniture	100.00
6185 · Deprec. Exp., Computers	60.00
6200 · Insurance Expense	200.00
6300 · Janitorial Expenses	125.00
6325 · Office Supplies Expense	150.00
6400 · Rent Expense	800.00
6450 · Telephone Expense	275.00
6475 · Travel Expense	950.00
6500 · Utilities Expense	450.00
6560 · Payroll Expenses	
6565 · Salaries and Wages Expense	8,880.00
6610 · Social Sec/Medicare Tax Expense	679.32
6625 · FUTA Expense	53.28
6630 · SUI Expense	355.20
Total 6560 · Payroll Expenses	9,967.80
Total Expense	13,537.80
Net Ordinary Income	9,197.58
Other Income/Expense	
Other Income	
6900 · Interest Income	10.00
Total Other Income	10.00
Other Expense	
7000 · Interest Expense	50.00
Total Other Expense	50.00
Net Other Income	-40.00
Net Income	9,157.58

FIGURE 11–FF Balance Sheet Standard Report May 31, 2021

EX11 [Your Name] Kristin Raina Interior Designs
Balance Sheet
As of May 31, 2021

Accrual Basis

	May 31, 21
ASSETS	
Current Assets	
Checking/Savings	
1010 · Cash - Operating	24,780.38
1020 · Cash - Payroll	5,593.68
1050 · Cash - Money Market	10,000.00
Total Checking/Savings	40,374.06
Accounts Receivable	
1200 · Accounts Receivable	13,980.00
Total Accounts Receivable	13,980.00
Other Current Assets	
1260 · Inventory of Carpets	800.00
1265 · Inventory of Draperies	1,000.00
1270 · Inventory of Lamps	1,000.00
1275 · Inventory of Mirrors	900.00
1300 · Design Supplies	200.00
1305 · Office Supplies	250.00
1410 · Prepaid Advertising	500.00
1420 · Prepaid Insurance	2,200.00
Total Other Current Assets	6,850.00
Total Current Assets	61,204.06
Fixed Assets	
1700 · Furniture	
1725 · Furniture, Cost	12,000.00
1750 · Accum. Dep., Furniture	-100.00
Total 1700 · Furniture	11,900.00
1800 · Computers	
1825 · Computers, Cost	3,600.00
1850 · Accum. Dep., Computers	-60.00
Total 1800 · Computers	3,540.00
Total Fixed Assets	15,440.00
TOTAL ASSETS	76,644.06
LIABILITIES & EQUITY	
Liabilities	
Current Liabilities	
Accounts Payable	
2010 · Accounts Payable	9,750.00
Total Accounts Payable	9,750.00
Other Current Liabilities	
2020 · Notes Payable	7,000.00
2030 · Interest Payable	50.00
2100 · Payroll Liabilities	
2110 · Social Sec/Medicare Tax Payable	538.56
2115 · FIT Payable	264.00
2120 · SIT Payable	122.00
2125 · FUTA Payable	21.12
2130 · SUI Payable	140.80
Total 2100 · Payroll Liabilities	1,086.48
Total Other Current Liabilities	8,136.48
Total Current Liabilities	17,886.48
Total Liabilities	17,886.48
Equity	
3010 · Kristin Raina, Capital	50,000.00
3020 · Kristin Raina, Drawings	-400.00
Net Income	9,157.58
Total Equity	58,757.58
TOTAL LIABILITIES & EQUITY	76,644.06

Reconciliation of Data to Reports

As you have seen in this chapter, income and expenses can be allocated to jobs either by entering data directly into the Create Invoices window and Payroll window or by activating the Time-Tracking feature and using the Weekly Timesheet. When data is entered manually or into the Weekly Timesheet, QuickBooks operates behind the scenes to calculate the amounts per job that appear in the Create Invoice window, Payroll windows, Job files, and Job reports. To better understand some of the behind-the-scenes computations, see Figure 11–GG, which displays how the amounts are calculated by QuickBooks.

FIGURE 11–GG Reconciliation of Data to Reports

RECONCILIATION OF DATA TO REPORTS

Design Services:

		Lakeside Hotel			Mountainside Hotel			Riverside Hotel		Total
May 15, 2021 Kristin Raina	(15 x $60) =	$900	(5 x $60) =	$300	(20 x $60) =	$1,200	$2,400
Richard Henderson	(25 x $40) =	1,000	(35 x $40) =	1,400	(28 x $40) =	1,120	3,520
		$1,900		$1,700		$2,320	$5,920
May 31, 2021 Kristin Raina	(11 x $60) =	$660	(10 x $60) =	$600	(19 x $60) =	$1,140	$2,400
Richard Henderson	(21 x $40) =	840	(28 x $40) =	1,120	(39 x $40) =	1,560	3,520
		$1,500		$1,720		$2,700	$5,920
Total Income		$3,400		$3,420		$5,020	$11,840

Payroll Expenses:

		Lakeside Hotel		Mountainside Hotel		Riverside Hotel	Total
May 15, 2021 Salaries Expense	(25 x $20) =	500.00	(35 x $20) =	700.00	(28 x $20) =	560.00	$1,760.00
PR Tax Expense		$61.25		85.75		68.60	215.60
		561.25		785.75		628.60	$1,975.60
May 31, 2021 Salaries Expense	(21 x $20) =	420.00	(28 x $20) =	560.00	(39 x $20) =	780.00	$1,760.00
PR Tax Expense		51.45		68.60		95.55	215.60
		471.45		628.60		875.55	$1,975.60
Total Expenses		1,032.70		1,414.35		1,504.15	3,951.20
Net Income		$2,367.30		$2,005.65		$3,515.85	$7,888.80

Allocation of Payroll Tax Expense:

Company Payroll Tax Expense:		Allocation of payroll tax expense based on hours to each job:				
May 15, 2021 Social Security Company	$109.12					
Medicare Company	25.52	Lakeside Hotel	(25 ÷ 88) x	$215.60 =	$61.25
Federal Unemployment	10.56	Mountainside Hotel	(35 ÷ 88) x	$215.60 =	85.75
MN - Unemployment Company	70.40	Riverside Hotel	(28 ÷ 88) x	$215.60 =	68.60
	$215.60	Total			$215.60
May 31, 2021 Social Security Company	$109.12					
Medicare Company	25.52	Lakeside Hotel	(21 ÷ 88) x	$215.60 =	$51.45
Federal Unemployment	10.56	Mountainside Hotel	(28 ÷ 88) x	$215.60 =	$68.60
MN - Unemployment Company	70.40	Riverside Hotel	(39 ÷ 88) x	$215.60 =	$95.55
	$215.60	Total			$215.60

Exiting QuickBooks

Upon completing this session, make a backup copy of your practice exercise company file to a removable storage device using the Back Up command. Be sure to change the *Save in* field to the removable storage device and then carefully type the correct file name. Close the company file and then exit QuickBooks.

Chapter Review and Assessment

Procedure Review

To add a job:

1. At the main menu bar, click Customers and then click *Customer Center.*
2. At the Customer Center window, select (highlight) the customer with which the job is associated, but do not open the file.
3. Click the New Customer & Job button.
4. At the New Customer & Job menu, click *Add Job.* The New Job window opens. The New Job window carries over information from the customer's file.
5. At the *JOB NAME* field, type the job name.
6. On the Job Info tab, type the appropriate data in the following fields:
   JOB DESCRIPTION
   JOB STATUS
   START DATE
   PROJECTED END DATE

7. If the information is correct, click OK.

To allocate payroll expenses to a job (without using the Time-Tracking feature):

1. At the main menu bar, click Employees and then click *Pay Employees.* Click *No* at the QuickBooks Payroll Services message, if necessary. The Enter Payroll Information window appears.
2. Enter the appropriate dates in the *PAY PERIOD ENDS* and *CHECK DATE* fields.
3. At the *BANK ACCOUNT* field, click the appropriate bank account.
4. Select the appropriate employee by inserting a check mark next to the name.
5. Click the Open Paycheck Detail button. You move to the Preview Paycheck window.
6. Confirm that the correct payroll item appears.
7. At the first line of the *HOURS* field, type the hours for the first job.
8. At the CUSTOMER:JOB drop-down list, click the job name.
9. Move to the second line of the *ITEM NAME* field and then click the payroll item at the drop-down list.
10. At the *HOURS* field, type the hours for the second job.
11. At the CUSTOMER:JOB drop-down list, click the second job name.
12. Repeat this procedure for all remaining jobs.
13. Complete the remainder of the window in the manner explained in Chapter 9 for company taxes and employee taxes.
14. If the information is correct, click the Save & Close button. You are returned to the Enter Payroll Information window.
15. Click Continue. The Review and Create Paychecks window appears, with the taxes columns completed.
16. If the information is correct, click the Create Paychecks button.
17. At the Confirmation and Next Steps window, click Close.

To create an invoice for a job (without using the Time-Tracking feature):
1. At the main menu bar, click Customers and then click *Create Invoices.*
2. At the CUSTOMER:JOB drop-down list, click the job name.
3. At the Billable Time/Costs window, choose *Exclude outstanding billable time and costs at this time?* and then click OK.
4. At the TEMPLATE drop-down list, click *Intuit Service Invoice.*
5. Enter the date and invoice number and accept the terms.
6. Click the appropriate items at the ITEM drop-down list.
7. Enter the quantity. Confirm that the *Print Later* and *Email Later* boxes do not contain check marks and the *Your customer can't pay this invoice online* command remains off.
8. Click the Save & Close button.

To set up the Time-Tracking feature:
1. At the main menu bar, click Edit and then click *Preferences.* The Preferences window appears.
2. In the left panel of the Preferences window, click the Time & Expenses icon.
3. Click the Company Preferences tab.
4. At the *Do you track time?* field, click the *Yes* option. Accept *Monday* as the first day of the work week.
5. Insert a check mark in the *Mark all time entries as billable* box.
6. If the information is correct, click OK.

To enter Time-Tracking data:
1. At the main menu bar, click Employees and then click *Enter Time.*
2. At the Enter Time submenu, click *Use Weekly Timesheet.*
3. At the NAME drop-down list, click the employee name and then click *Yes* at the Transfer Activities to Payroll message.
4. Click the Calendar icon. The Set Date dialog box appears.
5. Choose the start date.
6. Click the date on the calendar to return to the Weekly Timesheet window.
7. At the first line of the CUSTOMER:JOB drop-down list, click the job name.
8. At the SERVICE ITEM drop-down list, click the service item.
9. At the PAYROLL ITEM drop-down list, click the payroll item for this employee.
10. At the column for the first day of work, type the hours for that job.
11. Continue entering the hours for that job for the period of time displayed.
12. Confirm that the *BILLABLE?* box is checked.
13. Move to the second line, and at the CUSTOMER:JOB drop-down list, click the next job.
14. Repeat the process for all successive jobs for this time period.
15. If the information is correct, click the Next arrow.
16. Repeat the process for the employee for the next week.
17. If this is the final period of work, click the Save & Close button.

To pay an employee and allocate time using Time-Tracking data:
1. At the main menu bar, click Employees and then click *Pay Employees.* The Enter Payroll Information window appears.
2. Enter the appropriate dates in the *PAY PERIOD ENDS* and *CHECK DATE* fields. At the Pay Period Change message, click Yes to update the hours for the new pay period.
3. At the *BANK ACCOUNT* field, click the appropriate bank account.
4. Select the appropriate employee by inserting a check mark next to the name.
5. Click the Open Paycheck Detail button. You move to the Preview Paycheck window. Notice that the data for the hours worked on each job and for the pay amount have been filled automatically.
6. Complete the tax information in the usual manner.
7. If the information is correct, click the Save & Close button. You are returned to the Enter Payroll Information window.
8. Click Continue. The Review and Create Paychecks window appears with the taxes columns completed.
9. If the information is correct, click the Create Paychecks button.
10. At the Confirmation and Next Steps window, click Close.

To create an invoice using Time-Tracking data:
1. At the main menu bar, click Customers and then click *Create Invoices.*
2. Select the date, invoice number, and template.
3. At the CUSTOMER:JOB drop-down list, click the job name.
4. At the Billable Time/Costs window, choose the first option: *Select the outstanding billable time and costs to add to this invoice?*
5. Click OK. The Choose Billable Time and Costs window appears, and the hours billed by all the company employees for the job are displayed.
6. Click the Select All button. A check mark is inserted next to each item listed.
7. Click OK and then click OK at the message. You are returned to the Create Invoices window with all the billable hours entered at the appropriate rate and time.
8. Click the Save & Close button.

To create a customer statement:
1. At the main menu bar, click Customers and then click *Create Statements.*
2. At the *Statement Date* field, choose the statement date.
3. At the *Statement Period From* and *To* fields, enter the dates for the period of time covered by the statement.
4. In the SELECT CUSTOMERS section, click the option for the statement you wish to create.
5. Confirm that the *Intuit Standard Statement* is selected at the Template drop-down list and the *Print due date on transactions* box is checked.
6. If the information is correct, click the Preview button. The statement displays all the activity for this customer along with an aging of open receivables.
7. Click Print to print the report. If the statement printed OK, click *Yes* at the Did statement(s) print OK? window.
8. Close the report and the Create Statements window.

To view and print the *Profit & Loss by Job* report:
1. At the main menu bar, click Reports and then click *Jobs, Time & Mileage*.
2. At the Jobs, Time & Mileage submenu, click *Profit & Loss by Job*.
3. Enter the report dates.
4. Print the report and then close it.

To view and print the *Time by Job Summary* report:
1. At the main menu bar, click Reports and then click *Jobs, Time & Mileage*.
2. At the Jobs, Time & Mileage submenu, click *Time by Job Summary*.
3. Enter the dates of the report.
4. Print the report and then close it.

Key Concepts

Select the letter of the item that best matches each definition.

a. Job
b. Time Tracking
c. Customer Center
d. Job revenue
e. Time tab

f. Weekly Timesheet window
g. Job profit
h. *Profit & Loss by Job* report
i. *Time by Job Summary* report
j. Billable time

_____ 1. Tab at the Choose Billable Time and Costs window that lists billable hours worked for a specific job.

_____ 2. The center that contains a file for each customer job.

_____ 3. Report that displays the revenues, expenses, and net profit for each job for a specified period of time.

_____ 4. The time worked by company personnel that can be billed to customers.

_____ 5. The process by which a company maintains records of time worked by employees for various customers or jobs.

_____ 6. Job revenue less job expenses.

_____ 7. The report that displays employee time spent on each job.

_____ 8. It can be a project, assignment, or any identifiable segment of work for a customer.

_____ 9. The window where time worked by company personnel is entered.

_____ 10. The income earned for a particular job.

Procedure Check

1. Your company is a construction contractor and working on several projects for one customer. How would you use QuickBooks to determine which jobs are making money?
2. Describe the steps to add a job to the Customer Center.
3. Your company wishes to keep a record of the time worked by company personnel to bill customers for services provided. How would you use QuickBooks to track time information?

4. Upper management requests a report showing the profit or loss for each project on which the company is currently working. How would you use QuickBooks to obtain this information?
5. Explain to your company's new accounts receivable clerk how QuickBooks is used to inform customers of their account activity.
6. Explain why it is so important for a service business to keep accurate records of the time employees and others spend for each job or customer.

Case Problems

Demonstrate your knowledge of the QuickBooks features discussed in this chapter by completing the following case problems.

Case Problem 11–1

In July, the fourth month of business for Lynn's Music Studio, one of Lynn Garcia's clients, Highland School, has asked her to organize, coordinate, and supervise an eight-week intensive music program. All the classes will be held at the school, but they will be offered to three levels of students: beginner, intermediate, and progressive. Highland School needs a separate invoice each month for each level of students, so Lynn has decided that it is necessary to track income and expenses for each level. To aid in this process, she has decided to activate the Time-Tracking feature of QuickBooks so that the time spent by her and one of her employees, Michelle Auletta, can be tracked and allocated to each level of student and then billed to the client, Highland School. Lynn has added two service items to the Item List for Michelle Auletta's billable time as an assistant. The company file includes information for Lynn's Music Studio as of July 1, 2021.

1. Open the company file **CH11 Lynn's Music Studio.QBW**.
2. At the QuickBooks Desktop Login window, in the *Password* text box, type Student1 and then click OK.
3. Make a backup copy of the company file and name it **LMS11 *[Your Name]* Lynn's Music Studio**.
4. Restore the backup copy of the company file. In both the Open Backup Copy and Save Company File as dialog boxes, use the file name **LMS11 *[Your Name]* Lynn's Music Studio** and enter the password.
5. Change the company name to **LMS11 *[Your Name]* Lynn's Music Studio**.
6. Set up the Time-Tracking feature for Lynn's Music Studio. Monday is the first day of the work week.
7. Add the following jobs to the Customer Center:

CUSTOMER:	Highland School
JOB NAME:	Beginner Level
JOB DESCRIPTION:	Beginner Level Summer Program
JOB STATUS:	Awarded
START DATE:	07/01/2021
PROJECTED END DATE:	08/31/2021

JOB NAME:	Intermediate Level
JOB DESCRIPTION:	Intermediate Level Summer Program
JOB STATUS:	Awarded
START DATE:	07/01/2021
PROJECTED END DATE:	08/31/2021

JOB NAME:	Progressive Level
JOB DESCRIPTION:	Progressive Level Summer Program
JOB STATUS:	Awarded
START DATE:	07/01/2021
PROJECTED END DATE:	08/31/2021

8. Enter the following hours worked for Highland School in the Weekly Timesheet window. (Remember to click *Yes* at the Transfer Activities to Payroll message.)

Michelle Auletta: Piano Lessons—Assistant

Job	Hours per Job for July by Date									
	6	7	8	9	10	12	13	14	15	Totals
Beginner Level	2	2	2	2	2	2	2	2	2	18
Intermediate Level						2		2		4
Progressive Level				2					2	4

Lynn Garcia: Piano Lessons—Owner

Job	Hours per Job for July by Date									
	6	7	8	9	10	12	13	14	15	Totals
Beginner Level		2	2			2				6
Intermediate Level	2	2	2	2	2	2	2	2	2	18
Progressive Level	2	2	2	2	2	2	2	2	2	18

9. Process pay and allocate time for July 15, 2021, for Michelle Auletta. (Click *Yes* at the Pay Period Change window.)

Check No.:	6
Item Name:	Hourly Wages
Rate:	15
Company Taxes:	
Social Security Company:	24.18
Medicare Company:	5.65
Federal Unemployment:	2.34
PA - Unemployment Company:	15.60
Employee Taxes:	
Federal Withholding:	35.10
Social Security Employee:	24.18
Medicare Employee:	5.65
PA - Withholding:	11.70
PA - Unemployment Employee:	0.00

10. Create the following invoices:

Jul. 15   Create invoice for Highland School Beginner Level piano lessons provided by Lynn Garcia and Michelle Auletta for the period July 1, 2021, to July 15, 2021. Invoice No. 2020. Terms 2/10, Net 30 Days.

Jul. 15   Create invoice for Highland School Intermediate Level piano lessons provided by Lynn Garcia and Michelle Auletta for the period July 1, 2021, to July 15, 2021. Invoice No 2021. Terms 2/10, Net 30 Days.

Jul. 15   Create invoice for Highland School Progressive Level piano lessons provided by Lynn Garcia and Michelle Auletta for the period July 1, 2021, to July 15, 2021. Invoice No. 2022. Terms 2/10, Net 30 Days.

11. Enter the following hours worked in the Weekly Timesheet window:

Michelle Auletta: Piano Lessons—Assistant

Job	Hours per Job for July by Date										
	19	20	21	22	23	26	27	28	29	30	Totals
Beginner Level	3	3	2	3	2	3	2	2	2	2	24
Intermediate Level	3		3			3		3			12
Progressive Level		2		2	2		3		3	2	14

Lynn Garcia: Piano Lessons—Owner

Job	Hours per Job for July by Date										
	19	20	21	22	23	26	27	28	29	30	Totals
Beginner Level	2				2					2	6
Intermediate Level	2	2	2	2	2	2	2		2	2	18
Progressive Level	2	3	2	2	2	3	2	2	2	2	22

12. Process pay and allocate time for July 31, 2021, for Michelle Auletta:

Check No.:	7
Item Name:	Hourly Wages
Rate:	15
Company Taxes:	
Social Security Company:	46.50
Medicare Company:	10.87
Federal Unemployment:	4.50
PA - Unemployment Company:	30.00
Employee Taxes:	
Federal Withholding:	67.50
Social Security Employee:	46.50
Medicare Employee:	10.87
PA - Withholding:	22.50
PA - Unemployment Employee:	0.00

13. Create the following invoices:

Jul. 31   Create invoice for Highland School Beginner Level piano lessons provided by Lynn Garcia and Michelle Auletta for the period July 16, 2021, to July 31, 2021. Invoice No. 2023. Terms Net 30 Days.

Jul. 31   Create invoice for Highland School Intermediate Level piano lessons provided by Lynn Garcia and Michelle Auletta for the period July 16, 2021, to July 31 2021. Invoice No. 2024. Terms Net 30 Days.

Jul. 31   Create invoice for Highland School Progressive Level piano lessons provided by Lynn Garcia and Michelle Auletta for the period July 16, 2021, to July 31, 2021. Invoice No. 2025. Terms Net 30 Days.

14. Display and print a customer statement for Highland School for July 1, 2021, to July 31, 2021.
15. Display and print the following reports for July 1, 2021, to July 31, 2021:
    a. *Profit & Loss by Job*
    b. *Time by Job Summary*

Case Problem 11–2

In September, the fourth month of business for Olivia's Web Solutions, one of Olivia Chen's customers, Thrifty Stores, has decided to expand to three stores. Each store will need its own web page design services, as the stores carry different products. Olivia Chen has decided that it is necessary to track income and expenses for each store. In addition, she wishes to activate the Time-Tracking feature of QuickBooks so that the time spent by her and one of her employees, Gary Glenn, can be tracked and allocated to each job and then billed to the customer. She has added two service items to the Item List for Gary Glenn's billable time as an assistant. The company file includes information for Olivia's Web Solutions as of September 1, 2021.

1. Open the company file **CH11 Olivia's Web Solutions.QBW**.
2. At the QuickBooks Desktop Login window, in the *Password* text box, type Student1 and then click OK.
3. Make a backup copy of the company file and name it **OWS11 *[Your Name]* Olivia's Web Solutions**.
4. Restore the backup copy of the company file. In both the Open Backup Copy and the Save Company File as dialog boxes, use the file name **OWS11 *[Your Name]* Olivia's Web Solutions** and enter the password.
5. Change the company name to **OWS11 *[Your Name]* Olivia's Web Solutions**.
6. Set up the Time-Tracking feature for Olivia's Web Solutions. Monday is the first day of the work week.

7. Add the following jobs to the Customer Center:

CUSTOMER:	Thrifty Stores
JOB NAME:	Bronx Store
JOB DESCRIPTION:	Thrifty Bronx Store Web Page Design
JOB STATUS:	Awarded
START DATE:	09/01/2021
PROJECTED END DATE:	10/31/2021
JOB NAME:	Brooklyn Store
JOB DESCRIPTION:	Thrifty Brooklyn Store Web Page Design
JOB STATUS:	Awarded
START DATE:	09/01/2021
PROJECTED END DATE:	10/31/2021
JOB NAME:	Queens Store
JOB DESCRIPTION:	Thrifty Queens Store Web Page Design
JOB STATUS:	Awarded
START DATE:	09/01/2021
PROJECTED END DATE:	10/31/2021

8. Enter the following hours worked for Thrifty Stores in the Weekly Timesheet window. (Remember to click *Yes* at the Transfer Activities to Payroll message.)

> **HINT**
> You will need to start with the Weekly Timesheet for the week of August 30, 2021.

Gary Glenn: Web Page Design—Assistant

Job										
	1	**2**	**3**	**7**	**8**	**9**	**10**	**13**	**14**	**15**	**Totals**

Job	1	2	3	7	8	9	10	13	14	15	Totals
Bronx Store	4	3	1		5	2	4		1	2	22
Brooklyn Store		1	4	4	3	2	1	6	4	6	31
Queens Store	4	4	3	4		4	3	2	3		27

Olivia Chen: Web Page Design—Owner

Job	1	2	3	7	8	9	10	13	14	15	Totals
Bronx Store		2		2	2	2	1	4	2		15
Brooklyn Store		1	2		3		1	2	2	4	15
Queens Store	2	1	1	2		1	2	2	3		14

9. Process pay and allocate time for September 15, 2021, for Gary Glenn. (Click *Yes* at the Pay Period Change window.)

Check No.:	6
Item Name:	Hourly Wages
Rate:	25
Company Taxes:	
Social Security Company:	124.00
Medicare Company:	29.00
Federal Unemployment:	12.00
NY - Unemployment Company:	80.00
Employee Taxes:	
Federal Withholding:	360.00
Social Security Employee:	124.00
Medicare Employee:	29.00
NY - Withholding:	98.00

10. Create the following invoices:

Sep. 15   Create invoice for Web Page Design Services for Thrifty Bronx Store for services provided by Olivia Chen and Gary Glenn for the period September 1, 2021, to September 15, 2021. Invoice No. 1017. Terms Net 30 Days.

Sep. 15   Create invoice for Web Page Design Services for Thrifty Brooklyn Store for services provided by Olivia Chen and Gary Glenn for the period September 1, 2021, to September 15, 2021. Invoice No. 1018. Terms Net 30 Days.

Sep. 15   Create invoice for Web Page Design Services for Thrifty Queens Store for services provided by Olivia Chen and Gary Glenn for the period September 1, 2021, to September 15, 2021. Invoice No. 1019. Terms Net 30 Days.

11. Enter the following hours worked in the Weekly Timesheet window. (Remember to click *Yes* at the Transfer Activities to Payroll message.)

Gary Glenn: Web Page Design—Assistant

Job											

Job	**Hours per Job for September by Date**										
	20	21	22	23	24	25	27	28	29	30	Totals
Bronx Store	4	3	6	4	2		1	2	3		25
Brooklyn Store	2	3	1	2	4	6	5	5	4	1	33
Queens Store	2	2	1	2	2	2	2	1	1	7	22

Olivia Chen: Web Page Design—Owner

Job	**Hours per Job for September by Date**										
	20	21	22	23	24	25	27	28	29	30	Totals
Bronx Store	1	2	5	2	3	4		2	2		21
Brooklyn Store	2	2	2	2	2		4		2		16
Queens Store	4	3		3	1	4	2	1	1		19

12. Process pay and allocate time for September 30, 2021, for Gary Glenn:

Check No.:	7
Item Name:	Hourly Wages
Rate:	25
Company Taxes:	
Social Security Company:	124.00
Medicare Company:	29.00
Federal Unemployment:	12.00
NY - Unemployment Company:	80.00
Employee Taxes:	
Federal Withholding:	360.00
Social Security Employee:	124.00
Medicare Employee:	29.00
NY - Withholding:	98.00

13. Create the following invoices:

Sep. 30   Create invoice for Web Page Design Services for Thrifty Bronx Store for services provided by Olivia Chen and Gary Glenn for the period September 16, 2021, to September 30, 2021. Invoice No. 1020. Terms Net 30 Days.

Sep. 30   Create invoice for Web Page Design Services for Thrifty Brooklyn Store for services provided by Olivia Chen and Gary Glenn for the period September 16, 2021, to September 30, 2021. Invoice No. 1021. Terms Net 30 Days.

Sep. 30   Create invoice for Web Page Design Services for Thrifty Queens Store for services provided by Olivia Chen and Gary Glenn for the period September 16, 2021, to September 30, 2021. Invoice No. 1022. Terms Net 30 Days.

14. Display and print a customer statement for Thrifty Stores for September 1, 2021, to September 30, 2021.

15. Display and print the following reports for September 1, 2021, to September 30, 2021:
    a. *Profit & Loss by Job*
    b. *Time by Job Summary*

CHAPTER 12

Customization of Your Company File

Customizing the Desktop, Invoices, Letters, Memorized Transactions, Graphs, and Fiscal Year

Objectives

- Customize the desktop with the Home page and Icon bars

- Customize Lists/Centers (including subaccounts), merge entries, and create custom fields

- Customize Activities (including an Activity window display and related invoice), prepare QuickBooks Letter in Microsoft Word, and memorize transactions

- Customize Reports (including the appearance of reports), memorize settings, export a report into Microsoft Excel, process multiple reports, change report default settings, and view and print a graph

- View fiscal year closing, set closing date, and prepare for new fiscal year

At this point, you should have a good understanding of how to use QuickBooks and be able to create and set up a new company file, update the Lists and Centers, record transactions in the Activities windows, and view and print a variety of management reports, accounting reports, and financial statements.

In this final chapter, you will learn how to customize the desktop; customize Lists/Centers by changing subaccount default settings, merging entries, and creating custom fields; and customize Activities by personalizing the Create Invoices window and related printed invoices. You will then learn how to prepare a QuickBooks Letter in Microsoft Word and memorize transactions. Next, you will learn how to customize Reports and memorize the settings, export a report to Microsoft Excel, process multiple reports, change report default settings, and view and print graphs. Finally, you will conclude the accounting cycle in QuickBooks by viewing the fiscal year closing, setting the closing date, and preparing for the new fiscal year.

Chapter Problem

Begin by opening the company file **CH12 Kristin Raina Interior Designs**. Enter the password, *Student1*. Make a backup copy and name it **EX12** *[Your Name]* **Kristin Raina Interior Designs**. Restore the backup copy, enter the password *Student1*, and then change the company name to **EX12** *[Your Name]* **Kristin Raina Interior Designs**.

Customize the Desktop

There are many different ways to access Lists/Centers, Activities windows, and Reports in QuickBooks. Throughout the text, only the main menu bar was used, but you can customize your desktop to use the Home page and the Icon bars as alternative ways to access these items.

Home Page

By default, when you create a new company file and each time you open a company file, the Home page is displayed. If the default was changed and the Home page is not automatically displayed, it can be accessed for the current work session, or the default can be changed so that the Home page displays each time the company file is opened. In addition, the Home page can be customized according to your choices.

Using the Home Page

To display the Home page if it is not displayed:

1. At the main menu bar, click Company.
2. Click *Home Page*. The Home Page appears.

   QuickBooks provides two tabs on the Home page: the Home Page tab and the Insights tab. The Home Page tab is shown in Figure 12–A. The Insights tab provides information at a glance about the company's Profit & Loss, Income, and Expenses.

3. If necessary, click the Home Page tab. See Figure 12–A for the Home page—Home Page tab.

FIGURE 12-A

Home Page—Home
Page Tab

There are five sections of the Home page, and they are labeled with tabs: VENDORS, CUSTOMERS, EMPLOYEES, COMPANY, and BANKING. Recall that VENDORS, CUSTOMERS, and EMPLOYEES are the centers presented in prior chapters. If you click any of these tabs, you are moved to the respective center.

The Home page also displays icons for certain tasks and the workflow related to each center. You can click the icon to move to the respective window. In some cases, a drop-down menu will appear with additional choices.

To access a window using the icons on the Home page:
1. On the Home page in the VENDORS section, click the Enter Bills icon. The Enter Bills window appears.

    In Chapter 2, "Vendors," when a non-inventory item was purchased, the transaction was recorded in the Enter Bills window using the Expenses subtab. The Enter Bills window was accessed by using the Vendors menu and choosing *Enter Bills.*
2. Close the Enter Bills window.
3. In the VENDORS section, click the Receive Inventory icon. A drop-down menu displays two choices: *Receive Inventory with Bill* and *Receive Inventory without Bill.* See Figure 12–B.

FIGURE 12-B

Receive Inventory
Drop-Down Menu

HINT

Recall that there is only one Enter Bills window. To open it, choose *Enter Bills* or *Receive Items and Enter Bill* from the Vendors menu or the Home page. Then choose the Expenses subtab to record non-inventory purchases or the Items subtab to record inventory purchases.

4. At the Receive Inventory drop-down menu, click *Receive Inventory with Bill.* The Enter Bills window appears.

    In Chapter 5, "Inventory," when inventory was purchased and received, the transaction was recorded in the Enter Bills window using the Items subtab. The Enter Bills window was accessed by using the Vendors menu and choosing *Receive Items and Enter Bill.*
5. Close the Enter Bills window.

As previously noted, in addition to the VENDORS, CUSTOMERS, and EMPLOYEES sections on the Home page that represent the Centers, there is a section labeled COMPANY and a section labeled BANKING. These sections offer icons related to the Company and the Banking tasks.

Practice Exercise   12–1

On the Home page in the CUSTOMERS section, click the Create Invoices icon. The Create Invoices window appears. Close the Create Invoices window.

On the Home page in the EMPLOYEES section, click the Enter Time icon. At the drop-down menu, click *Use Weekly Timesheet*. The Weekly Timesheet window appears, as shown in Chapter 11. Close the Weekly Timesheet window.

On the Home page in the COMPANY section, click the Chart of Accounts icon. The Chart of Accounts List appears. Close the Chart of Accounts List.

On the Home page in the BANKING section, click the Reconcile icon. The Begin Reconciliation window appears, as shown in Chapter 10. Close the Begin Reconciliation window.

Customizing the Home Page

Icons are added to or removed from the Home page depending on the preferences for the company file. Recall in the New Company Setup chapters that when you create a new company file, the QuickBooks preferences, or features, are turned on (enabled) or turned off (disabled). In Chapter 6, the preferences were enabled or disabled as you answered questions in the EasyStep Interview window. In Chapter 7, you went directly to the Preferences window to enable or disable preferences. As a preference is enabled, choices appear on the drop-down menus on the main menu bar and also on the Home page. If a preference is enabled, you cannot remove the icon from the Home page.

In Chapter 12, most preferences for our sample company, Kristin Raina Interior Designs, have been enabled. If you look at the Home page for a company file in the earlier chapters, you will see fewer icons. For example, look at Figure 1–H on page 11.

Currently, Kristin Raina is not using the Estimates feature. Look at the company Home page (see Figure 12–A on page 479) and observe in the CUSTOMERS section that there is not an Estimates icon. Upon enabling the Estimates preference, the Estimates icon will appear on the Home page.

To enable a preference to customize the Home page:
1. At the main menu bar, click Edit and then click *Preferences*.
2. In the left panel of the Preferences window, click the Desktop View icon.
3. Click the Company Preferences tab. See Figure 12–C.

FIGURE 12–C
Preferences Window—
Desktop View—Company
Preferences Tab

The RELATED PREFERENCES section of this page indicates if a feature is enabled (on) or disabled (off). If a preference is enabled, you cannot remove the icon from the Home page. To remove the icon from the Home page, you would have to disable (turn off) the preference. The Estimates preference is turned off. When it is enabled, the Estimates icon appears on the Home page.

4. In the RELATED PREFERENCES section, click *Estimates*. You are moved to the Jobs & Estimates page.
5. In the DO YOU CREATE ESTIMATES? section, click the *Yes* option and then click OK. At the warning, click OK.
6. Open the Home page from the Company menu. The Estimates feature is now enabled, and the Estimates icon appears on the Home page in the CUSTOMERS section.

Along the right side of the Home page are three areas of information: ACCOUNT BALANCES, DO MORE WITH QUICKBOOKS, and BACKUP STATUS. While you cannot remove these categories from the Home page, you can minimize the detail below each heading by clicking the up arrow ⌃. When you click this arrow, only the information title is displayed. To see the information below the title, click the down arrow ⌄.

Changing the Default for the Home Page

The Preferences window is used to change the default setting for displaying the Home page when opening a new company file.

To change the default setting for the Home page:
1. At the main menu bar, click Edit and then click *Preferences*. The Preferences window appears.
2. In the left panel of the Preferences window, click the Desktop View icon.
3. Click the My Preferences tab.
4. Depending on your preference, insert or remove a check mark in the box to the left of *Show Home page when opening a company file*.
5. Click OK to save the setting.
6. Close the Home page.

Icon Bars

In addition to the Home page, there are two Icon bars that can be used to access Lists/Centers, Activities windows, and Reports.

Left Icon Bar

To view the Left Icon bar:

1. At the main menu bar, click View.

    On the View menu, when a check mark appears to the left of *Left Icon Bar*, the Left Icon bar is enabled. If there is no check mark, the Left Icon bar is disabled.

2. Click *Left Icon Bar* if there is no check mark. The Left Icon bar displays. See Figure 12–D.

FIGURE 12–D
Left Icon Bar

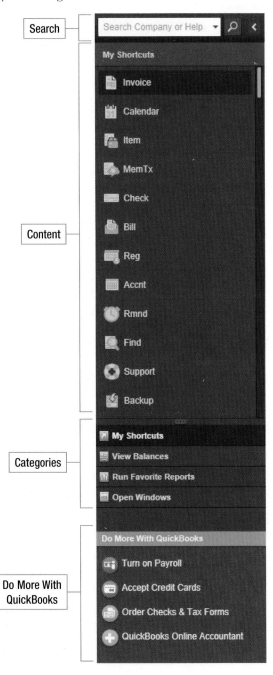

There are four sections on the Left Icon bar: Search, Content, Categories, and Do More With QuickBooks. The information in the Content section changes depending on which category is selected. By default, the My Shortcuts category is selected. The Left Icon bar can be customized to add, delete, or edit the icons in the My Shortcuts Content section.

3. In the Content section, with the My Shortcuts content displayed, scroll up and down the list.

   Notice that next to each icon in the Content section is part of the text name for the icon. Hover the mouse pointer over each icon listed in the Content section, and the entire text name for the icon is displayed. Notice the Accnt and Calendar icons. Also notice that the list of icons does not appear to be in any particular order.

To add an icon to the Left Icon bar:

1. At the main menu bar, click View and then click *Customize Icon Bar*. The Customize Icon Bar window appears. See Figure 12–E.

FIGURE 12–E
Customize Icon
Bar Window

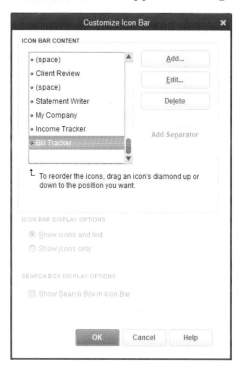

On the left in the ICON BAR CONTENT section is a list of the icons you just scrolled through on the Left Icon bar. Notice that at the bottom of the list is an option to reorder the icons. Buttons are also provided to Add, Edit, and Delete icons from the Left Icon bar.

2. At the Customize Icon Bar window, click the Add button. The Add Icon Bar Item window appears.
3. At the Add Icon Bar Item window, scroll through the list on the left until you see *Calculator*.
4. Click *Calculator*.

5. Click OK at the Add Icon Bar Item window and then click OK at the Customize Icon Bar window to save the change. The Calc icon is added to the Left Icon bar at the bottom of the list in the Content section.

6. On the Left Icon bar, scroll to the bottom of the My Shortcuts content to see the addition of the Calc icon.

You can also add icons to the Left Icon bar when a QuickBooks window is open. For many windows, when the window is open, you can click the View menu and there will be a choice to *Add Window to Icon Bar.*

To edit an icon on the Left Icon bar:

1. At the main menu bar, click View and then click *Customize Icon Bar.*

2. At the Customize Icon Bar window, in the ICON BAR CONTENT section, scroll through the list, click *Accnt* once to highlight it, and then click the Edit button.

3. At the Edit Icon Bar Item window, at the *Label* field, delete the text *Acct* and then type Chart Accts.

4. Click OK at the Edit Icon Item Bar window and then click OK at the Customize Icon Bar window. In the Content section of the Left Icon bar, the Accnt icon text changes to Chart Accts.

To remove an icon from the Left Icon bar:

1. At the main menu bar, click View and then click *Customize Icon Bar.*

2. At the Customize Icon Bar window, in the ICON BAR CONTENT section, scroll through the list and then click *Calendar* once to highlight it.

3. Click the Delete button. The Calendar icon is removed from the Left Icon bar.

4. Delete the following items from the Left Icon bar:
   Reg
   Rmnd
   Feedback
   Services
   Add Payroll
   Docs

5. Click OK to save the changes.

In the Categories section of the Left Icon bar, after My Shortcuts, other choices are View Balances, which allows you to view the balances in cash/bank accounts, accounts receivable, and liabilities accounts; Run Favorite Reports, which allows you to list customized reports that have been saved as favorites; and Open Windows, which provides a list of windows that may be open.

The last section, Do More With QuickBooks, provides additional features that QuickBooks offers online. The Account Balances and Do More With QuickBooks sections also appear on the Home page when the Left Icon bar is not displayed.

Top Icon Bar

To view the Top Icon bar:

1. At the main menu bar, click View.

On the View menu, when a check mark appears to the left of *Top Icon Bar*, the top icon bar is enabled. If there is no check mark, then the Top Icon bar is disabled.

2. Click *Top Icon bar* if there is no check mark.

The Top Icon bar is displayed under the main menu bar when it is enabled. When the Top Icon bar is chosen, the Left Icon bar is no longer displayed. Under each icon is the text name for the icon on the Top Icon bar. See Figure 12–F.

FIGURE 12–F Top Icon Bar

The Top Icon bar can be customized to add, edit, and delete icons the same way the Left Icon bar was customized. Changes made to the icons on the Left Icon bar carry over to the Top Icon bar. In addition, the Top Icon bar can be customized to add spaces and vertical lines between the icons. This is done using the Add Separator button at the Customize Icon Bar window. The background color of the Top Icon bar can be changed using the Preferences window, Desktop View icon, and My Preferences tab.

To remove the Left Icon bar or Top Icon bar:

1. At the main menu bar, click View.
2. Click *Hide Icon Bar.*

Lists/Centers ——→ ## Customize Subaccounts Presentation

As you know, accounts in the Chart of Accounts List can be denoted as subaccounts. When an account is a subaccount, the account of which it is a subaccount is referred to as the *parent account.* Accounts are marked as subaccounts to show a subtotal or net amount of the parent account on the financial statements. This procedure was illustrated with fixed assets, where the accumulated depreciation account (subaccount) was deducted from the fixed asset cost account (subaccount) to show the net book value of the fixed asset account (parent) on the *Balance Sheet.*

When there is a parent account and related subaccounts in the Chart of Accounts list, *Account Listing* report, and some activity windows, by default QuickBooks displays the parent account followed by the subaccount on one line. Sometimes when you are reviewing the *Account Listing* report or choosing an account in an Activity window, the default listing of first the parent account and then the subaccount can be cumbersome. Therefore, you can change the default settings to simplify the presentation of the parent account and subaccounts.

Chart of Accounts List Window Presentation

Open the Chart of Accounts List window by clicking Lists and then clicking *Chart of Accounts.* Scroll down to the fixed asset section. Look at the cost and accumulated depreciation accounts. These subaccounts are indented under the parent accounts. This is referred to as the *hierarchical view.* See Figure 12–G.

FIGURE 12–G
Chart of Accounts Window—Hierarchical View

parent accounts and subaccounts for fixed assets

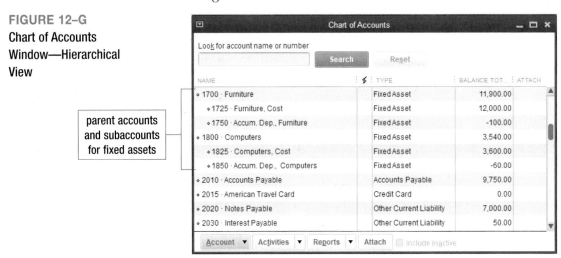

If you do not like the subaccounts indented, you can change the format to list all the accounts aligned at the left of the window. This is referred to as the *flat view.*

To change to the flat or hierarchical view:
1. At the Chart of Accounts List window, click the Account menu button. Notice that *Hierarchical View* is checked.
2. Click *Flat View.*
3. Scroll down the Chart of Accounts List window until the fixed assets are again displayed. The subaccounts are no longer indented; they are now left-aligned in the window. Notice that each line lists both the parent account and the subaccount. See Figure 12–H.

FIGURE 12–H
Chart of Accounts Window—Flat View

parent accounts and subaccounts for fixed assets

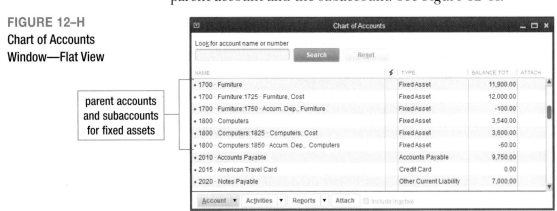

4. Click the Account menu button and then click *Hierarchical View.* If you receive the Hierarchical View message, insert a check mark in the box to the left of *Do not display this message in the future* and then click Yes. The presentation changes back to indent the subaccounts.
5. Close the window.

These changes to the view settings in the Chart of Accounts List window affect only this window.

Lists and Activities Windows Presentation

Open the *Account Listing* report by clicking Reports and then clicking *List*. See Figure 12–I.

FIGURE 12–I
Account Listing Report—
Parent Accounts Listed to
Left of Subaccounts

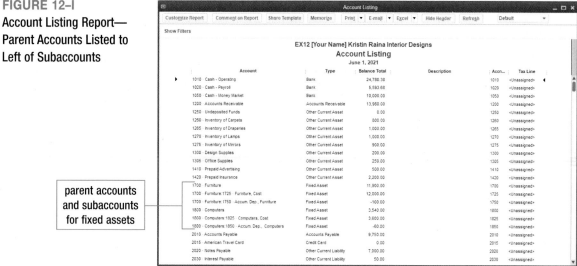

parent accounts
and subaccounts
for fixed assets

Review the subaccounts listed in the *Account Listing* report in Figure 12–I. Notice that the subaccounts 1725, 1750, 1825, and 1850—the cost and accumulated depreciation accounts—are listed next to their respective parent accounts, 1700 and 1800. Close the *Account Listing* report.

Open the Make General Journal Entries window by clicking Company and then clicking *Make General Journal Entries*. At the *ACCOUNT* field, on the first line, click the account *Furniture 1725, Cost,* and then tab to the next field. In the *ACCOUNT* field, the parent account is listed first. Because the field is small, you see the parent account and only a small part of the subaccount. See Figure 12–J.

FIGURE 12–J
Make General Journal
Entries Window—
Subaccount Selected—
Parent Account Displayed

Close the Make General Journal Entries window.

In the Activities and Reports windows, the default setting is to display the subaccounts to the right of the parent account. This default setting can be changed in the Preferences window.

To change the default setting of subaccounts:
1. At the main menu bar, click Edit and then click *Preferences.*
2. In the left panel of the Preferences window, click the Accounting icon.
3. Click the Company Preferences tab.
4. In the ACCOUNTS section, insert a check mark in the box to the left of *Show lowest subaccount only.* See Figure 12–K.

FIGURE 12–K
Preferences Window—
Accounting—Company
Preferences Tab

5. If the information is correct, click OK.

To see the effect of this default setting change, reopen the Make General Journal Entries window, and on the first line of the *ACCOUNT* field, click the account *1725 Furniture, Cost.* Notice that the parent account is no longer listed, only the subaccount. See Figure 12–L.

FIGURE 12–L
Make General Journal
Entries Window—
Subaccount Selected—
Subaccount Displayed

6. Close the Make General Journal Entries window.
7. View the *Account Listing* report. See Figure 12–M.

FIGURE 12–M
Account Listing Report—
Subaccounts Listed
without Parent Accounts

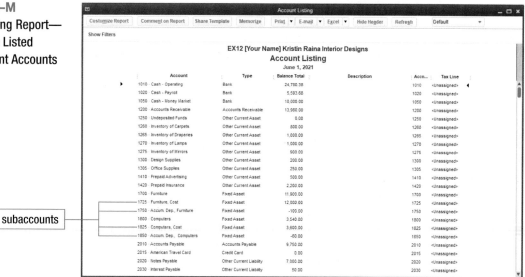

subaccounts

The subaccounts are listed on lines without the parent accounts. Compare Figure 12–M to Figure 12–I on page 487.
8. Close the *Account Listing* report.

Lists/Centers

Merge Entries

You have previously learned to add, delete, and edit vendors, customers/jobs, accounts, service items, and inventory part items in the appropriate Lists/Centers. You can also combine or merge vendors, customers, accounts, service items, and inventory part items. To do so, you simply use a name or number already in use, and QuickBooks will inquire if you wish to merge the two items.

Kristin Raina currently has a 6450 Telephone Expense account and a 6500 Utilities Expense account. She decides to combine—that is, merge—the two accounts into 6500 Utilities Expense.

Open the *Journal* report from 02/28/2021 to 02/28/2021. Scroll through the journal entries until you see the TwinCityTelCo journal entry (Trans #18), which records $275 to the account 6450 Telephone Expense. Leave the *Journal* report open.

To merge two accounts:
1. Open the Chart of Accounts List by clicking Lists and then clicking *Chart of Accounts*. Scroll down the accounts and notice the accounts 6450 Telephone Expense and 6500 Utilities Expense.
2. Select *6450 Telephone Expense*, but do not open it.
3. Click the Account menu button and then click *Edit Account*. The Edit Account window opens.
4. At the *Number* field, change the account number to 6500 and then click Save & Close. A Merge message informs you that the account is already in use and asks if you wish to merge the accounts.

5. At the Merge message, click Yes. Look at the Chart of Accounts List. Notice that there is no longer an account 6450 Telephone Expense.
6. Close the Chart of Accounts List.

Look at the *Journal* report for February 28, 2021. Notice that the transaction for TwinCityTelCo (Trans# 18) now has the transaction recorded as 6500 Utilities Expense instead of 6450 Telephone Expense. Close the *Journal* report.

The same process can be used to combine vendors, customers/jobs, service items, and inventory part items. QuickBooks will update all the information based on the merge.

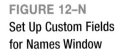

Create Custom Fields

In prior chapters, you displayed and printed reports, including filtering reports using fields of information already included in the report. QuickBooks allows you to create your own custom fields of information for later display in a report. Custom fields for customers, vendors, employees, and items can be created in the appropriate List or Center.

Most of Kristin Raina's customers are located in either Minneapolis or St. Paul. She would like to sort her customers by region so when she and her assistant visit the customers, they can each go to all the customers in one city at a time. To do this, Kristin Raina will create a custom field named *Region* and then edit each customer's account to identify the region for that customer. Finally, Kristin Raina will filter the Customer Center to list only the customers in a specified region.

To create a custom field:
1. Open the Customer Center by clicking Customers and then clicking *Customer Center*. Choose the first customer, Alomar Company, by double-clicking the customer name. The Edit Customer window appears. Notice that the city in the ADDRESS DETAILS section for this customer is Minneapolis.
2. Click the Additional Info tab.
3. On the Additional Info tab, in the CUSTOM FIELDS section, click the Define Fields button. The Set up Custom Fields for Names window appears.
4. On the first line in the *Label* column, type Region.
5. At the *Use for:* field, insert a check mark in the *Cust* (customer) column. See Figure 12–N.

FIGURE 12–N
Set Up Custom Fields for Names Window

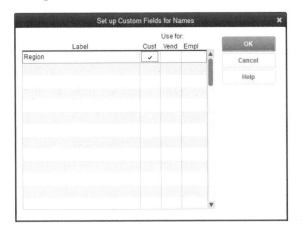

6. If the information is correct, click OK.
7. At the Information message, insert a check mark in the box to the left of *Do not display this message in the future* and then click OK. The *REGION* text box is now displayed in the CUSTOM FIELDS section on the Additional Info tab.
8. In the *REGION* text box, type Minneapolis. See Figure 12–O.

FIGURE 12–O

Edit Customer Window—
Additional Info Tab—
REGION Text Box Added
and Completed

9. If the information is correct, click OK to save it.
10. Edit each customer and type in each customer's city in the *REGION* text box on the Additional Info tab.
11. Close the Customer Center.

The Customer Center can now be customized to display only the customers in a specified region.

HINT

The *REGION* text box can also be viewed in the *Customer Contact List* report. Open the report and click the Customize Report button. In the Modify Report dialog box, click the Filters tab. In the *FILTER* field, scroll through the list and choose *Region*. In the *REGION* text box, type **Minneapolis** and then click OK. The *Customer Contact List* report is updated to display only the six customers that have Minneapolis as their region.

To display customers in the Customer Center in the Minneapolis region:
1. Open the Customer Center, if necessary.
2. On the Customer & Jobs tab, click the Search icon 🔍. The Custom Filter dialog box appears.
3. In the Customer Filter dialog box, click or type the following information:

Search:	Active Customers
in:	Custom fields
For:	Minneapolis

4. Click Go. The Customer Center is updated to display only the six customers that have Minneapolis as their region on the Additional Info tab. See Figure 12–P.

FIGURE 12–P Customer Center Filtered for Minneapolis Region

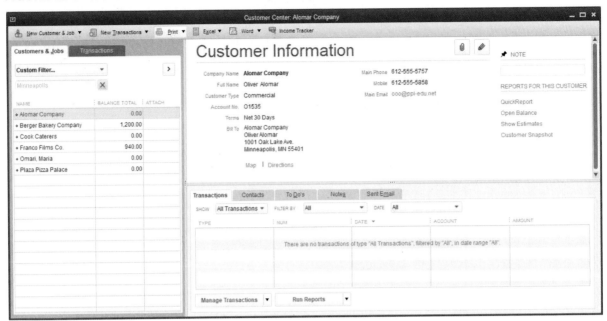

5. At the field where *Minneapolis* is displayed, click the X. The Customer Center returns to the list of all Active Customers.
6. Close the Customer Center.

Practice Exercise   12–2

In the Customer Center, display the customers in the St. Paul region.

QuickCheck: Five customers and jobs should be displayed in the Customer Center.

Similar procedures can be used to create custom fields for vendors, employees, and items. If you want to include the *REGION* field in the Vendor Center, open any vendor in the Edit Vendor window. On the Additional Info tab, click the Define Fields button. The Set up Custom Fields for Names window will appear with the *Region* label listed. Insert a check mark in the *Vend* (vendor) column and then click OK, which will activate the *REGION* text box on the Additional Info tab for each vendor.

Activities →
Customize Activities Windows and Printed Documents

In all chapters, the Activities windows displayed were based on default settings. QuickBooks allows you to change the default settings of a window as well as those of a document that can be printed as a result of data entered in a window.

Recall in Chapter 11 that when you used the Time-Tracking feature, the data you entered in the Weekly Timesheet window was carried forward to the Create Invoices window. The Create Invoices window displayed by default did not show all the relevant information carried over to that window. By changing the default settings in the Create Invoices window, more of the important information can be displayed.

To view the default settings and preview an invoice:
1. At the main menu bar, click Customers and then click *Create Invoices.*
2. Click the Find Previous button to display Invoice No. 1016. Click the Formatting tab. See Figure 12–Q.

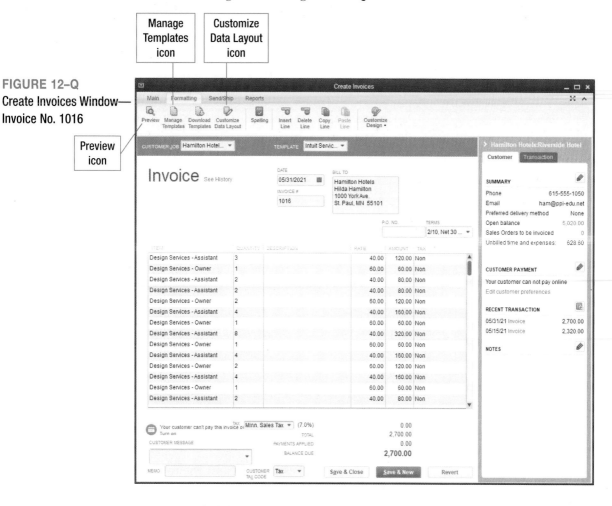

FIGURE 12–Q
Create Invoices Window—
Invoice No. 1016

In QuickBooks you can preview and print invoices that can be sent to customers.
3. On the Formatting tab, click the Preview icon. The invoice should look like Figure 12–R.

FIGURE 12–R
Invoice No. 1016

EX12 [Your Name] Kristin Raina Interior Designs

Invoice

25 NE Johnson Street
Minneapolis, MN 53402

Date	Invoice #
5/31/2021	1016

Bill To

Hamilton Hotels
Hilda Hamilton
1000 York Ave.
St. Paul, MN 55101

P.O. No.	Terms	Project
	2/10, Net 30 Days	Riverside Hotel

Quantity	Description	Rate	Amount
3		40.00	120.00
1		60.00	60.00
2		40.00	80.00
2		40.00	80.00
2		60.00	120.00
4		40.00	160.00
1		60.00	60.00
8		40.00	320.00
1		60.00	60.00
4		40.00	160.00
2		60.00	120.00
4		40.00	160.00
1		60.00	60.00
2		40.00	80.00
3		60.00	180.00
2		40.00	80.00
4		60.00	240.00
2		40.00	80.00
1		60.00	60.00
6		40.00	240.00
3		60.00	180.00
	Sales Tax	7.00%	0.00

Total $2,700.00

In both the Create Invoices window and the invoice itself, all the detail information is not displayed. In addition, the printed invoice does not indicate the items for which you are billing. This is not an invoice you would want to send to a customer. You can customize both the Create Invoices window and the invoice so that all the detailed information is adequately displayed. QuickBooks provides several pre-established invoices. Two invoices previously used are the Intuit Service Invoice and Intuit Product Invoice. These invoices are based on templates. You can create your own invoice by customizing a template. To do this, you will first make a copy of the existing template and then customize the copy. This is done using the Manage Templates icon on the Formatting tab at the Create Invoices window.

4. Close the Print Preview window.

To customize the Create Invoices window and a printed invoice:

1. With the Create Invoices window open and Invoice No. 1016 displayed, on the Formatting tab, click the Manage Templates icon. You are moved to the Manage Templates window.

2. In the SELECT TEMPLATE section, select *Intuit Service Invoice* and then click the Copy button. A copy of the Intuit Service Invoice is made. It is labeled *Copy of: Intuit Service Invoice* in both the SELECT TEMPLATE section and the PREVIEW section—*Template Name* field. See Figure 12–S.

FIGURE 12-S
Manage Templates Window—Template Name—Copy of: Intuit Service Invoice

You will create your own invoice using the Copy of: Intuit Service Invoice as a guideline. But you will first assign a new name to the invoice.

3. In the PREVIEW section, at the *Template Name* field, delete the text *Copy of: Intuit Service Invoice*, type Job Invoice, and then press the Tab key. Notice that the invoice name is also changed in the SELECT TEMPLATE section. See Figure 12–T.

FIGURE 12–T

Manage Templates
Window—Template
Name—Job Invoice

4. If the information is correct, click OK. You are moved to the Basic Customization window.
5. Click the Additional Customization button. You are moved to the Additional Customization window.
6. At the Additional Customization window, click the Columns tab.

    The Columns tab lists the pre-established settings for the service invoice. Next to each pre-established setting, you will see four columns of boxes. The *Screen* column applies to the settings that appear in the Create Invoices window. The *Print* column applies to the settings that appear on the printed invoice. Whether a specific setting will appear on the screen in the Create Invoices window, on the printed invoice, or both is indicated by which box or boxes contain check marks. The *Order* column applies to the order of display on both the screen and the printed invoice. The *Title* column is the title for the column to be displayed on both the screen and the printed invoice.

    Since nothing was listed in the *Description* field, we will remove this column from both the Create Invoice window and the printed invoice; this will allow more room for the columns in which data is displayed. In addition, we will indicate that the *Item* field should appear on the printed invoice.

7. At the *Description* field, in the *Screen* column, remove the check mark. At the Layout Designer message, insert a check mark to the left of *Do not display this message in the future* and then click OK.
8. At the *Description* field, in the *Print* column, remove the check mark.
9. Insert a check mark in the *Print* column box to the right of the *Item* field. At the Overlapping Fields message, click Continue.
10. At the *Service Date* field, insert a check mark in both the *Screen* and the *Print* columns. At the Overlapping Fields message, click Continue. QuickBooks automatically assigns an order number of *4*. See Figure 12–U.

FIGURE 12–U
Additional Customization
Window—Columns Tab

11. If the information is correct, click OK. You are returned to the Basic Customization window.

12. Click OK. You are returned to the Create Invoices window. The *TEMPLATE* field displays the new format created: *Job Invoice*. The *Description* column has been removed, and the *Serviced* column has been added. See Figure 12–V and compare it with Figure 12–Q on page 493.

FIGURE 12–V
Create Invoices
Window—Job Invoice—
Serviced Dates Added

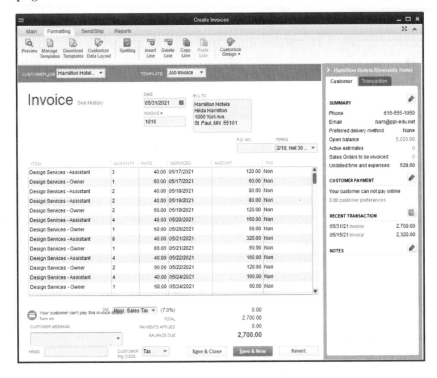

Upon reviewing the Create Invoices window, you realize that the order of data fields should be different. You will further customize the Job Invoice you just created.

HINT

On the Formatting tab, you could also click the Manage Templates icon. In the Manage Template dialog box, select *Job Invoice* and then click OK. At the Basic Customization window, click the Additional Customization button.

FIGURE 12–W

Additional Customization Window—Columns Tab—Order

HINT

If the revised order does not appear in the PREVIEW section, at the Additional Customization window for the Job Invoice, click the Columns tab, recheck the *Description* field in the *Screen* and *Print* columns, uncheck them, and then click OK. The order will be updated.

13. On the Formatting tab in the Create Invoices window, click the Customize Data Layout icon. You are moved to the Additional Customization window for the Job Invoice.
14. At the Additional Customization window, click the Columns tab.
15. Change the order of the data fields as follows:

| *Service Date:* | 2 | *Quantity:* | 3 |
| *Item:* | 1 | *Rate:* | 4 |

The *Amount* field remains at 5. See Figure 12–W.

16. If the information is correct, click OK. You are returned to the Create Invoices window, with the updated Job Invoice data displayed. See Figure 12–X.

FIGURE 12–X

Create Invoices Window—Job Invoice— Updated Order

17. If the information is correct, on the Formatting tab, click the Preview icon. If the Recording Transaction message appears, click Yes to save the Job Invoice format for this invoice.
18. The invoice is displayed using the custom-designed Job Invoice format. See Figure 12–Y and compare it with Figure 12–R on page 494.

FIGURE 12-Y
Invoice No. 1016—
Job Invoice Format

Item	Serviced	Quantity	Rate	Amount
Design Services - Assistant	5/17/2021	3	40.00	120.00
Design Services - Owner	5/17/2021	1	60.00	60.00
Design Services - Assistant	5/18/2021	2	40.00	80.00
Design Services - Assistant	5/19/2021	2	40.00	80.00
Design Services - Owner	5/19/2021	2	60.00	120.00
Design Services - Assistant	5/20/2021	4	40.00	160.00
Design Services - Owner	5/20/2021	1	60.00	60.00
Design Services - Assistant	5/21/2021	8	40.00	320.00
Design Services - Owner	5/21/2021	1	60.00	60.00
Design Services - Assistant	5/22/2021	4	40.00	160.00
Design Services - Owner	5/22/2021	2	60.00	120.00
Design Services - Assistant	5/24/2021	4	40.00	160.00
Design Services - Owner	5/24/2021	1	60.00	60.00
Design Services - Assistant	5/25/2021	2	40.00	80.00
Design Services - Owner	5/25/2021	3	60.00	180.00
Design Services - Assistant	5/26/2021	2	40.00	80.00
Design Services - Owner	5/26/2021	4	60.00	240.00
Design Services - Assistant	5/27/2021	2	40.00	80.00
Design Services - Owner	5/27/2021	1	60.00	60.00
Design Services - Assistant	5/28/2021	6	40.00	240.00
Design Services - Owner	5/28/2021	3	60.00	180.00
			7.00%	0.00

HINT

If the revised order does not appear on the printed invoice, go back to the Additional Customization window for the Job Invoice, click the Columns tab, recheck the *Description* field in the *Screen* and *Print* columns, uncheck them, and then click OK.

19. Close the Preview and Create Invoices windows. If the Recording Transaction message appears, click Yes.

After creating this new format for an invoice, you could review the other invoices in the Create Invoices window that used Time-Tracking data and apply the new Job Invoice format to those invoices.

Practice Exercise   12–3

In the Create Invoices window, change Invoice #1015 and Invoice #1014 to the Job Invoice format by selecting *Job Invoice* at the *TEMPLATE* field. Save the changes.

QuickBooks Letters

QuickBooks provides preformatted letters that may be used in certain business circumstances. You can use these letters as they are or customize them based on your personal preferences. You must have Microsoft Word installed on your computer to use the QuickBooks Letters feature.

Kristin Raina wants to send a letter to Berger Bakery Company regarding the check that was returned as non-sufficient funds (NSF) with the April 30 bank statement. She will use QuickBooks Letters to do this.

To prepare a business letter using QuickBooks Letters:

1. At the main menu bar, click Company and then click *Prepare Letters with Envelopes.*
2. At the Prepare Letters with Envelopes submenu, click *Customer Letters.* If the Find Letter Templates message appears, click the Copy button. The Letters and Envelopes window appears.
3. At the Review and Edit Recipients page, click the Unmark All button to remove all the check marks from the customer names.
4. Click *Berger Bakery Company* to select that customer and then click Next.
5. At the Choose a Letter Template page, click *Bounced check* and then click Next.
6. At the Enter a Name and Title page, enter the following data:

Name:	*[Your Name]*
Title:	Assistant Accountant

7. Click Next. Microsoft Word opens, and the bounced check letter is displayed with your company name, the current date, and the customer name included. See Figure 12–Z.

HINT

To refresh your memory, open the Create Invoices window and click the Previous arrow until you come to the transaction of 04/30/2021, Invoice # NSF1. This transaction was recorded when the bank reconciliation was prepared in Chapter 10. Close the Create Invoices window.

HINT

If a warning that the letters cannot be found appears, go to the default path: C:\Users\Public\Public Documents\Intuit\QuickBooks\Company Files and locate the folder Letters_Templates. Copy the Letters_Templates folder and Paste it in the folder where the Exercise (EX) files are stored.

FIGURE 12–Z
QuickBooks Bounced Check Letter Exported to Microsoft Word

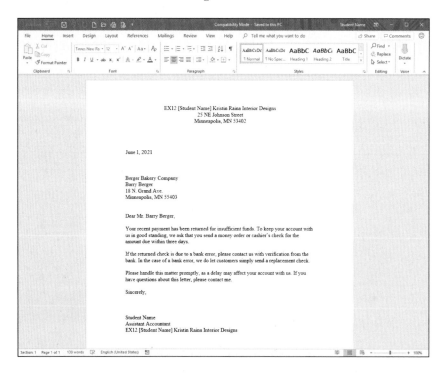

8. Close Microsoft Word. Do not save the letter.
9. Close the Letters and Envelopes window.

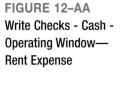

Memorized Transactions

Many routine business activities are repeated, often at daily, weekly, and monthly intervals. QuickBooks allows you to memorize repetitive transactions. Once a transaction has been memorized, you can recall the transaction at the appropriate time to record it, or you can have QuickBooks automatically record the transaction on certain dates.

An example of a transaction that could be memorized is the monthly rent Kristin Raina Interior Designs pays for its space. On June 1, 2021, Kristin Raina Interior Designs is ready to pay the monthly rent of $800 to Nordic Realty. Because this is a routine bill, Kristin Raina decides to have you set it up as a memorized transaction. To memorize a transaction, you first enter the data for the transaction as a regular transaction, and then before saving it, you set it up as a memorized transaction.

To set up and memorize a transaction:

1. At the main menu bar, click Banking and then click *Write Checks*.
2. Enter the following data for the rent expense, as you have previously learned:

Bank Account:	1010 - Cash - Operating
No.:	14
Date:	06/01/2021
Pay to the Order of:	Nordic Realty
Amount:	800
Memo:	(none)
Account:	6400 Rent Expense

See Figure 12–AA.

FIGURE 12–AA
Write Checks - Cash - Operating Window— Rent Expense

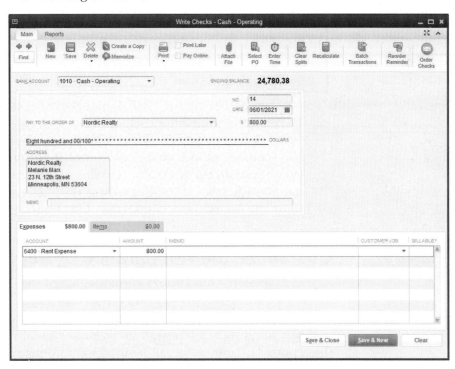

3. If the information is correct, click Edit at the main menu bar and then click *Memorize Check*. The Memorize Transaction dialog box appears.
4. At the *How Often* field, click *Monthly*.
5. At the *Next Date* field, choose *07/01/2021*. See Figure 12–BB.

FIGURE 12–BB
Memorize Transaction
Dialog Box

6. If the information is correct, click OK. The transaction is memorized.
7. At the Write Checks window, click the Save & Close button.

Assume that it is now July 1, 2021, and time to pay the rent for July. You can recall the memorized transaction.

To recall a memorized transaction:
1. At the main menu bar, click Lists and then click *Memorized Transaction List*. The Memorized Transaction List window appears. See Figure 12–CC.

FIGURE 12–CC
Memorized Transaction
List Window

2. To recall the transaction, select *Nordic Realty* and then click the Enter Transaction button. The Write Checks window appears, with the correct date and the next check number automatically entered.
3. Do not record the transaction at this time. Close the Write Checks window. Click No at the Recording Transaction message.
4. Close the Memorized Transaction List window.

Reports

Customize the Appearance of Reports

As you have seen, QuickBooks contains a large variety of pre-established management reports, accounting reports, and financial statements, many of which you have displayed and printed throughout this text.

When you display a report, there is a row of buttons along the top of the report. These buttons can be used to customize the presentation of a report, make comments (notes) on a report, share a customized report template, memorize settings in a report, email a report, export a report into an Excel spreadsheet, hide the header of a report, and collapse or expand the numbers on a report. In prior chapters, you displayed and printed reports using the pre-established settings—except in Chapter 4, in which you modified the report using the Filters and Header/Footer tabs of the Customize Report button. In this chapter, you will use most of the remaining buttons along the top of the report.

Customize Report Button

The Customize Report button is used to adjust the appearance of the report. The Customize Report button moves you to the Modify Report dialog box, which has four tabs: Display, Filters, Header/Footer, and Fonts & Numbers. A report can be modified to add or delete fields of information displayed in a report (Display tab); to filter (select) which categories of information should be included in a report (Filters tab); to indicate which information should be displayed in the headers or footers (Header/Footer tab); and to indicate the fonts and formats of the numbers in the reports (Fonts & Numbers tab).

Modify Report—Display Tab

Open the *Account Listing* report by clicking Reports and then clicking *List*. See Figure 12–DD.

FIGURE 12–DD

Account Listing Report

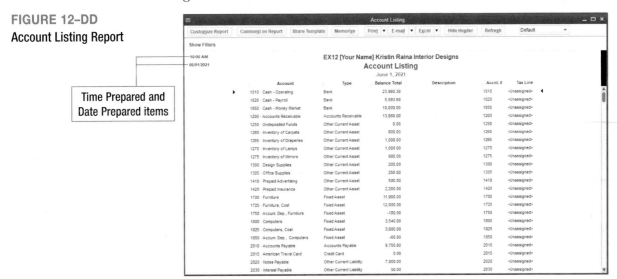

Time Prepared and Date Prepared items

To modify a report using the Display tab:

1. In the *Account Listing* report, click the Customize Report button at the top of the report. The Modify Report: Account Listing dialog box appears.

    In the Modify Report dialog box, the default tab is Display. The Display tab is used to indicate the fields of information that can be displayed in the columns in a report. Any column title that is checked is displayed.

    When adding new accounts to the Chart of Accounts List, you did not use the *Description* field; therefore, this field of information is blank. In the *Tax Line* field, all the accounts are marked unassigned. Since you do not need the information in these two fields, you can remove them from this report.

2. Remove the check marks from the field titles *Description* and *Tax Line.*
See Figure 12–EE.

FIGURE 12–EE
Modify Report: Account
Listing—Display Tab

3. If the information is correct, click OK. The report is revised to exclude those two fields of information.
4. Widen the *Account* and *Accnt. #* columns to display the entire account names and the *Accnt. #* title. See Figure 12–FF.

FIGURE 12–FF
Account Listing—
Customized

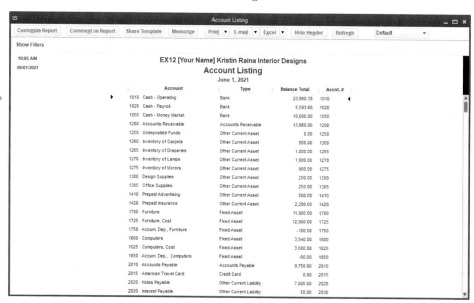

HINT

To change the width of the column, click and drag the vertical dotted bar next to the column title.

Modify Report—Header/Footer Tab

The Header/Footer tab is used to establish the presentation of the headers (including titles) and footers (including page numbers) to be displayed in a report. Two items in the heading of a report you can format are the Date Prepared and Time Prepared items. You may have noticed that when reports are displayed, by default, the date and time the report is prepared are always displayed in the upper left corner. The *Date Prepared* and *Time Prepared* fields are where you tell the software to display the current date and time on each report. This field is activated by default, which tells the software to display the current date and time as maintained by your computer.

If you print reports often, it is useful to have the date and time you print a report listed to avoid confusion among the many printouts. But there may be times you do not want the date or time displayed on a report. None of the printouts reproduced in this text included a current date or time because the *Date Prepared* and *Time Prepared* fields defaults were disabled.

To disable or change the format of the Date Prepared and Time Prepared items and change a title in a report:

1. In the *Account Listing* report, click the Customize Report button at the top of the report. The Modify Report: Account Listing dialog box appears.
2. In the Modify Report: Account Listing dialog box, click the Header/ Footer tab. The Header/Footer tab appears.
3. Click the Date Prepared drop-down list. You can use this drop-down list to change the format of the date.
4. To disable the Date Prepared item, remove the check mark from the box to the left of the *Date Prepared* field.
5. To disable the Time Prepared item, remove the check mark from the box to the left of the *Time Prepared* field.

   In the Header/Footer dialog box, you can also change or remove the company name, report title, subtitle, and footer information of the report.
6. At the *Subtitle* field, delete the date provided and then type June 30, 2021. See Figure 12–GG.

FIGURE 12–GG
Modify Report: Account Listing—Header/Footer Tab

7. If the information is correct, click OK. You are returned to the *Account Listing* report. The Date Prepared and Time Prepared items have been removed, and the subtitle date has been changed. See Figure 12–HH.

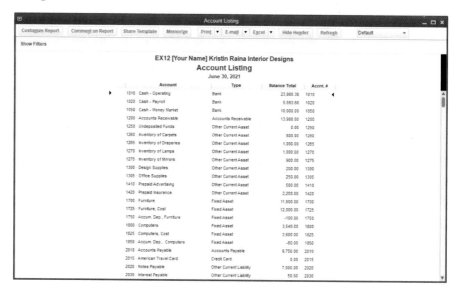

Keep the *Account Listing* report open for the next activity.

Memorize Button

The changes you just made to the report remain in place as long as the report is displayed. However, as soon as you close the report, those changes are lost. When you reopen the report, the original default settings are again displayed. Instead of having to change the settings each time you open the report, you can save the changes to a report by using the Memorize button.

To memorize the settings for a report:
1. With the *Account Listing* report open, the *Description* and *Tax Line* fields removed, and the heading format changed, click the Memorize button at the top of the report. The Memorize Report dialog box appears.
2. In the Memorize Report dialog box, at the *Name* field, type Account Listing - Custom. See Figure 12–II.

3. If the information is correct, click OK.
4. Close the *Account Listing* report.

Reopen the *Account Listing* report by clicking Reports and then *List*. Notice that all the original default settings are used to display the report.

Close the *Account Listing* report. If you wish to see the memorized report, you must open it.

To open a memorized report:
1. At the main menu bar, click Reports and then click *Memorized Reports*.
2. At the Memorized Reports submenu, click *Memorized Report List*. The Memorized Report List appears. See Figure 12–JJ.

FIGURE 12–JJ
Memorized Report List

The first report on the list is the *Account Listing - Custom* memorized report. The other reports listed are the same reports that can be accessed from the Reports menu, but QuickBooks has organized them into groups for easy retrieval.

HINT

The memorized report can also be accessed at the Memorized Reports submenu.

3. Double-click the report *Account Listing - Custom*.

The *Account Listing* report appears with all the changes intact. If you make any changes to a memorized report, they will be stored only while the report is displayed. If you wish to memorize the new changes, you must click Memorize again. You will then be given a choice to replace the memorized report with the new changes or to create an additional memorized report.
4. Close the report and then close the Memorized Report List.

Collapse/Expand Button

Open the *Balance Sheet Standard* report for June 30, 2021, by clicking Reports and then clicking *Company & Financial*. Notice that the Date Prepared and Time Prepared items appear in the report window. Remove the Date Prepared and Time Prepared items using the Customize Report button (Header/Footer tab) at the top of the report. Notice how the fixed assets section appears on the screen. See Figure 12–KK.

FIGURE 12–KK

Balance Sheet Standard
Report—Fixed Assets
Section Expanded

Fixed Assets	
1700 · Furniture	
1725 · Furniture, Cost	12,000.00
1750 · Accum. Dep., Furniture	-100.00
Total 1700 · Furniture	11,900.00
1800 · Computers	
1825 · Computers, Cost	3,600.00
1850 · Accum. Dep., Computers	-60.00
Total 1800 · Computers	3,540.00
Total Fixed Assets	15,440.00

Recall that in the fixed assets section, the fixed asset account is the parent account, and the related cost and accumulated depreciation accounts are subaccounts of the fixed asset. On the *Balance Sheet Standard* report displayed on the screen, in the fixed asset section, the parent account is listed as a heading, the two subaccounts are listed under the parent account, and the parent account is listed again—this time with a subtotal of the two subaccounts. This format is referred to as *expanded.* As an alternative, you can collapse the accounts and numbers, so that only the net amount for each fixed asset account is displayed.

To collapse and expand the numbers in a report:

1. In the *Balance Sheet Standard* report, click the Collapse button at the top of the report. Notice how the fixed assets are now displayed. Only the net amount for each fixed asset is displayed. See Figure 12–LL.

FIGURE 12–LL

Balance Sheet Standard Report— Fixed Assets Collapsed

▼ Fixed Assets	
▶ 1700 · Furniture	11,900.00
▶ 1800 · Computers	3,540.00
Total Fixed Assets	15,440.00

Notice that the Collapse button at the top of the report changed into the Expand button.

2. To expand the numbers, click the Expand button at the top of the report. The report returns to the original presentation. Do not close the report.

Share Template Button

In addition to the Reports menu, QuickBooks includes a Report Center. The Report Center provides the same choices of reports that appear on the Reports menu. The Report Center also allows you to memorize reports, save favorites, and view recent reports. An added feature to the Report Center is a forum where customized report templates can be shared among QuickBooks users. The customized report templates are provided by both Intuit and QuickBooks users. An internet connection is required to use the Report Center.

To access the Report Center, click Reports and then click *Report Center.* The customized report templates are accessed on the Contributed tab in the Report Center. By default, the Intuit report templates are displayed. To access report templates prepared by other QuickBooks users, in the Report Center, on the Contributed tab, at the *SORT BY* field, choose *Community created* at the drop-down menu. When you customize any of these reports, the Share Template button in the report is activated, which then allows you to share your report with the community. Only the format of a report is shared, not the financial details. Close the Reports Center.

Excel Button

QuickBooks allows you to export a report to a Microsoft Excel worksheet, where you can incorporate the report into another Excel file you may have or create a new worksheet. You can then use Excel to further customize the report. Excel must be installed on your computer to export the report.

To export a report to a new Microsoft Excel worksheet:

1. With the *Balance Sheet Standard* report (expanded) for June 30, 2021, displayed, click the Excel button at the top of the report. A drop-down list appears that offers two choices: *Create New Worksheet* and *Update Existing Worksheet.*

2. Choose *Create New Worksheet.* The Send Report to Excel dialog box appears. See Figure 12–MM.

FIGURE 12–MM
Send Report to Excel
Dialog Box

HINT

If you previously made an incorrect choice at the drop-down list, you can change to the correct choice in this dialog box.

In this dialog box, you also have these choices: *Create new worksheet in new workbook* or *in existing workbook, Update an existing worksheet, Replace an existing worksheet,* and *Create a comma separated values (.csv) file.*

3. Click the Advanced button. The Advanced Excel Options dialog box appears. See Figure 12–NN.

FIGURE 12–NN
Advanced Excel Options
Dialog Box

The Advanced Excel Options dialog box allows you to carry over formatting from QuickBooks to Excel and to turn on Excel options and printing options. You can make these choices in QuickBooks, or you can make them directly in the Excel worksheet after the report is exported into Excel.

4. In the Advanced Excel Options dialog box, click Cancel.

5. In the Send Report to Excel dialog box, with *Create new worksheet* and *in new workbook* selected, click Export. Excel opens and a worksheet is prepared, with the *Balance Sheet Standard* report exported into the worksheet. See Figure 12–OO.

FIGURE 12–OO
Balance Sheet
Standard Report
Exported to Microsoft
Excel

If you are familiar with Excel, you may revise the report according to your preferences.

6. Close Excel by clicking the X.

7. At the Want to save your changes message, click Save. You are moved to the Save As dialog box.

8. In the Save As dialog box, choose the folder where you save your files, and in the *File name* text box, type EX12 *(Your Name)* QB-BS. Click Save. If you receive a Microsoft Excel message, click Yes. The Excel worksheet is saved, and Excel closes.

Assume that at a later date, after more activities have been recorded in QuickBooks, you wish to record the updated information in the Excel worksheet you just created and saved.

To export a report to an existing Microsoft Excel worksheet:

1. Open the *Balance Sheet Standard* report, if necessary, and use the date *July 31, 2021.*

2. Click the Excel button.
3. At the drop-down list, click *Update Existing Worksheet.*
4. In the Send Report to Excel dialog box, click the Browse button. You are moved to the Open Microsoft Excel File dialog box.
5. Select the folder where you save your files, select the file **EX12 *(Your Name)* QB-BS**, and then click Open. You are returned to the Send Report to Excel dialog box, with the path filled in the first box in the *Select workbook* field.
6. In the second box in the *Select workbook* field, click the drop-down list, choose *Sheet1*, and then click Export.

   An Export Report Alert message appears, inquiring if you want the existing worksheet updated with new data. If you want to update the existing worksheet, click Yes. If you prefer to retain the existing worksheet intact, click No, which will end the process. Start over again using the previous steps to export a report to a new worksheet.
7. At the Export Report Alert message, click Yes. Excel opens the existing worksheet updated with the new data. The only change in this worksheet is that the date has been updated to *July 31, 2021.* Any previous changes in the formatting of the Excel worksheet will have been retained.
8. Close Excel. Do not save the changes.
9. Close the *Balance Sheet Standard* report.

Process Multiple Reports

In each chapter, as various reports were displayed, each report was opened one at a time. QuickBooks also allows you to open several reports at the same time. For example, Kristin Raina wishes to display the *Trial Balance, Profit & Loss Standard,* and *Balance Sheet Standard* reports for the period January 1, 2021, through June 30, 2021.

To display multiple reports:
1. At the main menu bar, click Reports and then click *Process Multiple Reports.* The Process Multiple Reports window is displayed.
2. At the Select Memorized Reports From drop-down list, click *<All Reports>*. See Figure 12–PP.

FIGURE 12–PP
Process Multiple Reports Window

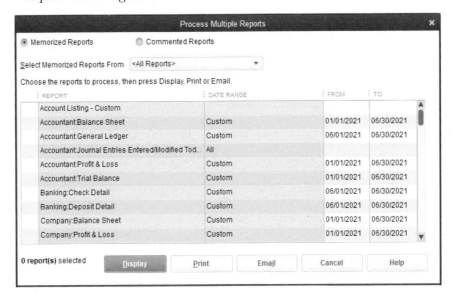

All the reports are listed. In the *From* and *To* fields, the current month or the current fiscal year-to-date is displayed. QuickBooks includes pre-established groups with which reports are classified. Custom groups can be created and reports can be memorized in a custom group. The name to the left of each report lists the pre-established group where QuickBooks locates the report. These classifications do not affect the display of the report.

3. Insert a check mark to the left of *Accountant: Balance Sheet*, *Accountant: Profit & Loss*, and *Accountant: Trial Balance*.

4. At the *From* and *To* fields for each report, choose *01/01/2021* and *06/30/2021* and then click Display. All three reports are displayed for the period of time indicated.

5. Close all the reports.

Reports → ## Set Default Settings in Reports

You saw that each time you display a report, you can modify the display by using the Customize Report (Display, Filters, Header/Footer tabs) and Collapse/Expand buttons. You also saw that these changes are only temporary. To save the changes, you can memorize the report. Or you can change the default settings for *all* reports using the Preferences window. For example, you can change the Date Prepared and Time Prepared items default settings.

To turn off or change the Date Prepared and Time Prepared items default settings:

1. At the main menu bar, click Edit and then click *Preferences*.
2. In the left panel of the Preferences window, click the Reports & Graphs icon.
3. Click the Company Preferences tab. See Figure 12–QQ.

FIGURE 12–QQ
Preferences Window—
Reports & Graphs—
Company Preferences
Tab

4. Click the Format button. The Report Format Preferences dialog box appears; it has two tabs: Header/Footer and Fonts & Numbers.

5. Click the Header/Footer tab, if necessary. You can change the default formats or disable any field of information for all the reports on this tab.
6. To disable the Date Prepared item, remove the check mark from the box to the left of the *Date Prepared* field.
7. To disable the Time Prepared item, remove the check mark from the box to the left of the *Time Prepared* field. See Figure 12–RR.

FIGURE 12–RR
Report Format
Preferences Dialog
Box—Header/Footer
Tab—Date Prepared and
Time Prepared Items
Disabled

8. Click OK in the Report Format Preferences dialog box. You are returned to the Preferences window.
9. Click OK.

The steps you used to disable the Date Prepared and Time Prepared items using the Preferences window are the same steps you took when you disabled the Date Prepared and Time Prepared items while a report was opened. By changing the settings of the Date Prepared and Time Prepared items in the Preferences window, you changed the default settings. Now, each time you open any report, the date and time prepared are no longer displayed. However, if you wish to see the date or time prepared in an individual report, you can activate it for that specific report.

Reports

Graphs

QuickBooks allows you to display financial information in graph format. Graph presentations are available for the *Income and Expense, Net Worth, Accounts Receivable, Sales, Accounts Payable,* and *Budget vs. Actual* reports.

To view the Income and Expense graph:
1. At the main menu bar, click Reports and then click *Company & Financial.*
2. At the Company & Financial submenu, click *Income & Expense Graph.*
3. Click the Dates button.
4. In the Change Graph Dates dialog box, choose from *01/01/2021* to *05/31/2021* and then click OK. The Income and Expense graphs for that period of time appear. See Figure 12–SS.

FIGURE 12–SS
Income and Expense
Graph Window

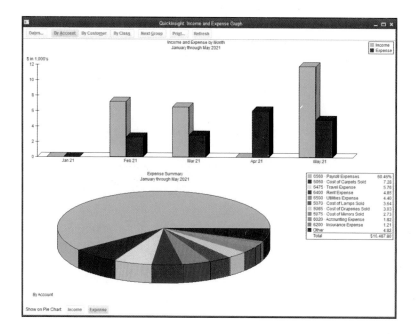

The bar graph displays a comparative analysis of income and expenses. The pie chart, by default, displays the Expense Summary.

5. To display the Income Summary as a pie chart, click the Income button at the bottom of the window. The pie chart changes to display the Income Summary.

6. Close the graph.

All graphs are displayed in the same manner. The graphs that are available can be accessed using the Reports menu at the main menu bar or the Reports button in the List windows.

Fiscal Year

Businesses must prepare their financial statements, including the *Profit & Loss* report and the *Balance Sheet* report, at least once per year. The year can be the calendar year or any other 12-month period. This 12-month financial reporting year for the company is called the **fiscal year**.

fiscal year the 12-month financial reporting year of the company, which can be the calendar year or any other 12-month period

In QuickBooks, the start of the fiscal year is displayed in the Company Information—Report Information window.

To view the fiscal year for Kristin Raina Interior Designs:

1. At the main menu bar, click Company and then click *My Company*.
2. At the My Company window, click the Edit icon. The Company Information window appears.
3. At the Company Information window, click *Report Information*.
    The fiscal year for this company begins in January, which implies that the fiscal year for Kristin Raina is January 1 through December 31.
4. Close the Company Information and My Company windows.

Fiscal Year Closing

In a manual accounting system and in most other computerized accounting software packages, the books are closed on fiscal year-end. When the books are closed, each of the temporary accounts—usually revenues, expenses, and some equity accounts—is brought to a zero balance, and the net income for the year is transferred into a capital or retained earnings equity account for the next year. After the books are closed, preclosing balances in the temporary accounts are no longer accessible.

QuickBooks does not require you to close the books on fiscal year-end. However, QuickBooks automatically creates an Owner's Equity system default account, and at the start of a new fiscal year, automatically transfers the net income for the previous fiscal year into it. In addition, at the beginning of the new fiscal year, all the revenue and expense accounts will begin with zero balances so the net income for the new fiscal year can be accumulated.

When the new company file was created for Kristin Raina Interior Designs, the fiscal year was designated as beginning on January 1, which is displayed in the Company Information—Report Information window, as previously illustrated. Recall that in New Company Setup (Chapters 6 and 7), the Owner's Equity system default account created by QuickBooks was renamed *Accumulated Earnings*. When you move to the new fiscal year, January 1, 2022, QuickBooks transfers the net income for 2021 into the equity account called *Accumulated Earnings*. For example, look at the *Profit & Loss Standard* report for the period January 1, 2021, to June 30, 2021. There is a net income of $8,357.58. See Figure 12–TT.

FIGURE 12–TT

Profit & Loss Standard Report— January 1, 2021– June 30, 2021— Net Income Section

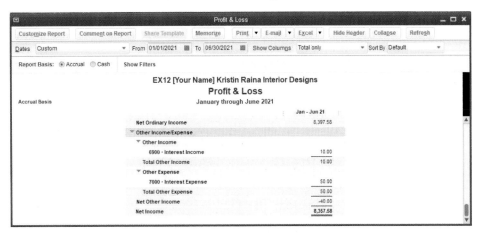

The net income is carried over to the *Balance Sheet Standard* report for June 30, 2021. See Figure 12–UU.

FIGURE 12–UU

Balance Sheet Standard Report— June 30, 2021— Equity Section

Assuming no other activity for the year 2021, look at the *Balance Sheet Standard* and *Profit & Loss Standard* reports for the first day of the new fiscal year, January 1, 2022. Notice that there is no longer a line labeled *net income*, but the $8,357.58 has been transferred into the Accumulated Earnings account. See Figure 12–VV.

FIGURE 12–VV
Balance Sheet
Standard Report—
January 1, 2022—
Equity Section

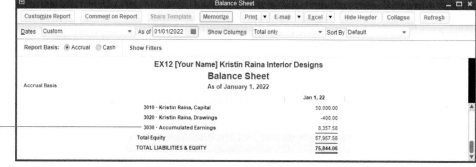

Accumulated
Earnings

In addition, the revenue and expenses accounts all begin with zero balances for the start of the new fiscal year. Since there are no revenues or expenses on January 1, 2022, there is no income. See Figure 12–WW.

FIGURE 12–WW
Profit & Loss
Standard Report—
January 1, 2022

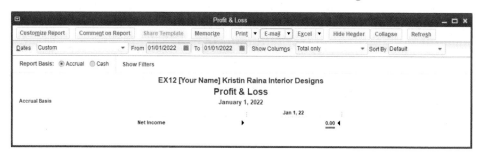

At this point, if you wanted to close the Drawings account, you would have to record an adjusting journal entry in the Make General Journal Entries window. Close all the windows.

Set the Closing Date

HINT

You may want to make a backup copy of the company file and label it *preclosing* before following the steps to set the closing date or condense the company file.

Because QuickBooks does not actually close the books, you still have access to all the records for prior years. As a precaution, however, you can protect the data for a fiscal year by restricting access to the records so no changes can be made after fiscal year-end. This is accomplished when you set the closing date.

To set the closing date:
1. At the main menu bar, click Company and then click *Set Closing Date*. The Preferences window appears at the Accounting page—Company Preferences tab.
2. Click the Set Date/Password button. The Set Closing Date and Password dialog box appears.
3. Read the page, and then at the *Closing Date* field, choose *12/31/2021.*

4. In the *Closing Date Password* and *Confirm Password* text boxes, type Student1 or a password of your choosing. See Figure 12–XX.

FIGURE 12–XX
Set Closing Date and
Password Dialog Box

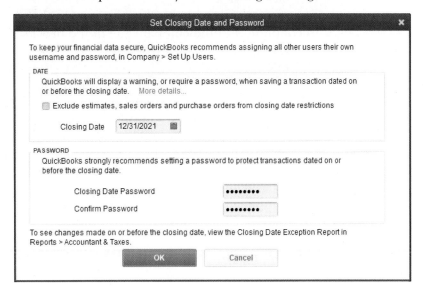

5. If the information is correct, click OK.
6. At the Preferences window, click OK.

If you need to make a change to a transaction in the company file after you set the closing date, you will receive a warning that the company file is closed, and you will need to enter the password to save any changes.

To enter updated information in a company file that is closed:
1. Open the *Journal* report and enter the dates from *01/01/2021* to *12/31/2021*.
2. Double-click the transaction for Minneapolis Electric and Gas dated 02/02/2021 (Trans# 3). The transaction appears in the Enter Bills window.
3. Change the amount to $500 and then click the Save & Close button.
4. At the Recording Transaction message, click Yes.
   The QuickBooks message appears informing you that you are modifying a transaction in a closed accounting period. If you still wish to record the transaction, you must enter the closing date password (*Student1*).
5. Do not save the change. Click Cancel at the QuickBooks message and then close the Enter Bills window.
6. At the Recording Transaction message, click No.
7. Close the *Journal* report.

New Fiscal Year

In QuickBooks, the accounting records are not closed, so all the activities previously recorded will be retained in the company file. If you wish to continue with the company file in the new fiscal year but do not want to carry forward the prior fiscal year activities into the new fiscal year, QuickBooks provides the Condense Data utility. When you condense the data in a company file, the prior year activities are removed from the company file, but all the preferences previously established remain intact.

As part of the process, QuickBooks makes a copy of the company file before condensing it. Note that this process is normally done in the year after the fiscal year-end. The company file for Kristin Raina Interior Designs is for 2021. If you attempt to do this process before January 1, 2022, it may not be completed.

To condense the company file to prepare for the new fiscal year:
1. At the main menu bar, click File and then click *Utilities*.
2. At the Utilities submenu, click *Condense Data.* The Condense your company file window appears with the How do you want to condense your company file page? displayed.
3. Accept the default *Remove the transactions you select from your company file* and click Next. The Condense Data dialog box appears with the What transactions do you want to remove? page displayed.
4. Choose the *Transactions before a specific date* option and choose *January 1, 2022.* See Figure 12–YY.

FIGURE 12–YY
Condense Data
Dialog Box

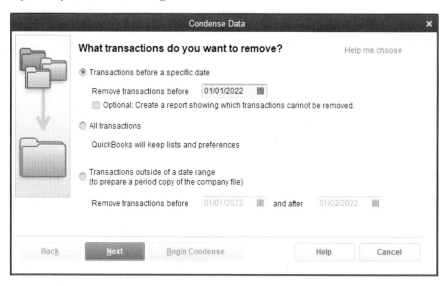

5. If the information is correct, click Next.
6. At the How Should Transactions Be Summarized? page, accept the default *Create one summary journal entry (recommended)* and then click Next.

7. At the How Should Inventory Be Condensed? page, accept the default *Summarize inventory transactions (recommended)* and then click Next.

8. At the Do You Want To Remove The Following Transactions? page, accept the defaults and then click Next.

9. At the Do You Want To Remove Unused List Entries? page, accept the defaults and then click Next.

10. At the Begin Condense page, click Begin Condense. It will take several minutes, and then you will see a QuickBooks Desktop Information message. Note that QuickBooks makes a copy of the company file. See Figure 12–ZZ.

11. At the QuickBooks Desktop Information message, click OK.

12. In the condensed company file, if you view the *Balance Sheet Standard* report for January 1, 2022, you will notice that QuickBooks created an equity account 32000 Retained Earnings. Edit the account in the Chart of Accounts List and change it to 3030 Accumulated Earnings to match the company's pattern for numbering accounts.

The effect of condensing the file is similar to making the closing entries in a manual accounting system. A closing journal entry is recorded in the general journal. Balances in asset, liability, and equity accounts are carried forward into the new fiscal year in the general ledger. Balances in revenue and expense accounts are closed, and these accounts begin with zero balances in the general ledger in the new fiscal year. The company file is now ready for the activities for the new fiscal year.

Exiting QuickBooks

Upon completing this session, make a backup copy of your practice exercise company file to a removable storage device using the Back Up command and label it postclosing. Be sure to change the *Save in* field to the removable storage device and then carefully type the correct file name. Close the company file and then exit QuickBooks.

Chapter Review and Assessment

Procedure Review

To display the Home page, if it is not displayed:
1. At the main menu bar, click Company.
2. Click *Home Page* and then click the Home Page tab.

To access a window using the icons on the Home page:
1. On the Home page, click an icon. Either a window opens or a drop-down list appears.
2. If a drop-down list appears, select the appropriate option.

To enable a preference to customize the Home page:
1. At the main menu bar, click Edit and then click *Preferences*.
2. In the left panel of the Preferences window, click the Desktop View icon.
3. Click the Company Preferences tab.
4. In the RELATED PREFERENCES section, click the item marked *off*, and you are moved to the window to enable the preference. When you enable a preference, the icon or icons appear on the Home page.
5. Click OK to save the changes in the Preferences window.

To view the Left Icon bar:
1. At the main menu bar, click View. At the View drop-down menu, when a check mark appears to the left of *Left Icon Bar*, the Left Icon bar is enabled. If there is no check mark, the Left Icon bar is disabled.
2. Click *Left Icon Bar* if there is no check mark.

To view the Top Icon bar:
1. At the main menu bar, click View. On the View drop-down menu, when a check mark appears to the left of *Top Icon Bar*, the Top Icon bar is enabled. If there is no check mark, the Top Icon bar is disabled.
2. Click *Top Icon Bar* if there is no check mark. If the Left Icon bar was displayed, it would be removed when the Top Icon bar was displayed. (Only one Icon bar can be displayed.)

To add an icon to an Icon bar:
1. At the main menu bar, click View and then click *Customize Icon Bar*. The Customize Icon Bar window appears.
2. At the Customize Icon Bar window, click the Add button. The Add Icon Bar Item window appears.
3. At the Add Icon Bar Item window, scroll through the list on the left until you see the icon you wish to add.
4. Click the icon you wish to add.
5. Click OK at the Add Icon Bar Item window and then click OK at the Customize Icon Bar window to save the changes. The icon is now added to the Icon bar.

To edit an icon on an Icon bar:
1. At the main menu bar, click View and then click *Customize Icon Bar*. The Customize Icon Bar window appears.
2. At the Customize Icon Bar window, in the ICON BAR CONTENT section, scroll through the list and then click once on the icon you wish to edit to highlight it.

3. Click the Edit button.
4. At the Edit Icon Bar Item window, at the *Label* field, delete the name and then type the edited name.
5. Click OK at the Edit Icon Bar window and then click OK at the Customize Icon Bar window. The icon text is updated to the edited name on the Icon bar.

To remove an icon from an Icon bar:
1. At the main menu bar, click View and then click *Customize Icon Bar*. The Customize Icon Bar window appears.
2. At the Customize Icon Bar window, in the ICON BAR CONTENT section, scroll through the list and then click once on the icon you wish to delete to highlight it.
3. Click the Delete button.
4. Click OK to save the changes. The icon is removed from the Icon bar.

To change to flat or hierarchical view at the Chart of Accounts List window:
1. At the Chart of Accounts List window, click the Account menu button. By default, *Hierarchical View* is checked.
2. Click *Flat View*. The subaccounts are no longer indented; they are now left-aligned in the window.
3. Click the Account menu button and then click *Hierarchical View*. The presentation changes to indent the subaccounts.
4. Close the window.

To change the default setting of subaccounts:
1. At the main menu bar, click Edit and then click *Preferences*.
2. In the left panel of the Preferences window, click the Accounting icon.
3. Click the Company Preferences tab.
4. In the ACCOUNTS section, insert a check mark in the box to the left of *Show lowest subaccount only*.
5. Click OK. In the *Account Listing* report and the Activities window, only the subaccount will display (not the parent account followed by the subaccount).

To merge two accounts:
1. Open the Chart of Accounts List.
2. Select the account you wish to merge, but do not open it.
3. Click the Account menu button and then click *Edit Account*. The Edit Account window opens.
4. At the Edit Account window, change the name or number to the desired account to merge and then click the Save & Close button. A Merge message informs you that the account is already in use and asks if you wish to merge the accounts.
5. At the Merge message, click Yes. The two accounts are merged. All the information in QuickBooks is updated accordingly.
6. Close the Chart of Account List.

To create a custom field:
1. Open a center and then choose a customer or vendor by double-clicking the name. The Edit window appears.
2. Click the Additional Info tab.

3. On the Additional Info tab, in the CUSTOM FIELDS section, click the Define Fields button. The Set up Custom Fields for Names window appears.

4. On the first line in the *Label* column, type the name of the new field you wish to create.

5. At the *Use for:* field, insert a check mark in the appropriate column.

6. If the information is correct, click OK.

7. At the Information message, insert a check mark in the box to the left of *Do not display this message in the future* and then click OK. The new field text box is now displayed in the CUSTOM FIELDS section on the Additional Info tab.

8. In the new field text box, type the appropriate information.

9. If the information is correct, click OK to save it.

10. Edit each customer or vendor and type in the information in the new field text box on the Additional Info tab.

11. Close the center.

To display customers or vendors in the Customer Center or Vendor Center for the custom field:

1. Open the Center.

2. Click the Search icon. The Custom Filter dialog box appears.

3. In the Custom Filter dialog box, click or type the appropriate information.

4. Click Go. The Center is updated to display only the customers or vendors that have been identified for the custom field on the Additional Info tab.

5. To remove the custom filter, click the X that replaced the Search icon.

6. Close the Center.

To customize the Create Invoices window and a printed invoice:

1. With the Create Invoices window open, on the Formatting tab, click the Manage Templates icon.

2. In the SELECT TEMPLATE section, make sure that *Intuit Service Invoice* is selected and then click the Copy button.

3. In the PREVIEW section, at the *Template Name* field, type Job Invoice.

4. Click OK.

5. At the Basic Customization window, click the Additional Customization button.

6. At the Additional Customization window, click the Columns tab.

7. Add or delete check marks for the different fields of information.

8. Change the order of the fields, if necessary.

9. Click OK at the Additional Customization and Basic Customization windows.

10. At the Create Invoices window, click the Save & Close button.

To prepare a business letter using QuickBooks Letters:

1. At the main menu bar, click Company and then click *Prepare Letters with Envelopes.*

2. At the Prepare Letters with Envelopes submenu, click *Customer Letters.* If the Find Letter Templates message appears, click the Copy button. The Letters and Envelopes window appears.

3. At the Review and Edit Recipients page, click the Unmark All button to remove all the check marks from the customer names.
4. Select the desired name and then click Next.
5. At the Choose a Letter Template page, select a letter and then click Next.
6. At the Enter a Name and Title page, enter the appropriate data.
7. If the information is correct, click Next. Microsoft Word opens, and the chosen letter is displayed with your company name and customer name included.
8. Save and print the letter and then close Microsoft Word.
9. Close the Letters and Envelopes window.

To set up and memorize a transaction:
1. Record a transaction as usual in an Activity window but do not click Save.
2. At the main menu bar, click Edit and then click *Memorize Check.*
3. At the *How Often* field, click *Monthly.*
4. At the *Next Date* field, choose the date to start the memorized transaction.
5. Click OK. The transaction is memorized.
6. At the Activity window, click the Save & Close button.

To recall a memorized transaction:
1. At the main menu bar, click Lists and then click *Memorized Transaction List.*
2. At the Memorized Transaction List window, select the transaction you wish to record and then click the Enter Transaction button.
3. The Activity window appears with the correct date and other information automatically entered. You may make changes, if necessary.
4. If you wish to record the transaction, click the Save & Close button.
5. Close the Memorized Transaction List window.

To modify a report using the Display tab:
1. Open the report and then click the Customize Report button at the top of the report.
2. In the Modify Report dialog box, the default tab is Display.
3. Insert or remove check marks from the column titles you wish to add or hide.
4. Click OK in the Modify Report dialog box.
5. Memorize the report if desired and then close the report.

To disable or change the format of the Date Prepared and Time Prepared items and change a subtitle in a report:
1. Open the report and then click the Customize Report button at the top of the report.
2. In the Modify Report dialog box, click the Header/Footer tab.
3. Remove the check marks from the boxes to the left of the *Date Prepared* and *Time Prepared* fields.
4. At the *Subtitle* field, delete the date provided and then type the new subtitle.
5. Click OK in the Modify Report dialog box.
6. Memorize the report if desired and then close the report.

To memorize the settings for a report:
1. Open the report and then make the desired changes.
2. Click the Memorize button at the top of the report.
3. In the Memorize Report dialog box, type the new report name in the *Name* field.
4. Click OK.
5. Close the report.

To open a memorized report:
1. At the main menu bar, click Reports and then click *Memorized Reports.*
2. At the Memorized Reports submenu, click *Memorized Report List.* The Memorized Reports List appears.
3. At the Memorized Reports List, double-click the desired report name. The memorized report appears.

To collapse and expand the numbers in a report:
1. Open the report and then click the Collapse button at the top of the report. Any account that has subaccounts is collapsed into one net amount. The Collapse button changes to the Expand button.
2. To expand the numbers, click the Expand button at the top of the report. The report returns to the original presentation, which lists the amounts for the subaccounts along with the net amount.
3. Close the report.

To export a report to a new Microsoft Excel worksheet:
1. Open the report and then click the Excel button at the top of the report. A drop-down list appears.
2. Choose *Create new worksheet.* The Send Report to Excel dialog box appears.
3. In the Send Report to Excel dialog box, click the Advanced button if you wish to review any Excel options and then click OK or Cancel.
4. In the Send Report to Excel dialog box, with *Create new worksheet* and *in new workbook* selected, click Export. Excel opens, and a worksheet is prepared using the report.
5. If you are familiar with Excel, you may revise the report according to your preferences.
6. Close Excel by clicking the X.
7. At the Do you want to save the changes message, click Save. You are moved to the Save As dialog box.
8. In the Save As dialog box, choose the folder where you save your files, and in the *File name* text box, type the file name and then click Save. The Excel worksheet is saved and Excel closes.

To export a report to an existing Microsoft Excel worksheet:
1. Open the report and enter the correct dates.
2. Click the Excel button. A drop-down list appears.
3. Click *Update Existing Worksheet.* The Send Report to Excel dialog box appears.
4. In the Send Report to Excel dialog box, with *Update Existing Worksheet* selected, click the Browse button. You are moved to the Open Microsoft Excel File dialog box.

5. Select the folder where you save your files, select the file, and then click Open. You are returned to the Send Report to Excel dialog box, with the path filled in the first box in the *Select workbook* field.
6. In the second box in the *Select workbook* field, choose *Sheet1* at the drop-down list and then click Export.
7. At the Export Report Alert message, click Yes. Excel opens the existing worksheet updated with the new data. Any previous changes in the formatting of the Excel worksheet will have been retained.
8. Close Excel and then close the report.

To display multiple reports:
1. At the main menu bar, click Reports and then click *Process Multiple Reports*. The Process Multiple Reports window is displayed.
2. At the Select Memorized Reports From drop-down list, click *<All Reports>*.
3. Insert a check mark to the left of each report you wish to view.
4. At the *From* and *To* fields for each report, choose the appropriate dates and then click Display. All the reports are displayed for the period of time indicated.
5. Close all the reports.

To disable or change the Date Prepared and Time Prepared items default settings:
1. At the main menu bar, click Edit and then click *Preferences*.
2. In the left panel of the Preferences window, click the Reports & Graphs icon.
3. Click the Company Preferences tab.
4. Click the Format button.
5. Click the Header/Footer tab. You can change the default formats or disable any field of information for all the reports on this tab.
6. To disable the Date Prepared item, remove the check mark from the box to the left of the *Date Prepared* field.
7. To disable the Time Prepared item, remove the check mark from the box to the left of the *Time Prepared* field.
8. Click OK in the Report Format Preferences dialog box. You are returned to the Preferences window.
9. Click OK.

To view a graph:
1. Use the Reports menu from the main menu bar or the Reports button in a List window to choose a graph.
2. Click the Dates button.
3. Choose the dates and then click OK. The graph for that period of time is displayed.
4. At the Income and Expense graph, to display the income as a pie chart, click the Income button. The pie chart changes to display the income analysis.
5. Close the graph.

To view the fiscal year:
1. At the main menu bar, click Company and then click *My Company.*
2. At the My Company window, click the Edit icon. The Company Information window appears.
3. At the Company Information window, click *Report Information.*
4. Close the Company Information and My Company windows.

To set the closing date:
1. At the main menu bar, click Company and then click *Set Closing Date.* The Preferences window appears at the Accounting page—Company Preferences tab.
2. Click the Set Date/Password button. The Set Closing Date and Password dialog box appears.
3. Read the page, and then at the *Closing Date* field, choose the closing date.
4. In the *Closing Date Password* and *Confirm Password* text boxes, type a password of your choosing.
5. If the information is correct, click OK.
6. At the Preferences window, click OK.

To enter updated information in a company file that is closed:
1. Open the *Journal* report and enter the appropriate dates.
2. Double-click the transaction. The transaction appears in the appropriate window.
3. Change the information and then click the Save & Close button.
4. At the Recording Transaction message, click Yes.
5. The QuickBooks message appears informing you that you are modifying a transaction in a closed accounting period. If you still wish to record the transaction, you must enter the closing date password.
6. Click OK or Cancel.
7. Close the Activity window and then click No at the Recording Transaction message.
8. Close the report.

To condense the company file to prepare for the new fiscal year:
1. At the main menu bar, click File and then click *Utilities.*
2. At the Utilities submenu, click *Condense Data.* The Condense your company file window appears with the How do you want to condense your company file? page displayed.
3. Accept the default *Remove the transactions you select from your company file* and then click Next. The Condense Data dialog box appears with the What transactions do you want to remove? page displayed.
4. Choose the *Transactions before a specific date* option, click the date of the new fiscal year, and then click Next.
5. At the How Should Transactions Be Summarized? page, accept the default *Create one summary journal entry (recommended)* and then click Next.
6. At the How Should Inventory Be Condensed? page, accept the default *Summarize inventory transactions (recommended)* and then click Next.
7. At the Do You Want To Remove The Following Transactions? page, accept the defaults and then click Next.
8. At the Do You Want To Remove Unused List Entries? page, accept the defaults and then click Next.

9. At the Begin Condense page, click Begin Condense. It will take several minutes, and then you will see a QuickBooks Information message. Note that QuickBooks made a copy of the company file.
10. At the QuickBooks Information message, click OK.
11. In the condensed company file, QuickBooks has created an equity account 32000 Retained Earnings. Edit the account in the Chart of Accounts List and change it to 3030 Accumulated Earnings to match the company's pattern for numbering accounts.

Key Concepts

Select the letter of the item that best matches each definition.

a. Excel button
b. Additional Customization window—Columns tab
c. Header/Footer tab
d. Edit menu - Memorize Check
e. Accumulated Earnings

f. Display tab
g. Memorize button at the top of the report
h. Prepare Letters with Envelopes
i. Manage Templates icon
j. Collapse/Expand button

_____ 1. Used to choose fields of information and order of appearance in the Create Invoices window and on a printed invoice.
_____ 2. Command choice to use preformatted business letters available in QuickBooks.
_____ 3. Button used to save the changes made to the settings in a report.
_____ 4. Used to customize a pre-established invoice in QuickBooks.
_____ 5. Buttons used in a report to display all the parent accounts and their respective subaccounts or to display only the net value of the parent accounts and subaccounts.
_____ 6. Command used to save a routine transaction so you can recall it for later use.
_____ 7. Tab used to add or delete the fields of information displayed in each column in a report.
_____ 8. Account created and used by QuickBooks at the start of the new fiscal year to automatically transfer the net income of the previous year into it.
_____ 9. Button used to export a report into a spreadsheet.
_____ 10. Tab used to establish or edit the headers and footers to be displayed in a report.

Procedure Check

1. In the Activities windows, when you choose an account with a subaccount, the parent account is displayed first in the account field followed by the subaccount. How can you modify this display of account names?
2. You would like to prepare a list of all of your customers that live in the New York City area. How would you do this?
3. On the first of each month, you write a check for $100 for the liability insurance premium. How can you use QuickBooks to simplify this monthly process?

4. You change the columns of information displayed in the Customer Contact List every time you display it. What steps could you take to eliminate this repetitive formatting each time you view the List?
5. You wish to display a graph representing the sales for the first quarter of the year. How can you use QuickBooks to accomplish this?
6. Your manager is new to QuickBooks and has just used the Time-Tracking feature. However, when the data was transferred into the Create Invoices window, your manager found it difficult to read the information in the window. Explain how QuickBooks can be used to display the information in a more meaningful presentation.

Case Problems

Demonstrate your knowledge of the QuickBooks features discussed in this chapter by completing the following case problems.

Case Problem 12–1

Lynn's Music Studio recorded the income earned on the Highland School jobs for the month of July 2021 in the Create Invoices window, but Lynn Garcia has not yet sent the invoices to the school. It is now August 1, 2021, and she is ready to send the invoices for the first half of July but wishes to present the detail in a more desirable format. You have been requested to prepare a Job Invoice format and print Invoice Nos. 2020, 2021, and 2022.

1. Open the company file **CH12 Lynn's Music Studio.QBW**.
2. At the QuickBooks Desktop Login window, in the *Password* text box, type Student1 and then click OK.
3. Make a backup copy of the company file and name it **LMS12 *[Your Name]* Lynn's Music Studio**.
4. Restore the backup copy of the company file. In both the Open Backup Copy and Save Company File as dialog boxes, use the file name **LMS12 *[Your Name]* Lynn's Music Studio** and enter the password.
5. Change the company name to **LMS12 *[Your Name]* Lynn's Music Studio**.
6. Open the Create Invoices window and then display Invoice No. 2020.
7. Create a Job Invoice based on the Intuit Service Invoice, using the following information:
   a. Save the new invoice as *Job Invoice*.
   b. Delete the *Description* column.
   c. Add the *Item* column (Print).
   d. Add the *Service Date* column.
   e. Put the invoice columns in the following order:

Item:	1
Service Date:	2
Quantity:	3
Rate:	4

   The *Amount* field remains at 5.

8. Print Invoice No. 2020 and then save the invoice.
9. Open Invoice No. 2021, change it to the Job Invoice format, print the invoice, and then save the change.
10. Open Invoice No. 2022, change it to the Job Invoice format, print the invoice, and then save the change.

Case Problem 12–2

Olivia's Web Solutions recorded the income earned on the Thrifty Stores jobs for the month of September 2021 in the Create Invoices window, but Olivia Chen has not yet sent the invoices to the store. It is now October 1, 2021, and she is ready to send the invoices for the first half of September but wishes to present the detail in a more desirable format. You have been requested to prepare a Job Invoice format and print Invoice Nos. 1017, 1018, and 1019.

1. Open the company file **CH12 Olivia's Web Solutions.QBW**.
2. At the QuickBooks Desktop Login window, in the *Password* text box, type Student1 and then click OK.
3. Make a backup copy of the company file and name it **OWS12 *[Your Name]* Olivia's Web Solutions**.
4. Restore the backup copy of the company file. In both the Open Backup Copy and Save Company File as dialog boxes, use the file name **OWS12 *[Your Name]* Olivia's Web Solutions** and enter the password.
5. Change the company name to **OWS12 *[Your Name]* Olivia's Web Solutions**.
6. Open the Create Invoices window and display Invoice No. 1017.
7. Create a Job Invoice based on the Intuit Service Invoice, using the following information:
   a. Save the new invoice as *Job Invoice.*
   b. Delete the *Description* column.
   c. Add the *Item* column (Print).
   d. Add the *Service Date* column.
   e. Put the invoice columns in the following order:

Item:	1
Service Date:	2
Quantity:	3
Rate:	4

   The *Amount* field remains at 5

8. Print Invoice No. 1017 and then save the invoice.
9. Open Invoice No. 1018, change it to the Job Invoice format, print the invoice, and then save the change.
10. Open Invoice No. 1019, change it to the Job Invoice format, print the invoice, and then save the change.

Appendices

Open or Restore a Company File

On the Open or Restore Company window, there is a significant difference between the *Open a company file* option and the *Restore a backup copy* option of a company file. The following summarizes and compares opening a company file with restoring (opening a backup copy) a company file. Compare Figure 1–F with Figure 1–N, and compare Figure 1–G with Figure 1–O below and on the next page. (These figures are the same illustrations that appear in Chapter 1.)

To *open* a company file, at the Open or Restore Company window, choose the *Open a company file* option. See Figure 1–F.

FIGURE 1–F

Open or Restore Company Window— Open a Company File Selected

Open a company file option

This window is followed by the Open a Company dialog box. See Figure 1–G.

FIGURE 1–G

Open a Company Dialog Box

Notice that all the company files have the extension .QBW.

Conversely, when you want to open a backup copy of a file, you must restore the file. To *restore* a company file, at the Open or Restore Company window, choose the *Restore a backup copy* option. See Figure 1–N.

FIGURE 1–N
Open or Restore
Company Window—
Restore a Backup Copy
Selected

Restore a backup copy option

This window is followed by the Open Backup Copy dialog box. See Figure 1–O.

FIGURE 1–O
Open Backup Copy
Dialog Box

Notice that all the company files have the extension .QBB.

If you do not see your backup copy file listed, you may be in the wrong dialog box. Go back to the Open or Restore Company window and be sure you selected the *Restore a backup copy* option.

Manual Accounting versus QuickBooks

A manual accounting system uses journals and ledgers. QuickBooks uses Lists/Centers, Activity windows, and Reports. Table B–1 summarizes and compares the journals and ledgers used in a manual accounting system with the Lists/Centers, Activity windows, and Reports used in QuickBooks, as explained in the chapters.

TABLE B–1

Manual Accounting versus QuickBooks

Manual Accounting System	QuickBooks
Accounts Payable Subsidiary Ledger	Vendor Center
Purchases Journal	Enter Bills window
	Enter Credit Card Charges window
Cash Payments Journal	Pay Bills window
	Write Checks window
	Pay Sales Tax window
Accounts Receivable Subsidiary Ledger	Customer Center
Sales Journal	Create Invoices window
Cash Receipts Journal	Receive Payments window
	Enter Sales Receipts window
General Ledger	*General Ledger* report
General Journal	*Journal* report
	Make General Journal Entries window
Inventory Subsidiary Ledger	Item List (inventory part items)
Payroll Journal or Register	Pay Employees windows
	Pay Payroll Liabilities window
Jobs Subsidiary Ledger	Customer Center

APPENDIX C
Journal Report Types

In a *Journal* report, the *Type* column indicates the window in which the activity was recorded. The System Default Account indicates the account that QuickBooks automatically uses to record activity. Table C–1 summarizes the Activity window and system default accounts for each journal entry type.

TABLE C–1
Journal Report Types

Type	Activity Window	System Default Account	
		Debit	Credit
Bill	Enter Bills		Accounts Payable
Credit	Enter Bills	Accounts Payable	
Bill Pmt — Check	Pay Bills	Accounts Payable	Cash — Operating
Check	Write Checks		Cash — Operating
Invoice	Create Invoices	Accounts Receivable	
Payment	Receive Payments	Undeposited Funds	Accounts Receivable
Sales Receipt	Enter Sales Receipts	Undeposited Funds	
Deposit	Make Deposits	Cash	Undeposited Funds
General Journal	Make General Journal Entries		
Inventory Adjust	Adjust Quantity/ Value on Hand		
Sales Tax Payment	Pay Sales Tax	Sales Tax Payable	Cash
Paycheck	Pay Employees	Salaries and Wages Expense Payroll Tax Expenses	Payroll Liabilities Cash — Payroll
Liability Check	Pay Payroll Liabilities	Payroll Liabilities	Cash — Payroll
Transfer	Transfer Funds Between Accounts		
Credit Card Charge	Enter Credit Card Charges		Credit Card Liability
Credit Memo	Create Credit Memos/Refunds		Accounts Receivable
Discount	Receive Payments		Accounts Receivable

APPENDIX D
Purchase Orders

Businesses commonly use a purchase order document as part of the inventory process. The purchase order (PO) initiates an order from a supplier of goods and services and at the same time gives the purchasing company a record of goods on order but not yet received. In QuickBooks, the information contained in the PO documents (items ordered, quantity, cost, vendor name, and so on) serves as the basis for completing the Receive Items and Enter Bill or Write Checks windows when goods are received.

Appendix Problem

Before you begin, open the company file **APP D Kristin Raina Interior Designs.QBW**. Enter the password, *Student1*. Make a backup copy of the file, name it **EXD** *[Your Name]* **Kristin Raina Interior Designs**, and then restore the file and enter the password. Finally, change the company name to **EXD** *[Your Name]* **KR Interior Designs**.

Note: The company name is changed to KR Interior Designs *to fit the name in the* PO ship to *field.*

Activities

Creating a Purchase Order for Inventory Items

On April 1, 2021, Kristin Raina orders 10 carpets from Bell Carpet Design, as the *Stock Status by Item* report indicates that there are only 4 carpets in inventory. The Purchase Order No. is 1.

To create a purchase order:
1. At the main menu, click Vendors and then click *Create Purchase Orders*.
2. At the VENDOR drop-down list, click *Bell Carpet Design*.
3. At the *Date* field, choose *04/01/2021*.
4. At the *P.O. NO.* field, type 1, if necessary.
5. Complete the balance of the window in the same manner as you would the Receive Items and Enter Bill window. Note that the *Ship to* field contains the shipping address for Kristin Raina. See Figure D–1.

FIGURE D–1
Create Purchase Orders Window—Completed

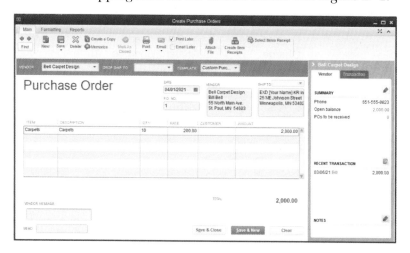

6. If the information is correct, click Save & Close.

The creation of a purchase order is not a transaction that changes general ledger posting accounts. No balances are affected. Kristin Raina can track open purchase orders through the *Open Purchase Orders* report contained in the Purchases submenu of the Reports menu. See Figure D–2.

FIGURE D–2
Open Purchase Orders
Report

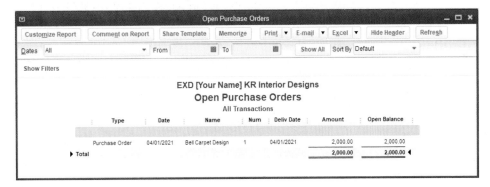

Recording Receipt of Inventory on Purchase Order

On April 5, 2021, Kristin Raina receives the carpets ordered on April 1 from Bell Carpet Design, its Invoice 12-5791. The bill is due May 5, 2021.

HINT
You can also access the Open Purchase Orders window by clicking the Select PO button at the Receive Items and Enter Bill window.

To record a purchase and receipt of inventory on order:
1. At the main menu bar, click Vendors and then click *Receive Items and Enter Bill.*
2. At the VENDOR drop-down list, click *Bell Carpet Design.* A window appears alerting you that open purchase orders exist for this vendor and asking *Do you want to receive against one or more of these orders?*
3. At the message, click Yes. The Open Purchase Orders window appears.
4. Choose the open purchase order by clicking in the ✓ column. See Figure D–3.

FIGURE D–3
Open Purchase Orders
Window—Open Purchase
Order Selected

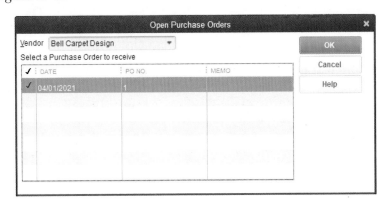

5. Click OK. The information from the Purchase Order window fills the appropriate fields in the Enter Bills window. See Figure D–4.

6. Complete the *DATE, REF. NO., BILL DUE,* and *TERMS* fields in the same way as illustrated in Chapter 5.
7. If the information is correct, click Save & Close.

The same procedure can be employed if the purchase is recorded in the Write Checks window.

APPENDIX E
Customer Credits and Bad Debt Write-Offs

In Chapters 3 and 5, you learned to record sales of services and inventory on account in the Create Invoices window. This transaction created an accounts receivable from the customer, which you tracked through the *Customer Center* and *Customer & Receivables* reports. Collection of receivables was recorded in the Receive Payments window.

In Appendix E, you will record a credit memo for a customer return of inventory in the Create Credit Memos/Refunds window. The credit memo will reduce the balance owed by the customer and reduce sales revenue, while restoring the returned item to inventory.

In addition, in this appendix you will record the write-off of an accounts receivable that is determined to be uncollectible using the Receive Payments window. The write-off will result in the elimination of an accounts receivable and the recognition of a bad debt expense.

Appendix Problem

Before you begin, open the company file **APP E Kristin Raina Interior Designs.QBW**. Enter the password, *Student1*. Make a backup copy of the file, name it **EXE *[Your Name]* Kristin Raina Interior Designs**, and then restore the file and enter the password. Finally, change the company name to **EXE *[Your Name]* Kristin Raina Interior Designs**.

Activities ── **Record a Sale of Inventory on Account**

1. Record the following transaction at the Create Invoices window. Refer back to the procedure in the section "Recording a Sale of an Inventory Item on Account" in Chapter 5 on pages 160–161.

Mar. 31, 2021	Sold the following on account to Maria Omari. Invoice No. 1020, Terms Net 30 Days.	
	4 lamps	$ 800.00
	2 carpets	800.00
	Total sale of merchandise	$ 1,600.00
	sales tax (.07 × $1,600)	112.00
	decorating services (6 hrs)	300.00
	Total sale on account	$ 2,012.00

See Figure E–1.

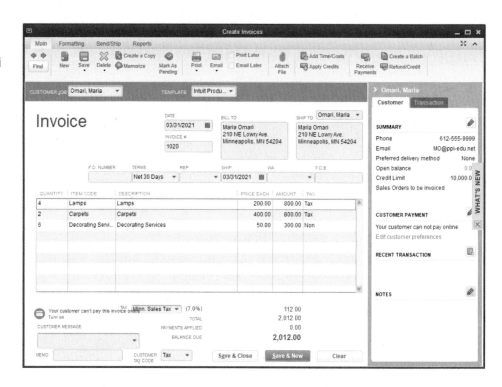

2. If the information is correct, click Save & Close.

Record a Customer Credit in the Create Credit Memos/Refund Window

The Create Credit Memos/Refund window is used to record a credit to a customer's account as a result of transactions such as returned inventory items from prior sales and allowances against prior invoicing. The credit can be in the form of a cash refund or credit available for use against future sales, or it can be applied to a specific open invoice. If a cash refund is made, a check can be created as part of the credit memo process. If the credit is applied to an open invoice, accounts receivable for that customer will be reduced.

The journal entry is as follows:

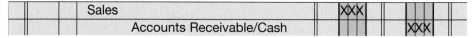

	Sales	XXX	
	Accounts Receivable/Cash		XXX

If the credit is a result of a returned inventory item, an additional journal entry will be made to return the item into the inventory account:

	Inventory asset	XXX	
	Cost of Goods Sold		XXX

On April 15, 2021, Maria Omari returns a lamp purchased on March 31, 2021, and a credit memo will be issued, No. 001. Because Invoice No. 1020 is still open, the credit memo will be applied against the unpaid balance.

To record a credit memo:

1. At the main menu bar, click Customers and then click *Create Credit Memos/Refunds.*

2. At the CUSTOMER:JOB drop-down list, click *Omari, Maria*. The invoice of March 31 is listed in the RECENT TRANSACTION section on the right, and the open balance of $2,012.00 appears in the SUMMARY section. See Figure E–2.

FIGURE E–2
Create Credit Memos/
Refunds Window—Maria
Omari

3. Enter the information provided on page 540 at the *DATE* and *CREDIT NO.* fields.
4. At the ITEM drop-down list, click *Lamps*.
5. At the *QTY* field, type 1. The word *Tax* should appear in the *CUSTOMER TAX CODE* field, and the *Print Later* and *Email Later* boxes should not be checked. See Figure E–3.

FIGURE E–3
Create Credit Memos/
Refunds Window

6. If the information is correct, click Save & Close. The Available Credit window appears and asks you how this credit should be used. See Figure E–4.

FIGURE E–4
Available Credit Window

6. Select the invoice by clicking in the ✓ column next to the open invoice.
7. Click the Discount and Credits button. This displays the Discount and Credits window.
8. At the *Amount of Discount* field, type 940.
9. At the Discount Account drop-down list, click *6075 Bad Debt Expense*. See Figure E–8.

FIGURE E–8

Discounts and Credits Window—Completed

10. Click the Done button to accept the discount (write-off) calculation. You are returned to the Receive Payments window, with the write-off amount in the *DISCOUNT* field. See Figure E–9.

FIGURE E–9

Receive Payments Window—Completed

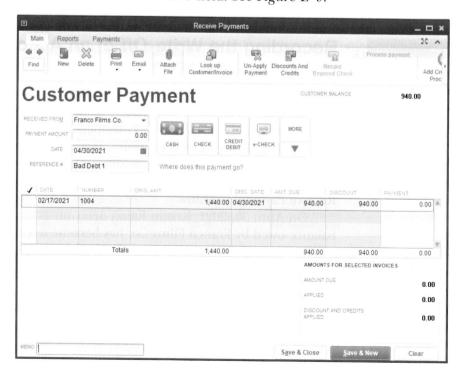

11. If the information is correct, click Save & Close.

Customer Balance Detail Report and Profit & Loss Standard Report

1. View the *Customer Balance Detail* report. Refer back to the procedure on page 98, if necessary. See Figure E–10. Note that the balance for Franco Films Co. is now 0.

FIGURE E–10
Customer Balance
Detail Report

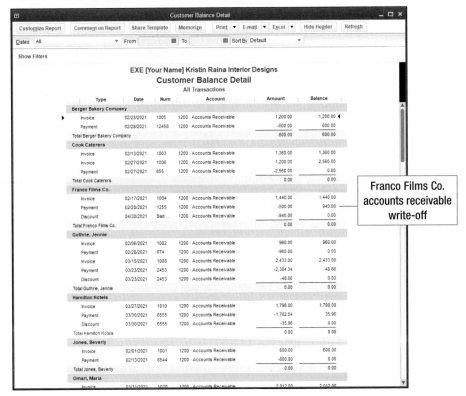

2. View a *Profit & Loss Standard* report for the period January 1, 2021, to April 30, 2021. Note the Bad Debt Expense for $940. See Figure E–11.

FIGURE E–11
Profit & Loss Standard
Report January 1,
2021–April 30, 2021

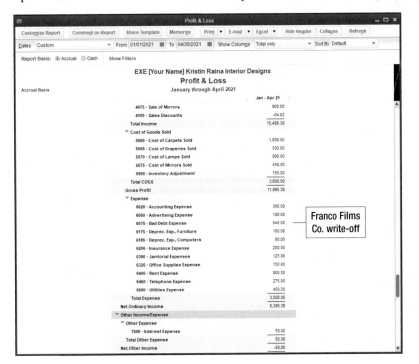

New Company Setup Methods

Reports

There are two methods of New Company Setup: Detailed Start and Express Start. Chapter 6 illustrates the Detailed Start method, which uses the EasyStep Interview window. In addition, Chapter 6 illustrates using the QuickBooks Desktop Setup window to enter information for customers, vendors, service items, and inventory part items. Chapter 7 illustrates the Express Start method. However, it did not use the QuickBooks Desktop Setup window to record customers, vendors, service items, and inventory part items. The following charts summarize and compare the methods used in Chapter 6 and Chapter 7 for New Company Setup.

Chapter 6—Detailed Start	*Chapter 7—Express Start*
↓	**↓**
EasyStep Interview Window	*QuickBooks Desktop Setup Window*

• Enter company information
• Select industry
• Select company organization
• Select first month of fiscal year
• Set up password
• Create company file
• Answer questions to establish preferences
  ➢ What do you sell? (choosing products enables inventory)
  ➢ Do you charge sales tax? (choosing Yes enables sales tax)
  ➢ Do you have employees? (choosing No disables payroll)
• Provide start date for using QuickBooks
• Review income and expense accounts
  ➢ Creates accounts in the Chart of Accounts List
	• Enter company name
	• Select industry
	• Select company organization (company type)
	• Enter company information
	• Create company file

	↓
	Create Company File Password • Enter password • Enter challenge question • Enter answer
	↓
	Establish Preferences • Add account numbers • Enable inventory • Enable sales tax • Disable payroll
↓	
QuickBooks Desktop Setup Window*	
• Enter customer information and opening balances • Enter vendor information and opening balances • Enter service items • Enter inventory part items and opening balances	
↓	**↓**
Customize Chart of Accounts List	*Update Chart of Accounts List*
• Add account numbers • Edit account numbers and names of accounts created by QuickBooks as part of the EasyStep Interview and QuickBooks Desktop Setup window	

continues...

...continued

Customize System Default Accounts
- Edit account numbers and names of system default accounts created by QuickBooks
- Open and close windows to force QuickBooks to create additional system default accounts
- Edit additional system default accounts created by QuickBooks

Customize Payment Terms

Update Chart of Accounts List

Update Item List
- Edit accounts
- Edit tax codes
- Edit sales tax

Update Item List**
- Enter service items
- Enter inventory part items and opening balances

Update Customer Center
- Edit information entered in the QuickBooks Desktop Setup window, if necessary

Update Customer Center**
- Enter customer information and opening balances

Update Vendor Center
- Edit information entered in the QuickBooks Desktop Setup window, if necessary

Update Vendor Center**
- Enter vendor information and opening balances

Adjust for the Accrual Basis of Accounting
- Enter opening balances
- Reverse uncategorized income
- Reverse uncategorized expenses

*   The QuickBooks Desktop Setup window can be used with either the Detailed Start method or the Express Start method of New Company Setup to enter information for customers, vendors, service items, and inventory part items, or it does not have to be used at all.

** All the information and balances can be entered directly into the Item List, Customer Center, and Vendor Center if you choose not to do so using the QuickBooks Desktop Setup window.

QuickBooks Payroll Setup Window

Chapter 8 illustrates the steps to activate the payroll feature in QuickBooks, update the Chart of Accounts List for payroll, choose the *Process Payroll Manually* option, and customize and add payroll items to the Payroll Item List. Chapter 9 illustrates the steps to add employees to the Employee Center and then process payroll.

In QuickBooks, you can customize and add items to the Payroll Item List and set up the Employee Center, as illustrated in Chapters 8 and 9 (custom setup), or you can use the QuickBooks Payroll Setup window. In this appendix, the basic features of the QuickBooks Payroll Setup window are described.

Appendix Problem

Before you begin, open the company file **APP G Kristin Raina Interior Designs.QBW**. Enter the password, *Student1*. Make a backup copy of the file, and name it **EXG** *[Your Name]* **Kristin Raina Interior Designs**. Restore the backup copy, enter the password *Student1*, and then change the company name in the file to **EXG** *[Your Name]* **Kristin Raina Interior Designs**.

Lists/Centers

QuickBooks Payroll Setup Window

HINT

See Chapter 8 (pages 331–337) for the procedures on how to activate the payroll feature and set up processing payroll manually.

Once the payroll feature has been activated and you have chosen to calcu late payroll manually—which has been done in this Appendix Problem—you can then access the QuickBooks Payroll Setup window. As part of this activation process, the Payroll Item List was created, as seen in, the section "The Payroll Item List" in Chapter 8 on pages 337–339. View the Payroll Item List in **EXG** *[Your Name]* **Kristin Raina Interior Designs**. The Payroll Item List includes typical federal tax items that generally apply to most payroll situations, such as Social Security, Medicare, federal withholding, and federal unemployment. As you enter information in the QuickBooks Payroll Setup window, additional items will be added to the Payroll Item List. In addition, in the Payroll Setup window, employees are added to the Employee Center.

To update the Payroll Item List and the Employee Center using the QuickBooks Payroll Setup window:

1. At the main menu bar, click Employees and then click *Payroll Setup*. The QuickBooks Payroll Setup window appears. See Figure G–1.

FIGURE G–1
QuickBooks Payroll Setup Window

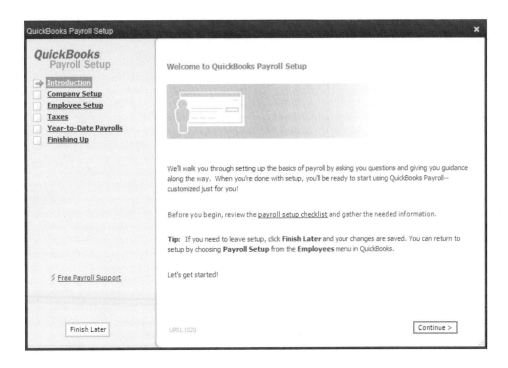

2. Read the page.

    At the QuickBooks Payroll Setup window, you move through pages; enter information when appropriate; and click Continue, Next, or Finish. As you proceed, you complete the six steps listed in the left panel of the QuickBooks Payroll Setup window. Notice the *payroll setup checklist* link. You can click this link to review a checklist provided by QuickBooks. (An internet connection is needed.)

3. Click Continue. You are moved to the Set up your company compensation and benefits page.

4. Read the page and then click Continue. You are moved to the Add New window—Tell us how you compensate your employees page. At this window, you add employee compensation items, which are added to the Payroll Item List.

5. At the Tell us how you compensate your employees page, choose *Salary* and *Hourly wage and overtime,* if necessary. Remove any other check marks. See Figure G–2.

6. If the information is correct, click Finish (or Next). You are moved to the Review your Compensation list page.
7. Choose the Hourly compensation item by double-clicking *Hourly*. You are moved to the Edit: Hourly window.
8. At the Edit: Hourly window, at the *Show on paychecks as* field, type Hourly Wages.
9. In the Expense account section, at the Account name drop-down list, choose *Payroll Expenses: Salaries and Wages Expense*. See Figure G–3.

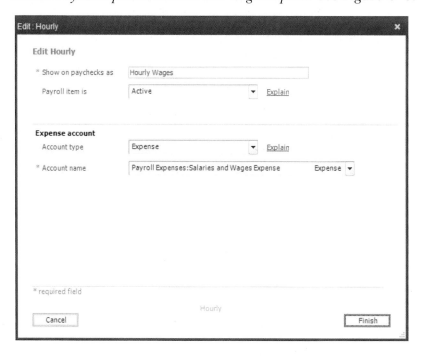

10. If the information is correct, click Finish. You are returned to the Review your Compensation list page.

11. Edit the Salary item at the Review your Compensation list page, choose the Account name *Payroll Expenses: Salaries and Wages Expense,* and then click Finish. You are returned to the Review your Compensation list page.

    Our sample company, Kristin Raina Interior Designs, uses only the Salary and Hourly Wages compensation items. QuickBooks created the Double-time hourly and Overtime (×1.5) hourly items, which Kristin Raina will not use. You will delete these two items.

12. Click Double-time hourly once to select the item and then click the Delete button. At the Delete Payroll Item message, click Yes. The Double-time hourly item is deleted.

13. Delete the Overtime (×1.5) hourly item.

14. After you edit or delete each compensation item, click Continue. You are moved to the Set up employee benefits page.

15. Read the page and then click Continue. You are moved to the Add New window—Set up insurance benefits page.

16. Accept the default *My company does not provide insurance benefits* and then click Finish. You are moved to the Review your Insurance Benefits list page.

17. Click Continue. You are moved to the Add New window—Tell us about your company retirement benefits page.

18. Accept the default *My company does not provide retirement benefits* and then click Finish. You are moved to the Review your Retirement Benefits list page.

19. Click Continue. You are moved to the Add New window—Set up paid time off page.

20. At the Set up paid time off page, choose *Paid sick time off* and *Paid vacation time off.* See Figure G–4.

FIGURE G–4
Add New Window—Set Up Paid Time Off Page

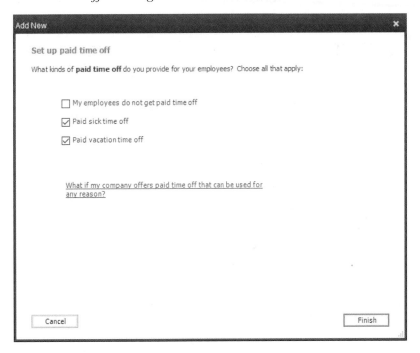

21. If the information is correct, click Finish. You are moved to the Review your Paid Time Off list page.

22. Choose the Hourly Sick paid time off item by double-clicking *Hourly Sick*. You are moved to the Edit: Sick Taken window.
23. At the *Show on paychecks as* field, type Hourly Wages Sick Pay.
24. At the Account name drop-down list, choose *Payroll Expenses:Salaries and Wages Expense*. See Figure G–5.

FIGURE G–5
Edit: Sick Taken Window

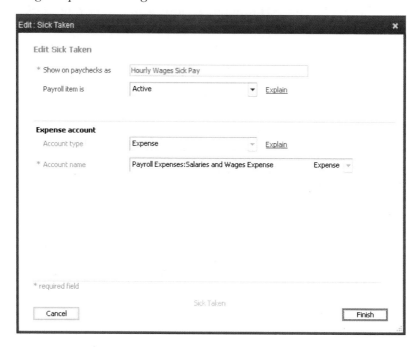

25. If the information is correct, click Finish. You are returned to the Review your Paid Time Off list page.
26. Repeat the steps to edit the remaining items at the Review your Paid Time Off list page as follows:

QuickBooks	Edited Name	Expense Account
Hourly Vacation	Hourly Wages Vacation Pay	Payroll Expenses: Salaries and Wages Expense
Salary Sick	Salary Sick Pay	Payroll Expenses: Salaries and Wages Expense
Salary Vacation	Salary Vacation Pay	Payroll Expenses: Salaries and Wages Expense

HINT
In the QuickBooks Payroll Setup window, at any time, you can click the Finish Later button, which will close the QuickBooks Payroll Setup window. To return to the QuickBooks Payroll Setup window, click Employees and then click *Payroll Setup*. You will be returned to the page where you left off.

27. After completing all the editing, click Continue. You are moved to the Add New window—Set up additions and deductions page.
28. Make sure that no items are checked and then click Finish. You are moved to the Review your Additions and Deductions list page.

Look in the left panel of the QuickBooks Payroll Setup window. You have completed the Company Setup part of the QuickBooks Payroll Setup.

29. Click Continue. You are moved to the Set up your employees page.
30. Read the page and then click Continue. You are moved to the New Employee window. The information you enter here will be entered in the Employee Center.

31. Type in the following information:

First name:	Harry
Last name:	Renee
Print on check as:	Harry Renee
Employee status:	Active
Home Address:	323 S. Main Ave.
City:	St. Paul
State:	MN
Zip Code:	54120

See Figure G–6.

FIGURE G–6
Employee Harry Renee Window—Enter Employee's Name and Address Page

32. If the information is correct, click Next. You are moved to the Employee Harry Renee window—Enter Harry Renee's hiring information page.
33. Enter the following information:

Employee type:	Regular
Social Security #:	112-55-9999
Hire date:	4/1/2021
Birth date:	2/17/1988
Gender:	Male

See Figure G–7.

34. If the information is correct, click Next. You are moved to the Tell us how you plan to pay Harry Renee page.

35. Enter the following information:

How often?:	Twice a month (Semimonthly)
	Salary
Salary amount:	24,000
Per:	Year

See Figure G–8.

36. If the information is correct, click Next. You are moved to the How is sick time off calculated for Harry Renee? page.

37. Enter the following information, using the drop-down lists when necessary:

Calculation

Harry Renee earns:	48 hours at beginning of year
Unused sick hours:	must be used or lost by end of year
Sick time accrual year starts:	January 1
Harry Renee earns:	no time off until
Earn sick time hours starting:	4/1/2021

Current balances

Hours available as of (current date):	48
Hours used as of (current date):	0

See Figure G–9.

FIGURE G–9
Employee Harry Renee Window—How Is Sick Time Off Calculated for Harry Renee? Page

HINT

The date for the current balances will be the date on your computer.

38. If the information is correct, click Next. You are moved to the How is vacation time off calculated for Harry Renee? page.

39. Enter the following information, using the drop-down lists when necessary:

Calculation

Harry Renee earns:	96 hours at beginning of year
Unused vacation hours:	must be used or lost by end of year
Vacation accrual year starts:	January 1
Harry Renee earns:	no time off until
Earn vacation hours starting:	4/1/2021

Current balances

Hours available as of (current date):	96
Hours used as of (current date):	0

See Figure G–10.

FIGURE G–10

Employee Harry Renee
Window—How Is
Vacation Time Off
Calculated for Harry
Renee? Page

40. If the information is correct, click Next. You are moved to the Set Up Harry Renee's direct deposit information.

41. Do not enter any information at this page and click Next. You are moved to the Tell us where Harry Renee is subject to taxes page.

42. Enter the following information, if it does not already appear:

State subject to withholding:	MN - Minnesota
State subject to unemployment tax:	MN - Minnesota
While working for you in (current year),	
did Harry Renee live or work in another state?	No

See Figure G–11.

43. If the information is correct, click Next. You are moved to the Enter federal tax information for Harry Renee page.
44. Enter the following information:

Filing Status:	Single
Allowances:	1
Subject to Medicare and Medicare Employee Addl Tax:	✓
Subject to Social Security:	✓
Subject to Federal Unemployment:	✓

See Figure G–12.

FIGURE G–12
Employee Harry Renee Window—Enter Federal Tax Information for Harry Renee Page

45. If the information is correct, click Next. You are moved to the Enter state tax information for Harry Renee page.
46. Enter the following information:

Filing Status:	Single
Allowances:	1
Subject to MN - Unemployment:	✓
Subject to MN - Workforce Enhancement Fee:	✓
Is this employee subject to any special local taxes not shown above?	No

See Figure G–13.

47. If the information is correct, click Finish. You are moved to the Review your Employee list page.

48. Click Add New. The New Employee window appears. Using Practice Exercise 9–1 on page 368, along with the information in Steps 49 and 50 below, enter the information for Richard Henderson, who was hired April 1, 2021.

49. At the Employee Richard Henderson window—How is sick time off calculated for Richard Henderson? page, enter the following information:

Calculation

Richard Henderson earns:	48 hours at beginning of year
Unused sick hours:	must be used or lost by end of year
Sick time accrual year starts:	January 1
Richard Henderson earns:	no time off until
Earn sick time hours starting:	4/1/2021

Current balances

Hours available as of (current date):	48
Hours used as of (current date):	0

50. At the Employee Richard Henderson window—How is vacation time off calculated for Richard Henderson? page, enter the following information:

Calculation

Richard Henderson earns:	96 hours at beginning of year
Unused vacation hours:	must be used or lost by end of year
Vacation accrual year starts:	January 1
Richard Henderson earns:	no time off until
Earn vacation hours starting:	4/1/2021

Current balances

Hours available as of (current date):	96
Hours used as of (current date):	0

Do not enter any information on the Set Up Richard Henderson's direct deposit information page. Complete the tax information.

51. After entering the information for Richard Henderson, click Finish. You are moved to the Review your Employee list page that lists both Harry Renee and Richard Henderson.

    Look at the list in the left panel of the QuickBooks Payroll Setup window. You have completed the Employee Setup part of the QuickBooks Payroll Setup.

52. Click Continue. You are moved to the Set up your payroll taxes page.

53. Read the page and then click Continue. You are moved to the Here are the federal taxes we set up for you page.

    The federal taxes that QuickBooks set up on the Payroll Item List are the ones common to most companies. While you have the choice here to edit these payroll items, you are not able to edit all the information at this time. Therefore, the federal taxes will not be edited here but later in this Appendix.

54. Click Continue. You are moved to the Review your state taxes page, and the Set up state payroll taxes window—MN - Minnesota UI Fund payment page appears. If the MN - Minnesota UI Fund payment page does not appear, double-click *MN-Unemployment* and then click Next.

55. At the *MN-Unemployment Company Rate* field, type 2.16.

56. Click Finish. You are returned to the Review your state taxes page.

57. Click Continue. You are moved to the Schedule Payments—Set up payment schedule for Federal 940 page.

    QuickBooks provides a Schedule Payments feature if you subscribe to one of the QuickBooks payroll services. The Schedule Payments feature allows you to keep track of your payroll tax and other payroll liabilities amounts, due dates, and payments.

58. At the Schedule Payments window—Set up payment schedule for Federal 940 page, enter the following information, if necessary:

    Payee: United States Treasury
    Payment (deposit) frequency: Quarterly

    See Figure G–14.

See Figure G–14.

FIGURE G–14

Schedule Payments Window—Set Up Payment Schedule for Federal 940 Page

59. If the information is correct, click Next. You are moved to the Schedule Payments window—Set up payment schedule for Federal 941/944/943 page.

60. Enter the following information:

Payee:	United States Treasury
Payment (deposit) frequency:	After Each Payroll (Semiweekly)

61. Click Next. You are moved to the Schedule Payments window—Set up payment schedule for MN Withholding page.

62. Enter the following information:

Payee:	Minn. Dept. of Revenue
MN Dept of Revenue Tax ID No.:	4777781
Payment (deposit) frequency:	After Each Payroll (Semiweekly)

See Figure G–15.

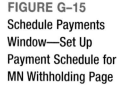

FIGURE G–15
Schedule Payments Window—Set Up Payment Schedule for MN Withholding Page

63. Click Next. You are moved to the Schedule Payments window—Set up payment schedule for MN UI and Workforce Enhancement Fee page.

64. Enter the following information:

Payee:	Minnesota UI Fund
MN Dept of Emp and Economic Dev UI Tax Acct No:	04777781-0123
Payment (deposit) frequency:	Quarterly

65. If the information is correct, click Finish. You are moved to the Review your Scheduled Tax Payments list page.

   Look at the list in the left panel of the QuickBooks Payroll Setup window. You have completed the Taxes part of the QuickBooks Payroll Setup.

66. Click Continue. You are moved to the Year-to-date payrolls page. If you are setting up payroll in QuickBooks and have paid employees for the current year, you will have to enter the year-to-date payroll information for each employee.

67. Read the page and then click Continue. You are moved to the Determine if you need to set up year-to-date payroll page.

68. At the question Has your company issued paychecks this year?, click No and then click Continue. You are moved to the You have finished payroll setup! page.

Look at the list in the left panel of the QuickBooks Payroll Setup window. You have completed the Year-to-Date Payrolls part of the QuickBooks Payroll Setup.

69. Click Go to Payroll Center.

If you subscribe to a QuickBooks Payroll Service, you are moved to a Payroll Center window. If you compute payroll manually, you are moved to the Employee Center window. The Employee Center should be the same as was updated in Chapter 9. See Figure 9–H on page 368.

70. Close the Employee Center.

Reports → ## Payroll Item List

As previously noted, when you activate the payroll feature, QuickBooks creates the Payroll Item List, which includes typical federal tax items that generally apply to most payroll situations, such as Social Security, Medicare, federal withholding, and federal unemployment. As you entered information in the QuickBooks Payroll Setup window, additional items were added to the Payroll Item List, such as Salary, Hourly Wage, and State Taxes.

To open the Payroll Item List:

1. At the main menu bar, click Lists and then click *Payroll Item List*. See Figure G–16.

FIGURE G–16 Payroll Item List

ITEM NAME	TYPE	AMOUNT	LIMIT	TAX TRACKING	PAYABLE TO	ACCOUNT ID
Salary	Yearly Salary			Compensation		
Salary Sick Pay	Yearly Salary			Compensation		
Salary Vacation Pay	Yearly Salary			Compensation		
Hourly Wages	Hourly Wage			Compensation		
Hourly Wages Sick Leave	Hourly Wage			Compensation		
Hourly Wages Vacation Pay	Hourly Wage			Compensation		
Advance Earned Income Credit	Federal Tax			Advance EIC Payment	United States Treasury	33-4777781
Federal Unemployment	Federal Tax	0.6%	7,000.00	FUTA	United States Treasury	33-4777781
Federal Withholding	Federal Tax			Federal	United States Treasury	33-4777781
Medicare Company	Federal Tax	1.45%		Comp. Medicare	United States Treasury	33-4777781
Medicare Employee	Federal Tax	1.45%		Medicare	United States Treasury	33-4777781
Social Security Company	Federal Tax	6.2%	128,400.00	Comp. SS Tax	United States Treasury	33-4777781
Social Security Employee	Federal Tax	6.2%	-128,400.00	SS Tax	United States Treasury	33-4777781
MN - Withholding	State Withholding Tax			SWH	Minn. Dept. of Revenue	4777781
MN - Unemployment	State Unemployment Tax	2.16%	32,000.00	Comp. SUI	Minnesota UI Fund	04777781-0123
Medicare Employee Addl Tax	Other Tax	0.9%		Medicare Addl Tax	United States Treasury	33-4777781
MN - Workforce Enhancement Fee	Other Tax	0.1%	32,000.00	Co. Paid Other Tax	Minnesota UI Fund	04777781-0123

Payroll Item ▼ Activities ▼ Reports ▼ ☐ Include inactive

In the QuickBooks Payroll Setup window, you were generally but not always able to edit item names and account names. If there are item names and account names that you were not able to edit in the QuickBooks Payroll Setup window, you can do so in the Payroll Item List.

Follow the steps in the section "Customizing the Payroll Item List" in Chapter 8 on pages 339–343, including Practice Exercises 8–1 and 8–2, to customize the federal tax items of Social Security (Company and Employee), Medicare (Company and Employee), Federal Unemployment, and Federal Withholding.

After customizing the federal tax items, use the same procedures to customize the state tax items that were created in the QuickBooks Payroll Setup window:

State Tax Item	Liability Account	Expense Account
MN - Withholding	2120 SIT Payable	
MN - Unemployment	2130 SUI Payable	6630 SUI Expense

2. Close the Payroll Item List.

Payroll Item Listing Report

The *Payroll Item Listing* report lists the payroll item, type, rate, and limit for some of the mandatory taxes, as well as the expense and liability accounts relating to the payroll item.

To view the *Payroll Item Listing* report:
1. At the main menu bar, click Reports and then click *Employees & Payroll.*
2. At the Employees & Payroll submenu, click *Payroll Item Listing.* See Figure G–17.

FIGURE G–17 Payroll Item Listing Report

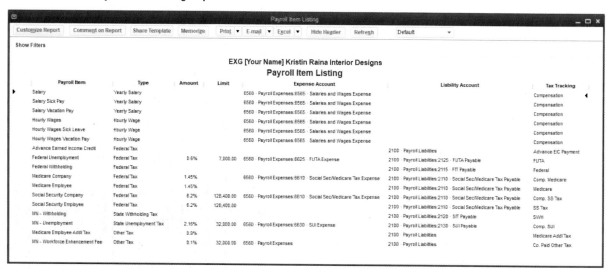

3. Close the report.

Sick and Vacation Paid Time

In Appendix G, you learned to set up paid time off for Kristin Raina's employees. In this appendix, you will process payroll when one employee uses sick or vacation time. You will also process payroll reports that track paid time used and paid time available.

Appendix Problem

Before you begin, open the company file **APP H Kristin Raina Interior Designs.QBW**. Enter the password, *Student1*. Make a backup copy of the file, name it **EXH** *[Your Name]* **Kristin Raina Interior Designs**, and then restore the file and enter the password. Finally, change the company name to **EXH** *[Your Name]* **Kristin Raina Interior Designs**.

Activities

Process Payroll

In Chapter 9, you learned to process payroll for Kristin Raina's two employees. Employee sick and vacation hours were not available at that time. In this appendix, paid time off has been established for each employee. The amount of available paid time appears in the Preview Paycheck window every time you process payroll. See Figure H–1.

FIGURE H–1 Preview Paycheck Window—Paid Time Off Hours Displayed

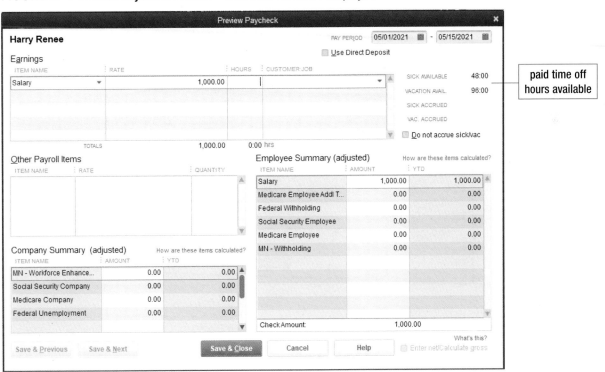

Using Banked Vacation Time Off Hours

Harry Renee plans to take a one-week vacation during the pay period ending May 15, 2021. Because he has 96 hours of paid vacation time available, he will use 40 of those hours and be paid during his time off.

To record the use of paid vacation time off:

1. At the main menu bar, click Employees and then click *Pay Employees.* The Enter Payroll Information window appears.
2. At the *PAY PERIOD ENDS* and *CHECK DATE* fields, choose *05/15/2021.*
3. At the *BANK ACCOUNT* field, click *1020 Cash - Payroll.*
4. At the *CHECK OPTIONS* field, choose the *Handwrite & Assign check numbers* option and then type 5 at the *First Check#* field.
5. Select *Harry Renee* by inserting a check mark next to the name.
6. If the information is correct, click the Open Paycheck Detail button. The Preview Paycheck window appears.
7. At the *ITEM NAME* field, confirm that the *Salary* item automatically fills for Harry Renee and that the *VACATION AVAIL.* hours are 96.
8. Move to the next line and choose *Salary Vacation Pay* at the *ITEM NAME* field. Notice that the $1,000 salary is now split between regular salary and vacation pay. See Figure H–2.

FIGURE H–2
Preview Paycheck Window—Salary Vacation Pay Entered

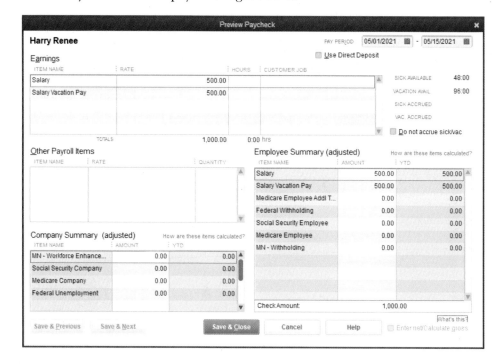

9. On both the *Salary* and *Salary Vacation Pay* lines at the *HOURS* field, type 40.

When you move to the next field, the *VACATION AVAIL.* hours will be reduced from 96 to 56, as 40 hours of paid vacation time have now been used. In addition, the $1,000 salary for the period is now divided between the Salary item and the Salary Vacation Pay item in the Employee Summary (adjusted) section. See Figure H–3.

FIGURE H–3
Preview Paycheck Window—Vacation Hours Used

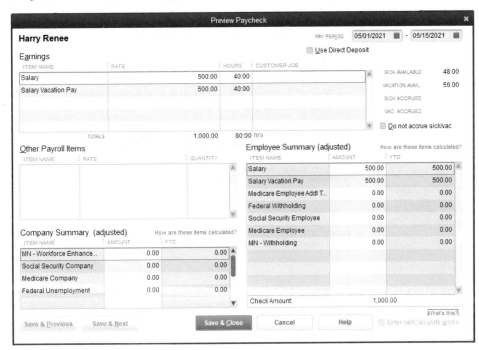

10. Complete Harry Renee's pay information:

Company Taxes:
    Social Security Company: 62.00
    Medicare Company: 14.50
    Federal Unemployment: 6.00
    MN - Unemployment Company: 40.00
Employee Taxes:
    Federal Withholding: 120.00
    Social Security Employee: 62.00
    Medicare Employee: 14.50
    MN - Withholding: 46.00

QuickCheck: The check amount should be $757.50.

11. Complete the process for Harry Renee's pay.

Activities

Using Banked Sick Time Off Hours

During the pay period ending May 15, 2021, Richard Henderson used two days (16 hours) of paid sick time. His pay will be processed for that pay period with 16 of the 80 hours allocated to Hourly Wages Sick Pay and only 64 hours allocated to Hourly Wages.

To record the use of paid sick time off:

1. At the main menu bar, click Employees and then click *Pay Employees*. The Enter Payroll Information window appears.
2. At the *PAY PERIOD ENDS* and *CHECK DATE* fields, choose *05/15/2021*. The Bank Account should be *1020 Cash - Payroll*, and the Check# should be *6*.
3. Select *Richard Henderson* and then click the Open Paycheck Detail button. Note that *SICK AVAILABLE* hours are 48.
4. At the *HOURS* field, on the *Hourly Wages* line, type 64.
5. Move to the next line and choose *Hourly Wages Sick Pay* at the *ITEM NAME* field.
6. At the *HOURS* field, type 16.

Note that the *SICK AVAILABLE* hours are now 32, reduced from 48. In addition, in the Employee Summary (adjusted) section, the gross pay is now split between Hourly Wages of $1,280 (64 hours at $20 per hour) and Hourly Wages Sick Pay of $320 (16 hours at $20 per hour). See Figure H–4.

FIGURE H–4
Preview Paycheck Window—Sick Hours Used

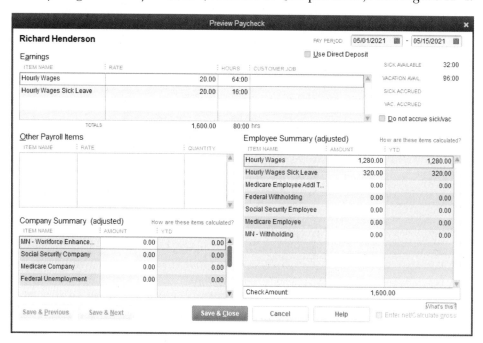

7. Complete Richard Henderson's pay information:

   Company Taxes:
Social Security Company:	99.20
Medicare Company:	23.20
Federal Unemployment:	9.60
MN - Unemployment Company:	64.00

   Employee Taxes:
Federal Withholding:	120.00
Social Security Employee:	99.20
Medicare Employee:	23.20
MN - Withholding:	54.00

   QuickCheck: The check amount should be $1,303.60.

8. Complete the process for Richard Henderson's pay.

Tracking Paid Time Off

The *Paid Time Off List* is a report that allows you to track the sick and vacation time used and the time available for each employee.

To view and print the *Paid Time Off List*:
1. At the main menu bar, click Reports and then click *Employees & Payroll*.
2. At the Employees & Payroll submenu, click *Paid Time Off List*. The report is displayed with the updated information. See Figure H–5.

FIGURE H–5

Paid Time Off List

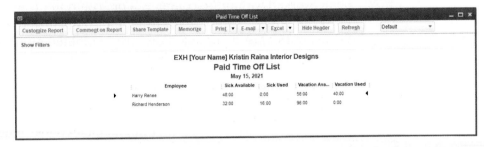

3. To print the report, click the Print button at the top of the report, check the settings in the Print Reports dialog box, and then click Print.
4. Close the report.

APPENDIX I
Setting Up QuickBooks for Multiple Users

There are many examples of businesses in which multiple employees need access to company files to record information. QuickBooks Pro and QuickBooks Premier allow up to three or five people, respectively, to access the company files, each from his or her own computer. This is referred to as *multi-user mode.* Computers for all the users must be networked within the company. One computer is designated as the host computer. To prepare for using the company file by multiple users QuickBooks must be installed on each computer, multi-user access must be set up, and the company files must be prepared for multi-user access.

Install QuickBooks

> **HINT**
>
> To view the number of user licenses, press the F2 function key or Ctrl + 1.

To use QuickBooks in multi-user mode, QuickBooks must be installed separately on each computer. Additional license fees are required for each computer. A company usually purchases the multi-user QuickBooks software, which includes the license fees for the additional users. If a company purchased single-user QuickBooks software, additional licenses can be purchased from QuickBooks.

Install QuickBooks on each computer, as described in Chapter 1. For the computer designated as the host computer, select *Multi-User Host Installation* when prompted. For all the other computers, select a standard installation.

Set Up Multi-User Access

There are several ways to set up multi-user access for a company file. One way, as stated above, is to choose *Multi-User Host Installation* when installing QuickBooks. If QuickBooks was previously installed, you can set up the host computer for multi-user access.

Complete the steps below with QuickBooks open but with no company file open.

> **HINT**
>
> If the choice is *Stop Hosting Multi-User Access*, then you are already in multi-user mode. Move to the next section, "Scan Company Files for Multi-User Access."

To set up the host computer for multi-user access:
1. At the main menu bar, click File and then click *Utilities.*
2. At the Utilities drop-down menu, click *Host Multi-User Access.* The Host multi-user access window appears.
3. Read the Start hosting multi-user access message and then click Yes.
4. If the Company file must be closed message appears, click Yes.
5. If the Administrator Permissions Needed message appears, click Continue.
6. If a User Account Control message appears, click Yes.
7. You are moved to the Set up multiple users information window. Read the message and then click OK.

The host computer is now set up in multi-user mode. The company files need to be scanned for multi-user access.

Scan Company Files for Multi-User Access

QuickBooks provides a database server manager to scan the computer files and prepare them for multiple users.

To scan the company files:

1. In Windows 10, click the Windows Start button, and then in the apps menu, scroll down and click *QuickBooks File Manager 2019.*

   In Windows 8, click the Search charm. In the *Search* text box, type QuickBooks Database Server Manager. The QuickBooks Database app tile should appear. Click the QuickBooks Database app tile.

   In Windows 7, on your desktop, click the Start button and then click *All Programs.* At the Programs menu, click *QuickBooks* and then click *QuickBooks Database Server Manager.*

2. At the QuickBooks File Manager 2019 window, click the Launch QuickBooks File Manager button.

3. If the Create Password Vault Login dialog box appears, type or select the following:

Username:	Admin
Password:	Student1
Confirm Password:	Student1
Challenge Question:	First college roomate's name
Answer:	Friend
Alternate Question:	Favorite restaurant in college
Answer:	Local Place

   See Figure I–1.

FIGURE I–1
Create Password
Vault Login Window—
Completed

4. If the information is correct, click OK.
5. If the User Account Control message appears, click Yes.
6. At the Building your client list and adding shortcuts to their files...
   1 - How should we name your clients? page, click Next.

7. At the Building your client list and adding shortcuts to their files...
   2 - From QuickBooks File Names page, click the Browse button.
8. At the Browse for Folder window, select the folder where your
   QuickBooks files are located and then click OK. You are returned
   to the Building your client list and adding shortcuts to their
   files...2 - From QuickBooks File Names page with the path for your
   QuickBooks files listed.
9. Click Finish. The Updating Client List window appears. It will take
   a few minutes for the list to populate. The files now appear in the
   Clients section of the QuickBooks File Manager 2019 window. The
   company files are now ready to be used in multi-user mode.
10. Click the X to close the QuickBooks File Manager 2019 window.

You then set up the users that are allowed access to the company files.
See Appendix J for setting up users.

Accessing the Company File in Multi-User Mode

After the host computer has been set up to allow multi-users and the
company files have been set up to be accessed in multi-user mode, when
opening a company file, you must indicate that you will use the company
file in multi-user mode. You do this at the Open a Company window. In
the lower left corner of the Open a Company window, insert a check mark
in the box to the left of *Open file in multi-user mode.*

You may be prompted to enter a user name and password or to Create
New Users. (If you are prompted, click No.) When the file opens, you will
have access to the company file as a multi-user.

If you did not open the company file in multi-user mode, you can
switch to multi-user mode when the company file is open. Click File and
then click *Switch to Multi-user Mode.* If the choice is *Switch to Single-user
Mode,* then you are already in multi-user mode.

Setting Up Users

As you have seen throughout this book, a company file password is set up to protect the company file. In addition, a company can further protect the company file by allowing limited access to the company file by users. The original person who creates the company file is the Administrator (Admin) of the file. The Administrator is the person who determines and sets up users so they may access the company file. When the Administrator creates a user, the Administrator can then restrict access to parts of the company file or restrict access to former company information.

To set up users in a company file:

> **HINT**
>
> You can use any Company File or Exercise File to set up users in a company file. You many want to use a File from one of the later chapters, and you may want to make a copy of the Company File or Exercise File.

1. At the main menu bar, click Company and then click *Set Up Users and Passwords.*
2. At the Set Up Users and Passwords submenu, click *Set Up Users.*
3. At the QuickBooks Desktop Login, type in the password Student1 and then click OK.
4. In the User List dialog box, click *Add User.* The Set Up user password and access dialog box appears.
5. In the Set Up user password and access dialog box, at the *User Name* field, type User1.
6. At the *Password* and *Confirm Password* fields, type User1PW. See Figure J–1.

FIGURE J–1

Set Up User Password and Access Dialog Box—User Name and Password Page Completed

7. If the information is correct, click Next.
8. At the Access for User: User1 page, choose the *Selected areas of QuickBooks* option and then click Next.
9. At the Sales and Accounts Receivable page, choose the *Full Access* option and then click Next.

> **HINT**
>
> Depending on which features are enabled in a company file, some of these pages may not appear.

10. At the next several pages—Purchases and Accounts Payable, Checking and Credit Cards, Inventory, Time Tracking (if displayed), and Payroll and Employees (if displayed)—choose the *No Access* option and click Next.

11. At the Sensitive Accounting Activities page, choose the *Selective Access* option, choose the *Create transactions and create reports* option, and then click Next.

12. At the Sensitive Financial Reporting page, choose the *No Access* option and then click Next.

13. At the Changing or Deleting Transactions page, choose *Yes* at the first option, choose *No* at the second option, and then click Next. You are moved to the Access for user: User1 page, which summarizes the user's access rights. See Figure J–2.

FIGURE J–2
Set Up User Password and Access Dialog Box—Access for User Page

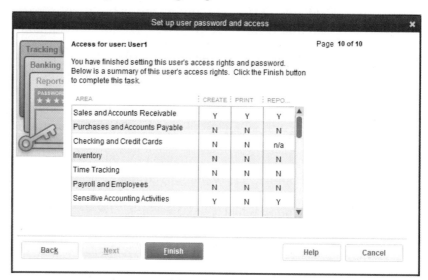

14. If the information is correct, click Finish. If you receive a warning, click OK.

15. Close the User List dialog box.

16. Close the company file.

Open the same company file as User1:

1. Open the company file. The QuickBooks Login dialog box appears.

2. In the QuickBooks Login dialog box, at the *User Name* field, type User1; at the *Password* field, type User1PW; and then click OK.

3. If the Sensitive Data Protection Setup dialog box appears, type the following:

User Name:	User1
Current Password:	User1PW
New Password:	U1PassW
Confirm New Password:	U1PassW

4. Click OK.

5. At the QuickBooks Desktop Information message, click OK.

   Recall that for User1, permission was granted only for Sales and Accounts Receivable. Open the Create Invoices window and the Enter Sales Receipts window. These windows can be opened by User1. Now try opening other windows, such as Enter Bills, Pay Employees, *Journal* report, *Profit & Loss Standard* report, and so on. A message warns that you need permission to open these parts of the company file.

6. Click OK at the warning and then close the company file.

7. Close QuickBooks.

APPENDIX K
Accrual Basis of Accounting versus Cash Basis of Accounting

You may have noticed in many of the reports that there is an *accrual basis* label in the upper left corner of the report. In QuickBooks, by default, the accounting reports (such as the trial balance) and financial statements (such as the Profit & Loss and Balance Sheet) are prepared using the **accrual basis of accounting**, which records revenue when earned and expenses when incurred regardless of cash receipts and cash payments. The accrual basis of accounting follows generally accepted accounting principles and is the basis used in this text.

An alternative accounting method is called the **cash basis of accounting**, which records revenue only when the cash has been received for services provided or for a product sold and records expenses only when cash payments have been made. QuickBooks allows you to switch individual reports from the accrual basis to the cash basis of accounting. When you convert the financial statements to the cash basis of accounting, the accounts that are typically affected are Accounts Receivable, Accounts Payable, revenues, and expenses.

accrual basis of accounting
an accounting method that requires the recording of revenue when it is earned and the recording of expenses when they are incurred regardless of cash receipts or cash payments

cash basis of accounting
an accounting method that records revenue when cash is received for services provided or for a product sold and records expenses only when payments have been made

To view a report using the cash basis of accounting:
1. Open the company file, **EX5 *[Your Name]* Kristin Raina Interior Designs**.
2. Open the *Profit & Loss Standard* report for the period 01/01/2021 through 03/31/2021.
   The report should match Figure 5–DD on page 177. Notice that the Net Income is *$8,285.38*.
3. In the *Profit & Loss Standard* report, click the Customize Report button.
4. In the Modify Report: Profit & Loss window, click the Display tab, if necessary.
5. On the Display tab, in the REPORT BASIS section, click the *Cash* option. See Figure K–1.

FIGURE K–1

Modify Report: Profit & Loss Window—Display Tab—Cash Report Basis Selected

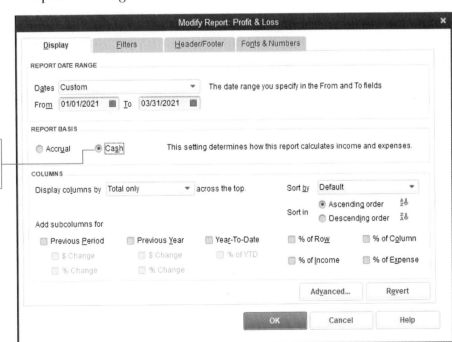

6. Click OK. The *Profit & Loss Standard* report is converted to the cash basis of accounting. See Figure K–2.

FIGURE K–2
Profit & Loss Standard
Report January 1, 2021
–March 31, 2021—
Cash Basis

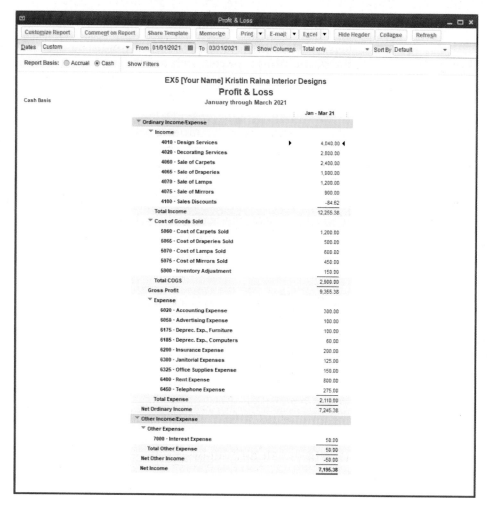

In Figure K–2, the Net Income is *$7,195.38*. Compare this to Figure 5–DD on page 177, which displays a Net Income of *$8,285.38*. There is a difference in the Net Income values of $1,090.

The difference consists of the Total Income of $1,540, ($13,795.38 – $12,255.38), which is the amount of the Accounts Receivable balance (this balance represents non-cash income), and the Utilities Expense of $450, which is part of Accounts Payable because this expense has not yet been paid. The difference of the Total Income and Expenses is the difference in the Net Income ($1,540 – $450 = $1,090).

Now open the *Balance Sheet Standard* report for March 31, 2021. The report should match Figure 5–EE on page 178. Convert the *Balance Sheet Standard* report to the cash basis of accounting following Steps 3–5. See Figure K–3.

FIGURE K–3
Balance Sheet Standard
Report March 31, 2021—
Cash Basis

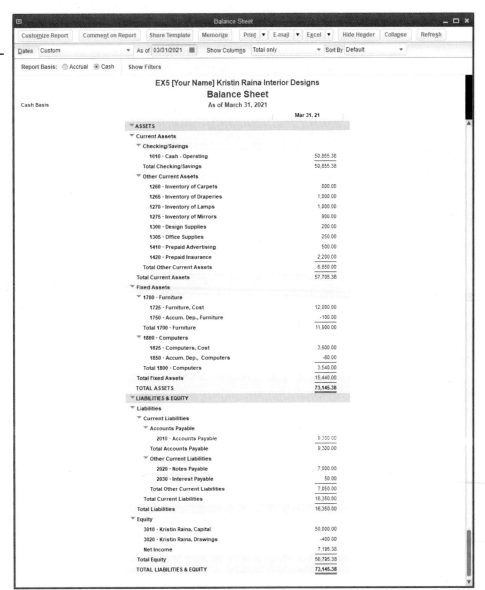

In Figure K–3 the balance is *$73,145.38*. Compare to Figure 5–EE on page 178, which displays a balance of *$74,685.38*. The difference is *$1,540*.

In the Asset section of the *Balance Sheet Standard* report, the difference consists of the difference in Accounts Receivable of $1,540. This balance is not included on the cash basis *Balance Sheet Standard* report because this balance relates to non-cash income.

In the Liabilities and Owner's Equity section of the *Balance Sheet Standard* report, the difference consists of the difference in Accounts Payable of $450, which is the not-yet-paid Utilities Expense (this expense is removed from Accounts Payable on the cash basis *Balance Sheet Standard* report) and the difference in the Net Income of *$1,090*, which is the cash basis Net Income reflected in Figure K–2 ($450 + $1,090 = $1,540).

When QuickBooks converts the *Profit & Loss* and *Balance Sheet* reports to the cash basis, it adjusts only the items that affect revenue and expenses and the related Accounts Receivable and Accounts Payable accounts.

The reports in Figures K–2 and K–3 were adjusted to the cash basis. When you close the report, the conversion to the cash basis of accounting is not retained. As shown in Chapter 12, if you wish to preserve these settings, you will need to memorize the report.

Alternatively, if you wish for the reports to always display the cash basis of accounting, you can change the default settings for the reports in the Preferences window. To change the report defaults, click Edit and then click *Preferences.* Choose the Reports & Graphs icon and the Company Preferences tab. The *SUMMARY REPORTS BASIS* field can be used to change to the cash basis of accounting.

Index

A

account(s)
   adding new, 115–118, 279–281
   creating in Chart of Accounts List, 196–197
   defined, 2
   deleting, 118–119, 221–222
   editing, 119
   examples of, 2
   merging two, 489–490
   operating account, 398
   reconciling account with bank statement, 407–411
   view in Edit mode, 219
   viewing specific, 113–114
   write-off of uncollectible account, 543–545
ACCOUNT field, 122
accounting. *See also* accrual basis of accounting
   defined, 2
   levels of operation in QuickBooks, 3–4
   for payroll transactions, 361–362
   with QuickBooks versus manual system, 2–3, 534
accounting concept
   deposit of receipts as separate transactions, 97
   general ledger posting
      adjusting journal entry, 124
      bank reconciliation, 412
      cash payment of expense, 55
      cash sale, 94
      credit card charge, 417
      credit card payment, 419
      inventory adjustments, 169
      payment of exiting account receivable, 90
      payment of sales tax, 171
      payment on existing Accounts Payable, 52
      processing paycheck, 443
      purchase of expense on account, 45
      purchase of inventory on account, 157
      purchase of inventory with cash, 158
      receipt of payment within discount period, 167
      sale of inventory for cash, 164
      sale of inventory on account, 162
      transfer funds, 403
      vendor credit, 48
accounting reports. *See also* reports
   Adjusted Trial Balance Report, 128–132
   General Ledger Report, 127
   Journal Report, 61–62, 100–101, 125–127, 175–176, 241–242
   Transaction Detail by Account Report, 422–423
   Trial Balance, 242–243
Account Listing Report
   changing subaccount display in, 487–489
   parent account and subaccounts in, 112–113
   viewing, 112–114
account name
   editing in Chart of Accounts List, 119, 220–221
      system default, 223–224, 283
   field in Edit Account Window, 113–114
account numbers
   activate account numbers feature, 219–220, 274–275
   adding, 219–220, 274–275
   editing in Chart of Accounts List, 220–221

editing system default, 223–224, 283
account numbers feature, activating, 219–220, 274–275
Account QuickReport
   function of, 136
   viewing, 137
Account Settings tab, 35
Accounts Payable account
   Enter Bills window and adjustment to, 31, 177
   Pay Bills window and adjustment to, 31, 49, 50
   as system default account, 31, 222, 282
Accounts Payable Subsidiary Ledger, 534
Accounts Receivable account
   Create Invoices window and adjustment to, 73, 83
   Receive Payments window and adjustment to, 73, 87, 89
   as system default account, 73, 222, 282
Accounts Receivable Subsidiary Ledger, 534
account types
   in Chart of Accounts List, 111–112
   choosing when setting up new account, 116–117
   field in Edit Account Window, 113–114
   system default accounts, 112
accrual basis of accounting, 573
   completing New Company Setup-Detailed Start, 236
   completing New Company Setup-Express Start, 299–300
   defined, 236, 299
   entering opening balances, 237–239, 300–302
   reversing entries, 236, 300
      Uncategorized Expenses account, 240–241, 304
      Uncategorized Income account, 239–240, 303
Accumulated Earnings account
   fiscal year closing, 515
   Owners Equity account renamed as, 282
   as system default account, 282
Activities
   level of operation described, 3–4
   making adjustments to account balances, 122
Activities Window
   change subaccount presentation, 487–489
   customizing system default accounts for use in, 223–224, 284–286, 492–499
   updating Vendor Center from, 45–46
Additional Customization window, 496–497
Additional Info tab, 35, 77
Additional Medicare Tax, 330
Add New Account window, 116–118, 279
Add new payroll item window, 344–348
Address Info tab, 35, 37
Adjusted Trial Balance Report
   as period-end accounting reports, 128–132
   viewing and printing, 128–132
ADJUSTING ENTRY field, 122
adjusting journal entries
   assigning numbers to journal entries, 123
   defined, 110
   Make General Journal Entries window for, 121–124
   printing trial balance before, 121
   timing for, 110
   view and print in Journal Report, 125–127
Adjust Quantity/Value on Hand activity window, 167–169
   correcting errors in Journal report and, 215
Advanced Excel Options dialog box, 509–510
agency for employee-paid liability page, 338–339
Apply Credit to Invoices window, 542
Asset Account field, 149
Assets account type, 111–112
Assign Check Numbers window, 51–52
Assigning Numbers to Journal Entries message, 123

Attach icon, 34, 76
Auto Apply/Un-Apply Payment button, 88
Available Credit window, 541

New Company Setup-Express Start
   accrual basis accounting, completing with, 299–300
   Balance Sheet Standard report
      after completed, 307–308
      viewing for interim review of, 298–299
   Chart of Accounts List
      add new account, 279–281
      open and review, 278–279
   compared to Detailed Start, 268, 546–547
   Customer Center, adding customer with outstanding
      balance, 292–293
   entering company information, 270–271
   hybrid method and, 308–309
   information needed for, 269–270
   Item List
      adding inventory part item to, 290–291
      adding service item to, 289–290
   Journal Report
      after completed, 305
      viewing for interim review of, 296–298
   new company file
      creating, 270–272
      customizing, 281–289
   opening balances, entering, 300–302
   overview of, 190, 268–269, 546–547
   password, creating for company file, 272–273
   payment terms
      adding, 287
      deleting, 288
      editing, 288
   payroll feature
      activating, 331–332
      disabling, 277–278
   preferences
      account numbers feature, 274–275
      inventory feature, 275
      payroll feature, activating, 277–27331–332
      payroll feature, disabling, 277–278
      sales tax feature, 275–277
   Profit & Loss Standard (Income Statement) report
      after completed, 307–308
      viewing for interim review of, 298
   QuickBooks Desktop Setup window, 270
   QuickBooks versus manual accounting systems, 268–269
   reversing Uncategorized Expenses account, 304
   reversing Uncategorized Income account, 303–304
   Trial Balance after completed, 306
   Vendor Center, adding vendor with outstanding balance,
      294–296
New Customer & Job button, 76, 436
New Customer window, 78–80, 292
New Employee button, 363, 364
New Employee window, 364–367
New Item window, adding item, 150–151, 289–290
New Job window, 436–437
New Terms window, 229, 287
New Transactions button, 34, 76
New Vendor button, 34
New Vendor window, 36
   Account Settings tab, 38
   adding vendor, 36–38
   adding vendor with outstanding balance, 294–296
   Name Page and Address Info tab, 37
   Payments Setting tab, 37
   sales tax information, 276
Next arrow, 43
No Company Open window, 6, 7

non-sufficient funds (NSF) checks, 399, 404, 410
NOTES section, 43, 84
Notes tab, 34, 76

O

omission, bank reconciliation and, 399
online purchases, recording transactions, 56
Open a Company dialog box, 10, 532–533
Open Backup Copy dialog box, 18
opening
   company file, 10–12
   memorized report, 507
   QuickBooks 2019 , 6–7
opening balance
   entering
      in Make General Journal Entries window, 237–238,
         300–302
      in New Company Setup-Detailed Start, 237–238
      in New Company Setup-Express Start, 300–302
   making corrections to, 215
Opening Balance Equity account, as system default account,
   282
Open Invoices Report, 98
Open or Restore Company dialog box, 10, 17, 532–533
Open Previous Company submenu, 21
Open Purchase Orders window, 537
operating account, 398
   reconcile Cash-Operating account with bank statement,
      407–411
operations, levels of, 3–4
outstanding balance
   adding customer with, 292–293
   adding vendors with, 294–296
outstanding check, 399
Owner's Draw account, as system default account, 282
Owner's Equity account, as system default account, 282, 515

P

paid sick and vacation time
   tracking, 567
   using banked, 564–566
   viewing available paid time, 563
Paid Time Off List report, 567
parent account
   in Account Listing Report, 112–113
   in Chart of Accounts List, 115
   flowing into financial statements, 134–135
partial payment
   of invoice and recording, 90–91
   making, 52–53
passwords
   creating company file password in Express Start, 272–
      273
   setting up administrator password in Detailed Start, 194
   for specific sections of company file, 272
Pay Bill button, 43
Pay Bills window
   automatic adjustment to
      Accounts Payable account, 31, 49, 50
      Cash account, 49, 50
   elements and features of, 49
   making partial payment of bill, 52–53
   manual accounting counterpart, 534
   overview of, 48–50
   overview of function, 30